AIRLINES: MANAGING TO MAKE MONEY

For Paula

Airlines: Managing to Make Money

STEPHEN HOLLOWAY

Ashgate

Aldershot • Burlington USA • Singapore • Sydney

Published by
Ashgate Publishing Limited
Gower House
Croft Road
Aldershot
Hants GU11 3HR
England

Ashgate Publishing Company
131 Main Street
Burlington, VT 05401-5600 USA

Ashgate website: http://www.ashgate.com

British Library Cataloguing in Publication Data
Holloway, S. (Stephen) , 1952-
   Airlines : managing to make money
   1.Airlines - Management
   I.Title
   387.7'0684

Library of Congress Control Number: 2001094263

ISBN 0 7546 1558 8

Printed and bound in Great Britain by MPG Books Ltd, Bodmin, Cornwall

Contents

List of Figures   *viii*
Foreword   *ix*
Preface   *xi*
Acknowledgements   *xiii*
List of Abbreviations and Definitions   *xv*

1. **Strategic Service Management: What is Meant by 'Strategic'?**   1
   What is strategy?   1
   The strategy-making process   5
   The content of strategy   12
   Summary   19

2. **Competitive Advantage**   23
   Definition and sources of competitive advantage   23
   The rest of the book   55
   Summary   58

3. **Competitive Scope and the Service Concept**   61
   Identification and segmentation of available markets   64
   The competitive scope decision   76
   The service concept   87
   Summary   101

4. **Designing the Service-Price Offer**   109
   The distinguishing characteristics of services   111
   Service design: competitive strategy in action   119
   The elements of service design   123

	The service design and development process	127
	Price	139
	The service-price offer	143
	Bridging the perceptions gap	145
	Summary	148
5.	**Service Attributes**	151
	Passenger airline service attributes	152
	Service processes	158
	Service encounters	164
	Servicescapes	178
	Conclusion	184
6.	**Managing Communications**	185
	Brand identity and image revisited	185
	Communication objectives	205
	External communications: customers	210
	External communications: other stakeholders	221
	Internal communications	223
	Development of an integrated communications programme	228
	Conclusion	232
7.	**Managing Service Delivery**	233
	Processes	235
	Resources, tasks, and activities	249
	Organizational architecture	263
	Conclusion	276
8.	**Managing Relationships**	279
	Stakeholder networks	279
	Employee relationships	281
	Customer relationships	299
	Collaborative relationships	321
	Conclusion	336
9.	**Managing Performance**	337
	Performance management systems	337
	The micro-level: service failure and recovery	341
	The macro-level: organizational performance as a whole	352

Conclusion   380

10. **Change, Creativity, and Innovation**   383
   Change   383
   Creativity   391
   Innovation   392
   Conclusion   401

   References   *403*
   Index   *423*

List of Figures

Figure 1.1	Strategy research streams	21
Figure 1.2	Corporate strategy	22
Figure 2.1	Matching competencies to market needs	39
Figure 2.2	The service management 'wheel'	57
Figure 3.1	From corporate to competitive strategy	62
Figure 3.2	The development of competitive scope and the service concept(s)	63
Figure 3.3	The dimensions of competitive scope	81
Figure 3.4	Service scope: a portfolio of service concepts	83
Figure 3.5	Options for delivering wide-market service	86
Figure 4.1	Design of the service-price offer	110
Figure 4.2	Perceived delivery standards and customer satisfaction	146
Figure 4.3	The service-value loop	149
Figure 6.1	Communicating the service-price offer	186
Figure 6.2	Identity and image	193
Figure 7.1	Delivering the service-price offer	234
Figure 7.2	A possible approach to the classification of processes	237
Figure 7.3	Tasks, activities and processes: a practical example	238
Figure 7.4	Outline of a value chain	265
Figure 9.1	Cause-and-effect chart for airline departure delays	348
Figure 9.2	Service outcomes	353
Figure 9.3	The strategy-performance pyramid	354
Figure 9.4	Conceptual model of service quality	378

Foreword

The title of this book reminded me of that old airline joke: What's the quickest way to create a millionaire? Find a billionaire and get him to run an airline.

There is no doubt that our billionaire would achieve that particular own-goal if he were to pursue a strategy which did not place good customer service at the forefront of his airline managers' minds.

Steve Holloway's book recognises the importance of good customer service to successful aviation management. It is no coincidence that the world's most successful international airlines are invariably also a byword for service excellence. Airlines like Cathay Pacific, Singapore and, dare I say it, British Airways are prime examples.

Service excellence must lie at the heart of an airline's strategy. With world aviation ever more competitive and consequently passenger choice so varied, the standard of service becomes a key driver for customer choice.

At British Airways, we recognise that very clearly. With the emergence of the no-frills airlines, the full-service sector has to make sure it provides exactly that. One mantra our customer service people adhere to is "Making every contact count". Simple, but effective.

Although we are also actively looking at how the right mix of technology can deliver better customer service – the ability to check in for your flight on your home computer, for instance – ultimately it is how the customer's contact with your staff is managed that can make the biggest difference.

You can have the finest fleet and the perfect strategy, but if you have a demotivated staff delivering shoddy service it will hit your bottom line very quickly.

So it is not only how your staff handle the customers that is so important, but how your managers handle their staff. Steve's book also rightly recognises that internal element as a key ingredient of service excellence. At British Airways, particularly after our £600 million investment in the Club World flat beds, we found that pride in the company and its products also put a broader smile on the faces of our cabin crew and customer service agents. And that of course makes your customers happier. No better example of the marketeer's virtuous circle.

Get it all right and, as this thoroughly-researched book explains, you might manage to make money out of an airline after all.

Rod Eddington
Chief Executive Officer
British Airways

Preface

This is not a 'how to' book. Managing a complex organization is not as easy as opening a book and following a recipe. Like my earlier titles, this is a 'framework book'. I have taken research from the management literature, and adapted its theories and empirical findings to the specific circumstances of the airline industry. The outcome is a 'framework' to help organize thoughts on how the management of an airline might profitably be approached.

The particular framework put forward is heavily influenced by the services management literature, by recent research in strategic management, and by work in brand management. The relevance of each will be explained as the plot unfolds. Readers expecting reference to airlines on every other line will be disappointed. The rather worn cliche that airlines are just like any other type of service business is finally moving from the realms of fiction to fact, and this being the case we can no longer hide behind our industry's 'special features'; commercial air transport remains a special industry in many ways, but there are very few justifications left for people interested in its future to ignore what services management, strategy, and brand management researchers have been uncovering for the benefit of those in less 'different' industries. This book is, accordingly, one which exemplifies rather than describes the airline business.

Although its framework might interest readers outside the air transport industry, the principal audience for the book is students on masters-level aviation management programmes; final year undergraduates on similar programmes should also find it useful. The book has been written not as a course text, but as a 'linking text': the intention is that the services management approach around which it has been structured can be used to link courses in strategy, marketing, human resources management, and operations. The book can therefore be read in conjunction with primary course texts in each of these fields.

The framework put forward might also appeal to practitioners, notwith-standing the deliberate lack of prescriptive advice at anything more than the most general level. There is a reasonable amount of reference to theory, particularly in the early chapters, and practitioners might see this as remote from their needs. I personally subscribe to the old adage that there is nothing as practical as a sound theory. Be that as it may, there are two problems with ignoring theory. First, everything we do is guided by some theory, no matter how elementary; if I do X, then Y will happen. Theory is simply an attempt to explain and predict cause-effect relationships, and what most managers are actually managing much of their time is cause-effect relationships. Second, few airline managers today can escape concepts such as competitive advantage, market positioning, strategic resource, competence, brand, knowledge, learning, service quality, customer satisfaction, and shareholder value; these are all the progeny of theory. If we are going to build our professional lives around them, it can do no harm to give some thought to what they are assumed to mean and where they have come from.

Whilst standards are generally high and rising in premium cabins, particularly in long-haul markets, down the back many airlines are failing to meet customers' expectations (*Aviation Week*, October 25, 1999 and December 11, 2000). With sustained annual traffic growth in the region of five per cent putting strain on the industry's infrastructure and output increasingly dominated by a small number of global alliances which talk about 'seamless customer service' but look suspiciously like nascent oligopolists, it is easy to be pessimistic about the future role of the airline customer. I have taken a more optimistic, hopefully not naive, perspective by suggesting an approach which puts the customer firmly at the centre of the airline management universe. It is predicated on the observable fact that the industry as a whole, if not necessarily every participant, is well-advanced in transitioning from a business that manages fleets of aircraft and sells the output they generate to a multi-billion dollar global service business that responds to the expectations of customers and depends for its financial health upon competencies developed to meet and exceed those expectations (Holloway, 1998b).

I hope you find the framework in this book as interesting and stimulating to explore as I have found it to build. But if you find parts of it seemingly detached from the day-to-day reality of the contemporary air travel experience, remember Colin Powell's words: 'Optimism is a force multiplier.'

Acknowledgements

People throughout the industry who have offered insights and stimulated ideas are too numerous to mention, but special thanks are due to Rod Eddington for taking time to contribute the Foreword. Steve Double at British Airways also provided invaluable assistance. I want to thank John Hindley at Ashgate Publishing for supporting the initial concept for this book, and then showing patience as it evolved into something rather different. Eddie and Colette O'Connor deserve thanks for their superb hospitality at Melaleuca Homestead in Australia's Northern Territory, where much of the book was brought together. Finally, thanks to my wife Paula for encouraging me yet again to write another 'final', 'positively the last' book.

List of Abbreviations and Definitions

AOG	Aircraft-on-ground (i.e., unserviceable).
ASK	Available seat-kilometre: one seat flown one kilometre, whether occupied or not. A measure of output.
ASM	Available seat-mile: one seat flown one mile.
ATK	Available tonne-kilometre: one tonne of payload capacity flown one kilometre, whether sold or not.
ATM	Available ton-mile: one ton of payload capacity flown one mile.
BA	British Airways.
CFROI	Cash-flow return on investment.
CSI	Customer satisfaction index.
EDI	Electronic data interchange.
ERP	Enterprise resource planning.
EVA	Economic value added (a registered trademark of Stern Stewart & Co).
FCF	Free cash-flow.
FFP	Frequent flyer programme.
FSC	Firm-specific competence.
GDS	Global distribution system.
GSA	General sales agent.
HRM	Human resources management.
IFE	Inflight entertainment.
IO	Industrial organization (economics).
IRR	Internal rate of return.
IS	Information system.
IT	Information technology.

MRO	Maintenance, repair, and overhaul.
NPV	Net present value.
O and D	Origin and destination (markets).
OD	Organization development.
OEM	Original equipment manufacturer.
PR	Public relations.
RBT	Resource-based theory of competitive advantage/ strategy.
ROI	Return on investment.
RPK	Revenue passenger-kilometre: one passenger flown one kilometre. A measure of sold output.
RPM	Revenue passenger-mile: one passenger flown one mile.
RTK	Revenue tonne-kilometre: one tonne of payload flown one kilometre.
RTM	Revenue ton-mile: one ton of payload flown one mile.
SCP	Structure-conduct-performance approach to competitive advantage/strategy.
Seat pitch	The distance from where the back and pan of a seat join to the same point on the seat in front.
SSC	Strategy-specific competence.
TQM	Total quality management.
Unit cost	Operating cost per ASK/ASM or ATK/ATM.
Unit revenue	Operating revenue per ASK/ASM or ATK/ATM.
VFR	Visiting friends and relatives/relations.
Yield	Revenue per RPK/RPM or RTK/RTM.

1 Strategic Service Management: What is Meant by 'Strategic'?

> The people who get on in this world are the people who look for the
> circumstances they want and, if they cannot find them, make them.
>
> George Bernard Shaw

Strategy is a question of process and content. When we look at strategy-making processes we are interested in how decisions are made to pursue a particular course of action, and when we consider content we are concerned with the substance of these decisions – with what it has been decided should be done. I will open the chapter with a brief summary of what is meant by 'strategy', and then review the main themes in the process and content literatures. The intention is to help locate the idea of service strategy within a wider context, and in doing this set the scene for later discussion of important ideas such as competitive strategy, customer value, service positioning, and the service concept.

i. What is strategy?

During much of the first half of the twentieth century, leading US business schools taught catch-all, atheoretical 'capstone courses' with titles such as 'business policy'. The essential goal of these courses was to show how general managers should integrate the different functions of an organization – functions such as marketing, finance, and operations, for example. There was little explicit recognition that certain types of decision, taken outside the context of a single function and independent of any integrative purpose, might be 'strategic' in their own right insofar as they have a long-term impact on the future direction and performance of the organization. The finger of blame for this myopia can be pointed at the academic power of mainstream microeconomics, which assumed efficient resource allocation and output decisions to be driven by market prices and had little incentive to delve inside the 'black box' of the individual firm.

By the late 1950s, some organizations were going beyond simple extrapolations of the past by trying to forecast the future. The idea was that if the future were to be accurately forecasted, any gap between projected and desired sales performance could be identified and addressed. Shortly afterwards, Chandler (1962) adopted the metaphor of 'strategy' from military science to distinguish between decisions made in pursuit of greater functional efficiency, and 'strategic' decisions which affect the funda-mental direction of an organization and its ultimate performance. He defined strategy as 'the determination of the basic long-term goals and objectives of an enterprise, and the adoption of courses of action and the allocation of resources necessary for carrying out those goals' (ibid: 16). He therefore drew a distinction between decisions that are 'operational' and others that are 'strategic' – the former oriented towards optimising perf-ormance in the short term and the latter more concerned with long-term performance. This distinction was to be temporarily blurred in the 1990s when top-management focus was shifted back onto operational concerns by the popularity of strategically agnostic movements such as total quality management and business process re-engineering; it is not that these are without strategic implications, but they are not in themselves *strategic* initiatives.

From the early 1960s onwards, certain aspects of executive choice and decision-making therefore started to be regarded as distinctly 'strategic', and strategic change was seen as something different from change for the sake of improved functional efficiency. Strategic choice was considered purposive, driven by pursuit of articulated goals. The word 'strategy' came into use as shorthand for a series of mutually reinforcing decisions and actions intended to allocate resources and efforts towards the achievement of these specified goals. The external environment was characterised as a source of opportunities and threats to which an organization must adapt by 'fitting' itself to prevailing contingencies, having taken into account its own strengths and weaknesses.

Strategy had been given autonomous life as a field of management research. No longer was it synonymous with the mechanically planned integration of business functions. With this autonomous life eventually came academic status. By the late 1960s, a few tenure-track researchers at US business schools started devoting themselves to the study of strategy, joining the high-profile consultants who had been making much of the early running in the field.

One of the interesting anomalies apparent to anybody who studies the early years of business strategy as a distinct field of research and practice is that amidst all the forecasting, life-cycle analysis, and portfolio planning that went on, there was not much attention paid to competitors and their impact. This is not to say that through the 1960s and 1970s strategic managers were unaware they had competitors. Nonetheless, in part because the postwar decades had been an era of burgeoning consumer demand with little evidence of industrial overcapacity, the analytical techniques in widest use made very little *explicit* reference to competitive dynamics. Only in the 1980s did competitor analysis, competitive advantage, and competitive strategy – all with academic roots stretching back over a generation – assume any prominence in popular management literature.

Despite all the changes that have affected the field of business strategy since its emergence almost half a century ago, the distinct but related concepts of 'ends' and 'means' established within an influential external environment have remained centre-stage.

Strategic 'ends': what we want to achieve

> To accomplish great things, we must not only act but also dream;
> not only plan, but also believe.
> Anatole France

Commonly used synonyms for 'strategic ends' include vision, mission, goals, objectives, targets, purpose, and 'strategic intent' (Hamel and Prahalad, 1989). There is no agreed definition of any of these concepts which distinguishes them unequivocally from the others. One interpretation is that vision is an image of the future, mission addresses what an organization does here and now, objectives, goals, and targets identify what is to be achieved, and strategic intent suggests what could be achieved if aggressive, 'stretch' goals and targets are adopted.

In this chapter I will be using 'vision' to encapsulate strategic 'ends', and I am taking it to convey a mental image of what – in general and qualitative, rather than detailed and quantitative, terms – an airline is to be and is to achieve for its customers, for its people, and for other relevant stakeholders (notably owners). In this sense a vision might be constructed as an answer to the question, 'How do we want our customers and others to describe the airline in, say, five years time?' Customers' perceptions are particularly important because they strongly influence the extent to which specific goals such as profit or shareholder value can be achieved.

A vision might be the result of participative efforts involving groups of stakeholders, or its source might be a single visionary leader. According to O'Brien and Meadows (1998: 39-40),

> A vision is something which is created. Some visions are created deliberately, through controlled, conscious thought; others are created through a less conscious learning process. Some visions appear suddenly, while others build up gradually over time in an incremental process....
>
> A vision underpins and promotes change. It is a necessary precondition for strategic planning, and provides the key criteria against which all strategic options should be evaluated. A vision sets the agenda for the organisation, and gives it direction and purpose....A company which holds a unique and distinctive vision is capable of enduring changes in leadership as well as market conditions.

Not everybody has signed-up to the 'vision thing', however. Kay (1993: 4) refers disparagingly to vision as 'the product of wish-driven strategy' and contrasts it unfavourably with strategy based on '....a careful appreciation of the strengths of the firm and the economic environment it faces'. On the contrary, vision is not 'the product' of strategy but its driver, and neither does having a vision of the future necessarily preclude careful analysis. Vision can and should be informed by commercial understanding. Born from a synthesis of ideas, learning, and evaluation, vision might flow from experience and intuition, from analysis of hard data, or from a little of each – but it need not be 'wish-driven'. A vision should embody a perceived market opportunity framed within a strong opinion about the means necessary to seize it (Holloway, 1998a). There is nothing 'wish-driven' about the FedEx vision:

> We will produce outstanding financial returns by providing totally reliable, competitively superior, air-ground transportation of high-priority goods and documents that require rapid time-certain delivery. Equally important, positive control of each package will be maintained using real-time electronic tracking systems. A complete record of each shipment will be presented with our request for payment. We will be helpful, courteous, and professional to each other and the public. We will strive to have a completely satisfied customer at the end of each transaction.

The FedEx vision identifies a market opportunity and how in general terms it is to be exploited, and it identifies the needs and expectations of key stakeholders – employees, customers, and investors.

Means: strategic action necessary to realise the vision

> Never confuse movement with action.
> Ernest Hemingway

Having painted an 'artist's impression' of what we want to achieve, for our customers in particular, we need next to take action to achieve it. Common synonyms for 'means' include strategy, plan, programme, policy, and even budget. At the macro-level of analysis that we are engaged in here, 'strategy' is the most widely used word. Whereas the concept of strategic management or 'strategy' (without an indefinite article) encompasses both ends and means, '*a* strategy' (with an article) refers only to means – a set of actions taken in response to an unstructured, non-routine, non-programmable problem situation framed in terms of how to move the performance of the organization closer to some desired ends. A 'service strategy' is the means through which an airline's vision of the service it will offer to its customers is to be implemented – the means through which that vision is to be transformed into satisfied customers.

One way of looking at *a* strategy is to treat it as an unproven theory – a hypothesis that certain assumed cause-effect relationships exist between action and outcome: *if* we do X, *then* Y will happen. A strategy is a hypothesis that is being continually tested in the marketplace. This perspective highlights a debate that has been going on in recent years between people who consider it feasible to attain desired outcomes by formally planning what actions to take, and others who believe that organizations and their environments are simply too complex and unknowable to allow us to grasp all the cause-effect relationships that stand between action and outcome. We will return to this debate later in the chapter.

Having briefly outlined the terrain of strategy, we will next take a quick look at two distinct research streams flowing through the field: process and content. This dichotomy exists despite some signs of confluence in recent years, the reasons for which we will come to shortly.

ii. The strategy-making process

Research into strategy-making processes has drawn on a wider range of disciplines than has research into strategy content, engaging behavioural scientists – particularly those with interests in cognition and learning – as well as researchers from systems dynamics, decision science, political science, organization theory, and some of the more recently developed branches of economics such as evolutionary economics, new institutional economics, and game theory. The process stream has two principal currents: strategic choice processes, and the management of strategic change.

Strategic choice processes

> Ever notice that "what the hell" is always the right decision?
> Marilyn Monroe

We have a vision for our airline. What are the processes through which we make decisions regarding the best choice of action to get us from here to there? The question is relevant because it would be helpful to know whether a linkage exists between a firm's performance and the mode of strategy-making it adopts. The answer is likely to lie somewhere on a continuum bracketed by two models: the planning model and the learning model.

The planning model

> To write it took three months; to conceive it took three minutes;
> to collect the data in it took all my life.
> F. Scott Fitzgerald

The classical, distinctly untrendy, yet still widely used planning or 'rational choice' model of strategy-making appears in a lot of different forms, but most share the following deliberate, detailed, formalised, linear steps: specify objectives; analyse the external environment for opportunities and threats, and the internal environment for strengths and weaknesses; state assumptions and make forecasts; formulate possible alternative strategies; choose one of the alternatives (ideally one flexible enough to accommodate a number of plausible scenarios); implement the choice by deploying resources into programmes, action plans, and budgets; monitor implementation and make adjustments in response to any feedback suggesting a negative variance between objectives and performance. 'Facts' go in one end of the strategic planning process, and a formulated plan comes out of the other end; from this plan flow various projects, functional or processual action plans, and budgets. There is in principle cohesion, unity of purpose, and single-mindedness – notwithstanding that culture, human behaviour, and politics often in fact influence what should be a purely rational, almost mechanical exercise.

Formal strategic planning can only be meaningful if it is fully integrated into the running of the business rather than being a ritualised annual 'addendum', if it confronts and tries to resolve issues that are truly strategic rather than being a grandiose budgeting exercise, and if it recognises that analytical techniques are just one dimension of the planning process. On this last point, Piercy (1997: 436) usefully breaks the planning process into three dimensions.

1. **Analytical dimension** Techniques, procedures, systems, and planning models.
2. **Behavioural dimension** Participation, motivation, commitment, and strategic assumptions.
3. **Organizational dimension** Structure, information, management style, and culture.

Successful planning is about analysis and synthesis. Analysis requires analytical tools, techniques, and models. Synthesis – the bringing together of the results of analysis into actionable plans that people are willing and able to implement – depends upon the behavioural and organizational dimensions. To treat behavioural and organizational variables as contextual or peripheral to the 'main focus' of a planning exercise – that is, peripheral to external and internal analyses – is flawed.

Piercy's contribution also alerts us to the fact that there is no single, objective rationality but a multitude of rationalities grounded in each individual's mental model of the world around them. A formalised strategy-making process, even if apparently rational, might in fact be the construction and dissemination of a particular, local rationality; in this case, strategic change may not be the rational redirection of an organization that it is made to appear, but the displacement of one version of rationality – grounded in the perceptions of a single leader, a powerful coalition, a work-group or organizational culture, or an industry recipe, for example – by another (Spender, 2001: 31).

The learning model

> Life is what happens while you're making other plans.
> John Lennon

Although perhaps more so in the literature than in practice, the mechanistic approach to strategy-making fell from favour in the face of growing environmental complexity from the 1970s onwards. The term 'strategic management' came into use, to some extent eclipsing 'strategic planning' (which itself had earlier replaced 'long-range planning'). Quinn (1980) developed the concept of 'logical incrementalism' to highlight the fact that strategy is less a question of regular 'big-bang' changes emanating from the annual planning cycle than it is a series of incremental shifts which build on what has gone before, and which often tend to take place outside the annual plan. Stacey (1996: 35-36) summarises Quinn's concept as follows.

1. Effective managers do not manage strategically in a piecemeal manner. They have a clear view of what they want to achieve, where they are trying to take the business. The destination is thus intended.
2. But the route to that destination, the strategy itself, is not intended from the start in any comprehensive way. Effective managers know that the environment they have to operate in is uncertain and ambiguous. They therefore sustain flexibility by holding open the method of reaching the goal.
3. The strategy itself then emerges from the interaction between different groupings or people in the organization, different groupings with different amounts of power, different requirements for access to information, different time spans and parochial interests. These different pressures are orchestrated by senior managers. The top is always reassessing, integrating and organising.
4. The strategy emerges or evolves in small, incremental, opportunistic steps. But such evolution is not piecemeal or haphazard because of the agreed purpose and the role of top management in reassessing what is happening. It is this that provides the logic in the incremental action.
5. The result is an organization that is feeling its way to a known goal, opportunistically learning as it goes.

Nonetheless, logical incrementalism still assumes rational decision-making processes, so keeping managers in the driving seat and events on the sidelines (Mercer, 1997). More radically, researchers such as Mintzberg and Waters (1978) began developing the concept of 'emergent strategy' to convey a sense that strategy-making is less a matter of rationally formulated and implemented change than a multitude of small alterations in course – many of which in fact arise unplanned from what is learned through the experience of 'doing'. This model shifts the focus away from deliberate strategic (as opposed to operational) planning and control, emphasising instead the imperative of an organizational capacity for strategic thinking and learning.

Strategy from this perspective is not a pre-formulated plan choreographing all the various 'means' by which we will attain our 'ends', but a pattern of mutually-reinforcing decisions sharing a consistent strategic theme and taken under the tutelage of events as they arise – decisions which themselves may not have been fully understood as 'strategic' at the time, but are seen to have been so in retrospect. Strategy-making and strategic change are seen here as one and the same; shared values are assumed to be particularly important in order to keep strategy and change coherent in the context of an agreed vision. Some characterise this as strategy in a tail-spin; others prefer the analogy of fly-by-wire – dynamic responses to unforeseen environmental turbulence made by an open system oscillating between equilibrium and disequilibrium.

The role of top management is seen as articulating an overall direction for the airline, putting into place the organizational architecture (i.e., structure, systems, and relationships) required to support decision-making and action, and influencing the value system and culture within which decisions are made and action is taken. Beyond this, there can be no 'grand plan', simply because in a dynamic competitive environment events will conspire to ensure that what actually happens is never entirely predictable and therefore cannot be orchestrated. Strategic success rests on situational insight, creative thinking, and the effective execution of decisions rather than on detached long-term planning.

Strategy-making in practice

> I never discovered anything with my rational brain.
> Albert Einstein

There is recent research that shows strategic planning has not in fact fallen as far from grace as contemporary management folklore would have us believe, and that variants of both the planning and learning models co-exist within the same companies (Brews and Hunt, 1999). In practice, some of what is intended (i.e., planned) actually happens, and some of it does not; 'realised strategy' – that is, what does actually happen – is an amalgam of bits of intended strategy, together with unplanned action that emerges from learning driven by unfolding (and often unforeseen) events (Mintzberg, 1994). Despite its outwardly rational appearance, strategy-making is a complex process owing as much to cognitive – as well as social and political – influences as to 'rational' choice.

The five conclusions to draw from this discussion are that:

- although many of the comments in this book are couched in terms of rational analysis and decision-making, strategic service management is not in fact as uncomplicated as I hope I am going to make it seem;
- whilst planning remains vital in an environment as complex as the airline industry, strategic planning might need to take a back-seat to strategic thinking – a more open, flexible approach that places less emphasis on trying to predict the future and instead allows for the emergence of strategic actions unguided by explicit *a priori* intentions.

This idea fits well with Peters and Waterman's (1982) concept of simultaneous 'tight-loose' coupling: tight control of short- and medium-term operations and finances, allied to a more adaptable approach to strategy-making;

- even when a formalised, rational planning model of the strategy-making process is used, its objectivity is often more apparent than real – if only because managers normally insert their own intuitive judgements into chosen assumptions;

- there can be no strategy, planned or emergent, without consistency. Whether a strategy comes with an 'owner's manual' – a detailed document specifying programmes and action plans – is less important in a services management context than whether it provides 'a unifying theme that gives coherence and direction to the actions and decisions' through which individuals at all levels make organizations do what they do (Grant, 1998: 3). Porter (1996: 71) argues that, 'In companies with a clear strategic position, a number of higher order themes can be identified and implemented through clusters of tightly linked activities'. We will meet this idea again when discussing service delivery in chapter 7;

- subject to the overriding need for consistency in how it approaches its markets, an airline might want to imbue strategy with sufficient flexibility to allow scope for experimentation and/or 'learning by doing'. The more flexibility there is in the content of a strategy, the closer the strategy-making process that produced it has moved towards the 'learning model'.

It is probably better to think of strategy-making processes not as the *formulation* of strategy through planning, but as the *formation* of strategy through strategic thinking driven by a synthesis of rational planning and 'learning by doing'. Kay (op cit: 358) rejects the 'artificial polarization between a view of the world which sees it as potentially wholly receptive to rational control and planning and one in which events fall as they will'. He argues for 'guided adaptation and managed incrementalism', suggesting that, 'In this framework, the false dichotomies between the implementation and the formulation of strategy, between rational analysis and incremental evolution, and between analytical and behavioural approaches, quickly fall away' (ibid). The idea of strategic 'foresight' has gained currency in recent years: strategic thinking and industry insight help identify plausible scenarios and guide the development of strategic options, whilst extreme perspectives on the knowability of the future driven either by notions of prediction and control or by strategic agnosticism are avoided (Hamel and Prahalad, 1994; Joyce and Woods, 1996).

For a practical example, consider two near simultaneous strategic initiatives launched by British Airways (BA). In the late 1990s BA responded to declining yields and falling profitability by reversing capacity growth. This was a deliberate, planned strategy with clear implications for fleet, network, and product planning: aircraft were down-gauged (e.g., B747 orders were replaced by B777s, and the B757 fleet was earmarked for replacement by smaller Airbuses); low-yield traffic, particularly low-yield flow traffic, was de-emphasised in favour of high-yield – especially high-yield point-to-point – business; premium inflight products were upgraded, and a new full-fare economy cabin was introduced on long-haul flights. Shortly after the formulation of this strategy, BA and KLM began to explore a combination of their businesses. This latter initiative was emergent rather than planned, two unpredicted (although perhaps in hindsight not unforeseeable) circumstances having come together to make it feasible: KLM had terminated its 'virtual merger' with Alitalia, and a new CEO had just arrived at BA. Clearly, there is more to strategy than just planning, important though planning undoubtedly is.

The choice lies not between having a strategy or not having one, but between rigid planning on the one hand and a more flexible, adaptive approach on the other.

Management of strategic change

> You miss 100 per cent of the shots you never take.
> Wayne Gretzky

Earlier in the chapter we identified research into strategy-making processes and into the content of strategies as two important themes within the strategy literature; in both, a major ambition has been to discover linkages between process or content on the one hand and corporate performance on the other. Within the process stream we have just looked at different models of strategic decision-making. Staying within the same stream, a second current of research has focused not on questions of strategy formulation but on implementation issues. Some of this work examines particular implementation variables such as culture and the culture/strategy fit; we will return to the importance of culture in implementing service strategy at various points in the book, particularly chapter 8. Other work attempts to draw the process and content streams together under the umbrella of strategic change by arguing that strategy formulation and implementation cannot be separated in practice, the two being entirely symbiotic. This latter idea is consistent with the notion of strategy as an 'emergent' phenomenon that was outlined in the last section.

Having looked briefly at the process stream within strategy research, we will next turn to the content stream. Of course, the more 'emergent' we believe strategy to be, the less meaningful it is to distinguish between process and content – because content is from this perspective just a single, arbitrarily frozen frame in a continuously unfolding passage of events. Be that as it may, the distinction does help highlight different types of strategy. Thinking in terms of strategy content enables us to distinguish corporate from competitive strategy, for example, and allows links between a source of competitive advantage, a choice of competitive strategy, and ultimate performance outcomes to be hypothesised.

iii. The content of strategy

> The nicest thing about not planning is that failure comes as a complete surprise, and is not preceded by a period of worry and depression.
>
> John Preston

Research into strategy content has primarily tried to establish links between the strategic choices made by decision-makers on the one hand, and superior organizational performance on the other. Superior performance can be pursued down one or both of two avenues.

1. By locating in a high-return industry. Choosing *where to compete* is the arena of 'corporate' strategy.
2. By forging an advantage over competitors in the industry(ies) selected. Choosing *how to compete* is the arena of 'competitive' (or 'business') strategy.

Corporate strategy

There are two closely related decisions involved in corporate strategy: the industrial scope decision – 'Do we want to be a single-business firm or a diversified enterprise?' – and the vertical scope decision – 'In which parts of the value chains of each of our businesses do we want to participate directly?' Turning first to the industrial scope decision, if we want a diversified enterprise should its different businesses be related or unrelated to each other? If related, on what basis should we identify the one or more 'core businesses' around which we will build? Should our objectives in respect of industrial (or, for that matter, vertical) scope be achieved through internal/organic growth, acquisition or collaboration?

Researchers looking at how the strategic choices embodied in these questions might translate into superior performance have concentrated their work into two areas.

1. **Industry attractiveness** The question here is the qualities that make a particular industry an attractive target for investment. According to microeconomic theory, firms in perfectly competitive industries are unable to sustain above-normal returns because these would quickly be competed away by new entrants attracted to the industry. Firms in industries where conditions of monopolistic competition, oligopoly or monopoly prevail are able to earn above-normal returns, but how long this advantage endures will depend upon the nature of whatever barriers to entry are preventing entrants from moving in immediately; these barriers might, for example, be regulatory (e.g., route licensing), physical (e.g., slot shortages), economic (e.g., the scale and scope of incumbents' operations) or competitive (e.g., incumbents' brand images and general market presence).

    Research by industrial organization (IO) economists in the United States during the 1930s was used to help inform government policy by highlighting industries in which incumbents benefit from potentially anti-competitive barriers to entry; these industries were then targeted for commercial regulation. The US airline industry was also brought into the regulatory fold, although the reason in this case was supposedly the prospect that *too much* competition would contribute to financial and operational instability. Forty years later, economists used a new body of work called 'contestability theory' to back deregulation – including airline deregulation – by arguing that the mere threat of entry in a liberalised industry would be enough to discipline anti-competitive behaviour by incumbents; perfect competition, or something approaching its theoretical ideal, was no longer seen as a prerequisite for deregulation provided markets were openly contestable.

    Meanwhile, about the same time that US airlines were being deregulated in the late 1970s, a group of IO economists interested in business strategy were turning the purpose of earlier research on its head by trying to identify attributes of environmental structure which make industries less than perfectly competitive, and therefore potentially attractive arenas in which to invest. Foremost among them was Porter (1980), whose popular five-forces model analyses industry attractiveness by reference to: the bargaining power of suppliers and buyers, the intensity of competitive rivalry, and the threat from new entrants and substitute products.

2. **Diversification** The question in this case is whether investment of corporate resources should be concentrated in one industry or spread over several. Two research themes have addressed this question.

    *   *The portfolio theme* To be valuable, diversification strategies must exploit economies of scope unavailable to external investors; if a corporate portfolio does not benefit from these economies, it might be more efficient for it to be broken up and for investors to be given the freedom to choose whether or not to invest in each of the separate, independent businesses (Barney, 1997). Economies of scope are present within a portfolio when aggregate costs are reduced or revenues are enhanced by virtue of linkages between the operations, the support functions, and/or the financing of different businesses in that portfolio.

        -   *Operational economies of scope* Valuable linkages arise when different services can share inputs or processes. A good example from the airline industry is the economies of scope that can be generated by operating different types of passenger and cargo service within the same system. Operational economies of scope are usually available only under conditions of 'related diversification' – where businesses in the portfolio share inputs, technologies, distribution channels, and/or customers.

        -   *Support function economies of scope* These arise when support functions such as human resources, IS/IT, or marketing can be shared.

        -   *Financial economies of scope* Portfolios might offer either or both tax benefits or risk reduction opportunities. With regard to risk reduction, popular matrices such as the Boston Box and the Directional Policy Matrix were developed in the 1960s and 1970s – primarily by consultants and practitioners – to explore the performance benefits derived from creating synergistic portfolios of investments in businesses at different stages of their life-cycle and having complementary net cash-flow profiles: the idea was that mature businesses would be throwing-off cash for investment in younger, cash-hungry businesses. Strategic decision-making was reduced to choosing which businesses to 'build', which to 'hold', and which to 'harvest' or 'divest'. Appropriately balanced portfolios might also contain businesses whose revenue streams 'hedged' each other as a result of having different levels or types of exposure to economic cycles.

More generally, linkages might exist when a core competence is leveraged from one firm in a portfolio into another. Whereas older analytical approaches looked for the source of superior perform-ance in portfolios constructed on the basis of complementary net cash flows, the interest here is in improving performance by leveraging competencies across industry and product-market boundaries. (We will discuss competencies in the next chapter, in the context of competitive strategy.) Whatever the source of economies of scope, in order for them to underpin a sustainable source of superior performance they must be difficult for others to imitate.

- *The parenting theme* Whereas the portfolio theme investigates synergies between the individual businesses within a corporate portfolio, the parenting theme looks for performance benefits arising from synergies between the corporate centre and each of its businesses. The issue is whether or not the centre adds to or destroys the value that would arise were the businesses independent of the group (Campbell et al, 1995). Economies of scope can be generated if support functions are centralised, for example. Added value can also be created when strategic investment decisions are more efficiently made by a parent with access to detailed inside information on each of its businesses than by a less well-informed capital market trying to finance them independently. Where this is not being achieved, investments in the portfolio – particularly in non-core businesses – simply lock-up funds that could otherwise be invested in core businesses or returned to shareholders.

The essence of the industrial scope decision at the heart of any corporate strategy is whether and, if so, how far to diversify away from the core business. Empirical research suggests that the performance benefits available from related diversification exceed those available from unrelated diversification; research into the relative merits of diversification comp-ared with single-business strategies is widely held to favour the latter, although some researchers consider the evidence equivocal (Barney, 1997; Palick et al, 2000). However, does 'business' mean 'industry' (a supply side concept), 'market' (which marries supply and demand) or a little of both? Of many possible definitions of 'business', perhaps the most useful is to define it as a combination of activities and processes linked within a common supply technology, creating value for specific customers in specific markets. Isolating different production processes each delivering their different products into markets populated by different customers with different needs and wants allows us to distinguish between the passenger and cargo air transport businesses, the maintenance, repair, and overhaul (MRO) business, the flight catering business, the ground handling business, the inbound and outbound tour businesses, the travel products distribution business, and so on.

Many airlines, particularly large carriers, have a portfolio of businesses. Which of these is considered 'core' will depend upon a particular carrier's resource base, competencies, cost structure, history, stakeholders' expectations, and political dynamics. Some related industries traditionally looked upon as being integral to air transport operations are now treated as separate enterprises with their own industrial logic (e.g., MRO businesses). Despite being somewhat 'rough and ready', a useful definition of a 'core business' is one that performs strongly, or has a realistic prospect of performing strongly, in an attractive market in respect of which we have an identifiable and sustainable competitive advantage. Businesses which are weak performers in an attractive market and have little prospect of improving, or strong performers in unattractive markets are arguably 'non-core'. What represents 'strong' performance, of course, is a matter for an airline's stakeholders to sort out amongst themselves when setting objectives and priorities.

The industrial scope decision might result in:

- a single-business corporate strategy: this is the model adopted by carriers concentrating on the transport of passengers and/or cargo as their core business and outsourcing all activities considered 'non-core';
- a portfolio of businesses related to the core air transport business: Lufthansa, Swissair, and Singapore Airlines are just three carriers that have built strong third-party businesses in activities related to air transportation such as maintenance and flight catering, and Lufthansa in 1998 set itself the specific medium-term target of generating 50 per cent of group revenues from services other than the air transportation business;
- a portfolio of businesses both related and unrelated to the core air transport business: most airlines are now less inclined than some have been in the past to involve themselves in activities only tenuously linked to air transport, although several do still have hotel interests whilst other are developing areas such as e-commerce (e.g., United) and financial services (e.g., British Airways).

Whilst this break-down is analytically useful, we need to be aware of two definitional problems: first, what represents a 'core' business is a matter of opinion, with some airlines considering airframe, powerplant, and avionics maintenance to be 'core', and others choosing to outsource some or all of these activities, for example; second, there is no universally accepted definition of 'relatedness' in the context of corporate diversification – some observers thinking in terms of related industries, some in terms of related markets, and others in terms of related competencies.

The SAir Group prior to its 2001 strategic reassessment provides an excellent example of corporate diversification. Its structure is summarised in Box 1.1.

Box 1.1: The SAirGroup in 2000

The SAirGroup was designed during the second half of the 1990s for the explicit purpose of diversifying revenue and profits as an alternative to relying more heavily on the highly cyclical passenger transportation business. A change of management in 2001 halted the policy of taking minority stakes in small, primarily European, carriers as an alternative to joining one of the global alliances; most were underperforming financially, and so magnifying problems already faced by Swissair. There was also a reassessment of the diversification policy, which was felt to be placing too much strain on the Group balance sheet. At the time of this reassessment, the Group was structured as follows.

- *SAirLines: air transport operations (Swissair, together with full ownership of Balair/CTA, majority ownership of Crossair, and minority stakes in several members of the associated Qualiflyer Group of scheduled and charter airlines), distribution (Traviswiss), and financial support (Airline Financial Support Services, based in Mumbai).*
- *SAirServices: MRO activities (SR Technics), ground handling (Swissport), IT (atraxis), real estate (aviReal), and SAirServices Invest. An example of further portfolio diversification is provided by SR Technics' joint ventures engaged in line maintenance, heavy maintenance of Trent 500, 700, and 800 engines (with Rolls Royce), and component inventory management (with Cathay Pacific).*
- *SAirLogistics: air cargo (Swisscargo – the Swissair cargo operation – together with a shareholding in Cargolux and the cargo operations of Crossair and Sabena), and cargo logistics (Cargologic).*
- *SAirRelations: hotels (Swissôtel), catering (Gate Gourmet and Rail Gourmet), duty-free outlets (Nuance), restaurants (Restorama), and hospital catering (Restosana).*
- *Flightlease: aircraft leasing.*

Having considered the industrial scope decision (i.e., which businesses to be involved in), we will next look briefly at a second choice that also arguably falls under the heading of corporate strategy: the vertical scope decision. This is relevant because, as we will see in chapter 7, decisions regarding which part of the value chain to participate in directly – in other words, what to do inhouse and what to outsource – are part of the operating strategy that defines the architecture of an airline's service delivery system.

Vertical scope decisions

Once they have decided which businesses to invest in, strategic managers must next decide the extent to which they want to be involved in the various activities that together contribute to the final service output deliver-ed to the customers of each of these businesses. The activities and process-es that transform multiple inputs into a final service delivered to end-consumers together constitute an industry's value chain; the more of these activities and processes an airline chooses to handle inhouse – that is, within its own corporate value chain – the more 'vertically integrated' it is said to be.

Most start-ups either do not have, or choose not to invest, the capital required to build a well-integrated vertical structure – preferring instead to outsource a large proportion of their activities and processes. The vertical structure of an existing airline, on the other hand, is likely to owe much to that particular carrier's history and the institutional pressures it faces (e.g., to maintain inhouse jobs) as well as to explicit strategic choice. Readers with a predilection for theoretical explanations might prefer the reasoning put forward by an influential sub-field of economics known as transaction cost theory, which argues that the boundaries – indeed the very existence – of firms can be accounted for by the balance of economic benefits that accrue from internalising within the firm certain recurring transactions rather than externalising them into the market. The purpose of internalis-ation is to manage transactions better than they could be managed were the exchanges instead to take place in the external market; 'better' implies cost minimisation and an increase in the efficiency of overall resource allocation. According to this analysis, an organization exists because it is more efficient for it to exist than for the work (i.e., the recurring exchanges) it undertakes internally to be conducted in external markets, outside the framework of that organization. It exists as presently designed because this form is more efficient than any feasible alternative design; were the design not in fact the most efficient possible, the organization would under-perform and eventually be 'selected out' of existence.

Vertical integration may be 'backward' if control over the supply of inputs is sought, or 'forward' if control over distribution channels is acquired. By introducing e-ticketing, promoting online bookings, and in some cases banding together to form jointly owned Internet travel portals, many airlines are at the moment consciously engaged in a push towards forward integration.

There is clearly a degree of overlap between vertical and industrial scope decisions. For example, is an inhouse airframe maintenance capability a result of industrial or vertical scope decisions, and does it matter anyway? The answer is that a distinction can be drawn, blurred though it might sometimes be, and that it does matter: the decision to turn Lufthansa Technik into a major player in the global third-party maintenance market and to make it a stand-alone competitor with its own customers, strategies, and positioning – albeit under the Lufthansa master-brand – is an industrial scope decision that has very different strategic implications compared with a vertical scope decision taken by a carrier that wants to do most or all of its maintenance inhouse, but is not committed to the third-party market beyond selling spare capacity from time-to-time.

iv. Summary

We have identified strategy as a field concerned with decisions and actions oriented towards the long-term direction, the scope, and the competitive stance of organizations – decisions and actions which are essentially purposive and are driven by the airline's vision, albeit mediated by consideration of internal resources and competencies, the external environment, and the expectations of stakeholders. Within the field there are two distinct if overlapping streams of research exploring how strategic decisions are made, and how the content of strategy might contribute to superior performance. In the content stream we have looked at 'corporate' strategy, which examines linkages between industrial and vertical scope decisions on the one hand and performance on the other. We will be considering the second current in the content stream – competitive strategy – in the next chapter. Figure 1.1 outlines the discussion so far and previews our look at competitive strategy.

Figure 1.2 illustrates in a more practical sense what we have covered in the present chapter. The industrial scope – or 'where to compete' – decision that lies at the heart of corporate strategy might leave us with a single-business organization focusing on air transport and involved in nothing else, or with a more diversified group engaged in businesses which themselves might or might not be closely related to the air transport business.

The topic of this book is passenger air transportation, rather than any other business in which an airline might involve itself. We are therefore not concerned with the choice of business – which is a given case – but with

how to compete in that business. Competitive strategy and possible sources
of competitive advantage are the subject of chapter 2.

Figure 1.1 Strategy research streams

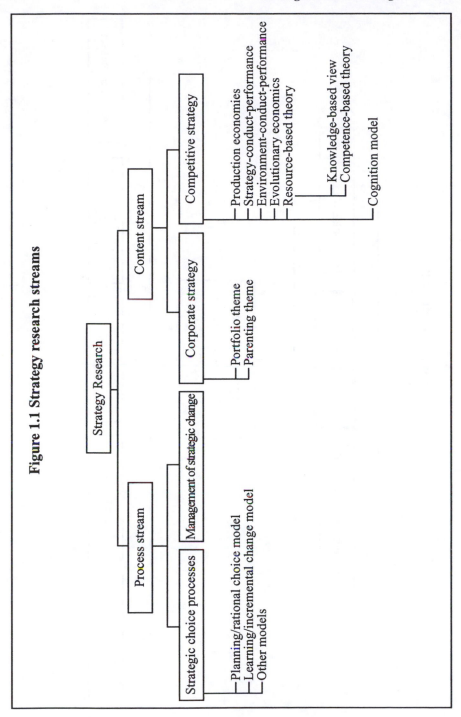

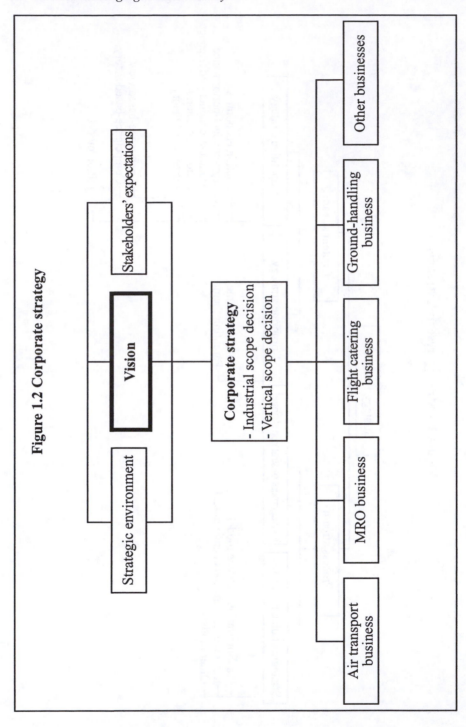

Figure 1.2 Corporate strategy

2 Competitive Advantage

> The danger in today's environment is that the competition may not attack
> you head-on, but eat away at growth opportunities over time
> until they've made you irrelevant.
> Gary Hamel

It is all very well having a vision, but if it leads to commercial success then sooner or later somebody will come along and either imitate or improve upon it. In order to sustain success it is necessary to have at least one source of advantage over the competition that gives rise to something which matters to customers and is difficult, or better yet impossible, for competitors to imitate or substitute.

i. Definition and sources of competitive advantage

> Competitive advantage is based not on doing what others already do well,
> but on doing what others cannot do as well.
> John Kay

Competitive advantage defined

'Competitive advantage' is an expression that is widely used, but often with imprecision. There is in fact no consensus definition. An economist might argue that competitive advantage is anything that permits a firm to earn 'economic rent' – that is, a profit in excess of returns available from equally risky investment alternatives. A more accessible proposition found widely in the strategic management literature is that competitive advantage is whatever allows one firm to earn and sustain a return that outperforms direct competitors. For an airline, this might show up as an ability to earn a larger surplus between unit revenues (i.e., revenue earned per ASM/ASK produced) and unit cost (i.e., cost per ASM/ASK) than direct competitors are able to earn.

However, because the airline industry is a network business, each carrier can potentially face a wide range of different competitors depending upon which city-pair market we choose to analyse; foreign exchange movements between the base currencies of international carriers established in different countries further complicate financial comparison. Competitive advantage is therefore variable from market to market. It is a useful concept rather than a precise number.

Sources of competitive advantage

> Being powerful is like being a lady. If you have to tell people you are, you aren't.
> Margaret Thatcher

Competitive strategy is a question of identifying, exploiting, and sustaining for as long as possible one or more advantages over competitors which enable the airline concerned to serve more effectively and/or efficiently customers that both it and its competitor(s) are targeting. Note that having a competitive orientation and a customer orientation are not the same; we need a balanced perspective that pays attention to both competitors and customers. If the scales must tip in one direction or the other, it should be towards customers.

Researchers from a variety of disciplines (particularly economics) have looked in a number of places for identifiable strategic behaviours and/or resources that can be empirically linked to superior performance. Their search has generated some attractive and in a few cases highly popular theories, but relatively little indisputable evidence of linkages that can be generalised beyond specific contexts at particular points in time. Competitive advantage is nonetheless a valuable concept insofar as it can help provide an intellectual foundation for strategic service management decisions. Note that here we are talking about the *content* of strategic choices rather than the *processes* (whether planned or emergent) through which the choices were arrived at.

Hypothesised sources of competitive advantage examined in the literature have included: market share and production economies; choice of strategic position; national environmental factors; innovation; organizational resources including, in particular, knowledge and competencies; and managerial cognition. We will look briefly at each of these.

Market share and production economies

Particularly during the 1960s and in the context of manufacturing industry, consultants pushed the merits of getting an early start and rapidly building market share. It was argued that benefits would accrue from unit cost advantages derived from economies of scale and from moving along the 'experience curve' ahead of competitors (Henderson, 1974). There is also more recent research from manufacturing industry suggesting that product differentiation used by early-movers to build market share can generate economies of scale and subsequent cost advantages (Womack et al, 1990). Economies of scale – the presence of which on the flight operations side of the air transport industry has been hotly disputed (Holloway, 1997) – arise when average unit costs decline from one period to the next as a function of increasing output volume (i.e., ASMs/ASKs). The experience curve effect – which was first discovered in the aircraft manufacturing business – is evident when unit costs decline as a function of total *cumulative* output over all time periods to date; there is also little empirical evidence to argue the presence of experience benefits in air transport operations.

Airlines as a whole have nonetheless proven themselves, until relatively recently, to be addicted to pursuit of market share. Current output has been seen as a powerful competitive tool insofar as a carrier offering the most capacity in a market (assuming its scheduling to be competitive) is often able to generate a proportionately greater share of sales than competitors can achieve (ibid). This could happen, for example, because that airline's higher frequencies are more likely to offer customers a convenient depart-ure time, and because its departures will dominate the first screens of CRS displays – which is where most agency sales come from; advantage might also arise from having a 'market presence' that is significant enough to curtail customers' search for alternatives by drawing them first to the airline concerned (via its web site, perhaps).

Strategic positioning

> Give me somewhere to stand and I will move the earth.
> Archimedes

Work in the strategic positioning school of competitive strategy is rooted in industrial organization economics (Bain, 1956). Its central argument is that the structure of an industry should shape organizational conduct (i.e., 'strategy'), and superior performance will result if the choice of strategy is sound relative to industry structure; this is sometimes referred to as the structure-conduct-performance (SCP) model. The unit of analysis is the industry rather than the individual firm. An industry's structure is defined by variables such as the number and size distribution of sellers and buyers, the presence of barriers to entry and exit, the scope for product different-iation, the nature of cost structures, and price elasticity of demand; conduct covers choices with regard to product and pricing strategy, advertising, and collusion amongst competitors; and performance refers not just to the results of any one particular firm, but to profitability, output growth, employment trends, and technological advance in the industry as a whole (Douma and Schroeder, 1998).

A variant of the SCP model popularised by Porter (1980, 1985) argues broadly as follows.

- What businesses do is create value. For example, manufacturing busi-nesses transform raw materials into tangible goods that consumers value more highly than the inputs, whilst airlines create 'place utility' by moving people and cargo to locations where their presence is more highly valued.

- The competitive structure of a particular industry influences how value created by the goods or services it produces will be divided between the end-consumer on the one hand, and those who contribute to production and delivery on the other (i.e., how it will be divided between participants in the industry's value chain).

- Industry structure can be modelled using five forces which between them determine the relative strengths of industry participants (i.e., their relative abilities to appropriate value): the bargaining power of suppliers; the bargaining power of buyers; the intensity of rivalry between existing competitors; the threat from new entrants; and the threat from substitute products. The configuration of these forces will vary both between industries and over time within any given industry – as, for example, when a fare war intensifies rivalry between existing competitors.

- Once we have an understanding of an industry's competitive structure, how it might change over time, and what impact changes could have on that industry's profitability and attractiveness as a target for invest-ment, it is possible – according to Porter – to decide on a strategy. For example, if presently outside the industry should the organization remain outside, enter it as currently structured by finding a gap in the market, or enter it and try to rewrite the rules of competition? If already inside the industry, should it remain and, if so, how should it compete? Can it, for instance, select customers, suppliers, and perhaps even competitors who have less power to adversely affect the organization's profitability than others? Superior financial performance, it is argued, comes from choosing and sticking consistently with one of a relatively small range of 'generic' competitive strategies: wide-market cost leadership; wide-market product differentiation; or either cost or differentiation focus within a niche. Cost leadership implies offering an essentially undifferentiated product off an industry-leading cost base, whereas differentiation implies offering something with added values for which customers are prepared to pay a premium. Selection of a strategy is keyed off an understanding of the industry and of the capabilities of the firm and its rivals; it is the result of a combination of initial conditions (in the individual firm and the industry) and executive choice under uncertainty.

- Cost leadership and differentiation – within either a wide-market or focused context – are, with some exceptions noted by Porter (1980), intended to be mutually exclusive. Clear decisions should be made with regard to how competitive advantage is to be sought in targeted markets. An organization choosing to adopt more than one competitive strategy should in principle house these different types of operation in separate units to avoid possible inconsistencies between the distinct approaches to the delivery of customer value that each presupposes.

- 'Sticking consistently' with a strategy means that every activity in the organization's value chain should be coherently orchestrated around the logic underlying the chosen strategy – in other words, around what is necessary to sustain cost leadership, product differentiation, or focus.

- Finally, barriers to entry must be created or, if they already exist, sustained in order to protect the chosen strategic position.

The IO analysis therefore begins with consideration of an industry's structural setting, moves on to a choice of strategic position within that setting, and finally to creation of competitive advantage through effective and consistent management of the firm's entire value chain in the context of whatever strategy is implied by the choice of strategic position. Advantage is contingent on selection of an appropriate strategic position. It is available if the competitive environment is understood, if its constituent forces are correctly diagnosed, if a competitive strategy is formulated which deals appropriately with the particular disposition of forces being confronted, and if the strategy is pursued consistently. Porter (1991: 104) has put the argument as follows.

Competitive advantage results from a firm's ability to perform required activities at a collectively lower cost than rivals, or perform some activities in unique ways that create buyer value and hence allow the firm to command a premium price. The required mix and configuration of activities, in turn, is altered by competitive scope.

The basic unit of competitive advantage, then, is the discrete activity. The economics of performing discrete activities determines a firm's relative cost, not attributes of the firm as a whole. Similarly, it is discrete activities that create buyer value and hence differentiation.

Activities take place within a firm's value chain, which itself is part of a wider value system encompassing also the value chains of upstream suppliers, horizontal partners, downstream distributors, and customers. Underlying each activity is one or more drivers which determine the way it contributes to cost and to product differentiation. Decisions regarding which activities to perform and which not to perform, together with the drivers associated with those activities that are performed, are the ultimate source of competitive advantage (ibid).

According to Porter, competitive strategy is in essence a two-dimensional construct: choice of market scope (niche focus or wide-market) and source of competitive advantage (which contributes to cost leadership or product differentiation). The theoretical prescription is straightforward: make an explicit choice of scope based on an explicit source of competitive advantage (i.e., choose a clearly defined strategic position), or risk getting 'stuck in the middle'. However, whilst Porter's model of competitive strategy has been profoundly influential on practitioners, its theoretical prescriptions have not been fully backed by empirical evidence (Campbell-Hunt, 2000).

National environmental factors

The focus here is on the role of country-specific variables in securing competitive advantage for firms in one country over those in another. The literature has identified several country-specific influences that might affect an airline's strategic decisions.

- **Pressure to innovate** Porter (1990) started this ball rolling by arguing that countries differ in the stimuli they provide to encourage innovation (e.g., competitive pressures, complementary resources, executive mind-sets), and others followed-up by examining differences in the diffusion of knowledge within and across borders as a source of country-specific advantage (Kogut, 1993). For example, deregulation of the US airline industry in 1978 created pressures to innovate far earlier there than elsewhere, hardening the winners for later international market liberalisation.

- **Factor markets** The proximate environment will influence, and in some cases define, the nature and quality of inputs (such as labour) that an airline is able to draw upon (Porter, 1990).
- **Government policy** Murtha and Lenway (1994) argue that companies can create competitive advantage over foreign rivals by aligning themselves with supportive government policies. For example, large US carriers have been well-served by aligning themselves behind their government's open skies policy.
- **Differences in cultural cognition** The argument here is that strategic decision criteria are weighted differently according to managers' home country cultural orientation (Hitt et al, 1997). It is certainly true that carriers in some countries have been slower than others to respond to the threats and opportunities of an increasingly competitive global marketplace, and have allowed more responsive competitors to establish an advantage.
- **Governance system** Thomas and Waring (1999) argue that institutional environments and stakeholders' expectations in different home countries directly influence strategic investment decisions. Even in a global industry different firms will have different views regarding optimal choice of strategy, influenced in part by the institutional environments of their respective home countries. In Anglo-American environments, for example, short-term equity market reaction is widely believed to rank high as a decision criterion, whereas elsewhere other criteria might be more significant. As we will see in chapter 6, there is an argument in the literature that the availability of resources such as external capital, labour, and public goodwill is in part dependent upon the legitimacy of a firm's strategic and other actions as perceived by the 'owners' of those resources (DiMaggio and Powell, 1983).

Innovation

'Evolutionary economics' places innovation at the centre of the search for competitive advantage (Nelson and Winter, 1982). Although it has made a significant contribution to the development of resource-based theory, which we will look at shortly, its unit of analysis is not the individual firm (as is the case in resource-based theory) but the population of competing firms. Whereas neoclassical microeconomic theory casts innovation as an exogenous technological change that is of interest primarily in terms of its contribution to efficiency and profit-maximisation, with the environment here playing a largely deterministic role, evolutionary economics delves deeper to examine the resources, capabilities, and history of a firm. In particular, it looks at entrenched 'routines'; these are patterns of activity which have at some time been deliberately chosen rather than being imposed by the environment and which, *inter alia*, encourage and maybe even incentivise or, alternatively, discourage and perhaps penalise innovative behaviour.

> Organizations develop particular ways of behaving which become 'the way we do things around here' as a result of repetition and reinforcement. These patterns reflect an underlying set of shared beliefs about the world and how to deal with it, and form part of the organization's 'culture'. They emerge as a result of repeated experiments and experience around what appears to work well – in other words, they are learned. Over time the pattern becomes an automatic response to particular situations, and the behaviour becomes what can be termed 'routine' (Tidd et al, 1997: 32-33).

Routines are created from a mixture of technologies, formal procedures, and informal conventions or habits, and they evolve in response to learning about what works and what does not (Levitt and March, 1988). In this sense they are part of corporate memory. More pertinent to our discussion in this chapter, they are 'what makes one organization different from another in how they carry out the same basic activity' (Tidd et al, 1997: 34). They might well be the bedrock of distinctive capabilities, but they can also be a force for inertia; whether or not they are open and adaptive is a significant factor determining how readily an airline responds to environmental change. In this sense evolutionary economics shares similarities with what is known as the Austrian school of economics, which focuses on the competitive process rather than on static equilibrium in markets and argues that decision-making improves over time as experience is gained in the face of endemic change and uncertainty. The eventual outcome is more competitive market conditions (Sinclair and Stabler, 1997).

Evolutionary economics encompasses several themes we will be picking up later in the book – notably capabilities and competencies, innovation, learning, and continuous improvement. Two of its concepts in particular need to be borne in mind.

1. **Path dependency** The route taken by an airline to get to where it is now will have a significant impact on where its search for competitive advantage can take it in the future. This is because learning is typically incremental rather than 'breakthrough'; routines that have worked well in the past tend to be more susceptible to incremental improvement than to being dispensed with in a single 'big bang'. One implication is that it might not be possible for a strategy to be rapidly changed, even when the need for change is correctly identified.[1]

2. **Firm-specific assets** These can be a particularly important source of competitive advantage. On the other hand, innovation is frequently constrained by over-attention to past expenditures already sunk into assets which might become redundant in the event that new routines, processes, or products were to be introduced.

We will meet these concepts again.

Organizational resources

> I have ten against one hundred, but I always attack ten against one.
> One hundred times. That way I win.
> Mao Tse-tung

The resource-based theory of competitive advantage (RBT) argues that whether or not a firm can earn above-average returns depends upon the distinctive qualities of the resources it has had the luck or acumen to acquire, together with what is done with those resources (Zou and Cavusgill, 1996). In other words, performance is contingent on possessing and correctly configuring strategically relevant resources. Whereas Porter's SCP approach looks to industry-wide factors and a firm's choice of strategic position to account for different levels of performance, the RBT looks to firm-specific factors; the firm, rather than the industry, is the unit of analysis in the search for sources of competitive advantage on which to build a competitive strategy. The core argument is that it is simply impossible for any firm to sustain a competitive advantage in an industry with homogenous and perfectly mobile resources: only a firm's heterogeneous and imperfectly mobile resources can lead to sustained competitive advantage (Barney, 1991). Basic propositions of the RBT are as follows.

- A firm is comprised of an integrated bundle of resources – human, physical, intangible, reputational, and processual, for example (Selznick, 1957; Penrose, 1959; Rumelt, 1984; Wernerfelt, 1984; Barney, 1991). The specialised linkages which integrate these resources imbue them with more 'value in use' to the airline concerned than their individual 'exchange value' in factor markets; some, such as organizational routines (Nelson and Winter, 1982) and unarticulated 'know-how', might be impossible to value outside the context of a particular firm.
- In contrast to the assumptions of SCP theory, resources are considered to be potentially – although not inevitably – both individually distinct and imperfectly mobile between firms. Each airline might therefore be

characterised as having a unique portfolio of resources, both tangible (e.g., physical and human) and intangible (e.g., hubs, networks, systems, practices, culture, and reputation). The way in which linkages within a vertically integrated airline and relationships with external parties – partners in a strategic alliance or within a looser network of co-operating firms – are co-ordinated can also be important resources that competitors might find difficult to imitate.

* The accumulation of resources is 'path dependent' – that is, whether through good fortune or sound investment, the portfolio of resources in each airline's possession today is shaped by its own particular history. Path dependency is closely associated with the concept of organizational learning insofar as firms are generally believed to learn better in domains that are close to existing activities than when they diversify away from their established 'path' (Foss, 1997).

* Competitive advantage can flow from having strategically relevant resources which are:
    - valuable, in the sense that they assist exploitation of opportunities and neutralisation of threats (and therefore make a specific contribution, over whatever timeframe, to either or both the revenue or cost side of the income statement);
    - unique or, at least, rare amongst current and potential competitors;
    - imperfectly mobile;
    - not susceptible to easy imitation or substitution (Barney, 1991).

If external environments in general and markets in particular are now in a constant state of flux, it is argued, there is more merit in developing a reservoir of resources available to cope with rapid and perhaps unforeseeable change than in attempting to maintain a constant position in that continuously shifting landscape (Elfring and Volberda, 2001).

* Competitive strategy is a conscious attempt to capitalise on the firm's endowment of strategic resources (Zou and Cavusgil, 1996). This is done by matching resources to available opportunities that can be exploited at an acceptable level of risk, and by using them wherever possible to neutralise threats (Foss, 1997). In other words, resources are exploited either by entering markets in which they convey an advantage, or by creating markets in which they can be deployed to advantage. Particular emphasis is often placed on the use of unique and hard-to-copy resources (Rumelt, 1984, 1987; Barney, 1986b; Conner, 1991). For example, Delta decided in the late-1990s to de-emphasise direct services to Asia and instead deploy scarce long-haul capacity to access Latin American markets; this was a classic example of a path dependent resource – in this case the carrier's Atlanta hub – being used

as a source of advantage to underpin a competitive strategy (the primary competitor in this case being American's smaller Miami hub).

- If a resource is to be a source of competitive advantage, it must contribute to something that an airline can do for its targeted customers that is valuable, non-substitutable, and difficult for competitors to imitate (Bogner and Thomas, 1994), or to something that enables the airline to satisfy customer needs at a lower cost than competitors (Barney, 1986a). In other words, it must yield positional advantage whether in terms of price, differentiation or both – *as perceived by customers*. Management has a responsibility to identify and invest in resources, particularly in hard-to-copy or inimitable resources, capable of yielding superior performance over a sustained period of time (Rumelt, 1987). Success flows both from accumulating and combining valuable resources, and from defending them against competitive attacks on their capacity to generate economic rent. A resource is valuable if 'it exploits opportunities and/or neutralises threats in a firm's environment' (Barney, 1991: 105). Proponents argue that a particular strength of RBT is its willingness to vest significance in socially complex resources – such as culture, teamwork, and internal and external relationship patterns – as potential sources of competitive advantage (Barney and Hesterley, 1996).

Within a diverse and not always consistent literature, we can highlight two concepts that will be met again at various points later in the book.

- **Tacitness** A resource (which, depending upon the definition adopted, can include a skill) is tacit if it is difficult to articulate and codify. The more tacit a resource – such as an organizational 'routine' or an established 'way of doing things' – the more likely it is to be 'path dependent' and the less likely it is to be imitated by a competitor (Nelson and Winter, 1982). This idea of tacitness draws on the concept of tacit knowledge developed by Polanyi (1962, 1966); tacit knowledge is now widely seen as an important potential source of competitive advantage because it is by definition difficult to articulate and imitate.
- **Causal ambiguity** When an airline's resources are tacit, highly firm-specific, complex, linked, and deeply embedded into the organization in an opaque, difficult-to-understand, hard-to-copy, and taken-for-granted way, the sources of its competitive advantage and the success attributable to that advantage can be said to be 'causally ambiguous' (Rumelt, 1984). For example, 'while new products at lower prices may be apparent, the strategic reasoning that led to the changes, the technological capabilities which made them possible, and the skills of

the people who executed the new strategy are likely to be much more difficult to define and copy' (Tallman and Atchison, 1996).

Box 2.1 describes how resources might be identified.

Box 2.1: Identifying resources

Nobody would remember the Good Samaritan if he'd only had good intentions.
He had money as well.
Margaret Thatcher

There is a lot of definitional imprecision in the literature regarding what exactly constitutes a 'resource' – a term which is variously taken to encompass skills, capabilities, and competencies (none of which is itself precisely defined to everybody's satisfaction) as well as tangible and intangible assets; some resources are subject to ownership or contractual rights, but many are not. Another problem is that nobody has yet proposed a widely accepted basis for deciding which of a firm's resources contribute – and contribute what – to competitive advantage. It can nonetheless be helpful to think of an airline as a bundle of resources (including skills) which can be used to produce a service valued by final consumers. Value chain analysis, touched upon in chapter 7, can provide a convenient frame-work within which to identify resources.

Resources might be tangible, such as gates at a congested hub, or a modern fleet benefiting from high levels of commonality and suited to the economics of the network being served; or they might be intangible, such as ready access to capital, possession of a route authority, workforce commitment, a service-oriented culture, or ownership of a well-regarded brand-name attracting a substantial and loyal customer base. They might belong to the airline concerned or, as is true of airport slots in many parts of the world, their legal ownership might be in doubt. Resources can be firm-specific *if controlled by the airline concerned, or* firm-addressable *if they are not controlled but are nonetheless accessible (e.g., through a formal alliance or a looser network of co-operating firms).*

What constitutes a strategic resource evolves over time, particularly when the competitive environment is being liberalised or deregulated. Wherever competing airlines have relatively equal access to markets and to the technologies needed to serve them, it is quite often the tacit, causally ambiguous intellectual resources available for deployment, and the effect-iveness with which they can be harnessed to deliver value to customers, that provide the foundation for competitive advantage.

In order to manage a resource we need to be able to do several things (Easton and Araujo, 1996).

- *Identify how it is or could be created, how it might depreciate or in some other way change over time, what its maintenance needs are, and whether it has a definable life and replacement cycle. Impending, as well as existing, resource gaps need to be identified.*
- *Evaluate its worth (in economic terms, its capacity to generate economic rent) in order to justify investments in building and/or maintaining it. Grant (1998: 128) attributes the profit-earning potential of a resource to three variables.*
  1. *The extent of any competitive advantage it embodies, which is a function of its scarcity and its relevance to key success factors in the market(s) being targeted.*
  2. *Sustainability of the competitive advantage it establishes, which is a function of its durability, its transferability (that is, its mobility – how easily competitors could get hold of it), and its replicability (or imitability).*
  3. *Appropriability, which determines who benefits from the returns generated by a resource and is a function of property rights (e.g., who 'owns' key organizational knowledge?), relative bargaining power (e.g., can key managers or labour groups appropriate a significant share of the airline's profit potential?), and embeddedness (e.g., is a resource – such as team spirit, service orientation, or customer understanding, for instance – too inseparable from the company's culture, brand image, or information systems to be separately attributed to any one individual or group?).*
- *Identify who controls it (whether inside or outside the airline), how readily accessible it is, and whether it is tradable.*
- *Understand how it might be combined with other resources in a strategically useful way. A resource might be a 'fundamental unit' (e.g., a slot at a congested hub) or a 'compound' created from other underlying resources (e.g., an airline's schedule). Whereas a compound resource can be broken down and its underlying units recombined in some way, a fundamental resource cannot be subdivided. Of course, it might not always be sensible to treat a compound resource as something that can be dismantled and rearranged (e.g., a brand image). The more readily a resource can be combined with other resources, the more 'versatile' it is. However, versatility is not just an innate property of a resource; it also depends upon an airline's people having sufficient insight to see merit in a particular combination of resources, as well as the management processes being in place to make*

> *it happen. The more a resource is tacit, causally ambiguous, and generally hard to recognise and comprehend, the more difficult it is likely to be to combine with other resources (and, on the other hand, the more difficult it is for competitors to imitate).*

Within resource-based theory (RBT), particular attention has been paid over the last decade to the impact of knowledge and competencies on corporate performance.

Knowledge Whilst RBT in general treats knowledge as one among many different resources, some researchers have put forward what they have called a 'knowledge-based view' of the firm and competitive strategy. They argue that heterogeneous stocks of knowledge, accumulated in a 'path dependent' way from both internal efforts and external sources, are the major determinants of performance differences between firms (Foss, 1996). From this perspective, the importance of knowledge lies not just in whether or not an airline has a current knowledge base that gives it certain competitive capabilities, but in whether it is able to create and transfer knowledge – in other words, whether it is able to organize in such a way that it can efficiently accumulate and deploy the knowledge necessary to give it a substantial competitive edge over time.

Competencies If knowledge is a special-case example of a resource, then competencies might be characterised as a special-case example of knowledge (Foss, 1997). The competence-based approach to inter-firm competition suggests that performance differences may result not just from choice of strategic position in the marketplace (i.e., low-cost or differentiation) or from heterogeneous resource endowments; it argues that they are also attributable to differences in the mental models of their industry's strategic logic held by decision-makers, and to the varying abilities of these decision-makers to co-ordinate resource deployment in response to the models they hold (Mahoney and Sanchez, 1997).

There is, of course, the question of what separates a 'competence' from a 'routine'. The strategy literature is nothing if not promiscuous in its use of conceptual language and – as so often noted in the early chapters of this book – there is no universally accepted answer. Grant (1998: 125-126) sees routines – that is, 'regular and predictable patterns of activity made up of coordinated [but not necessarily overtly directed] actions by individuals' – as 'the basis of most organizational capabilities' (and he treats 'capabilities' and 'competencies' as synonymous). Baden-Fuller and Volberda (1997: 96) have suggested the following plausible distinction.

We view *competence* as involving shared knowledge among a large group of units within the complex firm, whereas a *routine* is seen as the province of only one or, at most, a few units. A competence therefore draws on several routines which have been refined, stored, and codified, or socialized.

Presumably, though, the smaller and less complex an airline is, the more difficult it becomes in practice to distinguish competencies from routines.

Be that as it may, competence-based theory relies on two important concepts to which, it is argued, competitive advantage might be traceable.

- **Mental models** These are assumptions and generalisations adopted by managers to simplify the search, capture, processing, and organization of information and the prediction of decision outcomes (Morecroft, 1992). Useful though these models can be for coping with complexity, they may hinder the development of competencies in two ways: first, they might not change sufficiently rapidly to keep pace with environmental change and the need for competence-building this imposes – which means that they could be a force for inertia or for only incremental change when radical competence-building is actually required; second, it would be unusual for all members of an airline's management team to share precisely the same model of their business even if outwardly this appears to be the case – what is believed and acted upon not invariably being the same as what is espoused. (Scenario modelling can help overcome both problems; see van der Heijden (1996), and Ringland (1998), for example.)

  It needs to be borne in mind that an entire industry can develop a flawed mental model or mindset simply because its leaders look predominantly towards each other for standards of best practice. From time to time outsiders come along to challenge such 'meta-groupthink' (Senge, 1990).

- **Strategic logic** Sometimes also referred to as 'business logic', this is a belief system which links certain actions (notably deployment of resources) to targeted outcomes. Managers' strategic logic is in essence a 'theory of competition' that guides resource deployment in pursuit of a favourable response from the market. Highly complex in practice, a decision-maker's strategic logic is likely to encompass at a minimum 'the structure of needs which generates demand, the rational and irrational factors which define product quality, the identity and likely behaviour of competitors, barriers to entry and exit, the characteristics of different channels of distribution, and the skills and technologies which are essential for the provision of services' (Sutton, 1998: 12-13).

This strategic logic is being continuously tested in the marketplace (Sanchez et al, 1996).

According to competence-based theory, performance is contingent not simply on possession of resources (including skills), but on how effectively they are combined and deployed pursuant to a particular strategic logic of the way in which the business functions. In manufacturing companies, competencies are often technological; in service industries such as the airline business, they are more likely to be derived from operating systems, human resource policies, and corporate culture (Ind, 1997).

What drives strategically important differences between airlines according to this theory of competitive advantage is their different strategic logics, the different choices made with regard to leveraging existing competencies and building future competencies, and the different degrees of effectiveness they show in operationalising their choices. Carriers with broadly similar resource bases may therefore have very different competencies because their resources are deployed and co-ordinated in different ways. Figure 2.1 shows how competence leveraging and building fit within a product-market framework.

What are necessary to compete in any particular market are interrelated competencies managed as a system. The more opaque the manner in which these competencies are combined and the more causally ambiguous the performance to which they give rise, the less imitable they are likely to be. (Of course, causal ambiguity might also make an airline's own success more difficult to understand, sustain, and replicate.) As with resources, managers should identify strategically relevant competencies, protect them against imitation, substitution or neutralisation, leverage them, and build on them.

Competitive dynamics within an industry are from this perspective characterised as the result of management teams, each with their own cognitions and mental models of the competitive environment, creating new resource configurations and deployment patterns in pursuit of more favourable market responses. Competitive strategy from this perspective is a contest between managerial cognitions and mindsets in devising strategic logic (Sanchez, 2001). Stated formally, competence-leveraging generates current cash flows which – together with any additional capital raised from external sources – are potentially available to build further competencies; the building of competencies creates strategic options for the future which, if exercised, hold the prospect of generating incremental cash flows (Sanchez, 1993). Airline managers are therefore responsible for maximising both the NPV of current cash flows and their firms' options to

Figure 2.1 Matching competencies to market needs

MARKETS

	Existing	New
Existing	Can we leverage our competencies better to improve market penetration?	Can we leverage our competencies better to develop services for new markets?
New	What competencies must we build to defend the future of our current market position?	What competencies must we build to create new market opportunities under alternative scenarios?

COMPETENCIES

create future cash flows; in other words, they are responsible for maximising the 'economic value' of the firm. This view aligns competence-based theory with the mainstream of contemporary finance theory. It is a more dynamic concept of competitive advantage than characterising competition as a battle between products, a battle for strategic position, or a battle to accumulate resources (without any thought to their deployment).

Two concepts drawn from competence-based theory that have had wide currency and will be met at various points in the book are 'distinctive competencies' and 'core competencies'. There is no consensus definition of either. We will look at each in turn.

Tallman and Atchison (1996) have suggested a framework which can help in identifying 'distinctive' competencies.

- **Industry-specific competencies** These are 'qualifying competencies' that participants need in order to compete. Although they might act as entry barriers keeping players out of the industry, they are not a source of competitive advantage to any already competing within it.
- **Strategy-specific competencies (SSCs)** As the name suggests, these are required if an airline is to successfully pursue a particular strategy – say, product differentiation. Airlines implementing similar market strategies on the basis of similar SSCs share what is sometimes referred to as a 'strategic configuration'; strategic configurations are often used to help identify separate strategic groups, and in this context SSCs can be characterised as both a qualification for group membership and a mobility barrier limiting movement between groups. Drawing initially on industrial organization economics – the same research stream from which much of Michael Porter's widely recognised work has flowed – the strategy literature has for some time been concerned with the existence and competitive implications of 'strategic groups' of somehow similar firms within a particular industry. These groups have typically been taken to be comprised of firms clustered around distinct strategic positions chosen in response to shared environmental opportunities and threats or, more recently, similar resource combinations. More recently still, cognitive mapping has been developed as a technique for identifying groups on the basis of the cognitive frameworks and perceptions of managers – frameworks and perceptions that are both sense-making devices and, importantly, drivers of the modes of competition in the industry concerned (Gorman et al, 1996). As noted above, strategic groups might also be identified by the similar competencies of their members (Rispoli, 1996).

  There is a link between cognition-based and competence-based approaches to the definition of strategic groups insofar as individual managers in similar airlines are likely to share cognitive frameworks, perceptions of industry developments, and preferences for dealing with these developments – leading to similar strategic choices and the building and leveraging of similar strategy-specific competencies.

Whilst SSCs will be less visible, comprehensible, or imitable than industry-specific competencies, they may nonetheless not be sufficient in themselves to deter entry by competitors if the returns to any particular configuration grow far in excess of industry norms. In this sense, SSCs are a basis not for sustained *competitive* advantage but for *contestable* advantage.

- **Firm-specific competencies (FSCs)** These are close to the widely used but often loosely defined concept of 'distinctive competencies'. A distinctive competence is a strategically relevant competence about which it is possible to say either:
  - we are the only people able to do this; or
  - we do it better than anybody else.

As formulated by Selznick (1957), a 'distinctive competence' is something systemic and integrative – something unique to an individual business which allows it to integrate other competencies into a pattern of activities that competitors can see but not fully understand or imitate. Since then, the concept has been broadened through usage. According to Dosi and Teece (1998: 284), '[A] distinctive competence is a differentiated set of skills, complementary assets, and organization routines which together allow a firm to coordinate a particular set of activities in a way that provides the basis for competitive advantage in a particular market or markets.' To qualify as 'distinctive', a competence must pass the 'VRIO test' (Barney, 1997):
  - it must contribute to something of **V**alue insofar as it reduces costs and/or increases revenues;
  - it must be **R**are;
  - it must be **I**nimitable;
  - the airline must be **O**rganized to leverage it.

Truly distinctive competencies underpin competitive advantage. However, it is worth noting that distinctiveness might not arise from a single competence, but from a unique pattern of relationships established between competencies which individually are not in themselves distinctive; distinctiveness in this case is due to the synergies arising from the whole being greater than the sum of the parts (Eden and Ackermann, 1998).

Whereas industry- and strategy-specific competencies get an airline into its chosen 'game', it is firm-specific competencies that enable it to establish customer preference and earn a shot at 'winning' the game. FSCs are often path dependent (i.e., attributable to the specific history of a particular airline). More significant from the point of view of their resistance to imitation and so their sustainability, they are frequently tacit and causally ambiguous (Rumelt, 1984). FSCs can be opaque and difficult to understand, being deeply embedded in diffuse organizational processes (Reed and De Fillippi, 1990), 'ways of doing' and 'routines' (Nelson and Winter, 1982), culture, myriad sources of brand image, and the internal and external relationships that shape organizational architecture (Kay, 1993). It is the difficulty others have in comprehending FSCs that constrains imitation and keeps them 'distinctive'. Having said that, the higher the returns that an airline's FSCs appear to be earning, the more likely somebody is to try to imitate them; this is particularly true as an industry is liberalised, competition globalises, and competencies that were once distinct within a protected market are no longer distinct vis a vis new competitors. And if imitation proves impossible, an innovative competitor might instead substitute its own set of competencies – perhaps rewriting the 'rules' of industry competition, as low-fare start-ups have done in Europe and the Americas.

Turning now to 'core competencies', there is again no agreed definition. My interpretation is that a core competence is a distinctive competence that:

- defines a firm's fundamental business (Teece et al, 1997);
- makes a disproportionately high contribution to the delivery of customer value (a concept that will be discussed in chapter 3); and/or
- can be used across internal boundaries separating functions or strategic business units, or across product-market boundaries, to contribute to the building of a portfolio of related businesses (Hamel and Prahalad, 1994; Rumelt, 1994). It is this concept of tacit, knowledge-based routines (Nelson and Winter, 1982) being leveraged from one part of an enterprise to another that Prahalad and Hamel (1990) had in mind when they popularised the expression 'core competencies of the corporation'.

Whereas the core competence concept is commonly rolled out by strategists to rationalise organizational downsizing, it was in fact at birth used to argue in favour of building on the strength of an integrated whole rather than peeling it apart, layer by layer, in search of 'the core'. The concept is potentially much richer than the shrinkage and focus with which it became widely associated amongst practitioners of strategic management during the 1990s (Holloway, 1998a). Summarising Rumelt (1994: xv-xvi), Sanchez (2001: 152) notes that core competencies arise through the collective learning developed by a firm as it co-ordinates production skills, integrates different technologies, and learns from experience how best to use its resources (including human resources) and capabilities; the locus of competition shifts from product versus product to competitive acquisition of skills.

Box 2.2 outlines how competencies might be identified and used.

Box 2.2: Isolating and using competencies

We have seen that a competence is the ability to sustain deployment of a resource or a combination of resources, to do so intentionally, for a goal-oriented purpose according to a particular strategic logic of how the business functions (which is being continuously tested in the marketplace), and to attain these goals (i.e., targets which, if met, will help close the gap between the current situation and what is desired in respect of, say, growth, profits, or customer satisfaction). Lewis and Gregory (1996) have proposed a four-step procedure for isolating competencies.

1. *Identify and model the firm's activities and constituent resources.*
2. *Establish the firm's goals, and the strategies being pursued to attain them.*
3. *Relate identified activities and resources to the strategies and goals to which they contribute, then isolate combinations of resource deployment and activity as separate competencies.*
4. *Develop a 'competence map' to help monitor changes in the leveraging and building of competencies over time.*

A search for competencies could be co-ordinated on a functional basis – in marketing, sales, customer service, ground operations, flight operations or engineering, for example. This has the advantage of being conceptually straightforward, but recourse to vertically oriented functional 'silos' such as these ignores the fact that customer-serving processes tend to be horizontal and cross-functional. Extending a proposal by Chiesa and Manzini (1997), and amending somewhat their terminology, we can suggest that competencies might be found on three levels within an airline.

1. *Operational level An airline's most basic competencies lie in its ability to produce output marketable to target customers.*
2. *Value-defining level At this level specific knowledge, skill sets, and complementary assets are deployed in repeatable patterns to create customer value in distinctive ways that competitors cannot match.*

Both these levels are concerned with competence-leveraging. We will see in chapter 4 that they have parallels with the ideas that service itself is offered at different levels – with 'core service' and 'expected service' equating to the operational level above, and 'augmented service' fitting with the notion of added customer value being used to define and distinguish a service.

3. Cognitive level *Competencies here lie in the abilities of senior managers to perceive the evolutionary dynamics of their competitive environments, to develop an appreciation of the firm as a co-ordinated, integrated, goal-oriented system of resource flows, to develop industry foresight (Hamel and Prahalad, 1994), and to seize intellectual leadership by building competencies that will enable the firm to compete in future.*

A static analysis might look at competencies on each level. A more dynamic understanding would come from considering the often opaque organizational routines through which the three levels interact as competencies are leveraged and built. At any level, both resources and competencies can be firm-specific (i.e., internally controlled) or firm-addressable (i.e., accessible through relationships with external actors – relationships that might range from transactional through to partnerships).

The literature suggests that having identified competencies, management initiatives can then be grouped into three categories.

1. Competence-leveraging *According to competence-based theory of competitive strategy, it is the ability of some airlines to deploy their existing resources more effectively and efficiently than others that accounts for current differences in performance. An airline's initial resource endowment is only one of the ingredients; others include the way in which resources are nurtured, augmented (perhaps through collaboration with other organizations), combined, and concentrated in pursuit of clearly defined objectives. Any distinctive or core competence which contributes to competitive advantage is a particularly strong candidate for retention and investment rather than outsourcing: if a competence really is a source of competitive advantage for a particular airline, it is likely that no other organization would be in a position to accomplish the tasks involved more effectively and efficiently.*

2. Competence-building *An evolving portfolio of competencies is a more flexible platform with which to face the future than a portfolio of products alone. A competence portfolio can be built to provide flexibility in one or more of three dimensions (Volberda, 1996).*

- Operational flexibility *The ability of an airline's service delivery system to respond flexibly to demand changes in respect of volume and/or quality.*
- Structural flexibility *The ability of an airline's architecture of internal and external relationships, and of both its communication and decision-making processes, to adapt to changing conditions.*
- Strategic flexibility *The ability of an airline to shift goals and strategies in response to changing conditions, as well as to adjust its values and norms if necessary.*

3. Rigidity-stalking *Leonard-Barton (1992a) has drawn attention to the danger that a core competence might become a 'core rigidity'. Firms can find themselves trapped when the organizational routines that contribute to their current success channel learning too narrowly and inhibit the search for new ways of coping with change (Nelson and Winter, 1982; Teece, 1984). The concept of 'path dependency' met earlier alerts us to the danger that an airline's financial, political, and/or emotional investments in existing competencies might constrain its future behaviour. Like other organizations, airlines need to adopt a dynamic, questioning approach to the leveraging and building of competencies. As markets and technologies quickly change, it is often small or start-up carriers that have the flexibility to build the newly required competencies, whilst larger incumbents must not only try to do the same but do it whilst weaning themselves away from what has happened in the past.*

Thus, investment in competence-building 'buys' options for future action in pursuit of the airline's goals, whereas competence-leveraging involves exercising options for action created by earlier competence-building. Both competence-leveraging and competence-building should be consistent with the carrier's strategic logic – that is, the (explicit or implicit) rationale which is widely accepted by decision-makers as linking particular patterns of resource deployment with goal attainment. Either might be accomplished individually or within the context of competence-leveraging *or* competence-building alliances.

The concepts of competence-building and competence-leveraging are implicit in Hamel and Prahalad's (1994) three-tier approach to securing industry leadership.

1. *Compete to gain intellectual leadership by developing 'foresight'.*
2. *Compete to manage a better 'migration path' for the firm – which in essence means building the competencies that foresight suggests will be*

> *necessary to succeed in future, either alone or in partnership with other firms, whilst also maintaining strategic flexibility.*
> 3. *Compete for a profitable, and if feasible dominant, market share by leveraging existing competencies to meet customers' needs better than competitors are able to meet them.*

A caveat is in order, however. In the last chapter I introduced the 'learning model' of the strategy-making process and the associated concept of 'emergent strategy'. If we subscribe to this view of how strategies arise, it follows that we might not always be able to identify required competencies in advance of needing them; strategies that unfold in real time or are identifiable only in retrospect may depend on competencies that also emerge under the tutelage of events rather than out of formal strategic plans. Indeed, experimentation and learning have been argued to be a critical link between the identification of competencies and their transformation into day-to-day actions that 'get the job done' (Leonard, 1998). This takes us back to the need for industry foresight and the building of a portfolio of competencies adequate to provide strategic flexibility. Easy to write about in abstract, this is an organizational skill of some scarcity and value in most industries – and the airline industry is no exception.

Finally, it is worth noting that while some authors draw no distinction between the concepts 'competence' and 'capability' (Hamel and Prahalad, 1992), others do. Stalk et al (1992), for example, have defined a 'strategic capability' as an end-to-end, customer-serving process performed at a level of excellence that competitors find hard to copy. Their concept of capabilities-based competition embracing all an organization's processes complements, but is broader than, the competence-based approach (Lynch, 1997). There is also a school of thought referred to as 'dynamic capabilities' which extends the resource-based view by considering ways in which organizations identify, develop, and use resources (or 'strategic assets') to build competitive advantage and generate economic rent (Amit and Schoemaker, 1993; Teece et al, 1997); in this sense, 'dynamic capabilities' represent a way-point en route between resource-based theory and the competence-based approach.

I mention this here because the literature sometimes uses 'competencies' and 'capabilities' interchangeably, and sometimes distinguishes them as, respectively, a meta-technology or skill (a 'dynamic capability' or perhaps a 'competence') or a difficult-to-imitate combination of processes having a definable customer-serving outcome (a 'capability'). Neither capability nor competence can be bought 'off-the-shelf' or developed overnight – otherwise their value would readily be competed away. Their development usually requires a substantial investment of time and money in the promotion of learning and the building of a supportive cultural and systems infrastructure. Either way, we should know what each concept means when using these terms.

Managerial cognition

Another field in which research has looked for linkages between strategic choice and competitive advantage is managerial cognition. Managers (and other individuals) are constantly making sense of the world as they perceive it by incorporating new information into their cognitive frameworks. 'Cognition' is concerned with the mental processes through which knowledge is acquired, stored, transferred, and used (Matlin, 1998). We can see here a blending of the strategy process and content streams insofar as the nature of the strategy-making process – in this case driven by the cognitions of individual strategists – is seen as influencing the content of competitive strategy more than, say, market structure (cf the positioning school) or the firm's resources (cf resource-based theory).

Schneider and Angelmar (1993) have classified studies of cognitive processes in organizations into three bodies of research.

- **Cognitive structure** The categories, maps, and other knowledge structures into which information is processed, the cause-effect links established between different categories, the effect of categorisations upon the handling of complex situations by individuals, and the integration of shared cognitions within groups of decision-makers.
- **Cognitive processes** The ways in which new information is simplified and rationalised in order to make sense of it within a cognitive structure.
- **Cognitive style** The manner in which dimensions of cognitive structures (such as comprehensiveness and complexity) influence cognitive processes (such as information acquisition).

We saw above that competence-based competition can be characterised as a contest between managerial cognitions regarding what kind of resources and resource deployments will be required to satisfy future market needs, wants, and preferences – and therefore what kinds of competencies the firm should be building for the future (Sanchez, 1995). Competitive dynamics within an industry are seen as a product of the different mental models of their environment that managers hold, and how their sometimes conflicting perceptions of what is happening within it lead to different choices regarding how best to configure resources. In this way the competence-based approach offers a bridge between the economics-based theories that dominate much of the research into competitive strategy and have been seized upon by practitioners, and the managerial cognition perspective that has been slowly gaining ground amongst researchers over the last 20 years.

The focus of work in managerial cognition is the role managers' beliefs (about what is important and about the nature of cause-effect relationships, for example) and their perceptions of the competitive environment play in shaping strategic choice and action. The source of competitive advantage is argued to lie in the ability of some strategic decision-makers to understand, explain, respond to and sometimes even predict events in a way that enables their organization to outperform others. 'Responding' might take one or more of many forms, such as investing in new service specifications, process improvements, network expansion, alliance relationships, fleet upgrades, sharper marketing communications, better IS/IT, improved staff training, or a programme of culture change, for example. Whether superior performance is the result will depend upon the astuteness of managers' perceptions, the effectiveness with which strategic decisions are implemented, and the responses of others.

Where there is no differential 'sense-making' between managers in different airlines, an 'industry recipe' shared by most or all competitors is the likely outcome; conversely, an established recipe can powerfully influence individual cognition. Take, for example, the plethora of alliances presently being formed between airlines. One reason for the rapid growth in cross-border collaborations is that mergers between airlines in different countries are generally precluded by domestic laws (outside the European Union). That these collaborations have become a standard industry recipe in pursuit of network globalisation is beyond doubt. To argue that they are not always economically justified, that they often fail to provide customers with the 'seamless service' that is claimed, or that they are frequently anti-competitive would be looked upon within the industry as at best iconoclastic. Because being entrepreneurial is risky, managers sometimes prefer the comfort of imitation over innovation, and this caution often extends to choice of strategy.

Later in the book we will look at knowledge as an organizational resource, at culture, and at the importance of organizational learning. Regnér (2001: 49) links managerial cognition to these important topics in the following way.

> [An airline's] knowledge structure is a group of shared premises, beliefs, assumptions, etc. that shape the organization's comprehension of itself, its environment and the relationship between the two. It provides the organization's worldview and can be seen as part of the organizational culture. The knowledge structure can be viewed as a forceful learning foundation in the

sense that it controls the conditions suited for various learning mechanisms and also contains heuristics and routines that guide strategy. It provides a basis for mutual understanding within the organization and provides accessible knowledge accumulated over years, which can be used in given situations.

Taking the argument a step further, we can portray cognition as part of a politicised, negotiated, incremental decision-making process.

> Thus, decision-making and the strategies it produces can best be seen as the political, cognitive and cultural fabric of the organization. The expectation would be that strategic decisions could be explained better in terms of political processes than analytical procedures; that cognitive maps of managers are better explanations of their perceptions of the environment and their strategic responses than are analysed position statements and evaluative techniques; and that the legitimacy of these cognitive maps is likely to be reinforced through the myths and rituals of the organization (Mabey et al, 1998: 518, citing Johnson, 1987).

Strategic 'reality' is therefore not just an objective 'fact', but also a subjective construct built on the perceptions of managers and management teams. Who perceives what in an environment, an industry or an individual organization will depend on personality (e.g., optimistic, aggressive, pessimistic or cautious), past experience of actions that have worked out and others that have not, group biases, organizational context, hierarchical position, and both corporate and national cultures. Different people each have their own mental models which they use to evaluate 'reality' and the assumptions underlying alternative courses of action intended to cope with that 'reality'. They also have different levels of aversion to the risks inherent in these alternative courses of action.

> ....such constructs as markets, segments, competitive forces, and entry barriers are abstractions given meaning through processes of selective search and attention, selective perception, and simplification. Such processes are learned through experience, shared through industry conventional wisdom, warped by functional biases, and tempered by ready availability of data (Day and Nedungadi, 1994: 31).

Piercy (1997: 339) has the following to say about the importance of the meanings we impart to seemingly objective facts.

> ....marketing information is not just facts and figures, it is about the 'creation of meaning' or 'market sensing'. Now this may sound very high-blown and esoteric. It is not. It is about the basics of figuring out a few central issues

concerning markets: what do we actually *know*; what are the key *assumptions* we make about the outside world – customers, competitors, environmental change, and so on; who *shapes* and *controls* this model of the world that we assume to be true, and on which we base our decisions; and what are the opportunities for *re-shaping* and *re-defining* this model of the world to change how people think about the customer and to change what they think are the most important things to the business?

Box 2.3 develops some of these points by looking at the nature of organizations.

Box 2.3: The nature of organizations

Every airline is an organization, but what do we mean by 'organization'? To shed light on the answer to this question, we need to ask two more.

1. *Are organizations 'things' or 'social constructions'? There are broadly two views in the research community.*
   - *The typical view still advanced in many college-level textbooks is that organizations are purposefully structured, rational, goal-seeking decision-making systems with clear boundaries (Hall, 1996). They are identifiable, researchable, manageable 'things'.*
   - *A more recent, socio-cognitive view is that organizations are not real 'things', but social constructions. Both insiders and outsiders are constantly constructing and reconstructing their own ideas about what an organization means to them, based on their experiences of that organization and how they interpret those experiences (Checkland and Scholes, 1998). A 'social construction' arises when accommodation is reached between these multiple different cognitive frameworks and a generally accepted view of a particular organization emerges (Berger and Luckmann, 1966). Having ascribed meaning to what they interpret as happening in the world, most people then tend to forget that these meanings are subjective constructions and not objective things.*

   In other words, organizations are not static structures, but are instead the dynamically changing creations of human agents who constantly traffic in meanings and interpretations. Language – the manner in which information is conveyed, strategies are narrated, stories are told, organizational myths are created – is central to the process of constructing organizational reality. Language fuels the different discourses which dominate specific organizations – the discourse of 'theatre' that dominates Disney, the discourse of 'family' that dominates Hewlett-Packard, and the discourse of 'fun' that dominates Southwest, for example (Musson and Cohen, 1999); these discourses help create organizational reality. Customers experience this reality; managing it is an essential part of strategic service management.

We can broaden the discussion for a moment to the market as a whole. Perceptions of a situation drive action, which in turn helps fashion a deeper understanding of that situation but at the same time changes it. If we accept that every strategic act in some way shapes the competitive environment and stimulates future acts both by the same player and by competitors, we can argue that airlines not only experience environmental forces but help create or 'enact' them (Weick, 1995). 'Enactment' is driven by the behaviour of actors, who together help 'construct' the environment within which they compete. In this sense the competitive environment is not so much an objective 'thing' that is 'out there' waiting to be discovered – either by way of planning or through learning from experience – as it is a 'social construction' negotiated from the perceptions and interpretations of a myriad of managers and shaped by their actions.

2. *Narrowing the discussion back down onto the nature of organizations, the second question we need to address is how organizations are represented in our language. Because organizations are complex and intangible, we tend to rely on metaphors to represent them. Metaphor is being used when something is understood in terms of something else – as when we talk of an organization 'running smoothly' or being 're-engineered' as though it were a machine, or discuss its 'organic growth' as though it were a life-form (Morgan, 1997). Organizations are popularly represented as structures, machines, organisms, brains (e.g., the 'learning organization'), cultures, and networks of relationships. One highly influential representation of organizations which grew out of the organism metaphor is the systems perspective.*

I will summarise some of the points arising from all this ethereal stuff which are relevant to the rest of the book.

- *Although we tend to talk about individual airlines as though they are each goal-seeking 'things' with a unitary consciousness, this is only a convenience. In fact, they are complex social and political entities.*
- *An airline can 'mean' different things to different people. Internally, meanings help shape culture; externally, they help shape brand image.*

> *Both are, as we will see, highly significant service management variables.*

- *It is not only organizations that can be argued to be social constructions. Other candidates include concepts such as 'strategy', 'market', 'segment', 'brand', 'positioning', and 'service'. In fact, these concepts are sometimes taken to be neither real things nor imagined constructs, but 'enactments': strategists act on the basis of their perceptions (of market conditions, for example) rather than in response to some objective reality, and in doing this create a new 'reality' – which again is acted upon on the basis of perceptions. Bear all this in mind when I refer to each of these concepts as though they are real things that can be isolated and precisely managed.*

- *By representing an airline as a system, a structure, a machine, or a culture we are constructing something which would not otherwise exist in these terms. Our choice of metaphor could well shape how we gather, process, and respond to information, and how we frame issues.*

- *The systems metaphor in particular serves to underline the importance of interdependencies within airlines, and we will be using it at various places in the text. It emphasises the vital need for a coherent, holistic approach to the management of service design, communication, and delivery. It is, however, just a metaphor.*

Having in the last two sections defined competitive advantage and summarised some of the fields that have been investigated as potential sources, the next obvious question is whether once won it can be sustained.

How competitive advantage can be sustained

> In war, few things are as important as placing our army so that instead of being
> weak in many places it is strong in few.
> von Clausewitz

For over a decade after Porter (1980, 1985) first popularised the concept of competitive advantage, the fundamental means for protecting it was widely understood to be by building and/or exploiting barriers to entry – that is, things that prevent competitors from undercutting the advantage and eroding the superior performance it has made possible (Holloway, 1997). Since the mid-1990s, the idea of 'hypercompetition' has gained prominence on the back of an argument that advantage is in fact unsustainable because its sources can now be so much more quickly eroded or imitated (D'Aveni, 1994); in more extreme cases, the fact that competitive advantage is context-dependent means that nimble competitors with different and perhaps new perceptions of the marketplace can undermine it by changing an industry's context – that is, by rewriting the 'rules of engagement' in their own favour. Low-cost carriers have been doing this in some air transport markets for a number of years, and their impact on how the industry competes is continuing to snowball.

My own view is that there is something in each argument, and that airlines wanting to stay ahead of the pack need to be doing two things.

1. **Innovating** Whilst the airline business is hardly as 'hypercompetitive' as most hi-tech industries, there is still merit in keeping competitors off-balance with a rapid-fire succession of small innovations that create temporary advantage (Makadok, 1999). The economist Schumpeter argued back in the 1930s that competition is not something which brings about equilibrium in an industry, but is instead a dynamic force capable of altering industry structure. Referring to competition-induced change as 'creative destruction', he flagged the creativity of innovation as being responsible for the inevitable destruction of prevailing industry structures. More recently, Hamel and Prahalad (1989: 69) observed that, '[a]n organization's capacity to improve existing skills and learn new ones is the most defensible competitive advantage of all'. Because frequent service innovation can be an expensive business, however, low-cost carriers might have to look more often to innovative promotion and communication than service re-design initiatives.

2. **Defending** Infrastructural congestion and the remaining vestiges of the Chicago system of international regulation create effective barriers to entry in some air transport markets. But on the whole, developments such as operating leasing (which helps start-ups build their fleets and incumbents improve fleet management flexibility) and code-sharing (which allows airlines to create 'virtual networks'), together with the easy imitability of most service innovations, make a 'seize-and-deny' approach to competitive advantage dangerous at best. I will nonetheless be stressing throughout the book three sources of advantage which may be difficult to imitate and therefore can be sustained if nurtured.

   - *Organization culture* This cannot be precisely imitated by competitors and so, if service-oriented and relevant to the airline's vision of what it wants to achieve for its customers, can be a vital source of advantage. The style and tone of service delivery are much less straightforward to imitate than the functional attributes of a service.
   - *Causal ambiguity* Competitors might be able to see what an airline is doing, but not how it is being done. If the 'what' matters to

customers and the 'how' is inimitable, competitive advantage can be sustainable.

- *Brand image* This encapsulates everything an airline does and stands for, and is the foundation of its 'customer franchise'. If relevant to targeted customers, favourable, and actively nurtured, it can be a powerful and sustainable source of competitive advantage.

The nature of the airline industry is such that many sources of competitive advantage are ephemeral. On the other hand, some such as brand image, causally ambiguous process outcomes (based perhaps on tacit knowledge), and a service style attributable to inimitable aspects of corporate culture, can be more enduring.

Competitive advantage: a synthesis

Whilst researchers into the sources of competitive advantage who are working in the fields I have just summarised (and which were illustrated in figure 1.1 on page 21) tend to focus uniquely on linkages between superior performance and the decision variables in which they are interested (i.e., scale, strategic position, resource configuration, etc.), there is intuitive appeal in, and academic support for, the view that we can learn something from each (Rindova and Fombrun, 1999).

- Whether we are starting a new carrier or managing an incumbent, it is not unreasonable to believe that our *cognitions*, and those of others, will influence strategic choice.
- If we are establishing a start-up, we will probably be guided by a vision of what the new carrier is to achieve (i.e., the 'ends') and so try to carve out for it a particular *strategic position*. In order to do this we will need appropriate *resources*, including *knowledge*, and *competencies* (i.e., the 'means'). However, contrary to Porter's widely quoted assertion, there is no reason why circumstances that favour cost leadership (including high productivity, process efficiencies, and rapid organizational learning) should necessarily preclude service differentiation – based on, say, an insightful understanding of customers' expectations, a unique corporate culture, or a willingness to innovate (Murray, 1988).

  Managers of an existing carrier inevitably inherit resources, a strategic position, and a certain momentum (or, perhaps, inertia) born of past and current strategies. They might have a market position too weak to justify a significant commitment of additional resources, and so decide to focus on opportunities that can be successfully exploited with existing resources; they might, conversely, decide to strengthen their competitive position by increasing the commitment of resources, perhaps at the same time changing the nature of that commitment in some way; or they might move to take advantage of new opportunities – either in new or existing markets – that their competitors have not yet perceived, possibly influencing the 'rules of engagement' in those markets through being the first to respond to change (Sutton, 1998).

- In either case, the airline's *national environment* and the *economics of the industry* (Holloway, 1997) will influence performance outcomes.

- Over-focusing on a position in today's market and on the possession of today's required resources might constrain understanding of the trends and discontinuities that could open up new 'strategic space'. Being pro-active rather than reactive requires industry foresight (Hamel and Prahalad, 1994), and possession of a continuously evolving portfolio of *competencies* sufficiently flexible to facilitate the design, communication, and delivery of services that customers will expect in future.

- The capacities to *innovate* frequently while sticking to a consistent strategic theme and to be different in tacit and causally ambiguous ways that are difficult to imitate are likely to be critical.

Competitive advantage is not an equilibrium state arrived at as a result of single initiatives, but a richly complex, transitory situation that players endeavour to maintain for as long as its particular sources make possible – assuming, that is, that they understand those sources. In fact, there is a view that many – perhaps most – firms never actually secure a clear and sustained advantage over competitors (Porter, 1991). Those that do not may well be able to survive, perhaps quite comfortably, in favourable market environments and/or subject to some degree of regulatory protection; in unfettered and dynamic competitive environments, however, they are in for a turbulent ride and over the long haul their survival is likely to be in doubt.

ii. The rest of the book

Strangely, the various theories advanced to explain how competitive advantage can be achieved and sustained have very little to say explicitly about the role of customers, beyond their function of acting as willing buyers of whatever the firm's strategic position, unique resources and so on lead it to produce (Jenkins, 1997). In subsequent chapters we will try to remedy this by exploring the way in which some of the many concepts employed to identify competitive advantage can be used to define a service concept, and then to design, communicate, and deliver clearly specified services. The contents and structure of the book are broadly compatible with Doyle's (1997) argument that sustainable, robust growth strategies are in general based on four principles:

- the importance of delivering superior value to customers;
- recognition that no specific advantage is likely to be indefinitely sustainable;
- the importance of building sound relationships with stakeholders in general, and with customers, employees, and partners in particular;
- the need for learning and continuous innovation.

The distinction between goods and services on the basis of the latter's intangibility, perishability, inseparability, and versatility – all of which will be discussed in chapter 4 – has since the 1970s underpinned growth of an interdisciplinary services management literature. This literature recognises that practitioners of marketing, human resource management, and operations management in service firms face challenges that in significant respects are different from those faced by their counterparts in manufacturing industries. We will see evidence of these differences in each of the following chapters, and we will find that many of them flow directly from the fact that marketing, human resource management, and operations management overlap to a far greater degree in service firms than in most manufacturing businesses. Lovelock (1996) has coined the expression 'service management trinity' to highlight the critical interdependencies that exist between these three functions in a service business.

The structure of the rest of the book, outlined in figure 2.2, draws heavily on the services management literature. The attraction of this literature is that it allows us to think about the resources and competencies needed to manage an airline within a framework which both recognises the unique nature of services as opposed to goods, and yet also accommodates established knowledge in key functional areas such as marketing and operations management. Most importantly, however, 'services management is a total organizational approach that makes quality of service, as perceived by the customer, the number one driving force for the operation of the business' (Albrecht, 1988, quoted in Grönroos, 2000: 196).

We will also be drawing on the brand management literature, the strength of which is that it offers a guiding theme to provide practical help in the management of service design, communication, and delivery. The essence of this theme is consistency – about which much more will be said in the next few chapters.

But what does all this have to do with the title of a book called *Managing to Make Money*? Since the 1950s, there has been a divide in the

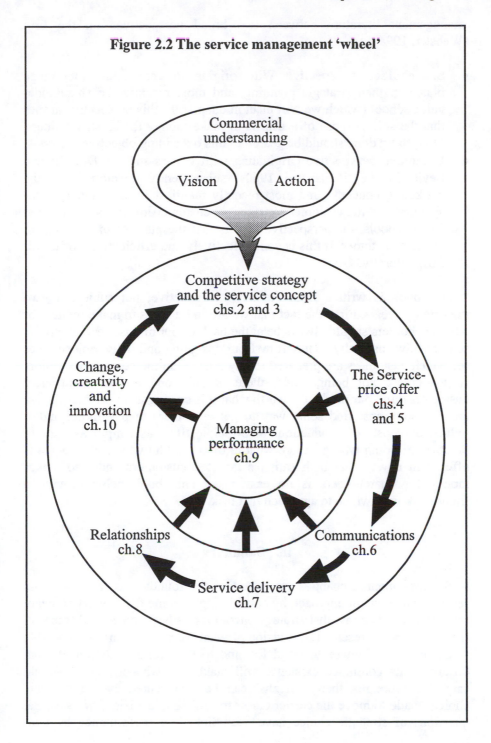

Figure 2.2 The service management 'wheel'

management literature between two broad perspectives on the firm (Webster, 1994).

- **Shareholder perspective** With origins in economics, long-range planning, then strategic planning, and most recently the shareholder value school (which we will meet in chapter 9), this perspective argues that the sole purpose of a firm is to make money for its shareholders. Everything done should be geared to this overriding objective.
- **Customer perspective** Originating with writers such as Drucker and Levitt in the 1950s and 1960s, subsequently developed as 'the marketing concept', and most recently manifest in total quality management and the customer satisfaction, customer loyalty, and customer value schools, the perspective here is that the purpose of a firm is to create a customer. If this is done effectively and efficiently, profits will flow naturally.

This book is written from the latter perspective, but subject to two important caveats. First, the fact that we are in business to make money for our shareholders should always be at the back of our minds. Second, profits seldom flow 'naturally'. They flow from designing and delivering services for which customers are prepared to pay more than the cost of production. If profits are not being made, there is only one reason: insufficient customers think our product is worth what it is costing us to produce. There are two solutions: find some way to get customers to pay more, and/or reduce our costs of production. In principle, it is as simple as that. In practice, deciding who to target, what to offer, and how to produce what is offered in a way that both satisfies targeted customers and also makes money for shareholders is no easy task. This book helps provide a framework with which to approach that task.

iii. Summary

In the two opening chapters we have laid the foundations for a strategic service management approach by considering in some depth what is meant by 'strategic'. We saw that strategy encompasses both 'ends' and 'means'. 'Ends' can be represented by a vision of what we want an airline to be able to do for its customers, to stand for, and to be – an articulation of what difference its continued existence will make and why customers should care if it were not there. 'Means' can be represented by the strategic choices made to move the carrier closer to fulfilling its vision. We saw that questions of strategic choice have been linked to performance by considering whether different choice processes and different strategy content might have a bearing on outcomes.

With regard to strategic choice processes, we noted that practice lies on a continuum bounded by the 'planning model' and the 'learning model': the management of airline service most certainly cannot be unplanned – not at any level, and particularly not at the operational level – but we equally certainly need the flexibility to learn from experience and adapt our plans. In this sense, strategy can more correctly be identified as a coherent 'theme' which binds choices into a mutually consistent pattern of actions rather than a rigidly implemented plan. With regard to the content of strategy, we distinguished between corporate strategy – which looks for superior performance in portfolio and parenting advantages – and competitive strategy. Because this is a book about service management within a single-business context – passenger air transport – we spent a fair amount of time looking at different bodies of theory, each hypothesising different routes to securing competitive advantage. Concepts that were introduced and that we will meet again, either explicitly or implicitly, later in the book include: competitive advantage, innovation, path dependency, differentiation, organizational resources, tacit knowledge, causal ambiguity, organizational routines and 'ways-of-doing', competencies, mental models, strategic logic, and the role of interpretation, meaning, and image in the creation of 'reality'. It was stressed that a key tenet of strategic service management is the importance of consistency in everything a service enterprise such as an airline does that might have an impact on how it is perceived in its markets.

We ended by synthesising an approach to competitive strategy: know who your customers are, what you want to achieve for them, how you want to set about achieving it, what resources (including knowledge and competencies) you will need to achieve it, what position that will place you in relative to competitors (as perceived by customers), and why you think customers should respond better to your offer than to what competitors are offering. To know these things we need to refine one or more service concepts out of our vision, our sense of the competitive strategy that the vision implies, and our understanding of the commercial environment. This is the subject of chapter 3.

Note

1. Readers familiar with economics (or with the Microsoft antitrust case) might have come across more precise usage of the expression 'path dependence'. In

modern monopoly theory, path dependence is the idea that a first-mover able to establish its product as an industry standard can create powerful barriers to entry amounting, perhaps, to a de facto monopoly.

3 Competitive Scope and the Service Concept

'The concept is interesting and well-formed, but in order to earn more than a 'C'
the idea must be feasible.'
Yale management professor responding to Fred Smith's paper proposing
a reliable overnight delivery service – eventually called FedEx

In the opening chapters we defined strategy as being a combination of vision and action moderated by commercial understanding – an understanding likely to be derived from both learning and rational analysis. We then narrowed our interest to the content of strategy rather than the process of strategy-making, and to the single-business case of competitive strategy rather than the multi-business case of corporate strategy. Our interest is in strategic service management within the context of a passenger air transport business; we are not directly concerned with how to manage other businesses that an airline or its holding company might be involved in, except insofar as they affect the ability to deliver air transport services to customers' satisfaction – an issue that will next arise in chapter 7. In this chapter, we will explore how a service concept can be moulded out of the ideas introduced in chapters 1 and 2. Figure 3.1 builds on figure 1.2 (page 22) to illustrate how far we have come in the discussion.

Figure 3.2 maps out the ground to be covered in the present chapter. The *competitive scope* decision outlines in broad terms:

- the type(s) of service to be offered (e.g., low-fare/no-frills, premium-fare services for business travellers, or a wide mix of different services);
- the type(s) of geographical market into which service(s) will be delivered (e.g., regional markets supporting aircraft with fewer than 100 seats, short- and medium-haul markets supporting mainline jet operations, or intercontinental markets).

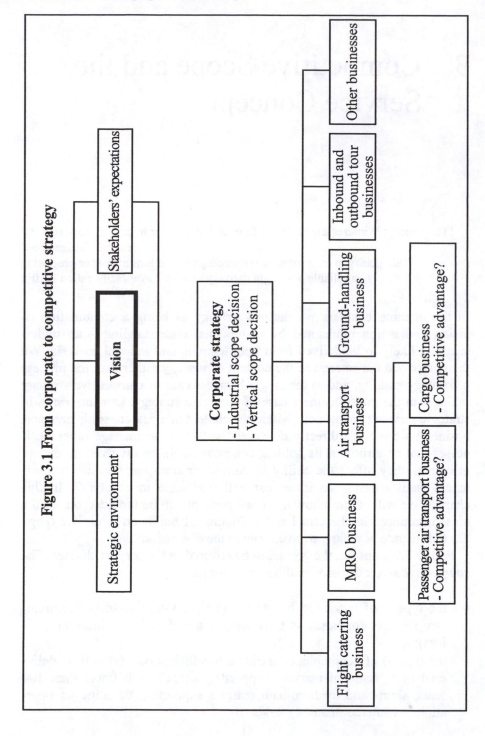

Figure 3.1 From corporate to competitive strategy

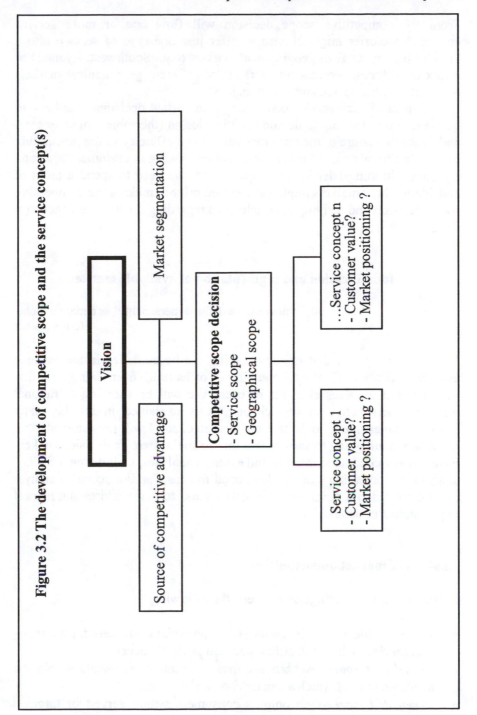

Figure 3.2 The development of competitive scope and the service concept(s)

From the competitive scope decision will flow one or more service concepts: a carrier might choose to offer just one type of service into a broadly similar range of geographical markets (e.g., Southwest, Ryanair) or a mix of different services into a range of different geographical markets (e.g., the US, European, and Asian majors).

In respect of each service concept, two important decisions that have to be made before moving to detailed service design (the subject of chapters 4 and 5) are the nature of the customer value to be offered and the positioning of the offer in customers' minds. We will be looking at customer value and market positioning later in the chapter. First, we need to spend a moment considering how markets might be assessed prior to making the competitive scope decision and arriving at conclusions regarding the service concept(s) to be developed.

i. Identification and segmentation of available markets

> At Southwest, we defined 'personality' as a market niche.
> Herb Kelleher

We saw in chapter 1 that strategy-making can be modelled in the extreme as either a process of rational planning or of learning-from-doing, and that in practice it involves elements of each. We will be adopting a 'rational planning' perspective in this chapter. It is explained in all the many strategic management books that are available, and I will not duplicate that work here. I am going to assume that our airline's strategic decision-makers have already conducted internal and external analyses, undertaken a SWOT analysis or something similar, developed forecasts and/or scenario analyses, and arrived at a point where it makes sense to begin addressing market opportunities in detail.

Analysis of market opportunities

It can be useful to distinguish between the following.

- *The available market* is comprised of potential customers for air transport services whom the airline could in principle access.
- *Served* or *targeted markets* are those markets or segments within the available market which a carrier chooses to target.
- *Penetrated markets* encompass consumers within served or targeted markets to whom sales have already been made.

Our interest here is in the available market. The availability of markets is constrained by barriers to entry. A barrier to entry is something which favours incumbent(s) already present in a market. It might be externally imposed (e.g., government unwillingness to license start-up airlines or grant additional route designations to existing carriers), it might grow over time through force of circumstance (e.g., slot constraints), or it might be deliberately created by an incumbent (e.g., network, brand, or distribution strengths, or a reputation for responding aggressively to new entrants). A barrier will either make entry impossible in a practical sense, or it will leave entrants with higher costs than incumbents. Higher costs suggest not only a weaker competitive position but a greater risk of commercial failure, and this perceived risk in itself is often sufficient to deter entry.

Existing airlines, particularly large carriers, generally find it considerably easier to overcome barriers to entry – except, perhaps, regulatory constraints and infrastructural congestion. Not only are they more likely to have the necessary marketing and operational resources, they are also betting proportionately less than a start-up or other small carrier on the success of any one route (Holloway, 1997).

At the highest level of aggregation, 'the available market' is comprised of passengers and cargo moving between geographical points the airline in question is free to serve. Because we are dealing with a network industry, however, airlines may also carry passengers making interline connections as part of journeys in markets which are only partly served by any one of the carriers used for those journeys. So what we are really discussing when referring to 'the available market' is demand at multiple points of origin for people or goods to be moved to multiple final destinations. Any airline, depending upon its particular geographical and commercial situation, might therefore have available as many 'markets' as there are traffic flows between points in its potential network, those of any code-sharing partners, and possibly even those of unaffiliated carriers with which significant interline relationships have been established.

Having identified which markets are potentially available and determined how to deal with any barriers to entry, two further steps should follow.

1. **Decide which markets to research** If a vision has been articulated, it can be used as a first-cut filter for assessing opportunities in potentially available markets. By running a market opportunity through this filter, one of two conclusions will emerge.
   - The opportunity is consistent with the airline's vision of what it is trying to achieve.

- The opportunity is inconsistent with the vision, and exploiting it will involve a significant change in strategic direction.
2. **Research selected available markets** Having decided that an available market is consistent with our vision of the airline or that sufficient just-ification exists for amending the vision, we need to look more closely at the market concerned.
   - *Market structure* Determinants of market structure include: the numbers of buyers and sellers present and their respective power; ease of market entry, mobility, and exit; the extent to which service offers can be differentiated in order to make competing services appear to be less obvious substitutes for each other; and the availability and cost of information about competing services. To analyse the strategic attractiveness of a given market, we can use the same industry attractiveness models we met in chapter 1:
     - the neoclassical microeconomic model, which recognises: monopolistic, oligopolistic, imperfectly competitive, and perf-ectly competitive market structures;
     - Porter's (1980, 1985) widely adopted five-forces model, which recognises as key variables in any market's structure the degree of rivalry between existing competitors, the threat of market entry, the threat from substitute products, and the power of buyers and suppliers.

     We would also want to consider potential synergies with existing activities, as well as the availability of resources (including know-ledge and competencies) appropriate to delivery of what customers in the market or segment concerned expect.
   - *Demand* Current and potential traffic (RPMs/RPKs) in a market will depend upon economic, political, and social variables, as well as the amount of output produced (ASMs/ASKs) and how it is offered (nonstop, multistop, or connecting routes); other important factors include the impact of whatever service (including schedule), price, promotional, and advertising stimuli are introduced into the market by competitors as a whole. An incumbent's share of current and potential traffic in a market will depend on the amount of capacity it offers as a proportion of total capacity, and the way in which it designs, communicates, and delivers its service-price offers relative to competitors.

     Traffic data should already be available for existing markets, but market research will be required to produce estimates of future demand potential; market research is the only way to generate data for potential markets that nobody is currently serving. Market research techniques can be used both to forecast demand, and to research the effectiveness of alternative service attributes and marketing communications efforts. The three are, of course, closely linked. Another important purpose of market research can be to profile a market with a view to gaining a better understanding of customers who are active, or potentially active, within it.

Understanding the customer

> Research is to see what everybody else has seen,
> and to think what nobody else has thought.
> Albert Gyorgyi

With governments progressively withdrawing from the economic regulation of commercial air transport, airlines have had to develop a better understanding of their customers – because it is customers who increasingly define the competitive terrain. Out of this understanding flow service concepts, and out of service concepts flow service offers that are designed, priced, and distributed in a manner which satisfies customers' – rather than regulators' – ideas of acceptable value. A corollary is that different customers seeking different value propositions can be served by more finely grained packages than was possible in a regulated marketplace; in other words, the availability of choice has increased.

An accurate and actionable understanding of customers – particularly how they define and perceive value – is an organizational resource. It can be derived from market research (which, in principle, anybody can buy), analysis of FFP databases, feedback from front-line personnel (which can be unique to any one airline, but is still too often ignored), and directly from customers via surveys, focus groups, and complaints as well as through direct and database marketing (the latter an expensive but potentially very useful source that is also not yet widely tapped within the industry). What all these have in common is that they involve listening. Another source of understanding is intuition born of experience and combined with a willingness to experiment – to go beyond what market research has to say and to be prepared to lead customers to a higher level of expectations than they themselves currently hold; both British Airways and Virgin Atlantic have been notably good at doing this – in their own distinct ways. (See Murley (1997), chapters 9 and 11, for useful introductions to the use of surveys and focus groups in a service environment.)

An understanding that is better than competitors' understandings, that leads to actionable knowledge, and that allows us to generate the desired customer behaviour – notably purchase and loyalty – is a potential source of competitive advantage. An understanding of what customers value and how they perceive different sources of value can feed through to revenues via the design of service attributes capable of generating benefits for customers that competitors, at least until they catch up, cannot offer; and it can help cost management insofar as a thorough understanding of the value targeted customers place on different service attributes might allow un-valued attributes to be stripped out of the offer, or over-delivered attributes to be scaled back.

Customer understanding is in fact a very complex resource, grounded in a number of underlying disciplines – notably economics, sociology, and psychology. Its raw material is economic concepts such as price and income elasticity and utility, sociological concepts such as culture, social-isation, roles, class, status, and group dynamics, and psychological concepts such as perception, attitude, and behaviour. These raw materials are mined using market research techniques that draw heavily from the 'scientific' methods of investigation developed in the social and behav-ioural sciences. And they are refined into insights that inform the design, pricing, distribution, communication, and delivery of services (Rice, 1997). For an international airline the strata to be mined are particularly complex because of national and cultural variations in the psychology and sociology of consumer behaviour; helpfully, there are global drivers at work – particularly advertising and print, television, and film media – which are in a growing number of markets gradually making lifestyle, self-image, and perceptions of value more relevant than nationality to the purchase of airline services. (See Usunier (1996) for an excellent textbook on the challenges involved in marketing across cultures.)

Consumption has both micro- (individual) and macro- (social and cult-ural) dimensions (Ward and Reingen, 1996). Customer understanding must therefore encompass an appreciation of the influences that each of these dimensions has on purchase behaviour in an airline's marketplaces. In fact, most consumer research has tended to focus on the individual level – specifically, on the cognitive psychology of information processing – with relatively little being undertaken at the social or cultural levels, and practically nothing being done to broaden our understanding of influences that intermediate all three (ibid).

In practical terms, customer understanding is a resource created by an iterative process which involves:

- understanding the market, its dynamics, and its segmentation possib-ilities;
- understanding the needs, expectations, preferences, attitudes, and aspir-ations of people in different segments;

- understanding how service and service attributes are perceived by consumers, and how these perceptions influence purchase behaviour;
- understanding the influence of communications, including promotional activities, on customers' perceptions and purchase behaviour;
- understanding how and why customers use different distribution channels;
- understanding consumers' levels of satisfaction with our services and with those of our competitors, and the reasons underlying them.

But consideration of customer understanding as an organizational resource begs two questions.

1. **How much detailed understanding of customers do we really need?** The answer is 'as much as we can afford'. It is clearly not practical for a low-cost start-up to look for the depth of insight that major network carriers might expect to have, and neither is it necessary. But even the needs, expectations, and preferences of customers in the most price-sensitive segments change over time, and these changes have to be understood if the service and – particularly – the communications programme of a low-cost carrier is to keep pace with customers' expectations; cost constraints might limit the scope of formal research, and might even limit 'research' to the intuitive understanding gained by management from simply keeping abreast of market and wider social developments, but customer understanding is nonetheless vital. For large, wide-market carriers competing on service innovation and highly focused marketing communications, a deep understanding of what their customers expect, how they perceive value, and how they make purchase decisions is particularly important.

2. **If everybody commissions market research into the same customers, what is the source of competitive advantage?** The worst-case answer to this question is that in some markets it is necessary to run in order just to stand still: market research might sometimes serve only to avoid the customer dissatisfaction that would follow from not keeping up with changed expectations that competitors have recognised. More positively, market research unearths data and refines it into information; the skill to turn that information into knowledge and a deep understanding of customers that can be used as a basis for an integrated, consistent, holistic approach to the design, communication, and delivery of services is not widely available. Insight and understanding are not commodity products. Furthermore, much customer understanding resides in the tacit knowledge held by each airline's customer-contact staff; a competitive advantage can be created where the tacit knowledge

of insightful staff is systematically tapped in conjunction with market research and used to refine or redesign services. Again, many airline managements seem to remain stubbornly resistant to the merits of listening to their own front-line people.

Another arguably under-exploited source of customer understanding is FFP databases. Zakreski (1998) argues that many carriers still adopt a mass-marketing approach to their FFP database members instead of responding to what is known about individuals' demographics and usage patterns (e.g., origins and destinations, types of destination, classes of service, fare classes, aggregate expenditures, frequencies of travel, miles earned, miles redeemed, redemption patterns, and responses to promotions) to tailor specific offers. Examples of 'mass marketing' in this context include award of bonus miles to promote a new service or meet enhanced competition, and the development of regional programmes offering different 'earn and burn' structures which have far more to do with addressing the relative strengths and weaknesses of the carrier's brand in the regions concerned than with meeting individual customer needs. Especially valuable is the development, use, and continuous updating – through dialogue and learning – of information on high lifetime value customers. Zakreski (ibid) contrasts this data-driven, relationship-oriented approach with the mass-marketing still widely used in the industry. (There will be more to say about customer relationships in chapter 8.)

Finally, research undertaken by separate airlines into requirements of a given customer group can yield different interpretations. For example, before redesigning their long-haul premium products at the turn of the decade both American and United conducted in-depth research into customers' requirements. American concluded that customers wanted to be able to interact with travelling companions and hold onboard 'meetings'; it therefore designed swivelling seats and a 'conferencing' capability into the onboard product. United, on the other hand, determined that the same customer group was looking for privacy and so adopted a different cabin design philosophy.

Once we feel we have a sound general understanding of our customers, there are broadly three approaches we can take to characterise them in a way that will help strategic (as well as tactical) service management decisions. One approach is to look at each customer individually. Although hardware and software capabilities are increasing at such a pace that it is in fact becoming possible to 'know' certain things about individual high-value customers such as major corporate and agency accounts and high-mileage frequent flyers, we are a very long way from being in an industry that knows – or, indeed, even needs to know – all of its customers. (Once customers enter the service delivery system, of course, an airline wanting to be a truly effective service business will endeavour to *treat* them as individuals; this is something different that will be touched upon in the next chapter.) We can for present purposes focus on two other approaches to customer characterisation.

- **Market level** In this case, we might choose to address all of our available markets as a whole and construct an 'average' characterisation of the customers and potential customers in those markets.
- **Segment level** Here what we do is construct 'average' characterisations applicable to groups of customers within each market or, more commonly in the airline industry, to groups that each span a wide range of geographical markets. Grouping customers in this way is called 'market segmentation'.

Market segmentation

> Those in the cheaper seats clap. The rest of you rattle your jewellery.
> John Lennon

Markets are rarely homogenous; they are simply made to look that way for statistical convenience. The more sharply that any apparently homogenous market is brought into focus, the greater the number of differences that can be identified amongst its participants. And in these differences lie the seeds of opportunity. Different groups of buyers in any market have unique requirements and will respond uniquely to variations in design of a service or service delivery system, changes in price, or new emphases in the marketing communications mix.

Market segmentation is a practical first use for customer understanding. Most industries – including air transport – have generic segments that everybody recognises and are part of the industry mindset and recipe; customer understanding that leads to identification of measurable, accessible, substantial, stable, and actionable segments of demand which competitors have failed to identify can be a valuable resource and, until it becomes more widely available, a potential source of competitive advantage. However, beyond having separate cabins onboard (which are in fact usually occupied by customers from a mix of different segments – albeit with one perhaps preponderant) and maybe recognising an 'elite' tier of FFP membership, many carriers still adopt a mass-marketing approach (Zakreski, 1998).

Conceptually, market segmentation assumes that customers are different, that certain of the differences between them account for behaviour which in turn affects demand and so accounts for the existence of multiple demand curves within the same market, and that groups of customers sharing these key differences and likely to respond in the same manner to any given marketing initiative can be isolated within the market as a whole. The purpose of market segmentation is therefore to identify groups of buyers who can be distinguished from other groups on the basis of their different responses to marketing mix variables such as service design, service delivery system design, price, choice of distribution channel, and marketing communications mix. The basic objective of the exercise is to identify what is being or might in future be bought, by whom, where, when, and why, as well as to identify specific competitors and how to out-compete them for segment dominance.

The more insightful an airline is in segmenting its markets, and the more precisely it can tailor its service design, communication, and/or delivery to what it has found out but competitors do not yet know, the more likely it is that segment knowledge – in this context a key organizational resource – will lead to competitive advantage. Bear in mind that segments are not simply 'out there' objects; they can also be characterised as the constructions of individual managers' perceptions. Managers whose perceptions of 'reality' take them outside the established industry mindset might unearth segment insights that others have not generated.

Segmentation procedure

The following procedure has been suggested by Zeithaml and Bitner (2000); for a full treatment of segmentation in the context of marketing planning, see McDonald and Dunbar (1998).

Identify segmentation variables   Market segments are groups of customers in a defined market who share characteristics relevant to the design, pricing, promotion, distribution, and/or delivery of a service; these characteristics make the segment broadly homogenous in its response to marketing stimuli, and also different from the rest of the market. We are interested in describing characteristics (such as demographics and socio-economics, psychographics, or spatial location) because, through the medium of attitudes, characteristics are believed to be a proxy for behaviour – and if we understand consumer behaviour, we can predict how it might change in response to particular marketing stimuli. Tapp (1998) has identified four particularly powerful approaches to segmentation.

- **Required customer value** Segment on the basis of the benefits that different types of customer expect and what they are prepared to pay for them. (A common proxy for benefits segmentation in the airline industry is purpose of travel – business, leisure, VFR, personal, etc.) At a strategic level, this is by far the most important segmentation variable (Piercy, 1997).

- **Predicted response** Segment according to how customers will react to variations in the marketing mix (i.e., product design, pricing, promotion, distribution, etc.). This has operational planning and resource allocation implications. It also increases our understanding of individual customers. (See Zakreski (1998) for a description of 'test cell marketing' within an FFP database – an experimental approach which uses different media (e.g., direct mail, statement inserts, e-mail, telemarketing) to target distinct groups of customers within a defined segment with information about a promotion; the purpose is to stimulate incremental purchases, investigate the cost-effectiveness of both the promotion as a whole and different communication media, and learn more about the behaviours of different members and different types of member – say, ranked by status – in response to promotions.)

- **Lifetime value** Segment on the basis of what customers are worth in terms of future revenue and profit potential.

- **Loyalty** Segment according to loyalty (ideally cross-segmenting with lifetime value, because there is clear merit in identifying loyal, high-value and non-loyal but potentially high-value segments). Loyalty segmentation is in fact the ultimate objective of branding: a strong brand manages to convey such meaning, such a powerful sense of its values and what it stands for that it generates loyalty amongst a significant segment of its targeted market. Loyalty is a particularly appealing basis for segmentation given its claimed linkage to profit (Reicheld, 1996; Heskett et al, 1997), but it can be difficult to measure (Tapp, 1998). There is certainly appeal in trying to 'ring-fence' the most loyal and the most valuable customers, relying perhaps on more aggregated approaches to others in the market. This is expensive stuff, however, so not only must the resources be available to achieve it but there should be reasonable confidence that real payback is likely to flow from the effort in terms of revenue and yield improvement.

Although a wide range of segmentation variables might be isolated for marketing communications, promotional, and pricing purposes, once customers enter an airline's service delivery system – that is, at airports and onboard aircraft – segmentation is a much blunter instrument simply because the system cannot be segmented as readily as can the consumers inside it (Holloway, 1997).

Profile the resulting segments Profiles of consumer segments are commonly based on demographic, psychographic, and lifestyle data; profiles of business buyers might use variables such as industry classification, travel-purchase decision-making processes, or size of travel budget. Profiling is driven by insight, the accessibility of primary and secondary data, and the research budget available; to be worthwhile, it must reveal meaningful and commercially actionable differences between identified segments.

Assess segment attractiveness The issues here are purchasing power, demand stability, competitive intensity, and segment accessibility. Taking into account factors such as size, growth, and profit potential, it might prove useful for certain segments to be sub-segmented – providing sufficient time, resources, and expertise are available. Not all sub-segments will necessarily be equally profitable; for example, there might be a potentially brand-loyal frequent flyer sub-segment that justifies a different marketing approach than other, less brand-loyal and/or less active, members of the business segment.

One caveat is that segment profitability can get blurred by the subjective nature of cost apportionment between different categories of ground and onboard service. Cost apportionment is difficult enough to argue convincingly in the case of direct costs such as fuel and crew salaries, but when indirect costs come into play the exercise can become very fraught indeed. The purpose of assessing segment profitability should be to get a feel for the numbers and therefore the implications of serving or not serving certain segments, rather than to craft a piece of fiction to two decimal places.

Target one or more attractive segments The issues here are whether the airline concerned has the competencies required to serve a segment effectively and profitably (i.e., whether it can match-up to the segment's key/critical success factors), the nature and sustainability of any competitive advantage it believes itself to have in serving particular segments, and whether doing so is consistent with its current 'strategic description' of itself and its vision for the future. Particularly given the fact that airlines are able to identify multiple segments for pricing, communications, and distribution purposes but only 'segment' aircraft into a small number of cabins (some not even doing this), the issue of segment compatibility within the service delivery system also arises; this is, however, an issue that most choose to ignore.

Summary

Drawing on what has been said in the first part of the chapter, I will now make some propositions that colour what follows.

- The demand for passenger air transport services can in most markets be segmented in several ways. Some segments will be relevant to service design and pricing decisions, some to service communication and promotion decisions, and some to both. The limiting factors in any segmentation exercise are the nature of demand in a given market, the resources available to research it, and the insight of the researchers. Having said this, segmentation costs money and some airline managements – particularly at small, low-cost carriers – might take the view that because they are offering a 'one-size-fits-all' service and because the benefits of segmented marketing communications do not repay the costs of segmentation, an undifferentiated approach to marketing within their niche is justified. From a product perspective they offer a single service concept targeted at a fairly broad market niche (e.g., cost-conscious travellers who want reliable service with minimal frills), and to the extent that they sub-segment this niche (e.g., into business and VFR or leisure) they use schedule (e.g., higher frequencies to attract business travellers) and revenue management (e.g., higher walk-up than advance-purchase fares – to make late-deciders, who are often business travellers, pay a premium for last-minute access to the seat inventory). The larger the airline and the more complex its customers' needs and purchase motivations, the more relevant segmentation is likely to be.
- Airlines can use segment information to help develop a competitive scope decision. This decision will be driven by:
  - top management's vision of what the airline is to be, what it is to do, and for whom;
  - the sources of competitive advantage available;
  - customer requirements in the markets and segments that the vision implies will be targeted.

Segmentation helps focus the product scope and geographical scope decisions which are implied by the airline's vision and which together comprise the 'competitive scope' decision.

ii. The competitive scope decision

There is only one airline mission statement: 'When people want to go somewhere that we can take them, we want them to think of us first; we want to be able to make a service-price offer that embodies the particular type of value they are looking for and which they will prefer over alternative offers made by our competitors; we want to deliver service that meets or (within reason) exceeds their expectations; we want them to come back and fly with us again; we want them to tell their friends and colleagues how good we are; and we want the cost of doing all this to be sufficiently less than the revenue we generate that our shareholders earn an attractive return on their investment.'

This of course begs several questions.

1. Where do we want to be able to take people – to a small country town 200 miles away, a holiday destination in the Mediterranean or Florida, a few major business centres, or everywhere we and our current or prospective service partners can fly? Are we going after transfer traffic or just point-to-point, and if transfer traffic should (or can) we pursue a single-hub or multi-hub network strategy? Are we interested in serving regional, short- and medium-haul mainline or long-haul markets, or all three? Will we serve thin or dense markets (however defined), or both?

2. What sort of service-price offer(s) do we want to make – full-service/ premium price, basic service/low price, something in between, or something for everybody? In other words, is our focus on premium, full-fare economy/coach, or price-sensitive demand or do we want a balanced mix? What about charter traffic? (The answers to these questions will of course largely depend upon the answers to question 1.)

3. How are we going to (profitably) meet or exceed expectations – through the friendliness of our customer-contact staff, the attention to detail in our service processes, a constant stream of value-adding innovations, simple but consistent and reliable service?

4. Is our cost base properly structured to achieve for our customers what we need to achieve and yet also allow us to be sufficiently profitable to meet or exceed shareholders' expectations?

5. How are we going to turn satisfied customers into loyal customers and, ideally, strong advocates?

The answers to these questions should be embedded in our vision of what we want to achieve, for whom, and how. They drive the competitive scope decision.

'Competitive scope' refers to the number of service concepts an airline chooses to offer to its customers; in large measure an output of market segmentation (whether formally undertaken or intuitive), competitive scope decisions are reflected in choices of product scope (i.e., the number of different types of service offered) and geographical scope (i.e., the number of different geographical markets into which services are offered). A customer purchasing any good or service (i.e., any product) is simultaneously participating in both a product market and a geographical market. Geographical and product scope are distinct but closely linked choices. Indeed, in a network industry such as commercial air transportation these two scope decisions are fundamentally symbiotic: every departure is in itself a product offered to one or more geographical markets, and different levels of ground and onboard amenities provided to customers travelling in whatever separate classes are available on each departure can be characterised as product attributes offered to different segments of those markets. An airline's network is, in fact, now widely perceived as a core attribute of its service – hence the rush to build alliances.

The characteristics of demand for air transport services in individual markets clearly determine to a considerable degree the services required to satisfy needs underlying that demand. A decision to enter a given geographical market will very often either require or preclude the offering of particular types of service; similarly, decisions to focus on a particular type of service frequently preclude entry into certain geographical markets. For example, a decision to offer a high-density, charter-type product with attributes designed primarily to attract short-haul leisure or VFR traffic is unlikely to have widespread appeal outside a fairly narrow spread of geographical markets. A decision to enter a long-haul market with high-frequency scheduled service has to date been assumed almost inevitably to require the offering of a wide range of onboard services (i.e., first and/or business class and economy/coach class, with the latter available at various different fare levels) in order to exploit the economies of density likely to be needed to help support a high level of frequencies using larger aircraft with low seat-mile costs (see Holloway, 1997); some observers now believe this will change, and that long-haul VFR/leisure and business segments will ultimately be carried on different airplanes.

Although in many ways quite distinct, airline product and geographical scope decisions are therefore intimately related. Together, they form the basis for a strategic description of any particular airline. At a very general level of abstraction, they can be categorised as follows.

1. **Product scope**
    *   *Wide-market* This approach offers a range of passenger (and usually cargo) transport services to entire markets or to multiple segments within the markets served. Some of these services might be offered outside the 'mainline operation' – by low-cost/low-fare divisions (e.g., Delta Express and Shuttle by United), or by charter subsidiaries (e.g., Japan Airlines' JALways and SAirLines' Balair/CTA) , for instance.
    *   *Niche* The offer in this case is limited to one or a small number of segments. Independent low-cost start-ups are a prime example. The problem is how precisely to define a product niche. Possibilities include number of enplanements (or percentage of enplanements at a specific airport or at a given city) or RPKs/RPMs flown (either in total or in particular markets). My preference is to treat a single-product service concept as a product niche; unfortunately, this leaves us casting Southwest as a niche player – something that is becoming increasingly implausible – and the growth of Ryanair and similar carriers in Europe looks likely to compound the definitional imprecision.

2   **Geographical scope**
    *   *Wide-market* In domestic markets, airlines can become wide-market carriers in a geographical sense. The problem with applying the analysis internationally is that the history of the industry's regulatory regime – based on sovereignty, reciprocity, and equal opportunity – has not left it with any truly global carriers; even international airlines with extensive networks remain focused on routes from, to, and – in the case of sixth freedom operations – through their home countries (Holloway, 1998a). The development of global alliances has been in part a response to the constraints on geographical growth imposed by the Chicago regulatory regime.
    *   *Niche* This involves offering either a wide or a narrow range of services into a small number of geographical markets. What constitutes a geographical niche and what represents a geographical wide-market strategy is obvious at the extremes (e.g., regional carriers) and unclear in the middle-ground. A large number of the world's international airlines make wide-market service offers into a relatively limited range of geographical markets, and are in this sense 'geographical niche carriers' – although they might not think of themselves as such. Some are moving out of their niches by joining global alliances; those that choose not to make this move will need confidence that they have distinctive and sustainable cost and/or service advantages with which to defend their niches.

Box 3.1 looks at how product and geographical scope decisions are shaping the contemporary airline industry. We will revisit the topic in chapter 6 when discussing brand hierarchies.

Box 3.1: The impact of product and geographical scope decisions

Product and geographical scope decisions within the air transport industry are leading to a business structured along the following lines.

1. Carriers within global alliances *The emerging alliances generally have one or more of the world's largest network carriers at their core, together with a variety of smaller network carriers and affiliates. Their geographical scope strategies aim to extend network reach into all major markets, establishing a presence in the most important nonstop markets and maximising connectivity between smaller points by constructing integrated, multi-hub systems. As well as attaining wide-market geographical scope, they also offer a wide range of products; full-service offerings on mainline routes are augmented by offers targeted at specific geographical or product segments, increasingly delivered by specialised units or service partners – such as low-cost subsidiaries, regional affiliates, franchisees, and code-sharing partners. In particular, global networks are battling for shares in long-haul business markets by enhancing service offers in respect of benefits valued by this segment. The ultimate objective of each alliance is to dominate as much point-to-point, inter-hub, and flow traffic as network geographies, competitive circumstances, and competition authorities allow, and in doing this regain some of the influence over pricing that regulatory liberalisation threatened to strip away. As well as revenue enhancement, the global networks are also looking for benefits on the other side of the income statement.*

    Their short-haul networks generally: feed medium- and long-haul routes; connect secondary short-haul points over a hub, where traffic densities between these points are insufficient to support nonstop service; and provide nonstop service in O and D markets to and from a hub, and on hub-bypass routes sufficiently dense to support point-to-point operations. Specialised affiliates may operate outside the network, offering low-cost/low-fare scheduled services in short-haul point-to-point markets and charter services in short-, medium-, or long-haul markets.

2. Network carriers outside alliances *Many existing and former flag carriers together with some more recent start-ups make wide-market*

service offers of various qualities into a range, often a relatively narrow range, of different geographical markets. These are essentially geographical niche carriers. Some endeavour to flow connecting traffic over their home bases or hubs, but many do not – either because they have failed to integrate their networks effectively, or because geography does not support extensive hubbing. The danger for a number of these airlines is that they are making ill-defined wide-market product offerings across networks which are not sufficiently large to compete for 'reach' with the biggest carriers or global alliances, nor sufficiently tightly designed to constitute an identifiable niche. Problems can arise from having to bear the expense of operating a network which although perhaps substantial, is not large enough to deliver the cost and revenue benefits available to the largest network carriers and alliances. To survive, these airlines need competitive cost structures and strong customer loyalty founded both on a sound image in their markets and on service-price positioning which is more relevant to those markets than alternatives being offered by competitors.

3. Non-network carriers *Independent low-cost carriers offering relatively basic, low-fare services into short-haul nonstop markets are a prime example of the non-network niche carrier. Some observers believe that with the possible exception of traffic feeding onto long-haul routes, low-cost/low-fare operations (some of which will of course be owned by network carriers) will eventually dominate enplanements in short-haul markets; this reflects the view that key consumer choice variables in these markets are now frequency, convenience, reliability, and price. European 'charter' carriers serving leisure destinations are another example of successful non-network airlines; the growth of seat-only sales on charter flights has resulted in some of them becoming in effect low-cost/low-fare scheduled carriers niching in medium- and long-haul leisure markets, whilst others are openly offering low-fare scheduled services. A number of regional carriers are prospering in Europe and elsewhere mixing their own services – sometimes 'networked' over a mini-hub – alongside code-sharing operations on behalf of larger airlines; their long-term future, however, looks likely to lead most of them more fully into network alliances (Holloway, 1998b).*

Figure 3.3 simplifies geographical and product scope decisions into two dimensions each.

*   Product scope: predominantly service-focused, selling primarily on an augmented level of service or predominantly price-focused, selling

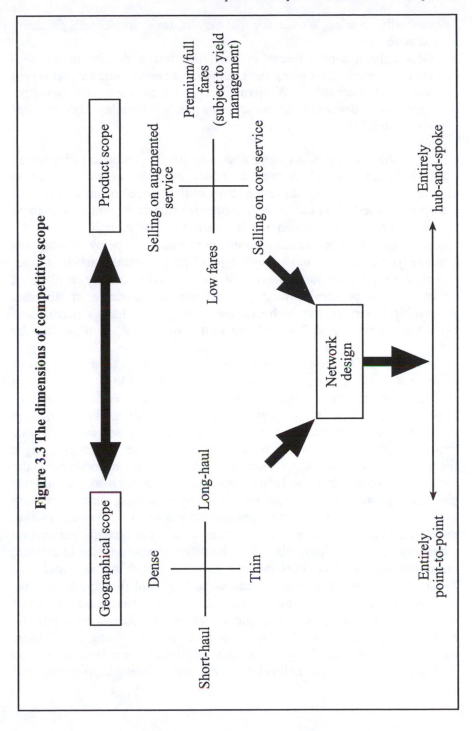

Figure 3.3 The dimensions of competitive scope

primarily on price. We can say that easyJet, for example, sells primarily on price.

- Geographical scope: length of haul, and traffic density in the segment(s) served. Continuing the example, we can say that easyJet serves short-haul markets in Western Europe which have price-sensitive segments of demand large enough to support reasonably high frequencies with B737s.

Geographical and product scope decisions have a profound influence on network design – which is itself a service attribute, as we will see in chapter 5. Together, they drive the 'competitive scope' of an airline's air transport business. The competitive scope decision is an outline statement of the business model through which a carrier asserts its right to exist. An airline might decide on pursuing limited competitive scope by offering just a single type of service into a single type of geographical market: in other words, it would have just one *service concept*. Alternatively, a range of different types of service might be offered into a range of different geographical markets, in which case the carrier would have a portfolio of service concepts. Figure 3.4, building further on figure 3.1, illustrates the point.

For a start-up, the competitive scope decision defines broadly what sort of product is going to be offered in which markets – a low-fare service in business markets or in leisure/VFR markets, a regional service concentrating on either or both hub-bypass or hub-feed, a wide-market service on dense point-to-point routes, a premium/business-only service, a service which complements or avoids incumbents or a service which challenges them in specific markets, for example. In the case of an incumbent, the competitive scope decision helps answer questions such as: Should we grow through market penetration alone (i.e., by expanding share in existing markets – through a frequency increase, for example), or through market development (i.e., selling existing services to new customers – perhaps by extending network scope)? Should we be offering new services to existing customers (i.e., product development – as when British Airways and SAS began offering premium economy cabins on long-haul flights)? Should we be diversifying away from the existing strategy by offering new types of service to new customers (a strategic choice which takes us back into the realm of corporate strategy)? How should we set about doing any of these things – through internal/organic growth, acquisition, or collaboration? Do we have the resources (including knowledge and competencies) to succeed?

Figure 3.4 Service scope: a portfolio of service concepts

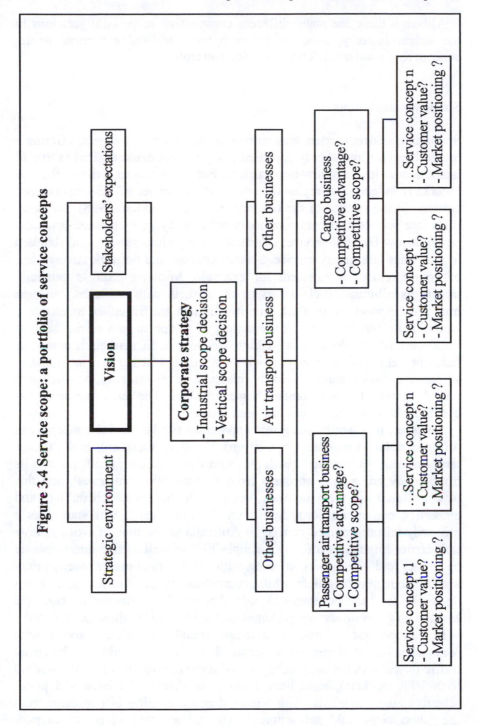

Although there are many different competitive scope configurations in the airline industry, most lie between two idealised extremes: single-concept focus and a portfolio of service concepts.

Single-concept focus

Some independent carriers concentrate on just a single segment, offering a focused service into clearly specified geographical markets. This is true of 'stand-alone' low-cost/low-fare carriers, European charter airlines, the few remaining independent regionals, and a small number of other specialised carriers. In the context of the US market, Gudmundsson (1998) has identified four service concepts commonly adopted by new entrants: low-fare/no-frills; low-fare/full-service; standard fare/premium service; and standard to first class fare/luxury service. Service concept and network strategy are, of course, closely connected: for example, Midwest Express generally targets its all-business-class service at markets with sufficient business traffic to support its product, but insufficient traffic either to attract a committed effort from one of the majors or to appeal to a carrier such as Southwest which looks to build high frequencies in markets it enters. A fundamental decision for any low-fare start-up is whether it is intending to stimulate a market that is currently unserved or underserved, or whether it intends going after an incumbent's market share. The latter can be an exceedingly bold strategy, but it has been done.

However, it is worth noting that apparently similar service concepts can differ in detail. Low-fare US start-ups Frontier, Vanguard, and Pro Air targeted business travellers (with the latter distinguishing itself, prior to its troubles, by going after accounts from Fortune 500 companies), and this was reflected in their network designs, frequencies, scheduling, and marketing communications; Spirit, on the other hand, was started as a primarily leisure-oriented carrier. In Australia at the time of writing, low-fare carrier Impulse is offering a simple FFP as well as free non-alcoholic beverages and newspapers in recognition of its orientation towards price-sensitive business travellers, whilst competitor Virgin Blue has no FFP but does offer food and beverages for sale. Apparently similar service concepts can and do generate service packages that are somewhat different in detail.

In Europe, most low-fare start-ups initially targeted markets with reasonably balanced year-round demand, and also directionally balanced traffic flows; with the early exception of Ryanair (which at first focused on Irish VFR markets), most have looked for a mix of leisure and price-sensitive business traffic, with leisure demand coming in particular from the 'short city-break' sub-segment. The introduction of routes to pure vacation markets such as Palma, Tenerife, and Malaga around the turn of the decade by some of these carriers broadened their focus to another sub-segment of the leisure market and brought them into direct competition with 'charter' operators' seat-only sales and recently introduced scheduled services.

Even apparently focused carriers are therefore sometimes operating with a broader scope than appears to be the case; their ground and onboard services will be undifferentiated, but different segments are separately addressed through other elements of the marketing mix – notably network design, pricing and, perhaps, marketing communications. Conversely, what is apparently a multi-niche strategy might in fact be more focused than it appears. VLM, an Antwerp-based regional, offers two-class service between uncongested secondary airports close to major commercial centres in Northwest Europe; although only 25 per cent of its revenues come from business class sales, approximately 80 per cent of aggregate sales are attributable to passengers travelling on business – emphasising the obvious but sometimes overlooked fact that purpose of travel and class of travel are not invariably synonymous.

A clearer example of a multi-niche approach, where a single carrier tackles a handful of distinct but related niches, is provided by American Trans Air (ATA) which at the time of writing offers low-fare scheduled services out of hubs at Chicago Midway and Indianapolis whilst also serving the military and passenger charter markets.

A portfolio of service concepts

Airlines that have made – or inherited – wide-market competitive scope decisions can operationalise those decisions in one or, increasingly, both of two ways. Figure 3.5 illustrates the alternatives.

1. **Segment specialisation** A wide-market airline or airline holding company might serve particular segments of demand through specialised divisions, subsidiaries, franchisees or other collaborative arrangements. When this approach to competitive scope is chosen, two key issues arise: the extent to which each specialised unit shares the service delivery system with other units or with the 'mainline' carrier itself; and whether or not the specialised units are to be separately branded with their own identities, or instead sub-branded under the larger airline's master-brand.

   One argument for separately branding different service concepts is to help more precisely manage customers' expectations, especially where

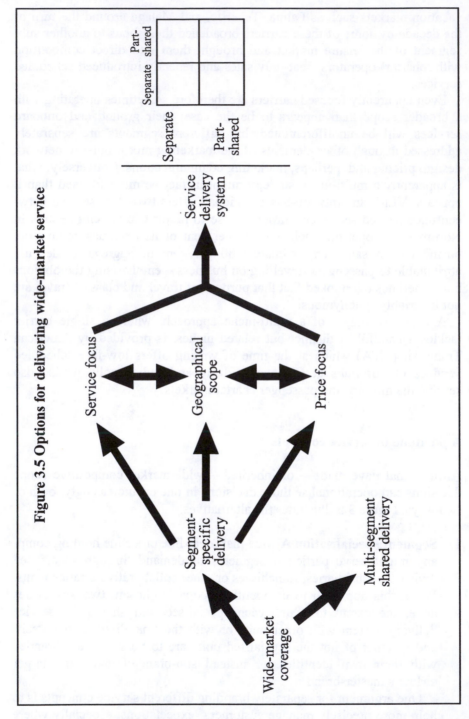

Figure 3.5 Options for delivering wide-market service

one concept (e.g., Buzz) is markedly different from the mainline parent's offerings (e.g., KLMuk); another reason is to leverage the loyalty of a customer segment and/or employee group to the subsidiary's brand (e.g., Crossair). On the other hand, some carriers prefer even highly distinct service concepts to receive endorsement from the corporate master-brand (e.g., Shuttle by United).

2. **Multi-segment service delivery** Serving multiple segments within the same airline's service delivery system – particularly, onboard the same aircraft – has long been the template for airline operations. In most US domestic markets, business and leisure segments are offered services that are distinguished from each other largely on the basis of price and ticket conditionality, with ground and inflight benefits common to all segments of what has increasingly been treated in this respect as a 'mass market'. (Some carriers addressed the problem at the beginning of the decade, with United for example reserving forward coach class rows with additional seat-pitch for medium-/high-mileage frequent flyers; overall, however, the point remains valid.) In other parts of the world, where segment price elasticities and customers' expectations are different, the segmentation exercise yields a range of service attributes offering benefits to the business segment, most notably in the form of priority check-in and baggage handling arrangements, airport lounges, and higher standards of inflight comfort and care; again, ticket conditionality to minimise revenue dilution is a feature of offers made to other, more price-elastic, segments of demand.

Even where airlines have 'spun-off' service in some segments to specialised units or partners, multi-segment mainline operations still carry the overwhelming majority of network traffic. Later in the book we will touch on the problems of serving different segments in the same service delivery system.

Clearly, how airline managements choose to tackle the issues raised here is a question of competitive strategy driven by many of the considerations we met in chapters 1 and 2 when strategic positioning, economies of scale and scope, and the availability of resources were introduced as potential sources of competitive advantage and contributors to organization performance. There are no prescriptive answers.

iii. The service concept

In chapter 1 we defined strategy, drew a distinction between research into the strategy-making process and the content of chosen strategies, and within the content literature drew a further distinction between corporate and competitive strategy. Corporate strategy was identified as broadly a question of deciding which industries to participate in, together with how and why they should be combined into a single corporate portfolio comprised of multiple business units. To survive and succeed in the long term, every business unit – whether involved in air transport operations, MRO businesses, catering, ground-handling, hotels, or any other activity – must have some competitive advantage. In chapter 2 we focused our attention on air transport operations and began to explore competitive strategy by looking at what the literature has to say about sources of competitive advantage. We opened the present chapter by arguing that competitive strategy is in fact a synthesis of the vision held for a particular business (in this case, an air transport business), identifiable sources of competitive advantage, and the needs of targeted market segments. We noted that market segmentation can be used to help design services, communication strategies, and distribution programmes, and that although there is considerable overlap the segments identified for each purpose are not necessarily identical.

The outcome of all this is a competitive scope decision which defines the types of service an airline will offer (i.e., product scope) and the geographical markets into which services will be offered (i.e., geographical scope). The competitive scope decision results in either a single service concept (i.e., the targeting of one type of ground and onboard service into broadly one type of geographical market) or a portfolio of service concepts; beyond these two extremes, we might find hybrid approaches. In this final part of the chapter we will look more closely at what is meant by 'service concept'. There is no universal definition. My interpretation is that it is a generalised idea of what we need to do for our targeted customers, and that as such it links segment targeting (discussed above) to the detailed design of a service package to be offered to the targeted segment (discussed in the next two chapters).

Grönroos (2000: 192-193) suggests the following definition.

> The service concept is a way of expressing the notion that the organization intends to solve certain types of problem in a certain manner. This means that the service concept has to include information about *what* the firm intends to do for *a certain customer segment*, *how* this should be achieved, and with *what* levels of resources. If there is no service concept agreed upon and accepted, the risk of inconsistent behaviour is high....Depending on how differentiated the operations are and how many different customer segments there are, there can be one or several service concepts. It is, however, important that they all fit the overall service vision....

A service concept addresses in broad terms what it is we intend doing, for whom, and how; it does this in narrower terms than a vision, but with less specificity than a fully designed and specified service. In contrast, a service is designed to provide identified solutions to the identified problems confronting an identified set of customers at a particular time, and to do this according to a set of design specifications relevant to the expectations of people whose problems are being solved.

I suggest that any service concept has two dimensions: the customer value to be offered, and the positioning of the offer in customers' minds. The two can be connected, of course, insofar as customers might derive social and psychological benefits – and therefore value – from buying-into a service positioned at the premium end of the market. We will, however, look at each in turn. Note that from this point through the end of chapter 5 we will be talking about just a single service concept and design of a single service package around that concept; for the purposes of the discussion it does not matter whether the concept and package are targeted at low-fare or premium segments and neither does it matter whether they are or are not part of a portfolio of service concepts and packages. Without ignoring possible synergies, managers need to consider each service concept and the service package designed around it separately from other concepts and packages.

Customer value

> Nothing can have value without being an object of utility.
> Karl Marx

Before developing this section of the chapter, it is worth emphasising that the people who consume an airline's services (i.e., passengers, freight shippers, and arguably also freight consignees) are not inevitably 'customers'; customers buy, and consumers consume. Often they are one and the same. In this book, the word 'customer' is used both generically and to refer to the buyers of a service, whilst 'consumer' refers to people directly experiencing some aspect of service delivery. Customers who do not consume the air transport service that they are buying include players as potentially important as corporate travel departments and freight forwarders. Not only might consumers and customers respond differently to variations in the marketing mix (e.g., where a corporate travel policy driven by price considerations overrides an executive's preference for a particular carrier's service), but there could also be others involved in the purchasing process who influence buying decisions – perhaps by commenting to potential buyers on the basis of their own perceptions of a product, or by setting a corporate travel or shipping policy.

A service concept is in essence a broad outline of a product-market strategy – a template for the type of value to be delivered, to whom, and how. 'Value' is a widely used but often loosely defined term (Woodruff, 1997). To put it into the context required here, consider the following propositions (Holloway, 1997).

1. A customer's **perceived benefit** from using a service is equivalent to the gross benefits offered by that particular service (e.g., safety, schedule convenience, ontime performance, inflight comfort, enhanced self-image through brand association, frequent flyer miles, etc.) less non-monetary costs (e.g., ticket conditionality, queues at various points in the service delivery system, elapsed journey time lengthened by having to connect over a hub, crowded airports and airplanes, etc.). This concept could in principle be monetised by equating it to the maximum price the customer is prepared to pay.

2. **Value created** by a service is the perceived benefit as just defined, less all the input costs that have been spent right along the 'value chain' in order to create that service and deliver value to the customer.

3. **Consumer surplus** is perceived benefit less the monetary price paid by the customer. This is widely referred to as 'customer-perceived value' or simply 'customer value'; although the terms are not always used synonymously, they can be treated as such for our purposes here. In effect this is the part of 'value created' that the customer is capturing. In some cases there might be no consumer surplus: the price paid in this case equates exactly to the value placed by the consumer on perceived benefits; this is likely only in the case where there is a monopoly supplier who knows each customer's valuation of the service and is able to price-discriminate accordingly (Bowen and Ambrosini, 1998). (Note that in principle there can never be a negative consumer surplus insofar as nobody is likely to pay for a service in respect of which they expect no net benefit.) Consumers in principle make purchase decisions that maximise consumer surplus (ibid).

4. **Seller's profit** is the monetary price paid by the customer less the cost of inputs. This is the portion of 'value created' that the airline – the final seller of the service fashioned out of all the inputs that went into creating and delivering it – is capturing. In terms of Porter's five-forces model, we could characterise this as the proportion of whatever value has been created that the airline is able to appropriate for itself given the bargaining power of customers and suppliers (including suppliers of

labour), the intensity of competitive rivalry, and whatever inroads are being made by substitutes and new entrants.

What airlines are, in principle, doing in the market is trying to win business by manipulating service-price offers – that is, by managing gross benefits, non-monetary costs, and price. Customer value can be enhanced by increasing perceived benefits whilst leaving price unchanged, or by reducing the price charged in return for the same perceived benefits. A brand offers good value relative to competitors when it provides one or more of:

- fewer benefits, sufficiently compensated by lower prices;
- similar benefits of similar quality at lower prices;
- unique benefits at the same price;
- unique benefits which justify premium pricing.

The fundamental objective is to pitch a better bid for customers' business than competitors are pitching, by offering perceptibly more customer value to targeted segments; the ultimate objective, of course, should be to do this and at the same time keep the price element of the service-price offer above input costs to ensure profitability. The critical point to remember is that customer value is defined by customers – not by airline employees; the 'value game' is played by the customers' rules, and in this game perception *is* reality. If customers perceive a service attribute to provide a benefit that has value, it has value – and if they don't, it doesn't.

All this might sound vague and academic set against the cut-and-thrust of an airline's real-time pricing environment in a highly competitive market, and it is in fact far from unproblematic.

- The concept of value is in itself highly subjective (Hardy, 1987).
- Any customer's perception of value will vary over time (Parasuraman, 1997; Ravald and Grönroos, 1996), perhaps depending upon mood or the context of the purchase (e.g., who is paying, purpose of travel, urgency of the journey, etc.).
- Perceptions of value available from the same service will vary from customer to customer (Wilkström and Normann, 1994).
- Perceptions of value will also vary between cultures (Assael, 1995).

Micromanagement of customer value is therefore precluded by the ambiguity and dynamism of the concept. The analysis above does, however, achieve two things.

1. It fixes attention firmly on the 'three Cs' – customers, costs, and competitors. Specifically, it requires airline managers to focus on:
   - what it is that customers need, want, and expect;
   - what it costs to deliver what customers need, want, and expect;
   - what competitors are doing to meet, exceed or change customers' wants and expectations.

   Critically important is the fact that consumers in most cases neither perceive nor value the resources, competencies or other sources of competitive advantage that enable an airline to price and/or different-iate its service(s) competitively. They perceive, value, and buy the ben-efits that these resources, competencies, and so on produce *for them*. This fact is what links the topics covered in the first two chapters to the customer-focused approach that guides the rest of the book.

2. The analysis also provides a sound model of the framework within which services should be designed and priced. The more competitive a market becomes, the greater is the volatility of service-price offers and the more difficult is the task of managing them without a framework. Intensified competition frequently leads to increases in customer value as prices come under downward pressure and/or the race to improve perceived benefits accelerates; it is useful to have a framework within which to order these developments.

Inherent in this proposition about customer value are two other tightly interlinked sets of strategic choices: revenue strategy and cost management strategy. Every decision affecting customer-perceived value needs to be considered in the context of its potential impact on *both* costs and revenues (Grönroos, 2000).

Revenue strategy

> To please people is a great step towards persuading them.
> Lord Chesterfield

Revenue strategy is based on an understanding of what targeted customers expect and an appreciation of whether and how a particular airline's resources and competencies can be leveraged to deliver service that at least matches these expectations (Grant, 1998). Some carriers offer relatively low levels of perceived benefit, compensating for this with low prices – prices that are nonetheless profitable because of low input costs and/or high productivity; this is the strategic path chosen by most low-cost/low-fare airlines. Others try to maximise perceived benefits, particularly for those segments of demand prepared to pay higher prices in return for improved benefits; this approach underlies the continuous cycle of product upgrades and re-launches in long-haul business and first-class cabins. It is also found in some short-haul markets. In Italy, for example, late-1990s start-up Gandalf targeted time-sensitive, high-yield passengers by offering service differentiation which notably included door-to-gate limousine service at its Bergamo base; it did not take on Alitalia head-to-head, as had the low-fare value proposition made by mid-1990s start-up AirOne. In the United States, 1999 start-up Legend set about carving a premium-service niche on routes out of Dallas Love Field using DC-9s configured with 56 seats (a limit set by arcane Federal legislation governing use of that particular airport for services beyond Texas and contiguous states); Legend, like most other start-ups focusing only on a full-fare/luxury service concept, failed to survive.

In India, private carrier Jet Airways has a service concept based around providing business travellers with reliable, customer-friendly service in modern aircraft – enough to carve out for itself a position that is clearly distinct from Indian Airlines. That Jet has been able to grow market share despite charging higher fares than the incumbent suggests that the value proposition embodied in its service concept has accurately identified the needs of a hitherto underserved, and not notably price-elastic, segment.

It is these choices about how customer value is to be created in product and geographical markets – the balance of emphasis between benefits and price – that help transform a vision-driven service concept into the service-price offers that reach individual marketplaces.

Cost management strategy

> My problem lies in reconciling my gross habits with my net income.
> Errol Flynn

In principle, each service concept should be supported by a cost structure capable of delivering costs per ASM/ASK that are low enough to allow profits to be earned given the revenues per ASM/ASK implied by that choice of concept. One of management's most important tasks is therefore to decide on the level of service to be offered into targeted segments, and then provide it at costs lower than the price that each segment is prepared to pay. If competitors can produce the same level of service more cheaply and choose to reflect this in their prices, or if competitors with lower cost structures can profitably offer a higher level of service at the same price, problems are likely to arise – unless nonprice determinants of demand such as brand image, network scope, frequent flyer programmes, and better marketing communications can be brought into play.

Life is not, of course, as easy as this in practice. Not only is the airline business a network industry with large carriers in particular serving multiple segments in multitudes of different city-pair markets, but even in individual markets demand varies enormously across daily, weekly, and seasonal peaks. Nonetheless, this analysis does highlight the fact that whereas cost-plus approaches to pricing start by considering costs and then turn to the market, in liberalised competitive environments it is in principle the market itself which decides the price that can be charged for a given level of service. The task is, accordingly, to design services for which customers are prepared to pay more than the cost of delivery.

There are certainly markets which, especially during cyclical upturns, can sustain a hardening of yields in the premium classes and at times even down the back as well. But overall, yields are in secular decline; stripped of regulatory protection, airlines are therefore having to become much more innovative in respect of their cost management whilst at the same time adjusting service design and delivery to constantly evolving customer expectations. Cost management efforts – whether aimed at lowering absolute input costs or raising input productivity – require a framework, and that framework is provided by the customer value being offered to each targeted segment.

'Cost management' frequently involves 'cost cutting', but the two are not necessarily synonymous. And neither is cost management, used in isolation, a strategy in itself; it is a fundamental management discipline which becomes a strategy only when linked to a defined revenue generation strategy within the context of a chosen competitive strategy that embodies the airline's competitive scope decision – as a low-cost/low-fare niche carrier, or as a full-service network carrier, for example. Cost structures should not have a life of their own. Their sole purpose is to make possible the delivery of a particular type of customer value. The idea of customer value can therefore be used to help determine which costs should be reduced, which eliminated, and which justifiably increased.

Box 3.2 looks at two extremes on the continuum of airline service concepts, each having very different implications for the type of customer value to be offered and the revenue and cost management strategies required.

Box 3.2: Low-cost/low-fare and premium service concepts

Premium brands should ideally justify their generally higher prices by offering a wider range of benefits – both tangible (e.g., better seat pitch) and intangible (e.g., more positive brand associations) – than low-cost/low-fare service concepts can offer, and competencies will be needed in the

*design, communication, and delivery of these benefits. Continuous innov-
ation is necessary as customers become more sophisticated and take
established benefits for granted. Costs also need to be managed coherently
in order both to maintain profit margins and resist undercutting by
competitors.*

*A price-driven service concept needs to be underpinned by competencies
that contribute to sustainably low costs, particularly given the industry's
recognised willingness to match prices. The following points are not a
recipe, simply a list of approaches widely pursued by low-cost/low-fare
start-ups which vary between essential (e.g., point 1) and optional, depending upon market circumstances.*

1. *Build a cost structure which, together with adequate capitalisation, can
   ride-out the fare wars that market entry is likely to produce and, over
   the longer term, can sustain low prices. To achieve this, low-cost/low-
   fare carriers require:*
   - *low absolute input costs;*
   - *a relatively simple service concept: cut out 'frills', but ensure that
     what is offered meets the highest feasible standards;*
   - *a highly efficient service delivery system: adopt an integrated appr-
     oach to the management of costs across the board, rather than
     arbitrary line-item cutting.;*
   - *high asset and workforce productivity: ensure the culture of the
     airline supports a low-cost/low-fare strategy (an essential ingred-
     ient being flexibility and a willingness to 'pitch-in').*
2. *Target unserved, underserved or badly served markets which have
   significant growth potential and price-elastic segments of demand
   likely to respond favourably to low-fare offers. When challenging an
   incumbent head-on, attack point-to-point markets that are sufficiently
   dense to sustain the high load factors likely to be necessary to compensate for relatively low yields.*
3. *Operate whenever possible and consistent with the requirements of
   targeted segments from uncongested airports (low-cost secondary
   metropolitan airports, for example), where slots are freely available to
   build whatever schedule is required by those segments, costs are lower
   than at congested major hubs, and the impact of traffic-induced delays
   on schedule integrity can be kept to a minimum.*
4. *Provided the approach is appropriate given the needs of targeted segments, use direct distribution (particularly web sites) to avoid GDS and
   agency costs; use e-ticketing to reduce processing costs.*
5. *Adopt a simple fare structure which does not require time-consuming
   (therefore expensive) explanations to customers from reservations staff.*

6. *Create an effective but appropriately sized reservations and revenue management system, using off-the-shelf software.*
7. *Maximise favourable PR coverage to reduce advertising costs.*
8. *Build brand image into a resource deployable against competitors which choose to match low fares. The purpose is to reassure customers that even though fares are low and competitors match each other, there are differences in quality. If this cannot be done, the product is en route to becoming commoditised.*

Whatever the value proposition being offered, there is a need for consistency, integration, and the development of a reinforcing pattern in everything the airline does – and, particularly, in every encounter its people and infrastructure have with customers and prospective customers.

Developing a value proposition

Within the context of each targeted (or potentially available) segment, and also given a thorough understanding of our vision and source(s) of competitive advantage, we can focus closely on the value that customers are and will be looking for by asking several questions. Citing Treacy and Wiersma (1995), Piercy (1997: 204-205) identifies a three-phase process to help develop a value proposition. (We are assuming that management of an incumbent carrier is asking these questions, but the approach can also be applied to a start-up situation.)

Phase One: Understanding the status quo
Develop a common understanding of the market based on five fundamental questions:
- What are the dimensions of value that customers care about?
- For each dimension of value, what proportion of customers focus on it as their primary or dominant decision criterion?
- Which competitors provide the best value in each of these value dimensions?
- How do we perform compared to our competitors on each value dimension?
- Why do we fall short of the value leaders on each dimension of value where we perform less well than they do?

Phase Two: Identifying realistic options
For each dimension of value, we should ask:
- ….what are the benchmark standards of value performance that will affect customer expectations, and how do firms achieve these?

- For the value leaders in this market, what will the standards of performance be in three years' time?
- How are the operations of the value leaders designed to attain these levels of performance?

Phase Three: Design and choices

If we have options for how we would close the gap, then we must ask:

- How will this operating model produce superior value?
- What threshold levels of value will the market require in the other value dimensions, and how will these be attained?
- How large will the market be for this value proposition?
- What is the business case – costs, benefits, risks – for pursuing this option?
- What are the critical success factors that can make or break this value proposition?
- How will the company make the transition?

Market positioning

> He who knows others is clever. He who knows himself is enlightened.
>
> Lao Tzu

There is insufficient space here to go in depth into competitor analysis (that is, who they are, what they can do for customers, what resources and competencies enable them to do what they do, and what they are likely to do in future); a thorough review of the field can be found in Fahey (1999). What I want to do is underline the importance of developing a clear idea of the position relative to competitors that we want to achieve for our value proposition(s) in customers' perceptions within targeted markets and segments. If we are dealing with a single-concept business (e.g., an independent low-cost carrier), the challenge is essentially one of corporate brand positioning; if the competitive scope decision gives rise to multiple service concepts, services targeted at individual segments need to be positioned as well as any corporate master-brand. Therefore, either an airline as a whole, a line of services, or a single service might need to be 'positioned'.

The purpose of positioning a service within the 'cognitive space' represented by customers' perceptions of the marketplace is to influence preferences with a view to stimulating purchase. This is done by positioning the corporate or service brand in respect of dimensions which contribute to customer value and are known to influence purchase behaviour. What these dimensions might be will become clearer when we look at service design and communications over the next three chapters. 'Market position' is not quite the same concept as the 'strategic position' in Porter's (1980, 1985) structure-conduct-performance (SCP) approach to competitive strategy that we met in the last chapter, although the two are certainly close cousins. The SCP school argues that superior performance comes from analysing the five forces that shape competitive dynamics (the bargaining power of suppliers and buyers, etc.), and then choosing an appropriate 'strategic position' – whether as the single lowest-cost operator in a market or niche or one of several differentiators. 'Market positioning', on the other hand, is a reflection of how a particular airline and its services are perceived by customers in targeted markets and segments relative to competitors. Choice of 'strategic position' in Porter's terms is clearly a strong influence on 'market positioning', but the concepts are not synonymous.

Market positioning links external analysis (what customers want, governments are allowing, and competitors are offering) with internal analysis (what we are capable of doing for our customers). Positioning should be arrived at with due regard to what it is that an airline believes gives it an advantage over competitors. It exploits rather than creates competitive advantage; returns to position cannot be earned simply by imitating a competitor's successful positioning. A market position is not in itself proprietary over the long term. It is sustainable only if underpinned by some competitive advantage – some unique combination of resources, for example – that makes it correct for the airline concerned.

Market positioning is concerned with the way in which people's perceptions of an airline and its services are managed relative to perceptions of competitors. The first step is to assemble a list of competing service propositions considered by customers to be viable alternatives (including, where appropriate, products offered by industries other than air transport). The second step is to understand the evaluative criteria used by customers – the benefits they assess, how they assess them, and the relative importance of each, for example. The third step is to locate the position of each competitor relative to others in respect of customers' composite evaluations; one method for doing this is 'perceptual mapping' (which is explained in Rao and Steckel (1998), and should be covered in other good marketing course-books). This type of exercise can identify overcrowding in certain market positions (which could justify repositioning), or isolate gaps that have yet to be exploited.

Positioning of a service concept should reflect the 'price/performance' combination inherent in the customer value chosen by the airline; it is a shorthand message which conveys to customers (and other stakeholders) what it is that a brand can do for them (Aaker, 1997). It needs to be accomplished along dimensions that are relevant to customers. Up-to-date market research is necessary to ensure that managers understand the evaluative dimensions used by customers, because these can change over time.

Every airline has a 'position'; the question is whether or not it is actively managed. Particularly in a crowded, competitive marketplace with low barriers to entry and mobility, it is essential that customers are aware of what an airline can do to satisfy their needs, wants, and preferences. In practice, positioning is a function of three things.

1. **The intended position** As already noted, this is a decision which should flow from consideration of competitive advantage, market requirements, and vision. It must reflect the value that the airline has decided to deliver to its customers. It is both communicated and at the same time built by marketing communications. Marketing communications must be integrated with service design and delivery, as well as with every interface between the airline and its stakeholders (e.g., the appearance of facilities and equipment, the appearance and behaviour of staff, and the presentation of both internal and external communications), in a coherent, consistent, and actively managed effort to locate (or relocate) the airline and/or its service(s) at a chosen place in consumers' minds relative to other offers competing in the same segment. The brand management literature refers to 'points of difference' and 'points of similarity' between brands – the balance of which can be important to consumer purchase decisions.

    The purpose of positioning is therefore to distinguish the airline and its individual service concept(s) from competing offers along one or more dimensions that matter to customers and influence their purchase decisions, and to establish the distinction firmly in customers' perceptions. In fact, the literature tends to assume more competitor analysis goes into this process than might actually be the case (Aaker, 1995). What is believed to happen in practice is that managers use their mental models of the competitive environment to simplify a complex 'reality' and filter information; these models may or may not in fact reflect the 'reality' of airlines' relative market positions, and neither are they necessarily shared in their totality amongst members of any one management team – unless, perhaps, specific efforts are made to surface, articulate, and accommodate variations.

2. **The actual perceptions of customers and potential customers** There are two relevant points here.
    *   It is not necessarily inexpensive to undertake the market research needed to establish what customers in specific segments expect and the extent to which they perceive the attributes of competing offers to be capable of satisfying those expectations. One approach, root-

ed in benefits segmentation, is *customer value analysis*. This technique requires market research to identify service attributes valued by customers in each segment, quantify and rank the attributes, and assess competitors' performances in respect of each.

- If there is a gap between the positioning outcome intended by the airline and the actual position as perceived by targeted customers, it has to be closed. This can be accomplished in two ways:
  - by addressing shortcomings in the actual design and delivery of the service(s) concerned;
  - by communicating the airline's positioning message more clearly. This will need to be done as part of a coherent, consistent, and fully integrated brand management effort.

  One other alternative, of course, is to change position. This option is potentially expensive in terms of service delivery system redesign and marketing communication expenditures, and risky in terms of possible customer confusion. It also requires explicit identification of whatever competitive advantage is expected to underpin the new position.

3. **The activities of competitors** There are three points here.
   - Competitors can come from outside the air transport industry (e.g., telecommunications and ground transportation) or from its fringes (e.g., the fractional ownership of business jets and the public sale of seats on fractionally owned or owner-operated business jets, and travel web sites which sell tickets without first identifying the carrier concerned).
   - Liberalised and deregulated markets are generally dynamic; positioning may achieve equilibrium over the short run, but changeable customer perceptions together with new entrants and aggressive incumbents inevitably make positioning against competitors an act more akin to juggling than to balancing.
   - Because larger airlines compete in so many discrete geographical markets, each with its own cast of competitors and each with its own particular service-price offers (in respect of schedule and routing, for example), the best they can achieve is to fix a position in these markets which is relatively consistent across their networks.

Although positioning is a highly complex topic, there are in fact only four fundamental rules underlying what must be done (Collier, 1995).

1. Convey a single unique message which captures the essence of the airline's service and what it stands for.

2. Even if it is not invariably factual, ensure that the positioning message is always credible when set against the reality of what the airline is able to deliver. Never overpromise.
3. Stress benefits – what the service can achieve, for whom, and why it achieves more than competitors – rather than service attributes/features.
4. Be consistent. Every aspect of the design, communication, and delivery of a particular service should be consistent with the position chosen for the underlying service concept in its markets.

In the final analysis, positioning is what gives customers in the targeted segment a reason to buy the services of one airline rather than those of another (Payne and Clark, 1995; McDonald and Payne, 1996). Both segmentation and positioning are dynamic rather than once-and-for-all analyses; the more rapidly customers' expectations of service and perceptions of different competitors change, the more dynamic these concepts are. They need to be revisited on a regular basis – or, put another way, customer understanding needs frequent if not continuous updating.

iv. Summary

This chapter has moved our discussion away from the ivory towers of strategy research and a little closer to the marketplace. We have seen how a market-oriented service concept can be distilled from an overarching vision and – once it has been clearly positioned in terms of the customer value to be offered to targeted markets or segments – used to drive competitive strategy. Competitive strategy is in this sense a series of mutually consistent and self-reinforcing decisions and actions taken to exploit an advantage over identified competitors who are also offering value to the same customers. It should at this point be possible to identify 'critical success factors' (CSFs) that will be important to the successful implementation of competitive strategy, and that will guide the next stage in the strategic service management process. The next stage is detailed specification of the service-price offers from which targeted customers will derive the value established for each service concept. We will look at service design in chapters 4 and 5, and then turn to the communication and delivery of services in subsequent chapters. But before proceeding, I want to advance three propositions drawn from the opening chapters that will guide much of what follows.

Proposition 1: Whether starting or already working within an airline, we need a clear vision of what we are trying to achieve

A vision of what we are trying to achieve allows us to develop a service concept – an articulation of what value we are going to offer to which customers in which markets and how that value will be positioned relative to the value offered by our competitors. It also allows us to develop a competitive strategy – a plan or a pattern of decisions intended to exploit one or more sources of competitive advantage, united around a consistent theme, and oriented to the design, communication, and delivery of services that can provide customer value more appealing in targeted markets and segments than the value offered by competitors.

A service concept is derived from an explicit competitive scope decision, itself a function of geographical scope and product scope choices based on clearly identifiable sources of sustainable competitive advantage.

1. Geographical scope can be wide-market or focused in orientation.
2. With regard to product scope:
    *   there is no such thing as a 'commodity' or 'standard' service (Payne and Clark, 1995). Air transport demand is highly susceptible to segmentation;
    *   either selected geographical markets as a whole or one or more segments within them can be targeted with specific service-price offers;
    *   the starkness of choice between being *the* lowest cost producer in the industry on the one hand and offering distinctive service on the other is intuitively appealing, but can obscure shades of grey. Low costs and service distinctiveness are not inevitably incompatible:
        -   distinctiveness need not necessarily add substantially to the cost base. For example, if the impact of an airline's particular culture on the style of service delivery contributes positively to customer satisfaction in some causally ambiguous way that competitors might find difficult to imitate, distinctiveness can be achieved at relatively low cost. Southwest comes to mind;
        -   cost is a function not of service quality alone, but of how that quality is achieved.
        The 'cost versus distinctiveness' challenge is perhaps better addressed as one requiring arrival at a balance, rather than resolution of an 'either/or' paradox (Stacey, 1996). We will return to this point in chapters 4 and 5;
    *   distinctiveness – being different from competitors – on one or both sides of an airline's service-price offer to customers is the only true

competitive strategy, because unless an airline distinguishes either its service, its prices or both it is giving customers in a competitive market no particular reason to buy from it rather than from competitors. Passengers in free markets do not choose an airline because its costs are low. They select on the basis of a service-price offer that appeals to them. This appeal can be based on one or both of service distinctiveness (i.e., offering higher levels of service than competitors) or price distinctiveness (i.e., offering lower prices, for either the same or lower levels of service). If an airline can charge premium prices for distinctive service, it is 'differentiating' in the sense meant by Porter (1980, 1985). We will explore in chapter 4 the subtle difference between being distinctive and being a differentiator;

- service distinctiveness occurs when augmented service is added over and above what is expected in the market concerned. One purpose of adding attributes is to be able to charge a premium price for the benefits they provide (i.e., to 'differentiate'), but this can only be done if consumers value the benefits in question enough to pay extra for them and they are not easily provided by competitors choosing not to charge a premium. Frequently, service distinctiveness is worthwhile insofar as it favourably influences consumer purchase decisions, but is nonetheless not sufficient to generate a price premium. Emotional benefits are less easily imitated than those *attribut*able to more tangible service features, and brand image and the manner in which corporate culture affects the style and tone of service delivery are two of the least imitable sources of benefit available in the industry;

- taking away expected benefits (either unbundling and eliminating certain service attributes or, alternatively, reducing the quality of one or more remaining attributes) may require downward price distinctiveness, and could imply repositioning of the service concept if the changes are significant. Conversely, a carrier with firm control over a competitive cost structure might be able to engage in downward price distinctiveness on a sustained basis without reducing or eliminating attributes. There will be much more to say about service attributes and the benefits they provide when we discuss service design in the next chapter;

- there is more to differentiation, distinctiveness, and positioning than service design alone. Grant (1998: 219) puts the holistic nature of the challenge as follows.

> [Distinctiveness] extends beyond the physical characteristics of the....service to encompass everything about [it] that influences the value customers derive from it. This means that [distinctiveness] includes every aspect of the way in which a company does business and relates to its customers....[Distinctiveness] is not an activity specific to design and marketing; it infuses all functions and is built into the identity and culture of a company. As a result, companies that supply seemingly basic, no-frills offerings such as....Southwest Airlines....may achieve highly [distinct] market positions in terms of customers' perceptions.

If this is all accepted, we can characterise competitive strategy as having two pillars:

- to sell, it is necessary to distinguish service and/or price in order to make the best service-price offer available to each targeted segment (however broad or narrow). This need not mean the best service or the lowest price – although it might. Service and price are better characterised as scales which need to be balanced than as an either/or choice;
- to make a profit, expenditure has to be managed actively and with commitment to ensure that the level of service being delivered costs less to produce than the price it can command in target segments. Having low costs relative to competitors targeting the same segment(s) or, indeed, relative to any potential challenger, is not so much a competitive strategy as a prerequisite for long-term survival.

These ideas underlie the title of the book: *Managing to Make Money*. Keeping the scales in balance requires deep commercial understanding. Specifically, it demands a profound understanding of targeted customers – their expectations and elasticities – and a constant monitoring of corporate resources and competencies. Resources and competencies, and the competitive advantage they underpin, have to be relevant to the type of customer value being offered and its positioning in customers' perceptions.

Proposition 2: Everything done within either a single-business airline or a business unit of a larger group needs to be consistent with vision and strategy

People rarely share precisely the same mental models, rarely perceive the same external stimuli in precisely the same way, and seldom have entirely congruent objectives. Consistent behaviour is therefore not easy to achieve. Consistency nonetheless needs to be sought in the following areas.

1. **Strategic and operational consistency** Everything an airline does and the way in which its people do it should be consistent with the concept(s) it has chosen for the service(s) it is offering to targeted segments. Some carriers try to limit deviations through heavily centralised planning and the tight 'scripting' of staff interactions with customers, whilst others rely more on shared values and a strong corporate culture to keep decisions and actions consistent with the strategic logic of the business.

2. **Communications consistency** Everything an airline communicates about itself, what it does, and how it does it should be consistent with the brand image it wants people to hold.

The brand management literature provides us with a lot of insight into the importance of consistency and how it can be achieved. As defined by de Chernatony and McDonald (1998: 205), 'a brand is a set of differentiated perceptions' [and] 'brand strength depends on the extent to which these perceptions are consistent, positive, and shared by all consumers'. Achieving consistency in consumer perceptions demands both strategic and operational consistency and communications consistency; it is particularly difficult in the case of a service business because of the intangibility of what is being offered, the simultaneity of production and consumption, and the potential for quality variations in the course of the multiple service encounters that take place between staff and consumers during service delivery. We will be exploring these challenges in the next chapter, and making reference to them throughout the book.

The brand management literature contains some important concepts to help orchestrate a commitment to consistency, and we will be meeting these at various points in the book. Three of the most vital are brand identity, brand image, and band personality.

* **Brand identity and image** Every point of contact between an airline and its customers or potential customers – the design and delivery of services, the tone of communications, the appearance of staff, equipment, and facilities, and the behaviour of staff – should be coherently managed so that a uniform *identity* is conveyed consistent with the service concept and the market position selected for it. What this effort will result in is a brand *image* held by customers and other stakeholders; the more successfully identity is managed, the more congruence there will be between the desired identity and the image actually held by customers. These concepts of identity and image can be related back to the point made in chapter 1 that some observers conceive organizations not as real 'things', but as constructs in people's

minds – socially negotiated human constructs derived from the interpretations and meanings people ascribe to their experiences of a particular organization.

A positive brand image relevant to targeted customers is a key intangible resource, and the ability to leverage it can be an important strategic competence. When several airlines' service quality, prices, and FFPs are perceived to offer similar benefits, brand image – especially in the case of airlines the corporate brand image – can have a casting vote in deciding purchase behaviour.

- **Brand personality** One approach frequently used by brand managers to help manage identity is to ask customers what personality they think a brand would have if it were to come to life and, particularly, what underlying *values* they associate with the brand. (It can be useful to ask the same question internally, in order to see whether there is any gap between what customers think and what the people responsible for designing and delivering services think.) The question of brand personality is of more than academic interest because not only can it help define market positioning, it can also be a key factor in moulding long-term customer relationships. We will look at customer relationships in chapter 8.

Proposition 3: Performance outcomes flowing from a choice of service concept are dependent on cognitive, position-related, and resource-related factors

Performance outcomes will depend upon the strategies and action plans developed to operationalise a service concept. More fundamentally, success is dependent upon the accuracy of our mental model of the commercial environment, and whether we have chosen a position in the market that properly balances insight into the present and future needs of targeted customers against the resources and competencies we can reasonably expect to make available to satisfy those needs. This is actually the very essence of marketing; too many managers still confuse marketing with advertising, promotion or sales when in fact the 'central idea of marketing is to match the organization's capabilities with the needs of customers in order to achieve the objectives of both' (McDonald and Payne, 1996: 4). The coupling which forges this link is the services marketing mix – a concept we will define in the next chapter and refer to, implicitly or explicitly, throughout the book. Key questions are: Does the airline have whatever resources and competencies are required to profitably deliver the particular type of value expected by customers in targeted segments? If so –

fine; if not, can the resource-/competence-gap be closed either through internal development or external acquisition of the missing piece(s) of the jig-saw, or through an alliance? If so – fine; if not, it is time to reassess the target segment (Bowman and Faulkner, 1997).

To win competitively, targeted segments should not be under-served; to keep costs in check, they should not be over-served. Services have to be designed, priced, promoted, distributed, and delivered with a keen eye on changing segmentation variables and segment membership, and they have to be positioned in consumers' minds with an equally keen eye on competitors. It is to the design and pricing of passenger air transport services that we turn next.

4 Designing the Service-Price Offer

> If you're not thinking customer, you're not thinking.
> Theodore Levitt

The starting point for this chapter is as follows.

1. We have identified, assessed, and segmented available markets.
2. We have refined our vision into a service concept that implies offering a certain type of customer value to one or more targeted segments.
3. We have chosen a position for the service concept in customers' minds which:
   - requires the projection of a certain brand identity;
   - leverages points of difference between our offer and the offers being made by competitors.
4. We have established that we possess:
   - the resources and, particularly, the strategy-specific competencies necessary to deliver the service embodied in our service concept;
   - the firm-specific competencies required to establish and sustain a competitive advantage over defined competitors.

The task now is to translate the type of customer value embodied in our service concept into a specific service-price offer pitched at targeted customers. Figure 4.1 illustrates where we presently stand; our interest here lies on the passenger side of the air transport business.

This chapter looks at: how a service concept (or 'benefit concept' – although I have not used the term elsewhere in the book) can be translated through service design into a set of service attributes (or 'features'), and then priced to become a 'service-price offer'; how these attributes get merged into brand image and a set of customer-perceived service benefits;

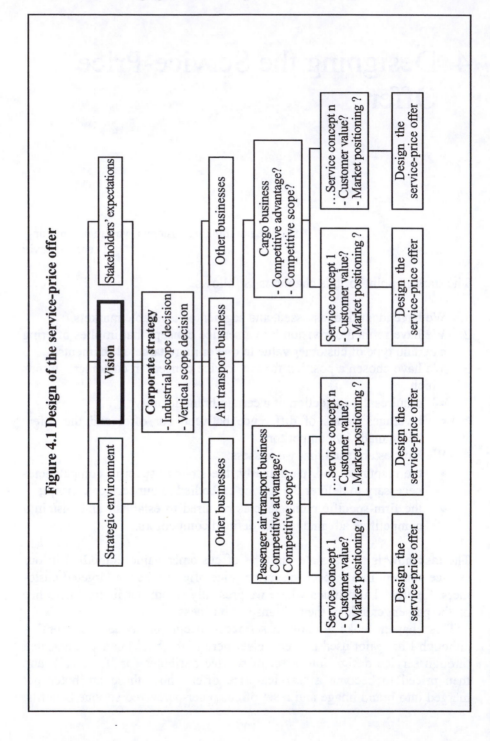

Figure 4.1 Design of the service-price offer

and how our success in delivering customer-perceived benefits, rather than just the attributes we have designed, is what actually determines whether or not we are delivering the type of customer value required by the service concept. We will begin by considering first what it is that distinguishes services from manufactured goods; we will then explore the importance to service design of having a good understanding of customers' expectations and of how they perceive service quality, before going on in chapter 5 to look at individual aspects of service design.

i. The distinguishing characteristics of services

Every *product* sold lies somewhere on a continuum that stretches from tangible *goods* such as a home appliance at one end, to intangible *services* such as legal advice at the other (Shostack, 1977). In fact, most tangible goods come with services attached – such as warranties, or the degree of helpfulness in the dealer's attitude. Similarly, the delivery of most services involves provision of 'physical evidence' – such as the documents prepared by a lawyer, or the decor selected for its lounges by an airline.

Because air transport products lie towards the 'intangible' end of the spectrum (albeit not as far along as services such as pension and insurance contracts), they share certain generic characteristics with other types of service: intangibility; perishability; inseparability of production and consumption; and variability in delivery standards. These characteristics not only distinguish services from tangible goods at a theoretical level; they have a profound influence on the ways in which service industries such as airlines attract, serve, and retain their customers (Holloway, 1998b).

Characteristics of services in general

Intangibility

A service offer is an offer to perform a process rather than to transfer ownership of a tangible good. This creates 'purchase risk' – particularly for first-time buyers – because the consumer cannot generally experience a service in advance and neither is past experience necessarily an accurate guide to future performance. It also creates a differentiation challenge for service firms. It is the reason why, as will be argued elsewhere in the book, brand image is so important in providing pre-purchase quality reassurance to prospective customers – even in the most price-sensitive segments of air transport markets. The essence of brand management is to establish a clearly distinct position for the brand, built on a platform of well-articulated values. A long-running example of positioning based on a theme designed to add tangibility to the essentially intangible attribute of high-quality service is 'Singapore Girl'; this has been used to convey intangible service attributes such as warmth, friendliness, efficiency, and professionalism. Tangible 'clues' such as the design of lounges, aircraft liveries, cabin decor, staff uniforms, and 'house style' in written communications and advertisements are used both to help shape image and add a tangible dimension to an airline's service. Another effect of intangibility is that the complexity of their price-quality relationship makes services difficult to price.

Perishability

Seats and cargo space on departing flights clearly cannot be produced and then inventoried ahead of sale, and are equally clearly lost if not consumed when produced. Service delivery systems have a tendency towards either overcapacity or overdemand – something which is particularly acute when the markets being served are as prone to peaking as most air transport markets. Because space unsold at the time of departure generates costs but not revenue, efficient capacity management is vital. (See Holloway, 1997.)

Inseparability (or 'simultaneity') of production and consumption

Whereas the majority of consumer goods are produced and then sold, scheduled air transport is committed, sold, then produced – and customers have to be present during the most important of the production activities. There is no separation in either space or time between consumption on the one hand and many of the production processes on the other. This, as we will see, should bring the marketing and operations functions into particularly close proximity – something that is happening at a growing number of airlines as market liberalisation forces them away from an operations focus and towards greater customer orientation. In fact, some pioneers writing early in the development of the services management literature used the somewhat inelegant but nonetheless quite graphic term 'servuction system' to emphasise the point that service consumption and production are closely bound and should not be looked at in isolation (Langeard et al, 1981).

Provided that the end products meet their expectations, most buyers of tangible goods neither know nor much care about the processes used to produce them. Airline passengers, on the other hand, must directly experience many of the production processes that contribute to the service they are buying. Indeed, passengers' experiences whilst they are present in the service delivery system are an important part of the service being bought. Airlines must therefore address not only *what* they want to offer target segments, but also *how* they want to deliver that offer; the style and tone of service delivery are service attributes in their own right. This makes the quality, training, motivation, commitment, and values of a carrier's people absolutely critical to effective service delivery.

Another implication of 'simultaneity' is that because passengers are present at the time of production, they are likely to feel immediately and directly the effects of any significant failure in the service delivery system. The buyer of a home appliance will likely never know about a breakdown in the production line or about a fault picked up during pre-shipment inspection, but a passenger will know immediately if a flight departs behind schedule or a service encounter with an employee is unsatisfactory (Holloway, 1998b). The positive side to this is that the 'simultaneity' characteristic of services can provide an almost real-time source of customer feedback if staff are trained and systems are in place to capture it.

Variability (or 'heterogeneity') in delivery

Because they are present during the production process, consumers experience multiple 'service encounters'; the management of service encounters is discussed in chapter 5. In this sense the delivery of services can be characterised as a multitude of one-off, unsupervised 'production runs' that are both affected by the presence of customers and, because of that presence, judged instantaneously (Irons, 1997b). It is not straightforward for service companies such as airlines to ensure consistent standards across all these 'moments of truth' (Normann, 1984). Some use 'the rule book' and/or tight scripting of service encounters to secure consistency, some rely more on the shared norms of organizational culture, whilst others are willing to empower their staff with the latitude to respond individually to each circumstance. Absolute consistency is impossible to achieve, and there is anyway an argument that many of today's consumers – particularly in premium segments – do not respond well to the 'industrialisation' of service delivery where it leads to service providers being deprived of the opportunity to treat customers as individuals. Empowering staff to be flexible (within realistic limits set by the nature of the industry's operating environment and the particular service concept) has the merit of recognising the fact that although service packages can be designed around the benefits thought to be expected by the average customer in a targeted market or segment, there is really no way of telling what any specific customer is actually going to expect until they present themselves for service.

Service inconsistencies can arise because:

- every individual service provider performs differently over time;
- different service providers encountered on different occasions each deliver the same service to different standards;
- any one customer's mood or emotions can vary between different journeys or different stages of the same journey;
- the presence of different customers can evoke different interactions between a customer and a service provider on different occasions.

We will see later in the book that this is where employees' skills and motivation interact with customers' expectations and behaviours. An airline averaging, say, eight service encounters per passenger and carrying 30 million passengers in a year has close to a quarter of a billion 'moments of truth' to get right (and this ignores potential customers who have not yet made a decision to purchase from that airline but nonetheless come into contact with its staff). In the case of an international carrier, many of these encounters cross cultural boundaries; employees from different cultural backgrounds might have contrasting views of their role in the service delivery system and distinct styles of delivery, whilst customers from different cultural backgrounds are very likely to have distinct, culturally influenced expectations (e.g., about the acceptability of waiting for service or about staff attitudes and behaviour). A final point to bear in mind is that a single service transaction in the airline business may require a passenger to remain within the service delivery system, interfacing with an airline's people, for up to 24 hours. Reducing service variability to an acceptable level is a challenge in such a 'high-contact' industry (Chase, 1978). Code-sharing and alliance-building do not simplify the task. This is why throughout the book I keep coming back to the importance of organizational culture (something that alliances, of course, do not yet have and are unlikely to develop for as long as it is the staff of their many different members who actually deliver service to customers).

Summary

I mentioned in chapter 1 that the model for this book is derived from the services management literature. This is a body of work that has expanded greatly over the last two decades in response to the rapidly growing importance of services in the modern economy and a widening recognition that the management of service businesses differs in significant respects from the management of traditional manufacturing industries. When I talk about service(s) management in this book, two different sets of contrasts need to be appreciated.

1. **Services versus goods** The delivery of services is distinguished from the manufacture and delivery of goods by the characteristics listed above: intangibility, perishability, inseparability/simultaneity, and variability/heterogeneity.
2. **Service versus customer service** Airlines are service businesses insofar as their core product is an intangible process (i.e., air transportation) as opposed to a tangible good. 'Customer service' is something different: customer service is something offered in support of the core product, and it can be offered by a service business such as an airline supporting its core air transportation product or by a manufacturing company supporting sale of its tangible product. 'Customer service' as the term is commonly used is therefore a narrower concept than 'service' when the latter is used in the context of 'service(s) management' – as is the case in this book. 'Customer service' is simply one attribute of a much wider package of services offered by any airline.

The characteristics of airline service

Looking at the passenger side of the airline industry, there are several important considerations that are derived from the nature of services generally and link through to much of what follows in the rest of the book. Drawing on a framework suggested by Rispoli (1996), I will break these down into two sets: supply-side and demand-side characteristics.

Supply-side characteristics

The following flow directly from the nature of service production and delivery operations in the passenger air transport industry.

1. Consumers (i.e., end-users of the service, who may or may not also be the customers who make actual purchase decisions) need to be physically present to receive the core transportation service.
2. Transportation is an experience derived from a mix of tangible and intangible elements that can be identified as separate service attributes.
3. Because production and consumption of the service can only occur simultaneously, there is a high level of contact between consumers on

the one hand and an airline's operational staff, facilities, equipment, and processes on the other.

4. Interpersonal contacts between consumers and service providers (i.e., an airline's front-line staff) are a significant part of the service experience and are highly significant service attributes.

5. As well as being people-intensive, airline service is also equipment-intensive and information-intensive, with the result that service delivery depends heavily on the effective management of both people and technology.

6. Airlines have generally high fixed costs (i.e., high operating leverage) that can cause profit volatility in unstable demand conditions (particularly when financial leverage is also high). (See Holloway (1997) for an explanation of these concepts.) The fact that a system comprised of capital equipment and highly trained people has to be in place to offer service on any significant scale means that fixed costs are high; this in turn puts airlines under pressure to adopt a volume-oriented approach to their business, which then exerts pressure to engage in 'marginal cost pricing' whenever this is what it takes to maintain traffic volume. The impact is often seen in weak yields, particularly when new capacity is added to a market or when the economy turns down.

7. Many airlines have transactional dealings with an overwhelming majority of their customers, but relationship dealings with a relatively small number of business customers who generate a disproportionately high percentage of their revenues.

8. Front-line personnel in direct contact with consumers can have a profound impact on the quality of service delivered, but often have little influence over the design of that service.

9. The level of customisation airlines are able to offer even to their high-value customers is very limited, with the result that the style of service delivery is often all that prevents a consumer feeling he or she is being anonymously processed.

10. Airline operations exhibit a great deal of short-run rigidity.

    • Whilst some airlines now manage their fleets much more flexibly than in the past, output (ASMs/ASKs) remains difficult to adjust on any significant scale over a short period of time – with upper limits imposed by capacity at full utilisation, and lower limits set by the sustainability of fixed costs associated with an underutilised fleet. A countervailing advantage is that because aircraft are mobile resources, they can be quickly reallocated in response to demand fluctuations in different markets.

    • Demand peaking on an intra-day, intra-week, and seasonal basis is an additional capacity management problem.

- Unsold output produced off-peak cannot be inventoried for later sale.
- It is difficult and expensive to quickly upgrade service quality levels because heavy investments are likely to be needed in facilities and equipment and, particularly, in staff training.

11. In some jurisdictions, competition authorities can influence output decisions which are deemed, for example, to be predatory or an abuse of dominant position. Output decisions in many, albeit a declining number of, international markets remain constrained by the terms of bilateral air services agreements (Holloway, 1998a).

Demand characteristics

The demand for airline service is both cyclically volatile and prone to heavy peaking. It is also a demand that is *derived* from customers' underlying requirements to be somewhere else; there is very little intrinsic demand for air services in their own right. There are several different players on the demand side, each of whom will have different expectations.

1. Consumers (i.e., end-users), who are also customers when they search for and choose the service they themselves use.
2. Influencers (e.g., executive secretaries, travel agents, and members within a consumer's social network from whom he or she hears word-of-mouth opinions on an airline's service), who may under certain circumstances have the power to affect individual consumer purchase behaviour.
3. Customers for airline services who do not actually consume the services bought include corporate travel departments negotiating rebates or special terms with particular airlines and obliging staff to comply with travel policies.
4. Wholesalers such as tour organisers and consolidators which buy blocks of seats directly from airlines and either package them with other travel-related services for sale to the public or retail them on a seat-only basis.

The services marketing mix

For several decades, the concept at the heart of marketing planning has been the '4Ps' of the marketing mix – a managed blend of *product* (i.e., attributes, quality, packaging, and length and breadth of lines, etc.), *price* (i.e., levels, discounts, conditions), *promotion* (i.e., advertising, PR, sales, and sales promotion), and *place* (i.e., distribution channels). The idea, developed originally from research in US fast-moving consumer goods markets, is that these need to be integrated in order to stimulate required behaviour – usually purchase behaviour – within the markets or segments for which they are designed. Management of the marketing mix is a dynamic process; equilibrium is rarely achieved in competitive markets.

More recently, the 'services marketing mix' has added three more 'Ps' in recognition of the particular characteristics of services (Booms and Bitner, 1981): *people* are a factor because service providers are a vital element in service delivery processes and in service outcomes (i.e., customer satisfaction and service quality assessments) and because customers themselves are people who also have a sometimes significant role to play in service delivery; *processes* are a factor because service delivery processes, as seen from each customer's perspective, are very much part of the product whenever they are directly experienced; and *physical evidence* (e.g., equipment, facilities, uniforms, signage, etc.) is a factor because it lends tangibility to an otherwise intangible service offer. The three additional 'Ps' are helpful, but arguably misleading. People (that is, an airline's people), processes, and physical evidence (sometimes referred to as 'tangible clues') are in fact an intrinsic part of the first 'P' – product. This has already been made fairly clear in the summary of service characteristics above, and will become clearer when we look at service design.

Note that marketing can be considered on two levels: strategic and tactical/operational (Bradley, 1995). This book is primarily oriented towards the strategic level, although it does touch upon tactical issues in respect of communications, service delivery, and one or two other topics. The marketing mix is generally considered a tactical tool, concerned more with stimulating immediate consumer responses than with long-term strategic issues. I am mentioning it here because tactical though it might be, everything that impacts upon an airline's service, communications, and pricing can in principle affect its brand positioning – and whether it does or not, it needs to be managed as though it does. Aside from ensuring that elements of the marketing mix are appropriate both to positioning strategy and to current competitive circumstances, it is important that they are internally consistent with each other and reasonably consistent over time.

ii. Service design: competitive strategy in action

> Who the hell wants to hear actors talk?
> Sam Warner, 1927

Chapter 9 will consider how to evaluate the overall performance of a service business such as an airline. It will look in particular at concepts such as customer satisfaction and service quality, both of which are driven by customers' expectations and perceptions of service. If customers' expectations and perceptions are important metrics for evaluating performance, they should logically be used to help guide the design of service-price offers.

Customer understanding revisited: expectations and perceptions

> Experience is not what happens to you;
> it is what you make of what happens to you.
> Aldous Huxley

We might need to get from Milan to New York. Ideally, we want to have 80-inch seat pitch and gourmet dining – all for a low fare. Realistically we know we cannot always have what we want, so we make either a sybaritic or an economical choice which leads us to have certain *expectations* with regard to the type of value we will receive. If during and after the service experience our *perceptions* are that expectations were met or exceeded we will probably be *satisfied*, but if not we are likely to be *dissatisfied*. Depending upon just how satisfied we are, how our future air travel requirements develop, and what other airlines offer us, we might become *loyal* customers of the carrier concerned.

Every service concept should be based on a distinct value proposition that is clearly positioned in the minds of customers in targeted segments. The customer understanding that was used to develop a service concept from the competitive scope decision (i.e., product scope plus geographical scope) is also used, albeit in sharper focus, to help design service-price offers: specifically, what we need in order to design these offers is an understanding of what customers in the segment concerned *expect* and the evaluative processes through which they arrive at *perceptions* of the service-price package actually delivered to them.

Customers' expectations

Unearthing the service expectations of targeted customers is in principle a relatively straightforward market research task that can be undertaken using established techniques such as surveys, focus groups, critical incident reviews (discussed later in the chapter), advisory panels, one-to-one conversations, and complaints (Scheuing, 1998). They can be isolated by asking the following types of question (Tenner and DeToro, 1997).

- What benefits do customers expect from the service concerned?
- At what level of performance is each benefit expected?
- What is the relative importance of each benefit?

In practice, the literature complicates matters by drawing a distinction between two different types of customer expectations.

1. **Expectation as prediction** Predictive expectations with regard to a specific service experience (i.e., what probably *will* happen on a given journey) are compared by customers against their perceptions of what actually does happen, and the outcome is either satisfaction or dissatisfaction. 'Expectation as prediction' is the perspective adopted in the customer satisfaction literature.
2. **Expectation as ideal** The service quality literature, on the other hand, sometimes treats expectations as customers' pre-purchase ideals (i.e., what ideally *should* happen on airline journeys in general). Ideal expectations of service are compared with perceptions of services actually received in order to arrive at service quality assessments.

Customer satisfaction and service quality are two different theoretical constructs (although they are often incorrectly treated as synonyms). Unfortunately, researchers have yet to conclusively isolate the component dimensions of each in particular industries, and neither is there any empirical evidence on which to base unequivocal assertions about how the two are linked. Because we have two different definitions of customers' expectations, it is possible to satisfy a customer by delivering a service which the same customer nonetheless feels in some way falls short of her ideal. This raises performance management issues, as we will see in chapter 9, and it also complicates the process of plugging customers' expectations into the service design process: it is important to know whether the 'predictive' or 'ideal/normative' definition of expectations is being used when surveying customers with a view both to designing and communicating service benefits, and also managing their expectations.

Zeithaml et al (1993) have modelled several levels of 'acceptable' service, using ideas that can help to organize initial thoughts about service design.

- **Ideal level** Most passengers would ideally like airports to be uncongested, flights to depart on time and arrive early, seats next to them to be empty, inflight catering to be enjoyable, and service providers to be universally helpful, courteous, and efficient.
- **Desired level** Knowing that life is rarely ideal, customers generally settle on a desired level of service which accommodates performance below the ideal level. Nonetheless, the drivers of customers' expectations (e.g., past experience, word-of-mouth endorsements, marketing communications, competitors' activities, increasingly demanding attitudes towards service standards in general) might work singly or in unison to edge the desired level closer towards the ideal level.
- **Adequate level** Between the desired level and the minimum adequate level of service is a *zone of tolerance* within which delivered service will be acceptable even if not up to the desired level. Below the 'adequate' level, service becomes unacceptable. Again, drivers such as those mentioned above will determine the width of the 'zone of tolerance' and the floor set by what is an 'adequate' level of service. Context is likely to be quite important here; for example, arriving two hours late on a vacation trip from London to Sydney might be acceptable, whereas a similar delay on a day-return business trip from London to Paris is likely to cause dissatisfaction. Predictive expectations also affect the boundaries of a zone of tolerance: what represents adequate service on the Thursday before Thanksgiving is likely to be very different from adequate service on a Tuesday in February, given the different predictions of airport congestion that passengers will make for each of the two days.

A customer might *ideally* expect 'good service' from a major transatlantic airline; more specifically, the same passenger travelling transatlantic in business class will in many cases have reasonably explicit *predictive* expectations of the benefits she can expect from her journey (e.g., fast and hassle-free check-in, a lounge to relax or work in prior to departure, generous seat-pitch, meal and entertainment services at or above a certain level of performance, etc.). Airlines must be able to design and deliver levels of service that are always at least 'adequate' from the perspective of a representative cross-section of targeted customers, and which in most cases far exceed the minimum level of adequacy. Managing zones of tolerance through service design is no easy matter, however.

1. Different service attributes each have their own separate zones of tolerance. For example, a check-in queuing time between five and ten minutes might be established through research as being within the zone of tolerance of most passengers in a particular segment, but how do we arrive at a similar determination for non-quantifiable service encounters such as the tone of greeting extended to boarding passengers? Also, the more important a particular attribute, the narrower its zone of tolerance is likely to be (Zeithaml and Bitner, 2000); flight safety has no zone of tolerance.

2. Different passengers have different zones of tolerance in respect of each attribute. Consider two alternative beverage-service processes in a long-haul business class cabin, one of which requires cabin attendants to take drinks orders prior to or soon after take-off and deliver them direct from the galley, whilst the other involves after-take-off preparation of a beverage trolley followed by the simultaneous taking of orders and delivery of drinks; assuming that a glass arrives in a given passenger's hand at precisely the same time in either case, the fact is that the early attention provided by taking orders in advance is likely to place the service attribute within most passengers' zones of tolerance whereas the other process – particularly if the passenger concerned is last in the cabin to be served – might leave him feeling ignored for longer than he finds acceptable.

3. Zones of tolerance are contextual. An executive travelling on business might have very different expectations of service compared to when she is travelling on vacation and has a more relaxed attitude.

Customers' perceptions

Whether or not customers are satisfied with our value proposition will depend in the final analysis on how they perceive it relative to their prior expectations. In addition to knowing what they expect, we therefore need to input into our service design process an understanding of the dimensions that customers use in evaluating the services we deliver to them. If customers perceive that we are failing to meet their expectations, we need to reassess our understanding of those expectations and the manner in which we are trying to satisfy them. The objective of every service design effort must be to have customers perceive that we have at least met, preferably exceeded, their predictive expectations. In the long run, and within the context of our particular service concept(s), we need to aspire to meeting their *ideal* expectations – although these inevitably represent a moving target.

iii. The elements of service design

> There is not much to say about most airplane journeys. Anything remarkable must
> be disastrous, so you define a good flight by negatives: you didn't get hijacked,
> you didn't crash, you didn't throw up, you weren't nauseated by the food.
>
> Paul Theroux

Paul Theroux's observations sometimes ring true; more often they do not, and they certainly do not have to. Whether or not they do will depend in the first instance on how a service is designed. Service is a performance from the perspective of those who deliver it, an experience from the perspective of those who receive it. It has two fundamental elements: what is done, and how it is done.

- **What is done** What people are actually buying from an airline is the solution to a problem: how to get themselves to another location. This problem gives rise to subsidiary problems, such as how to get to that other location in minimum time, in maximum comfort, at minimum cost, with maximum certainty, and so on. In this sense, service design is akin to problem solving; a service concept is a commitment, albeit often unarticulated, regarding which problems the airline wants to solve, for which customers, and how it intends to solve them; service design is a process that translates what is to be done into explicit service specifications.
- **How it is done** The issue here is the style and tone of service delivery. These intangible attributes can also be specified as part of the service design process; however, ensuring consistency is extremely difficult because 'delivery' in this case involves literally millions of human interactions between staff and customers. Appropriate staff training, a genuine and long-term commitment to a service ethic strong enough to resist knee-jerk cost cutting brought on by the last quarterly income downturn, and a corporate culture that reinforces desired behaviour can contribute enormously to consistent service delivery, but they can never guarantee it.

Important though it is to recognise service as a matter of 'what' and 'how', the fact is that the two are closely intertwined. For more practical help in designing a service we need to think in terms of the specific expectations we intend to meet or exceed for targeted customers, the benefits required to achieve this, and the service attributes needed to deliver those benefits. Some attributes will be largely a matter of 'what' (e.g., cabin decor), some a matter of 'how' (e.g., check-in style), and others a matter of both (e.g., inflight meal service).

Terminology varies, but there is reasonably widespread agreement in the services management literature that whatever segment it is targeted at, a service package will usually have attributes designed into it on three levels.

1. **Core service** This is the level of service to which we can apply the old but nonetheless apt axiom that people buy quarter-inch holes, not quarter-inch drills. In other words, we are here offering a core solution to a core problem. On the scheduled passenger side of the air transport business this means safe air transportation on selected routes, consistent with a published schedule. Industry-specific competencies are required to deliver core service. A common core can be the platform for a product line, with separate offers targeted at discreet segments and distinguished on the basis of different levels of expected and augmented service. However, individual carriers operating in product niches, particularly those making low-fare/no-frills offers, will not generally build complex product lines.

2. **Minimum expected service** 'Expected service' embodies the 'points of similarity' we met earlier in the book; the logic is that this level of service corresponds with what is widely known about customers' expectations. Acting on this common knowledge, every competitor provides at least the minimum expected service, so that in this regard their brands share 'points of similarity' (Levitt, 1980) or 'points of parity' (Keller, 1998). Initiatives in this area are frequently taken for revenue-protection purposes (i.e., to keep pace with customers' expectations and competitors' products) rather than to earn incremental revenue; profit-oriented carriers should want to earn at least their hurdle rate of return on investment when spending on revenue-protection, but this might need to be measured using 'net revenue not lost' as the numerator rather than 'incremental net revenue earned'. Strategy-specific competencies are necessary to deliver the minimum levels of service expected in any targeted segment.

3. **Augmented service** Following the same argument, 'augmented service' is said to correspond to whatever 'points of difference' there are between competing brands. Whilst every serious competitor in a segment should be delivering the expected service (which, along with core service, can be said to be commoditised), augmented service is unique to each carrier. Service augmentation occurs when an airline unearths and responds to latent customer needs – that is, offers something that customers either needed but were not previously getting, or never knew they needed until the offer was designed. Sometimes augmented

service can come from delivering an expected service in a better way than competitors deliver it – the 'what' is the same, but the 'how' is different; a lot of the competition between similarly positioned airlines is fought-out in this way. Firm-specific competencies – perhaps in intangible areas such as sustaining a particular organizational culture – are required to deliver augmented service and leverage a brand's 'points of difference'. However, what qualifies as 'augmented service' and what is 'expected' tends to vary along the following dimensions:

- over time: what was once considered a service augmentation tends over time to move closer to becoming 'expected' as consumers' expectations rise and they take more for granted, and as innovators add attributes in search of sustainable bases for differentiation. However, as the product differentiators ratchet-up their offerings, they leave behind niches for others (such as no-frills carriers) to fill (Trott, 1998);

- between geographical markets: the bundle of attributes actually expected varies in response to the history of individual markets, as well as the freedom and willingness of competitors to innovate. The different expectations of short- and long-haul passengers gen-erate further distinctions between geographical markets.

When people talk about 'adding value' for consumers it is usually in this area of augmented service that value is being added.

(These three levels were originally suggested by Levitt (1983), who also proposed a fourth which he called the 'potential product' and characterised as all potential added features and benefits that are or could be of use to buyers. I prefer to look upon this potential as the 'space' into which aug-mented service can be moved, rather than treat it as a separate level of service in its own right.)

A service package is in essence a bundle of attributes designed to provide benefits for targeted customers; any given attribute might contribute to one or more of core, minimum expected, or augmented service. These attributes and the benefits they are designed to offer can be of several different types (Bhat and Reddy, 1998).

1. **Functional** Utilitarian performance benefits can be derived from funct-ional attributes of an airline's service, such as seating configuration, meals, inflight entertainment, etc. Rationally assessed functional ben-efits can also be derived from service encounters between customers and staff. The functionality of service delivery is clearly affected by several of the characteristics of airline services mentioned earlier in the chapter – notably their experiential nature, the simultaneity of

production and consumption, and the inevitable variability in service delivery arising from the central role of the human dimension.

2. **Emotional/symbolic** These benefits can be psychological and/or social in nature.

- *Psychological* Positive inner emotions might be stimulated by the choice and experience of a particular service (e.g., empathy with the brand values that have been bought into, and confidence in the reliability of the brand, etc.). Consumers frequently look for reassurance – from advertising, from the service environment, from the style of service delivery, for example – confirming that this is the right brand for them. For some consumers, brand choice is a means of communicating something *about* themselves *to* themselves; in this sense, the brand image and self-image need to be congruent.

- *Social* Benefits can be derived from the symbolism associated with a particular purchase (e.g., the symbolism of success attached to a premium product, and the sense of belonging associated with membership of a particular executive club). Symbolic meanings are formed partly in response to marketing communications; they also arise through interactions between customers on the one hand and both airline staff and other customers (de Chernatony, 1999a). Word-of-mouth can be another important influence. Brand usage allows people to make statements about themselves, and also helps them interpret other people they meet (de Chernatony and McDonald, 1998). Purchase decisions might therefore be stimulated not just by perceptions of a brand held by the purchaser, but also by perceptions held by peers and a wider reference group. (Recall what was said in chapter 1 about an organization being, according to some definitions, a social construction rather than a real 'thing' – an image held by multiple different actors who have arrived at a sometimes implicitly negotiated consensus.)

Whereas emotional/symbolic benefits associated with tangible goods are to a large extent under management control because they are created and nurtured through marketing communications and packaging strategies, the importance to customer value of less readily controllable service encounters between customers and staff makes the design and consistent delivery of these benefits more challenging in a service industry (de Chernatony, 1999b).

It is worth emphasising that international airlines face an added cultural complication insofar as customers from different cultures might give different weightings to psychological benefits, while cultural frames of reference can affect the way symbolic information derived from a brand image is decoded.

The concept of product attributes links the idea of competencies to competitive advantage – in other words, it links the supply side to the demand side. If we take a service to be comprised of a bundle of attributes, the ability of an airline to deliver core, expected, and augmented levels of service at a given time will in large measure be determined by its resources and competencies. The better able an airline is to deliver attributes particularly valued by a targeted market or segment, the more likely it is that competitive advantage can be gained and sustained (Bogner and Thomas, 1996). Which attributes an airline needs to have competencies in delivering will depend upon the markets and segments it is targeting and, further back up the chain of analysis, upon its service concept(s).

iv. The service design and development process

In this section I will first briefly revisit the service concept and customer value, before moving on to discuss the service design process itself.

Service design and the service concept

Whether it is an independent operator or a unit within a larger group, an airline whose management has decided to focus on a single product niche is likely to offer a single 'package' of service attributes into that niche. It may or may not treat segments differently for the purposes of marketing communications, promotions, ticket conditionality and pricing, but within the service delivery system it will in most cases offer just a single service.

On the other hand, the norm for most carriers is to offer several different types of service within broadly the same service delivery system. The differences usually reflect different classes of travel and possibly membership or non-membership of the airline's FFP. In each case, the carrier's service design team will need to think carefully about the core, expected, and augmented levels of service appropriate to each service package both on the ground and in the air. In other words, they will need to consider the type of customer value to be offered.

Customer value as a service outcome

From this point I am going to assume that we are interested in designing a single package of ground and onboard services. This might be a niche-focusser's single-class product, or just one of several classes offered by a wide-market carrier. Within the group of people for whom our service is being designed there may well be multiple sub-segments when viewed from, say, a marketing communications perspective; but from a service design perspective, airport space and onboard cabin floor-space constraints limit the number of different variations that can be 'customised' for sub-segments. We touched on this in chapter 3, where I noted that however many segments are identified for other purposes, once a customer enters the service delivery system at the departure airport these segments are necessarily combined into a small number of categories distinguished by FFP membership (if this is relevant to lounge access, for example) and class of travel (which determines access to the different aircraft cabins and, in premium classes, to airport lounges). In other words:

- product niche-focussers offering a single service concept (particularly low-cost and charter carriers) in most cases treat passengers broadly the same once they enter the service delivery system;
- wide-market carriers offering multiple service concepts segment passengers within their service delivery systems as far as possible, although many service attributes – particularly core attributes such as safety, network, and schedule – are inevitably shared.

What we are trying to do for the customers for whom we are designing any particular service package is provide them with value consistent with what has been formulated – albeit perhaps only in the most general terms – in the service concept. 'Customer value' as I have defined it is a matter of offering customers at least the perceived benefits they expect (in a 'predictive' sense) at a price they consider acceptable given the level of service provided. We noted in the last chapter that if service is improved in some meaningful way without a corresponding rise in price or if price is lowered in respect of an unchanged level of service, value increases. It was also observed that low price and low levels of service do not necessarily equate to poor value; they could simply reflect a service concept which offers a value proposition different from what is being provided by another airline's higher-service, higher-priced offer.

Customer value is a measure of what customers perceive themselves to be getting out of an airline's service-price offer, not what the airline itself is putting into it. Whereas passenger-kilometres or enplanements are common measures of an airline's sold *output*, customer value is a less commonly measured *outcome*. Airlines in liberalised or deregulated markets have to be less concerned about raw outputs, and more focused on outcomes.

Clearly then, before designing a service it is necessary to understand what contributes to target customers' perceptions of value. A 'customer value analysis' might help; as we saw in chapter 3 this involves the listing and ranking of benefits which customers say contribute to value, and the rating of how airlines competing in the segment perform in respect of each. A first-cut customer value analysis will have been necessary in order to define a service concept relevant to the targeted segment. Another, more quantitative (and not yet widely practised) approach is 'conjoint analysis', which models the purchase behaviours of a sample of customers on the basis of the value weightings they give to different attributes (and also to price) combined into an actual or potential service offer (Rao and Steckel, 1998). Grant (1998: 223) summarises the technique as requiring

> first, an identification of the underlying attributes of a product and, second, a ranking of hypothetical products that contain alternative bundles of attributes. On the basis of these data, trade-offs can be analyzed and simulations can be run to determine the proportion of customers who would prefer a hypothetical new product to competing products already available on the market.

Once we know in detail what benefits we need to deliver in order to meet or exceed the expectations of targeted customers, we can set about designing the service-price offer – that is, we can begin to translate the service concept into a properly structured value proposition by putting together a coherent package of service attributes.

Differentiation or being different?

My working assumption is that in order to sell in a competitive market it is necessary to be different from competitors in some way that customers value. Difference might lie anywhere in a service-price offer. It might lie in lower prices, better functional service attributes (e.g., schedule or punctuality), excellent brand image, or an amalgam of these and other factors which makes the service-price offer as a whole better value in the eyes of targeted customers.

But 'being different' is not quite the same thing as what is meant by economists when they talk of 'differentiation'. The idea of differentiation, widely popularised by Porter (1980, 1985), in fact goes back to the 1930s. At that time, economists added the concept of 'monopolistic competition' to the microeconomic model of market structure which until then had recognised perfect competition, oligopoly, and monopoly (Chamberlin, 1933; Robinson, 1934). The basic idea of monopolistic competition is that by differentiating their offers in some way that is valuable to customers, firms gain a degree of freedom to raise prices they would not otherwise have in a perfectly competitive market; in effect, what they do is create a 'mini-monopoly' for the differentiated product.

When I talk of a service-price offer being 'distinct' in some way, I am not necessarily referring to differentiation as an economist would use the word. My perspective on service-price offers is as follows.

- **Service** An airline might offer a service that differs from competitors' offers in one or more ways which customers value. That difference could lie in functional attributes such as a better schedule or more comfortable cabins on long-haul services, or it might lie in less tangible but arguably more defensible emotional (i.e., psycho-social) attributes such as the style and tone of service delivery.
  - If customers are willing to pay a premium for this augmented service, we have a case of 'differentiation' as defined by economists. The next questions would then be whether the price premium covers any incremental costs – a rough calculation at best, in most circumstances – and how sustainable the competitive advantage on which the differentiation has been built will prove to be over time. Some airlines have been able to charge premia for nonstop services competing against connecting routes, for innovations such as sleeper-seats/flat-bed seats, for schedule strength at a dominated hub, and sometimes even for what they consider to be their 'high-quality' brand image. Sustaining such premia on a long-term basis can nonetheless prove challenging.
  - If customers will not pay a premium in return for functional or psycho-social attributes, other than perhaps temporarily, these attributes are not technically a form of 'differentiation'. They are certainly 'points of difference', but in this case the airline is not earning 'economic rent' from the resources or competencies that make it different – much though it might like to; it is nonetheless giving customers a 'reason to buy' in a competitive environment hall-marked by product 'sameness' and widespread price-matching. In general, few airlines possess the unique, rare, and costly-to-imitate resources required to sustain either 'differentiation' or 'points of difference' based on purely functional service attributes. There are exceptions, most notably those built on possession of critical mass at a hub or in a particular market; either can lead to the building of a dominant position in customers' perceptions within a geographical market. But on the whole, it is in respect of intangible attributes such as service style and brand image – providing predominantly psycho-social benefits – that sustainable points of difference can be found.

- **Price** This is where I diverge further from the economists' idea of differentiation, because I treat price as part of an overall service-price value proposition rather than as a reflection of whether or not an airline has been able successfully to differentiate itself in economists' terms. Take for example a low-cost/low-fare carrier. It might be able to establish clear points of difference between itself and competitors based on corporate culture and a positive brand image, as Southwest has done; but it cannot earn a price premium – that is, 'differentiate' in economists' terms – because low price is a fundamental purchase criterion in the segment it is targeting. This does not mean that the points of difference built on corporate culture and brand image are irrelevant, because all other things being equal – including price and schedule, for example – these give customers a reason to choose, and remain loyal to, Southwest rather than another carrier. In other words, although Southwest might for the sake of argument score equally with the competition on price and on functional attributes such as frequency and departure timings, the points of difference it has established by nurturing psycho-social attributes driven by culture and image give its overall service-price offer a winning edge.

  At this point we need another brief reality-check to remind us that price is in fact a complex concept with both tactical and strategic implications. We will look at these later in the chapter. But the fact that many airlines now use price in a very dynamic way to manage capacity and revenue does not detract from the argument here; at a strategic level, guided by a vision of the sort of carrier it is and by the service concept that has been developed, every airline should have a clear picture of where its service-price offer is to be positioned in customers' minds. The position might be that the carrier will sell primarily on price; revenue management may still be used to assist tactical pricing decisions and if competitors match it on price it must have some other 'points of difference' on which to sell rather than price alone, but overall the airline sees itself as serving a segment that expects low fares. Alternatively, the position might be that the carrier offers augmented service for which it feels it can charge fares as high as those of any comparable competitor or, perhaps, even slightly more than competitors are charging; if this is the strategic approach to pricing, on a tactical basis the airline will probably do no more in its premium cabins than offer occasional price promotions, and no more in its 'main cabin' than discount to sell off-peak or otherwise 'distressed' capacity.

In summary, when I talk about price or service 'distinctiveness' in this chapter or elsewhere, I am in fact talking about what the brand management literature refers to as 'points of difference' rather than what economists mean by 'differentiation'. I am talking about design variables in a strategic service-price offer which give customers a reason to purchase from us rather than from competitors.

The service design and development process

Unmet needs always exist.
Philip Kotler

The ability to design service attributes that customers value, that influence their purchase decisions and/or brand loyalty, and that can be delivered cost-effectively is an important competence founded on four sets of resources (Leonard-Barton, 1992b).

1.   Employee knowledge and skills.
2.   Technical systems.
3.   Managerial systems.
4.   Corporate values.

A competence in product development can be said to be grounded in 'a *dynamic and recursive* match between *technical capabilities* and *market knowledge* where individual [skills and learning] and organizational processes mediate the flow of information between these two' (Winterscheid and McNabb, 1996 – italics in the original). Less formally, we might say that service development in the airline industry is a complex process involving specialists from market research, engineering, flight operations, scheduling, catering, and passenger services to name just a few of the functions that could be involved. It requires resources in the form of accumulated knowledge, quite aside from the financial resources also needed to turn design into offer; it also requires excellent boundary-spanning competencies to co-ordinate the efforts of functional specialists, and possibly also external design teams and suppliers (of buyer-furnished equipment for aircraft cabins or of passenger services at outstations, for example). Critically, it requires all team members to be able to relate individual service attributes to the wider strategic context. Given what was said in chapter 2 about people possessing different mental models of reality and also players perhaps having different interpretations of the strategic logic underlying their business, getting this to happen is clearly not a simple task. The process through which complex service packages are designed or upgraded is quite likely to be 'causally ambiguous' and therefore, if replicable on a regular basis, is a core competence that could be a source of competitive advantage. Activities in a design management process may include the following (Bruce and Morris, 1998).

- Selection and commissioning of (inhouse and/or external) design expertise.
- Preparation of design briefs.
- Evaluation of design work.
- Project management.

Each activity might be underpinned by hard-to-copy tacit knowledge held by one or a small cadre of managers, co-ordinated by deeply embedded – perhaps taken-for-granted – organizational routines (Nelson and Winter, 1982).

The process in principle

Designing and developing a new service package or adding a new attribute to an existing package can in principle be reduced to the following steps. Clearly, when a new attribute rather than an entirely new service is under consideration, the degree of detail and formality in the process is likely to be lower. In either case, a good starting point is to ask one very simple question: What influences the purchase decisions of the particular customers we hope will be paying the next salary cheque?

Generate ideas Any reasonably detailed market segmentation exercise should provide a feeling for the way targeted customers make purchase decisions and the benefits they expect to derive. It is absolutely vital that we deliver at the very least what our targeted customers expect from a service – by which I mean that we deliver service at or above, preferably well above, the bottom end of their 'zones of tolerance'; these expectations are the baseline against which customers assess our performance, and this assessment can have a profound impact on repurchase intentions whenever there is a choice of alternative carriers. Ideas for new service attributes can come from several possible sources.

- **Creative service leadership** Some airlines pursue a policy of leading through innovation, sometimes brainstorming to create attributes that customers had not thought of but which generate relevant and substantial benefits.
- **Responsiveness** Valuable ideas can come from customers (through market research, or through paying attention to complaints and suggest-

ions), and from staff (particularly front-line staff). Suppliers and competitors can also be sources of ideas – but competitors' ideas will have to be improved upon if they are to lead to 'points of difference' rather than 'points of similarity'.

One approach that appears commonly in the literature and has been adopted by practitioners is the 'critical incident technique'. This involves asking customers (and staff) to recall in detail incidents during service delivery that caused either satisfaction or dissatisfaction (Bitner, 1992; Edvardsson, 1992). Its advantages are that specific areas for service improvement can be identified, whilst knowledge is also acquired regarding what aspects of service delivery generate most customer satisfaction. For example, research by Bitner et al (1990) highlighted the critical importance of having explicit systems in place to keep passengers informed about delays.

Two techniques that can be used to identify potential opportunities in unmet needs are *needs gap analysis* and *perceptual mapping*. Needs gap analysis relates what is known about customers' needs to the attributes currently being offered by the airline concerned and/or its competitors. Perceptual mapping relates what is known about customers' needs to what customers perceive to be on offer (irrespective of whether or not their perceptions are correct). A more comprehensive technique – developed within the total quality movement and used with increasing frequency in service industries – is *quality function deployment*. This is a sequential approach which starts by identifying customers' requirements and expectations, and then links each to one or more specific design elements in the service package and service delivery system (Bounds et al, 1994).

Screen ideas   The search for ideas must be conducted within a framework which recognises that airlines are in the business of delivering service outcomes rather than services. Every idea needs first to be subjected to some questions: What outcome will it deliver? For whom? How? What benefit does it offer targeted customers, why does this matter to them, and how does this benefit fit into the airline's service concept? Does provision of this benefit allow the airline to exploit a competitive advantage, or is it essentially imitable? What will it cost? Can the benefit be provided more efficiently or effectively by some other service attribute or, if not, can the attribute itself be delivered more effectively or efficiently? Each proposed service attribute should be linked directly to a customer benefit with the phrase, '….which means that….'; weak linkages and linkages to unimportant benefits need particular scrutiny. When major service innovations are being screened, 'concept tests' might be conducted using customers in a focus group format.

Every service attribute should provide one or more functional or emotional benefits. In addition, its specific characteristics need to be closely questioned.

1. Is the benefit it is designed to deliver valued by target customers? What need(s), want(s), or preference(s) does it satisfy? Something which does not contribute to an outcome valued by members of the targeted segment is unlikely to be a worthwhile service attribute.
2. Does the benefit it is designed to produce contribute to targeted customers' purchase decisions? Not all service attributes directly fuel purchase decisions, but to be worthwhile they must make enough contribution to justify the cost of providing them.
3. Particularly if the benefit it is designed to offer is relevant to customers' purchase decisions, is it unique to us? If so,
   - Is it protected by any barriers to market entry?
   - How readily could it be imitated or substituted?
4. If we choose *not* to offer an attribute offered by competitors, in what way would this disadvantage us?

A service attribute might offer more than one customer benefit. For example, compared to having to connect at a hub a nonstop routing might offer time savings, a better chance that schedules will be maintained, an improved probability that checked bags will arrive at the same time as the customer, and less overall hassle (e.g., by halving embarkations and disembarkations). On the other hand, an attribute providing benefits to one segment might be considered negatively by another: nonstop routings are generally well-received, especially by business travellers, but some leisure travellers might find a particular airline's network less attractive when stopover opportunities are lost.

If it passes this 'first cut' assessment for relevance and cost/effectiveness, the service attribute – or overall service package – should be examined by a cross-functional team looking at the following dimensions. Although the screening process can be formalised using techniques such as multi-attribute decision analysis, in fact much has to do with the judgement of team members.

1. **Feasibility**
   - *Marketing feasibility* Will it work in targeted markets?
   - *Operational feasibility* Is it technically possible? Does the service delivery system have the capacity to deliver it? Do we have the

required resources, and if not can we obtain them? Do we have the competencies required to execute the idea? If not, can they be secured and can the cost be justified?

- *Economic feasibility* Will customers absorb, or preferably pay a premium above, the incremental cost likely to be incurred? What is the business case?

2. **Compatibility** Does the idea sit comfortably with current corporate and competitive strategies, and if not what are the wider implications of adopting it? If we are talking about a particular service attribute, what would be its impact on other elements of the service package? Does it fit with the airline's overall image?

3. **Probability of success** Is it worthwhile to proceed with the proposal given the risks involved and the likelihood of success? Is it too similar (or too different) to what is already on offer to be a success?

Use a cross-functional team to specify the service package and how it is to be delivered Specification implies the designing of a package of attributes, asking in respect of each: What is the attribute and how should it be delivered? Designing specifications for a service package is complicated by some of the characteristics of services we met above, particularly their:

- **intangibility**: much of what a service provides is experiential, and experiences cannot be specified with quantitative precision. Words such as 'flexible', 'responsive', 'empathetic', and 'courteous' are open to a variety of interpretations, and a single service experience can anyway have very different meanings for different individuals;

- **variability**: the nature of interactions between consumers and service providers will inevitably vary from encounter to encounter, again making specification difficult.

This does not mean we should not try. Service specification is important because both consistent service delivery and effective monitoring of standards rely to some extent on the existence of specifications. Using a cross-functional team to specify service standards, blueprint service delivery, and fail-safe likely service failure points is also important because people in front-line functions who will be responsible for delivering services ought to be involved in their design in order to draw on practical input and secure commitment to on-specification delivery. For example, flight attendants should play a role in specifying inflight catering standards; they, after all, are on the receiving end of existing customers' reactions and will be on the receiving end of reactions to any new service attribute, whether tangible or processual. Cross-functional teamwork is also important to consistency: an airline letting cabin services managers specify onboard tangibles and processes, customer services managers specify ground service processes, facilities managers design terminal servicescapes, human resources people commission staff uniforms, marketing people make advertising and PR decisions, and revenue managers make pricing decisions with strategic implications (e.g., discounting in the premium cabins) all in isolation stands little chance of offering a coherent, consistent service package.

Service specifications comprise four elements (adapted from Anderson, 1999).

1. **Design specifications** These are standards which specify the tangible attributes (e.g., lounge availability, cabin design, meal presentation, etc.) and process attributes (e.g., embarkation and disembarkation procedures, inflight service, etc.) associated with each class of service. Within individual classes of service, different specifications might be required for each route (e.g., frequency/aircraft type, IFE variations reflecting the requirements of passengers travelling to particular regions of the world), and even for each departure (e.g., timing of meals and/or snacks).
2. **Status specifications** These establish required standards for each design specification directly or indirectly affecting customers' experiences (e.g., presentation of check-in areas, cleanliness of cabins, baggage reclaim times, etc.).
3. **Encounter specifications** The most difficult specifications to quantify, these establish standards for staff interactions with customers and are often articulated in imprecise – some would say 'warm and fuzzy' – terms. They can only be sustained on a consistent basis through frequent training, supported by an appropriate culture.
4. **Outcome specification** This is the standard that the airline wants to achieve in terms of customer satisfaction with service performance. One hundred per cent satisfaction is the ideal; although not attainable, it should nonetheless be the goal. We need a high and challenging minimum acceptable outcome specification – a bar which we should raise continuously, and which 'stretches' employees to improve standards of performance.

For a description of attributes important in each of the leisure/VFR and business segments, see Holloway (1998b).

Review the design This step will involve some combination of inhouse review, the use of customer focus groups, prototyping, and piloting or other forms of testing. It will end with detailed implementation planning (including any required staff training and both internal and external communications).

Launch, feedback, and amendment   What happens at this stage will depend upon whether we are talking about a major product upgrade or re-launch, or just minor additions or amendments to an existing product. When a strong 'learning by doing' ethos exists in an airline, and particularly when operating in rapidly changing competitive environments, the first four steps are sometimes time-compressed. Hamel and Prahalad (1994) coined the term 'expeditionary marketing' to describe the process of testing what customers value through an ongoing series of fast-paced experiments in service design and delivery.

The end result   When completed, service design should link attributes into a benefits-oriented package with explicit service specifications or standards.

Conclusion   Service design is about more than developing and specifying attributes consistent with the service concept; it is also about making considered cost/benefit trade-offs within a context provided by the customer value and market positioning embodied in that service concept. It involves asking what benefits our customers expect, what attributes delivered at what level can be offered to provide those benefits within their zones of tolerance, what those attributes will cost to produce, and how delivery costs can be kept below revenues likely to be earned from the segment concerned whilst at the same time maintaining or improving levels of customer satisfaction. Ethereal stuff this might well be, but it is the essence of how any airline *manages to make money*.

The fact that the airline business is a network industry complicates matters in two ways.

- The benefit requirements of ostensibly similar segments in different geographical markets can vary quite widely. For example, the business travel segment in different regions of the world does not inevitably expect the same benefits.
- The identities of competitors frequently differ in different markets, with the result that a competence in the delivery of certain service attributes sufficient to generate a competitive advantage in one market might not provide a similar advantage in other markets.

In general, the easier and cheaper it is to change a service attribute, the more readily imitable that attribute is likely to be and the shorter the span of time over which it can provide a meaningful 'point of difference'. Within any group of airlines competing for business in the same markets or segments, functional/performance value tends broadly to equalise over time because so many 'hard' airline service attributes are readily imitable. The style of service delivery and the emotional/symbolic benefits associated with a particular brand are more opaquely rooted, and therefore less imitable (Feldwick, 1991). Once again, this points to the importance of 'soft' attributes such as image, corporate culture, and service style. Put another way, what we are saying is that points of difference based on the contribution of functional attributes to customer value are often more difficult to sustain than those based on the more opaquely rooted, tacit, causally ambiguous, and less readily imitable contribution of emotional (i.e., psycho-social) attributes.

Expanding on the last point, it is not just the design of service attributes that determines whether or not they provide the benefits target customers want – it is also the manner in which service is delivered. It is the 'what' and 'how' together that transform a service concept into a detailed service package and, ultimately, a service outcome – ideally, satisfied and loyal customers. This can have quite far-reaching implications if taken to its logical conclusion. Whereas 'hard', functional service attributes can be specified and subjected to direct performance monitoring, emotional attributes are less easily specified and measured. This inevitability has repercussions on internal organizational relationships and structures insofar as the notion of supervisory control sits less comfortably in a genuine service culture than the idea that front-line personnel should be supported, coached, encouraged, and – perhaps within defined limits – empowered (Grönroos, 2000). We will look at this issue again in chapter 8.

v. Price

> They're only putting in a nickel, but they want a dollar song.
> Anon.

Having spent some time looking in depth at the service side of airline service-price offers, we turn next to price. By 'price' I mean 'monetary costs to customers'. It is not uncommon in the literature for nonmonetary costs, measured in terms of time or inconvenience for example, to be embodied in the concept of price. The view taken here is that high nonmonetary costs are better treated as low-quality service attributes; thus, a multi-stop or connecting service 'costs' more time than a nonstop service and so compares unfavourably in terms of the routing attribute.

The functions of price

Price has broadly the following functions.

1. To *generate revenues* in excess of costs, and in this way earn a profit. Airlines may have one of several overall pricing objectives in this context.
    *   Maximisation of profit, profitability, or shareholder value.
    *   Maximisation of revenue – ideally subject to a baseline profit, profitability or shareholder value target.
    *   Maximisation of market share – again, ideally subject to baseline targets.

    Peppard and Rowland (1995: 54) make the following important point.

    > Price should not be confused with cost. A company which has a lower cost base than its competitors can, all else being equal (which, of course, it rarely is), decide whether to lower its price and thus hope to gain market share, or operate at a higher margin. Thus, cost is a factor in considering a company's competitive advantage, but price is a mechanism by which it can compete and manage demand.

2. To *generate cash-flow* (both for general corporate purposes, and also in specific foreign currencies required to meet current obligations and service outstanding unhedged debt or lease rentals denominated in those currencies).
3. To *convey information* about the strategic positioning of the service and the brand. Price is one of the most important threads binding the service concept, marketing communications, and distribution strategy into a single, coherent, clearly positioned offer to the marketplace.
4. To contribute to *tactical objectives*, amongst the most important of which might be:
    *   *capacity management*, with a view to optimising asset utilisation;
    *   *competitive deterrence*, discouraging potential competitors from entering a market;
    *   *competitive response*, in reaction to the arrival of a new entrant or aggressive pricing by an incumbent;
    *   *competitive stability*, avoiding potentially damaging fare wars between competitors already present.

Tactical pricing can be influenced by revenue managers, sales executives negotiating rates with key accounts, and personnel responsible for promotional campaigns. Sometimes they act in unison, but often they do not.

Our interest here is in the strategic function of price. From a strategic perspective, pricing is not a separate decision but an outcome of the positioning choice we discussed in chapter 2.

Strategic pricing

We have seen that every 'service-price offer' should be keyed off an underlying notion of customer value. A value-based approach to pricing is oriented towards the buyer's perception of what she is getting for her money rather than towards the seller's costs. This perception is to a large extent moulded by the manner in which service design and the other marketing mix variables are managed to build value in the customer's mind. Having said this, we once again need a reality-check. Many air transport markets are fundamentally oligopolistic, and price leadership therefore remains a widespread influence on pricing even under liberalised regulatory regimes (Holloway, 1997; Zeithaml and Bitner, 2000); competition-oriented pricing is still more common than value-based pricing, and both price-signalling and price-matching remain rife.

And even when used strategically, pricing may have little to do with customer value. By offering more competitive joint fares to an alliance partner than to unaligned carriers, an airline might be able to deprive the latter of sufficient traffic feed to justify remaining on a particular route. For example, were Lufthansa to offer more competitive fares to passengers connecting over Frankfurt onto a United service to Miami than it was prepared to offer those preferring to connect onto American, it could make life difficult for an American Frankfurt-Miami service notwithstanding that carrier's strong Miami hub.

From a strategic perspective, the neoclassical microeconomic notion of supply and demand being matched to arrive at a single market-clearing price is no longer watertight. What we face instead in many air transport markets today is the following.

- A series of 'price platforms', each consistent with a particular service concept and supported by a relevantly designed marketing mix. We might call this 'strategic pricing'.

- Discounting off each price platform at any particular time, reflecting the exigencies of either or both market-specific competitive pressures and departure-specific revenue management. We can call this 'tactical pricing'.

When pricing any class of travel, we might want to think strategically about four possible price platforms.

1. **Premium pricing** This position could be associated with a carrier that believes itself to have a strong, high-quality brand image and a strong share in markets or segments that are broadly price inelastic. Because of the industry's penchant for price-matching, relatively few airlines can get away with positioning themselves as offering a service worth a significant premium above the full fare (i.e., the full 'IATA fare', where applicable). British Airways is one which has consistently tried to do this, most notably in its first and business class cabins.
2. **Parity pricing** In this case, the carrier is unable to offer a differentiated service which justifies a price premium. It might nonetheless still offer 'points of difference' that motivate customers to buy its service rather than the services of competitors, even though prices are at parity; if it does not offer any meaningful and attractive points of difference, it is putting forward no compelling reason to buy its services and is potentially in a weak long-term position even when pricing at parity with competitors. The situation might, of course, vary across an airline's network: a carrier strong in particular markets could be able to sustain a premium price in some of those markets, but only parity pricing in markets where its brand is less established.
3. **Discount pricing** Carriers making weak service offers, or having either or both a poor brand image or low market share, might need to adopt a discount price position. Inevitably, the facts of airline life mean that in certain markets at certain times most carriers will engage in some form of discounting to boost load factors and protect or build market share. The fact that the marginal cost of putting an extra passenger into an empty seat on an aircraft that is about to depart is practically zero also makes Internet auctioning of 'distressed' inventory a natural choice for airlines (albeit a choice that might in time erode established tariff structures if pursued without discipline). But this is different from adopting a long-term strategic position as a price discounter.
4. **Cost leadership** Airlines that make low fares a central element of their service-price offer – low-cost/low-fare carriers in particular – are positioning themselves not as discounters responding to weaknesses in their

service package, but as cost leaders trading heavily on the 'price' side of the service-price offer.

The most sophisticated approach to the formulation of a pricing strategy is to examine the range of potential service-price offers that could be made to available markets, then deliver those which fit the service concept and can be sustained given the airline's cost structure. The issue is then not whether a particular pricing strategy is good or bad in any absolute sense, but whether it is rational in terms of that carrier's chosen strategic position and source(s) of competitive advantage.

It is, of course, a clever trick to assess customers' needs correctly, design a service package which satisfies those needs and which the airline concerned is able to deliver effectively at a competitive cost, and then pitch the price in a way that reflects the value placed by the customer on either individually priced attributes (e.g., inflight communications and pay-per-view entertainment) or on the package as a whole. Not only does all this sound unnervingly subjective, but in dynamic liberalised markets it can be very difficult to keep strategic pricing from being subsumed by competitive necessity; the increasing sophistication of revenue management systems make some degree of convergence inevitable, as does the opportunity provided by the Internet for suitably competent carriers to make real-time adjustments to prices and promotions in response to customers' observed reactions. Nonetheless, pricing should never become entirely tactical in its orientation. An airline's strategic approach to pricing should convey information about its overall position in targeted markets, as well as providing a framework within which to act tactically.

vi. The service-price offer

> Better quality + lower price = value
> + spiritual attitude of our employees = unbeatable.
> Herb Kelleher

When demand evaporated from low-cost carriers in the US domestic market during the summer of 1996 after a fatal accident involving one of their number, this was because the core service they were perceived to be offering in respect of safety was being reassessed by customers. Despite the low prices they continued to offer, the service-price positioning chosen by these carriers had (with the exception of long-established and highly regarded Southwest) been unbalanced by changing consumer perceptions of that key attribute. Not even the most price-sensitive end of the US domestic market, it seems, is driven entirely by price; customer-perceived value is driven by both sides of the service-price offer, rather than by price alone. Customers may well buy into tight seat pitches and an absence of 'frills', but this does not mean that those service attributes that are in fact offered will necessarily be acceptable irrespective of quality; safety is perhaps the attribute which most strongly demonstrates this fact.

It is missing the point to assume that, say, Southwest sells on price alone. Southwest sells on value for money – on the right service-price offer. It has targeted customers who prefer not to pay as much as other carriers want them to pay, and it gives them good value for what they do pay. Many of the 'hard' service attributes offered by 'full-service' airlines, such as lounges, meals, seat assignment, and other amenities, are not a feature of Southwest's value proposition; but value is embodied in emotional benefits derived from using the brand (e.g., the corporate ethos of 'fun') and from a culture supporting consistent standards of personal service, as well as in high frequencies and low prices. Were a new competitor to undercut Southwest's fares but in the process offer low frequencies, patchy schedule reliability, and surly service, it is doubtful that more than a very small percentage of demand would be attracted: the reason is that customers are looking not just at price, but at the overall service-price offer. Midwest Express – a very different airline with a very different service concept – also sells on value for money. Different though their value propositions are, these highly successful carriers share one thing in common: clearly defined service concepts that have been effectively translated into service packages designed around targeted customers and supported by appropriate cost structures.

Whatever attributes are offered, the quality of what is delivered should be pitched to the highest feasible standard. There appears in some markets to be a trend towards polarisation of demand between low-price and full-service offers. (Indeed, early in 2001 the Chief Executive of Ryanair was quoted (*Financial Times*, February 7) as projecting a pull-back of their intra-European services by full-service carriers, leaving his own airline some ten years hence carrying upwards of 30 million people on a fleet of over 100 aircraft.) Low levels of service in terms of the number of attributes on offer might be necessary to help keep prices low, but this need not equate to low-quality service delivery; in particular, brand values, culture, and the service style they reinforce can qualify as augmented service just as readily as sleeper seats and chateau-bottled wine – and the 'soft stuff' is much less easily imitated.

Finally, consider figure 4.2. It is not, as far as I know, based on any empirical research. However, there is intuitive appeal in the belief that when it comes to satisfying customers the 'core' and 'expected' levels of service are more or less taken for granted; they are what Herzberg et al (1959) called 'hygiene factors' – their presence is often barely noticed, but their absence can be a source of sometimes intense dissatisfaction. It is in the area of augmented service – based on both 'soft' and 'hard' attributes and potentially offered by any type of carrier subject only to the context of its service concept – that the real battle to satisfy customers takes place.

vii. Bridging the perceptions gap

The service-price offer we make to targeted segments is not simply a bundle of service attributes with a price attached. It is part of a wider *brand identity* which, whether wittingly or not, is projected to the market. Ideally, brand identity should be projected 'wittingly' – that is, it should be consciously managed. Punctuality, a conversation between a flight attendant and a customer, the quality of an inflight meal, the comfort of a seat, and the cleanliness of an aircraft cabin are all service attributes which have a bearing on brand identity.

Clearly, a consistently presented brand identity that fits with the service concept is not something that happens by chance. The projection of a consistent brand identity requires careful integration and orchestration of everything the airline does, and specifically the following.

- **The service concept and the service-price offer** What the airline 'does' and the market position chosen for it are powerful forces shaping brand identity.
- **Communications** What we say about ourselves and our services, whether directly through the media (e.g., advertising and PR), through promotions, or through the condition of facilities and equipment, or indirectly through the way we manage internal relationships and our business as a whole, has a profound impact on the identity we project.
- **Service delivery** How we do what we set out to do for customers, both in terms of style and effectiveness, also influences brand identity.

Brand identity is something that we manage and project. This projection is filtered through customers' perceptions. What comes out the other side is a *brand image* – which we hope will be close to the identity we are trying to project, but which might not be. Brand image in turn has a bearing on whether the functional and, particularly, emotional attributes we have designed into our service package are capable of providing the benefits that targeted customers expect. (Some writers characterise 'image' as a relatively short-term and therefore unstable perception based on consumers'

Figure 4.2 Perceived delivery standards and customer satisfaction

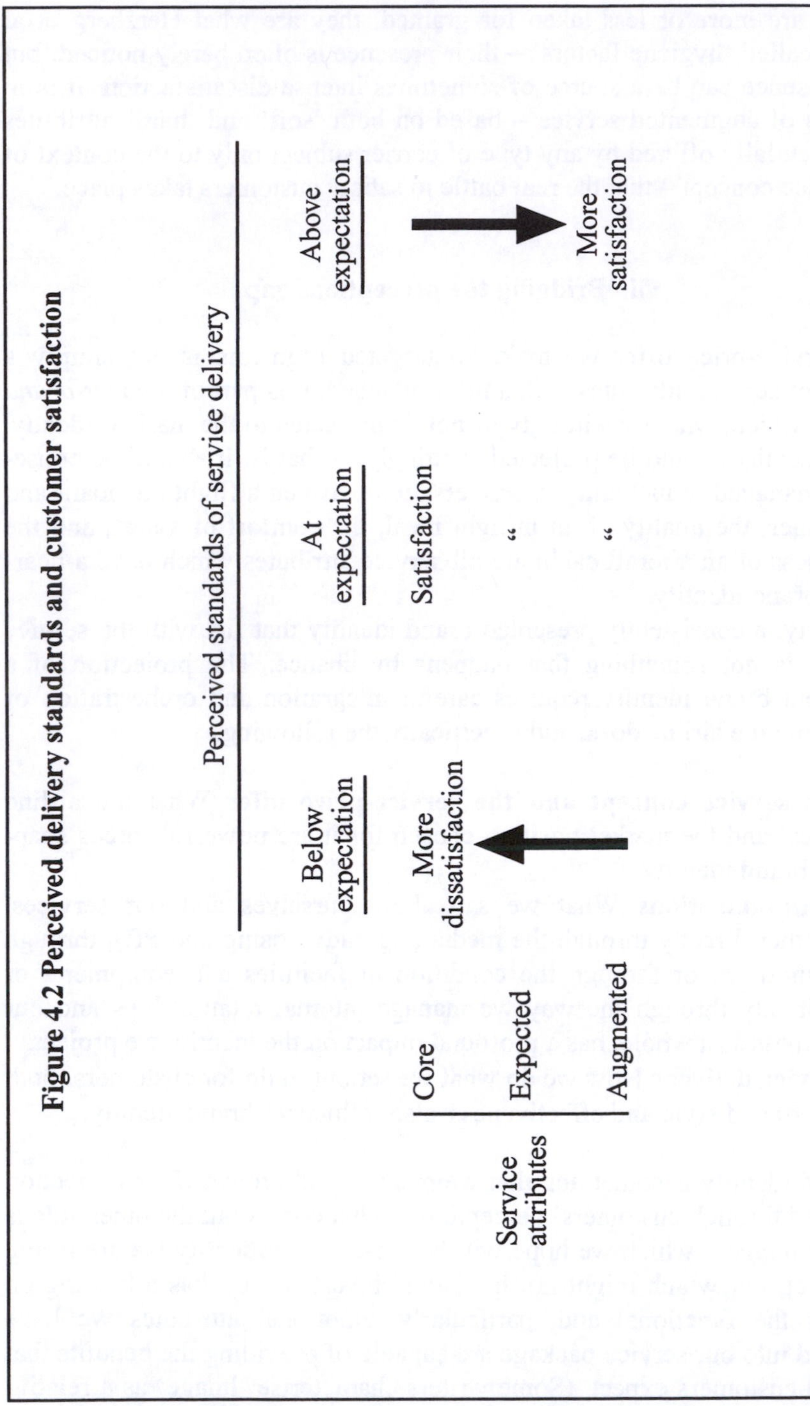

Perceived standards of service delivery

Below expectation	At expectation	Above expectation
More dissatisfaction	Satisfaction	More satisfaction

Service attributes

Core — Expected — Augmented

most recent experiences of an organization, and distinguish it from 'reput-ation' which is seen as a longer-term and therefore more stable amalgam of perceptions arising over time. Whereas everybody who has anything to do with an airline can have a separate image of it based on their own indiv-idual perceptions, 'reputation' is to a greater extent 'socially constructed' by people 'negotiating' their own individual images into a more generally accepted consensus. The point made in this paragraph is the same whether we talk about image or reputation.)

We can therefore draw the following conclusions about service attrib-utes.

1. They form an important part, but only a part, of the image any cust-omer holds of the airline concerned and of its general reputation.
2. What matters is how effectively customers, not marketers, perceive them to deliver benefits critical to success in the targeted segment. ('Success' in this context might be equated to influencing purchase decisions and brand loyalty.)
3. Although competition occurs across multiple dimensions, one attribute can be dominant as far as the purchase behaviour of certain segments is concerned. This might be price in the price-elastic leisure segment of a market, for example, or schedule in a short-haul business segment. More problematic is the fact that wherever one attribute is not clearly dominant, the trade-offs customers make between the presence, absence, and relative qualities of attributes are not always readily apparent; expensive market research might be required to arrive at a determination.
4. What also matters is how customers perceive the attributes being offer-ed relative to what competitors are offering – that is, how customers perceive 'points of difference' and 'points of similarity' and establish relative market positions in their minds.
5. Over time, attributes contributing to an 'augmented' level of service tend to slip down into the 'expected level' – particularly functional attributes. Airlines serving premium segments therefore have to be con-sistent innovators or, at the very least, 'fast followers' in respect of functional attributes.

There will be more to say about brand identity and image in chapter 6.

viii. Summary

Figure 4.3 links the discussion in this chapter through to what follows when we look at service communication and delivery in chapters 6 and 7. Before we turn to these two topics, the next chapter will develop the discussion in the present chapter, first by looking at the menu of possible service attributes from which an airline can draw in order to deliver the customer benefits required by a particular service concept and, second, by considering service encounters – the quintessential interface between service design and service delivery.

Figure 4.3 The service-value loop

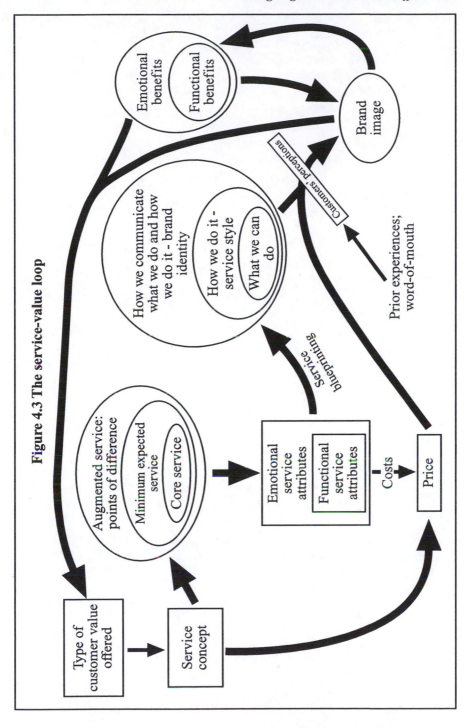

5 Service Attributes

640k ought to be enough for anyone.
Bill Gates, 1981

There is no denying the importance of price, particularly amongst coach/
economy class passengers and in certain geographical regions. Branding,
frequent flyer programmes, and – notably on long-haul routes – improved
amenities are nonetheless a constant feature of the battle between airlines
for customer loyalty, and there is also an argument that a service industry
which captures and retains clients in contact-intensive delivery systems for
anything ranging from two hours to 24 hours is never going to be entirely
commoditised. There will always be opportunities to distinguish not only
what is done, but how it is done. Air transport has certainly been 'demo-
cratised' since the 1970s. But no matter how commonplace flying becomes,
it will remain a unique enterprise in terms of its emotional impact on customers. As long as this is so, characterisation of an undeniably price-elastic
business as one which has become 'commoditised' could lead to missed
marketing opportunities.

In the first section of the chapter we will briefly consider the 'menu' of
service attributes available to airlines on the scheduled passenger side of
the industry. The second section will look at service process blueprinting,
and the third at service encounters – a critical attribute of any service offer,
but one that is difficult to manage. The final section will highlight the significance of servicescapes – the environments within which service delivery
takes place. Service attributes – including processes, encounters, and servicescapes – all contribute to communication of an airline's identity. Communication is the subject of the next chapter.

151

i. Passenger airline service attributes

The word 'attribute' can be taken to encompass any feature of a service that is able to deliver benefits to customers. We have already established that service delivery processes, service encounters between staff and customers, and the servicescapes within which encounters take place are all attributes of an airline's service package. Each will be covered in separate sections of the present chapter; the first section will contextualise the discussion by outlining a broad menu from which attributes of a scheduled passenger service design can be drawn.

The attributes menu

A comprehensive review of airline service attributes is available in Holloway, (1998b); the following summary draws from that source.

1. **Safety and security** These are core service attributes. Much of the battle to establish points of difference in customers' minds takes place elsewhere, although some carriers do implicitly embrace safety and security within consciously created images of 'reliability'.
2. **Network and schedule** Network and schedule design choices (including code-sharing) will reflect the need to balance airline economics with the service requirements that arise from the traffic mix in targeted markets and segments, and from the airline's choice of position within these markets and segments (Holloway, 1997). A network embodies both geographical and product scope decisions. Its design accesses targeted markets and at the same time makes a service offer (e.g., point-to-point or connecting, nonstop or multi-stop, etc.).
3. **Flight completion rate and punctuality** A high completion rate and good time-keeping are important service attributes in all markets, but none more so than those with a significant business travel segment.
4. **Ticket conditionality** The more conditions that are imposed as part of a particular tariff (usually to optimise capacity utilisation and maximise revenue), the more negative this service attribute becomes in the sense that it is moving away from the 'unrestricted' ideal.
5. **Brand identity** This provides information which, when filtered through customers' perceptions to become *brand image*, can have a positive, neutral or negative effect on buying behaviour. A positive brand image is an emotional (i.e., psycho-social) service attribute that can both attract new customers and impose a switching cost on existing customers. Through their effect on individual attitudes and behaviours,

both national and organizational cultures can be powerfully influential in shaping identity and image (Cray and Mallory, 1998).

6. **Distribution** Most marketing texts see distribution as something quite different from service design, but this is because they tend to focus only on the first of three purposes underlying distribution. These three purposes are: selling – that is, acting as a channel to market; adding value for the customer – in the form of convenience, information, or other value-adding attributes; and building a relationship with the customer – something that is difficult to achieve when a channel intermediary is involved. If we focus on the second and third of these purposes, the argument that distribution is a service attribute in its own right becomes clearer.

Distribution is a service attribute insofar as it affects the ease with which customers can do business with the airline concerned – the ease with which they can get the information they need and make or change reservations – and it forms part of whatever relationship might develop between the customer and the brand. The type of value that distribution should add for customers will be dependent upon what customers in the targeted segment(s) are looking for; the important point is that because distribution adds value it is part of the service package, and as part of the service package it should be both managed and costed within the context of the particular service concept. As with most other attributes, distribution design strategy needs to balance an airline's desire to cut costs (e.g., by reducing agency and GDS involvement) against customer benefits (derived, for example, from maximum access to a full range of channels or, more specifically, from the availability of a travel agent's information and advice to infrequent vacation travellers or travel management services to corporate clients); sometimes, as in the case of ticketless travel, the two can be congruent. E-ticketing, for instance, benefits the customer by making the airline more straightforward to deal with, may benefit the airline if the booking is made direct and avoids agency commission and GDS fees, and will certainly benefit the airline by reducing the revenue accounting costs associated with reconciling coupons.

An example of segment-targeted distribution is a portal for small and medium-size businesses introduced by British Airways early in 2001. In addition to giving customers access to BA's inventory, Internet offers, and any specially negotiated fares, 'Your Travel Manager' permits access to other travel service providers (including other airlines) and enables travel managers to enforce corporate policy with regard to choice of carrier and fare categories.

7. **Seat availability** There are four linked attributes affecting seat availability: accessibility (i.e., the probability of a seat being available on the preferred flight at the required tariff when booking is attempted); overbooking (i.e., the creation of 'artificial accessibility' by overselling, and the 'negative attribute' of involuntary denied boarding); ticket conditionality (referred to above and used in this context to combat revenue dilution); and wait-list and standby priority (accorded to high-value frequent flyers by some airlines). Although these do need to be set within the strategic context of an airline's service concept(s), in practice they are closely controlled on a day-to-day basis by revenue management systems.

8. **FFP benefits** It is clear that awards and other benefits can profoundly influence purchase behaviour and are seen as a significant benefit by many passengers. On the other hand, it is now equally clear that both multiple programme memberships and the importance of other service attributes (e.g., schedule convenience and punctuality in business segments) can in particular situations be countervailing influences.

9. **Ground experiences** Airlines are judged by a wide range of ground service attributes which, depending on the carrier, the service concept, and the class of travel, might include any of the following: convenience of the airport and attractiveness of its facilities; limousine service; valet parking; curb-side check-in; airport facilities (most of which are not in fact under direct airline control unless the terminal concerned is owned or leased); check-in style (e.g., positive-name, eye contact, etc.), technology (e.g., automated via booths, the Internet or wireless links), and location (e.g., concourse, gate, or off-airport); nature and size of baggage allowances; availability of 'fast-track' channels through security and immigration; smart-card facilitation; lounges (perhaps for use by certain categories of arriving, as well as departing, passengers); availability of complimentary hotel rooms during long layovers; response to delays; embarkation and disembarkation procedures; hotel day-room facilities on arrival off long-haul night flights; speed and accuracy of baggage-handing (again, often outside direct airline control); and the manner in which any problems or complaints are dealt with.

10. **Inflight experiences** These flow from the aircraft itself, the chosen cabin design, and the design of amenities and processes. A significant challenge facing any carrier with a multi-type fleet is maintaining a perception of service consistency across different gauges of aircraft and, with respect to any one type used on a variety of segments, across widely different lengths of haul; this can be a particular problem where different types, perhaps rated differently in the perceptions of frequent travellers, are mixed on a given route – as, for example, when regional

jets are used to supplement the mainline fleet during off-peak periods on a predominantly mainline route. (See Bauer (1998) for a description of work Boeing has done to investigate how variations in seat pitch can be used to equalise variations in passengers' perceptions of cabin comfort aboard different aircraft types.)

- *Aircraft-related attributes* Age of the aircraft might be an issue for some passengers, and a number of airlines use a modern fleet as a point of difference in their marketing communications; the external appearance of any aircraft is certainly a brand element irrespective of its age – an element contributing significantly to brand image. Relative cabin cross-sections have spurred lively debate in the ongoing Airbus versus Boeing battle; this can be a meaningful attribute to some frequent travellers, but probably has not entered too many customers' consciousness. Similarly, the wing loadings of different types carrying approximately the same payloads can be distinct enough to affect perceived ride quality, but it is doubtful that most passengers will be sufficiently well-informed to link any relative comfort or discomfort level to a particular airline's choice of aircraft.

- *Cabin-related attributes* A fundamental choice is clearly how many classes of onboard service are to be offered – a choice driven by the competitive scope decision discussed in chapter 3. In the design of any cabin, there is a balance to be struck between on the one hand the imperatives of airline economics – which require maximum utilisation of cabin floor-space – and the requirements of the airline's concept(s) for serving passengers travelling in that cabin. This balance is reflected most significantly in seating density – itself a reflection of seat pitch and width and the ratio of passengers to galleys, lavatories, and closets. Other cabin-related attributes include seat design and ergonomics, the decor, appearance, and cleanliness of the cabin interior (e.g., seats, carpets, side-wall laminates, bulkheads, bins, galleys, toilets, closets), the accessibility and design of overhead bins, the availability of quiet zones on long-haul flights, and whether or not smoking is permitted. Service attributes which are not in themselves cabin-related but can influence the in-cabin experience include the ability to pre-select preferred seats at the time of booking, and whether the airline's check-in system and procedures are set-up to maximise free adjacent seating within the constraints of each flight's load factor. Cabin air quality is also a service attribute over which airlines have control and in which passenger interest is growing in some markets. (See Favart-

Andrieux (1998) for an excellent overview of aircraft interior design issues and possibilities.)

- *Amenities and processes* Depending upon the class of service and each airline's particular service concept(s), and against the background of the imperative of courteous and efficient service at all times, attributes in this category include: cabin crew ratios; cabin crew language skills (and cultural awareness); passenger name recognition; visibility and responsiveness of flight attendants throughout the flight – not just during meal or beverage service; the extent to which cabin service procedures are tailored to the convenience of passengers rather than the convenience of the crew (e.g., meal times, and cabin lighting levels during night-flights); inflight entertainment and communication options; availability of lap-top power and networking facilities; food and beverage service (scope, quality, presentation, choice, and degree of sensitivity to route-specific customer requirements); availability (and language) of magazines and newspapers; amenity kits; hot and cold towels; pillows, blankets, and duvets; give-aways and other 'physical evidence'; children's amenities; special programmes on long-haul flights (e.g., Virgin Atlantic's massage option, and British Airways' 'Well Being' programme); duty-free goods; the onboard availability of specialised medical equipment and ground-to-air medical advisory services (e.g., MedLink); clarity and timeliness of information in the event of push-back, taxi, and inflight delays; and help with rescheduling missed connections.

By virtue of its nature, provision of a service has both functional and emotional dimensions, as we saw in chapter 4. It is very easy to focus on the functional attributes when designing a service package and ignore the mood, atmosphere, and tone of the service experience. Emotional – particularly interpersonal – aspects of the experience can often be a primary source of distinctiveness leading, if positive, to customer satisfaction and loyalty. This is why an airline's corporate culture and the attitudes and values of its employees – notably, but not only, those who have contact with customers in the 'front office' – are so important. It is these that underlie the tenor of the human interactions which help shape the emotional attributes of a particular service-price offer. We will return to this topic when service encounters are considered shortly. But emotional appeal is not solely a question of interpersonal contacts; both design concepts used in servicescapes such as cabins and lounges, and a carrier's overall image and reputation are part of its emotional appeal – or lack of it.

Conclusion on service attributes

The benefits provided by various attributes will be worth more to some customers than others. Treating safety as a given 'core' service, attributes such as network scope, schedule convenience, and punctuality are clearly important to business travellers, and the longer a journey is the more likely inflight service attributes are to factor into purchase decisions (although FFP membership will certainly distort the decision process). An airline's national origins are still important in some markets, but practically irrelevant in others. Market research should help in identifying the critical purchase criteria in each segment – criteria which we can assume fall into the 'core' and 'expected' service level categories. Research can also usefully track two other variables of interest to service design teams.

1. The value customers place on 'points of difference' in any augmented service offer. Do they influence purchase decisions and customer satisfaction levels sufficiently to be worth the cost of providing them?
2. The willingness of customers to 'trade-away' non-critical attributes in return for a lower price. If a mainline carrier faces a competitive threat in this area, one alternative to the tactical option of discounting price (and perhaps risking a dilution of brand image) might be to take a more strategic approach by establishing its own low-cost operation; this may cannibalise the existing customer base, but if properly planned the impact should be small and these customers might anyway have been lost to competitors.

In conclusion, the airline industry is not the commodity business it is so widely purported to be. It is a business wherein the economics of airborne real estate have been allowed for too long to dominate the imagination that can allow different carriers to use design in order to create 'points of difference'. We live in an increasingly design-obsessed era. This fact has begun to impose itself on the airline industry over the last few years; at the moment, relatively few airlines have been affected, and even then there has been an understandable tendency to concentrate first on bringing long-haul premium cabins into the 21st century. Over time, best practice will – within the context of the service concepts involved – find its way into service attributes further back down 'the tube'.

Alliance contributions

As a whole, alliances are considered by prevailing industry wisdom to be net contributors to the delivery of customer benefits insofar as they offer expanded network scope, higher frequencies, integrated schedules, proximate gates for hub transfers, reciprocal lounge access and general recognition for FFP members, as well as improved opportunities to earn and redeem FFP awards.

However, quite aside from their sometimes negative impact on competition in individual markets, they are not without disadvantages from a customer service standpoint. Perhaps the most knotty and widely cited difficulty is harmonising ground and onboard products and ensuring service consistency across a multi-company, multi-cultural alliance. Service consistency is a difficult enough target for individual airlines to strive towards. Stripping away the pro-alliance banter of pro forma press releases, we are a long way from seeing service consistency achieved across any of the global partnerships. The argument is quite straightforward: people buy into a service experience; they have certain service expectations; confidence that those expectations will be met is embedded in the image they hold of the brand they are purchasing from; take away consistent standards of service delivery and brand image is weakened; passengers who buy into one brand's service proposition but find themselves code-shared onto another carrier may or may not object, but particularly if frequent travellers they will almost certainly have a problem should the service they receive fall below the expectations they hold for 'their' brand. It is not yet clear that the notion of partners that are different but equally excellent in their own separate ways stands serious scrutiny. To airline managements, size clearly matters; to customers, so does consistency.

ii. Service processes

We have already established that service processes are themselves attributes of any service package and need to be carefully designed in the context of the relevant service concept. One widely used process design tool is service blueprinting; we will look at this first. But in addition to the attributes embodied in a service process, there is also the question of how long customers have to wait for service before or during a process; we will therefore consider the key variables of 'queuing' and 'waiting for service'.

Service blueprinting

Because service is a process rather than a tangible 'thing', tools developed to aid process design in other contexts need to be employed by service design teams. For example, process flow-charting has long been used by industrial engineers to analyse manufacturing, and more recently service, processes in pursuit of opportunities to improve efficiency. Service blueprinting is a similar, but more customer-oriented, technique first introduced by Shostack (1984). It involves mapping each step in every process used to deliver services to customers; 'mapping' means specifying the actions to be undertaken, by whom and in what sequence. It describes tasks, activities, and processes required to deliver each service as well as the environments within which they will be delivered (e.g., lounges and cabins) and what if any tangible attributes might be delivered (e.g., meals); it describes who does what, when, and how – the respective roles of customers and service providers, what they are expected to do and not do, and what options they have wherever options have been designed-in.

Process times and productivity targets might well be specified, but the fundamental point is that mapping takes place from the customer's perspective. The purpose of service blueprinting is to think through the entire customer experience from the customer's point of view.

Preparation of a service blueprint requires the following steps.

1. Identification of customer-facing, 'front-office' processes within the airline's overall service delivery system.
2. Identification of the activities which comprise each process.
3. Illustration of these activities in diagrammatic form.
4. Development of a clear understanding of what each process and every activity contributes to the customer value objectives designed into the airline's service package – the purpose being to ensure that there is no duplication or redundancy of effort.
5. Isolation of potential fail-points, specification of counter-measures to reduce the risk of failure, and development of service recovery procedures to cope with failures that do occur. According to Heskett et al (1997), fail-points can arise, inter alia, where:
   - customers' expectations of service have been inadequately conditioned in advance;
   - the potential exists for customers participating in a particular service delivery activity to become confused;
   - employee judgement has an important impact on customers' perceptions of service;

- available infrastructure, equipment or human resources might be insufficient or inadequate for the task.
6. The setting of process performance standards – usually in terms of time, quality, cost, and/or productivity, and always with a firm eye on how different levels of performance in respect of a particular variable are perceived by customers.

Being an explicit specification of service levels, a service blueprint or map should reflect an airline's service concept – the nature of the customer value being offered and its chosen market position. Low-cost/no-frills carriers will therefore have service blueprints which differ in many important respects from those of full-service network airlines, for example. Think how different the service blueprints are in a McDonald's outlet compared to a Michelin-rated restaurant.

Service blueprinting brings us face-to-face with the practical implications of several of the characteristics we met in chapter 4 which distinguish service from manufacturing industries: intangibility; simultaneity of production and consumption; and the inevitable variability in what is delivered.

After blueprinting and setting-up a process, the final stage should be a *walk-through audit*. The purpose of this is to evaluate relative to the airline's service concept(s) both the processes that have been blueprinted and the aesthetics and functionality of the servicescape. We will consider servicescapes later in the chapter.

Queuing and waiting for service

Capacity management in the context of an airline's operating strategy can be considered on two levels: the macro-level dealing with medium- and long-term fleet and facilities management, and the micro-level dealing with day-to-day issues; it is the latter with which we are primarily concerned here (although the two are evidently very closely linked). Even though capacity might over a span of time be capable of meeting demand, during peak periods there will often be too much demand for the service delivery system to accommodate. This will require customers to queue or in some other way wait prior to or during one or more service delivery processes. Queuing and waiting for service can have a profound impact on customers' perceptions of service quality, and on their mood going into subsequent service encounters.

Queue modelling

The customer value being offered – reflecting an airline's service concept and brand positioning – must be used to guide the inevitable trade-off between on the one hand inconveniencing customers in queues, and on the other hand spending money to raise service levels by boosting process capacity and reducing queues. This is an example of the efficiency/effectiveness trade-off that is a defining issue in operations management.

Queuing theory has been well developed over the last several decades, and there is now no shortage of queue modelling software. The basic parameters at check-in, for example, are as follows.

- Customer arrival patterns – usually irregular.
- Length of service encounter – usually variable.
- Number of services being delivered.
- Queue configuration (i.e., single or multiple lines).

Most comprehensive services management texts, and every good operations management text, should provide detailed examples of queue modelling techniques (see, for example: Fitsimmons and Fitzsimmons, 1998).

The management of waiting

Air transport operations involve the batch processing of customers within a capacity-constrained system; waiting is therefore an inevitable part of service delivery. It can involve a scheduled wait (e.g., between connecting flights), a queue to be processed (e.g., at check-in), or an unscheduled wait (e.g., a delayed departure), and it can occur preflight (e.g., during ticketing, check-in or boarding), inflight (much of which is a scheduled wait for arrival at the destination) or post-flight (e.g., immigration, baggage reclaim, and the solution of any problems that may have arisen during the journey).

The longer any period of waiting is, the greater the likelihood of customer dissatisfaction. Dissatisfaction might lead a customer to:

- leave the service delivery system, most notably at the enquiry/reservations stage;
- avoid repeat purchases;
- relay negative word-of-mouth comments about the airline's service.

There are two aspects to a wait.

1. **Actual waiting time** Techniques used to shorten an actual wait include the following.
   - More nonstop and hub-bypass services.
   - More efficient routings (e.g., trans-Pacific and trans-Asia).
   - Improved schedule integration.
   - Reservations (i.e., telephone waiting): online reservations; special numbers for FFP or club members, or for premium class travellers.
   - Ticketing (at agencies and airports): ticketless travel/e-ticketing.
   - Check-in: automated check-in.
   - Security and immigration: fast-track clearance lanes; smart-card recognition technologies.
   - Enplaning and deplaning: priority to premium class passengers.
   - Baggage reclaim: priority tagging for premium class passengers.
2. **Perceived waiting time** The following are believed to make a wait appear longer than it is.
   - Waiting to begin a process: some airlines have agents working the back of check-in queues to create the impression that customers are 'in the system'.
   - Waiting for a premium service: many airlines provide dedicated check-in and lounge facilities for their first and business class passengers.
   - Anxiety about the service, notably fear of flying: at least one large airline has run courses to help potential customers overcome their fear of flying, but in general having the carrier's staff, facilities, and equipment project a professional image is about all most airlines can do.
   - Unoccupied waiting: more airports today provide shopping and eating opportunities than was true in the past, and in the air both the design of food and beverage cycles and the provision of IFE are used to shorten perceptions of long-haul journey times. Research has shown that the negative causality between waiting and service evaluation can be ameliorated by the use of moderators such as activities (e.g., entertainment) or service information (including, perhaps, progress of the flight or descriptions of the destination) to fill time.
   - Unexplained waits: some airlines do now make an effort to explain the reasons for delays as soon as they become foreseeable. Research has proven that waits accompanied by ignorance are perceived to be longer – and are therefore likely to be more frustrating – than waits of the same duration accompanied by an honest explanation. To the extent that one school of thought on the nature

of service encounters characterises them as a battle for control between provider and consumer, information also helps those consumers who need to do so to feel more in control of the encounter.

- Uncertain duration: explanations of the reason for a delay should whenever possible be accompanied by an estimate of its length – although it is better to overestimate the delay or not to estimate it at all rather than to underestimate and have to revise it later.
- Comfort of the environment: the less comfortable the environment, whether an airport lounge or an aircraft cabin, the longer a perceived wait will be.
- Solo waiting: people waiting in groups generally perceive a wait of given duration to be shorter than a passenger waiting alone.
- Unfamiliar music: one of the reasons that anodyne 'musak' and house theme tunes are frequently encountered is that research has revealed unfamiliar music lengthens perceived waiting time.
- Negative customer attitude: the less goodwill a customer has towards an airline, either as a result of previous service experiences or of what has already happened during the present journey, the longer a wait will be perceived to be.
- Unfair waiting: perceived waiting periods lengthen if passengers see, for example, successful queue-jumping, unused airline facilities (e.g., unstaffed check-in desks), apparently idle employees, or favourable treatment of staff passengers.
- Situational factors: a business traveller in danger of missing a crucial meeting might perceive a given wait to be longer than a leisure traveller, whilst a leisure traveller off on a long vacation might be less concerned about, say, a four-hour delay than somebody going on a week-end break.

In principle, therefore, waiting can be managed in two ways.

1. Through management of operational processes.
2. Through the management of perceptions.

What this means in practice will depend upon the nature of any particular carrier's service concept and the reality of physical constraints within its service delivery system.

Service delivery processes are in fact cascades of service encounters (Zeithaml and Bitner, 2000), each of which provides a fresh opportunity for a customer to evaluate service. It is to consideration of service encounters that we turn next.

iii. Service encounters

A professional is a person who can do their best at a time when they don't
particularly feel like it.
Alastair Cooke

Service encounters are interactions between an airline and its customers.
They are the medium through which many of the attributes designed into a
service are actually delivered; they are also themselves 'process attributes'
insofar as they contribute significantly to the delivery of expected benefits
and therefore to outcomes – that is, to customer satisfaction or dissatisfaction. In this section we will first define what is meant by 'service
encounter', then look at how they can be designed and at the 'micro-
variables' that contribute to the outcome of each encounter.

Service encounters defined

A 'service encounter', as the term is widely used in the literature, is any
interaction between a service organization (its people, facilities, or equipment) and its customers (and, arguably, potential customers) – whether taking place face-to-face, by mail, over the telephone, or electronically. (This
definition is somewhat broader than the one used by Czepiel et al (1985)
who, in first coining the expression, referred primarily to interactions between humans – that is, between service providers and customers.) Each
encounter contributes to the forming of an impression about the organization by the customer. Service encounters delimit the 'front office' and
draw a 'line of visibility' between front- and back-offices. Those which
involve direct interpersonal contact are potentially very high in impact;
they also underline the inseparability/simultaneity of service production
and consumption first mentioned in chapter 4.

1. Potential customers could include:
    - people making reservations enquiries;
    - visitors to an airport or passengers of other airlines whose future
      decisions to become customers of the airline in question might be
      influenced by what they see of that airline's people, facilities, and
      equipment;
    - people exposed to the carrier's marketing communications progr-
      amme.
2. Actual customers have two perspectives on service encounters:
    - those they observe other customers engaged in;

- most importantly, those in which they themselves participate as consumers.

It can be useful to think in terms of the following types of service encounter.

1. **Person-to-person** This interaction has been widely referred to in the literature as the 'moment of truth'. (The expression was coined by Normann (1984), who borrowed it from bull-fighting, and was widely popularised by Jan Carlzon in the context of his turnaround of SAS in the mid-1980s.)
   - *Visible* (e.g., all stages of airport-to-airport transportation). Influences on success include: employees' skills, knowledge, attitudes and behaviours; facilities (i.e., the servicescape); equipment, and IS and other support systems; 'physical evidence' of service (e.g., meals, give-aways); the attitudes and behaviours of other customers; the customer's mood, loyalty to the airline, and expectations (both predictive and normative); and the context (i.e., circumstances and personal factors surrounding the trip).
   - *Invisible* (e.g., information search over the telephone, followed perhaps by a reservation). Influences on success are largely the same, except that servicescape and the behaviours of other customers are usually less of an issue.
2. **Person-to-machine** (e.g., automated check-in, speech recognition software used in telephone reservations systems). Influences on success: easy procedures; good ergonomics; speed; evidence of service performance; access to human back-up if required.
3. **Machine-to-machine** (e.g., reservations over the Internet). Influences on success: compatible hardware and software; ease of access; speed of transactions; record of transactions; verification; security.

Our interest here is in service encounters between employees and customers. Consistently successful service encounters are the building blocks of the customer retention and loyalty we will be discussing in chapter 8. But airlines face several challenges in this regard.

1. Maintaining consistency across multiple human interactions between multiple customers and multiple service providers is difficult at the best of times. This is the 'variability' characteristic of services that was first mentioned in chapter 4.
2. Peak periods in particular are not 'the best of times', and because service encounters cannot be rolled off a production line during slack

periods and inventoried for later distribution (i.e., production and consumption are 'simultaneous') there is a danger that they will be shorter, more 'pressured', and therefore less satisfying to customers when the service delivery system is stretched. To some extent, passengers may be prepared to make allowances – but the danger of dissatisfaction cannot be ignored.

Service delivery involves an 'activity cycle' through which each customer passes; this cycle begins with information search (prior to making a reservation) and ends either with baggage reclaim after arrival (or possibly an airline-supplied limousine service). Post-flight resolution of any problems might also be part of the cycle. Customers will then, often subconsciously, factor their perceptions of service received into the information search stage of the same cycle ahead of their next journey.

Positive encounters early in an activity cycle can in particular set the tone for the entire service experience. In the airline industry this can be difficult to achieve: reservations and passenger handling are often outside the direct control of individual carriers – being instead the responsibility of travel agents, airport authorities, government agencies, or passenger handling agents. At outstations it is in fact conceivable that the first encounter between a consumer and the airline whose ticket she has bought will be at the aircraft door – unless, of course, it is a code-shared flight in which case there might never be any contact at all!

Service encounters: the people involved

> You can be totally rational with a machine. But if you work with people,
> logic often has to take a backseat to understanding.
> Akio Morita

The quality of contact between an airline's people and its customers is central to success in competitive markets.

The consumer

Consumers as actors in the delivery of air transport services Consumer involvement in service delivery is an important consideration in service design for a number of reasons.

1. Customer involvement is the source of the experiences that surround delivery of both the core transportation benefit and many of the emotional/symbolic benefits being purchased.
2. It provides an opportunity for an airline to add 'tangible' attributes to an essentially intangible offer.
3. Consumers of services are likely to experience directly any change in the configuration of one or more of the processes comprising a service delivery system, particularly if they are physically present at the point(s) in the process being changed.
4. Consumers are affected by the presence of other consumers, some of whom might be from different market segments and therefore have different benefit requirements.

Consumers' involvement in service delivery can be both physical and emotional.

1. Physical involvement is often active, but much of the time it is passive:
    *   in the case of active physical involvement, the consumer is in reality a 'co-producer'. This happens, for example, at check-in (especially if it is automated), on boarding, and during disembarkation and subsequent baggage reclaim. The airline's objective in designing active customer involvement into a service package should be to improve resource productivity and reduce outcome uncertainty, whilst at the same time at least maintaining – ideally raising – customer satisfaction;
    *   passive physical involvement occurs whilst waiting at various times during service delivery. The flight itself is commonly the longest period of passive involvement, although new interactive cabin technologies are beginning to reduce passivity.
2. Emotional involvement in the service delivery process often stems from the effects on a consumer's self-image of the image of the airline she carries with her into the service delivery system. It is then further shaped by the effect of actual delivery experiences on that image. The same is true in respect of the use of a particular sub-brand such as first or business class.

Consumers looking for confirmation of decisions Consumers are therefore important participants in many service delivery processes. But they are also decision-makers. In respect of a service delivery process in which they are involved, most will consciously or subconsciously search for tangible 'clues' reinforcing the initial view that their decision to purchase the intangible and as yet uncompleted service experience was correct. This is part of a process of post-choice evaluation.

Service delivery processes give airlines opportunities to add tangibility to their service concepts which they therefore need to take. Two of the most important sources of tangibility are service providers, whom we look at next, and the service environment – which we will consider shortly.

The service provider

> All business is show business.
>
> Jan Carlzon

The focus here is on front-line personnel, although the fact is that every-body in an airline should be considered the provider of some sort of service – whether to internal or external customers. Research over the last decade has provided increasingly convincing evidence of a linkage between satisfied employees on the one hand and satisfied customers and higher revenue on the other (Heskett et al, 1994). Attention to employee well-being and a passion for service in an organization both appear to be highly correlated with customer satisfaction, and there is a widespread assumption that causality flows from the former to the latter; whatever the direction of causality, it seems that the ways in which employees and customers separately experience an organization have a direct bearing on each other (Schneider and Bowen, 1993).

Service providers are clearly a major potential source of distinctiveness in a high-contact industry such as the airline business. This is why their selection, training, acculturation, and motivation are so important. They are also a source of possible conflict; we therefore need to look briefly at several possible types of conflict in which they might be involved and which could affect the customer-perceived quality of service delivery.

Intra-organizational conflict There are three possibilities.

1. **Conflict between employee and organization** It is important to ensure that employees:
   - understand and are enabled (through training and the provision of adequate facilities, equipment, and systems) to carry out their resp-onsibilities within the context of the airline's strategies and goals;
   - are, as far as possible, motivated and satisfied;
   - know how much latitude they have in dealing with customer requ-ests for non-standard service, and the extent to which they are em-powered to solve customers' problems without upward referral.

2. **Conflict between employees** This requires attentive diagnosis and management: identify the source of conflict, then mutually explore the problem and how to solve it.

3. **Conflict between employee and role** The services management literature has suggested that a service delivery process can be seen as an enacted drama. The chosen *play* is the airline's service concept – something which defines in general terms what is being offered and to what type of audience. The *audience* is comprised of customers, most of whom will have been targeted by the service concept but some of whom will not. The *actors* are the service providers – front-line staff who have to be auditioned (i.e., selected) and rehearsed (i.e., trained) so that they can play their *roles* and are familiar with their parts in the *script*. There are different *acts*, marked by phases in the activity cycle such as check-in, lounge wait, gate wait, embarkation, flight (itself punctuated into several further acts on a long sector), and so on. The drama is played out against background *scenery* – the servicescape provided by lounges and cabins, both of which 'set the scene' for service delivery. Some parts of the play require *audience participation*, others do not. *Backstage*, processes comprised of activities and individual tasks are going on, in most cases unseen and unheard by the audience but vital nonetheless to the production. Although many airline executives will feel uneasy with the parallels, Disney – a very commercial organization with safety concerns of its own – has found the metaphor extremely helpful in practice.

   Be that as it may, some airline employees are having difficulty with the roles that changing market circumstances are requiring them to play. *Role conflict* can, for example, arise from the following transformations.

   • **Employee to entrepreneur** The empowerment of staff, particularly where it comes without clearly defined parameters, requires people to take quasi-entrepreneurial decisions rather than follow 'by-the-book' procedures – to 'ad lib' rather than follow rigid scripts.

   • **Servant or referee to friend or advocate** Some airlines have quite deliberately loosened the reins in recent years to provide staff with more scope to show their own personalities and relate to customers as individuals.

   Employees' roles will often vary in accordance with an airline's service concept. The role of flight attendants on a low-cost, short-haul carrier, for example, is likely in most cases to be simply to fulfil legal requirements (with their numbers being no more than the statutory minimum) and to provide just a basic level of inflight service. On the other hand, the role of cabin attendants on a full-service carrier will – in principle – be to deliver a high level of inflight service, particularly in business and first class cabins.

The use of concepts such as 'role' and ideas from dramaturgy might seem like an academic flight of fancy, particularly to more technically oriented readers. In fact, it is not (Grove et al, 2000). Consider the difference between a job description and a role. 'Job descriptions define work in terms of specific tasks or activities to be performed and *how* they are to be performed. Following the Taylor/Sloan models [of scientific management], they attempt to break the work down into repeatable, learnable components' (Chapman, 1997: 329). In contrast to detailed job descriptions defined in terms of specific activities or tasks, roles are described in terms of the responsibilities that need to be fulfilled for the role-holder to make the agreed contribution (ibid: 330). Front-line staff certainly have jobs to do, but to focus just on the doing of the job is to have an operational rather than a customer focus; particularly on the front line of a service industry where the doing of a job by a member of staff is in many cases part of the service experienced by customers, each job has to be seen as part of a wider role carrying with it responsibilities for meeting or exceeding customers' overall performance expectations in addition to any technical, task-related performance metrics that need to be met.

For example, knocking a few seconds off each service encounter in a cabin might make staff more task-efficient, but it will not necessarily fulfil their responsibility to deliver customer satisfaction; of course, this is a balance that can only be struck within the context of a particular service concept. The point is that 'job' and 'role' are not the same, and airlines committed to service need to be thinking, hiring, training, motivating, and rewarding in terms of both. Put another way, does a cabin attendant see himself as somebody paid to sit by an emergency exit on take-off and landing and deliver refreshments in between, or as one of a team of people responsible for ensuring customer satisfaction – as well as safety – during a critical part of service delivery? People can be drilled in emergency procedures and cabin service processes, but they cannot have commitment and a passion for satisfying customers trained into them; recruiting the right attitudes and nurturing them in the right culture are the only long-term answers – answers that are easier for a small start-up to fashion than for a major incumbent.

'Boundary' conflicts between customer and employee Service providers play a boundary-spanning role in each service encounter, interfacing between customers and the airline. This role requires them to deliver a

substantial part of the benefits package being offered by an airline to satisfy customers' expectations. Ideally it should also involve them in the receipt and processing of information from consumers that can be fed back to shape future service redesign and delivery system reconfiguration. This type of boundary-spanning can create in service providers a conflict between the demands and expectations of consumers on the one hand, and any restraints imposed either by service design or by configuration of the delivery system on the other. Conflict can arise from customers' attitudes and behaviours (manifested in extreme form as 'air rage'), a poor understanding of customers' expectations on the part of service providers, or from shortcomings in staff attitudes, accessibility, knowledge, or appearance as perceived by customers. If a passenger perceives a flight attendant's role to include lifting carry-on bags into an overhead bin and this does not happen, one possible source of misunderstanding could be **role ambiguity**.

Front-line personnel need to have a clear idea not only about *what* they are supposed to do, but also *how* they should do it; they need a thorough understanding of their roles in the context of the specific service concept within which they are working and how to cope with customers' demands that go beyond what can reasonably be expected. As much as anything, this calls for sound internal communications and a strong commitment to training and retraining.

According to Hoffman and Bateson (1997: 93), this role theory perspective implies two key managerial tasks:

1. to design roles for the service encounter that are acceptable and capable of fulfilling the needs of both customers and service providers; and
2. to communicate these roles to both customers and employees so that both have realistic perceptions of their roles as well as those of their partners in these interactions.

Staff experiencing role conflict or role ambiguity are unlikely to be satisfied, which in turn will lower the likelihood of customers being satisfied. 'Scripts' can help reduce role ambiguity, although scripting human interactions is never going to completely avoid unforeseen encounter outcomes simply because of the 'variability' characteristic inherent in all service delivery.

Boundary conflicts can also arise when staff willing to deliver the expected benefits are unable to do so because of an inadequately configured service delivery system – perhaps one in which efficiency/effectiveness trade-offs inappropriate to the service concept have been made (e.g., too few staff checking-in business class passengers, leading to unacceptable queues).

Several steps can be taken to help eliminate stress arising from boundary conflicts.

- Actively involving front-line staff in the design of services and the configuration of the processes through which they will be expected to deliver the attributes specified. This can be important where the structure and tenor of service encounters have an impact on employee motivation, performance, and satisfaction; in cases such as these, it may be particularly advisable to design service encounters with employees' as well as customers' requirements in mind.
- Giving front-line staff the information, facilities, equipment, and training they need in order to do their jobs efficiently and effectively.
- 'Empowering' front-line staff, within clear limits, to deal flexibly with service failures or to modify the service in response to unique customer needs. Empowerment is a tricky concept, particularly in an organization such as an airline where strict adherence to procedures is often necessary to keep what is a highly complex system functioning smoothly and, in many cases, also to ensure safety.
- Better managing customers' expectations – perhaps by making more realistic promises in advertising, for example.

In the final analysis, appropriate selection, training, and motivation of staff are likely to be critical factors in the reduction of boundary conflict. A few carriers now promote the view that if employees are not satisfied it is highly unlikely that they will be motivated to ensure that customers are satisfied. This is reflected in the sequencing of the FedEx philosophy: 'people, service, profits'; Virgin Atlantic has been explicit in adopting a similar philosophy. Enlightened human resource policies are increasingly seen by some airline managements as an important source of workforce satisfaction, and therefore an integral part of any corporate culture oriented strongly towards high levels of customer satisfaction.

Of course, few airline managements would admit to being anything other than customer service oriented. As competition intensifies, however, so do pressures to back lip-service with action. Airlines' different histories, cultures, service concepts, and resource availabilities will shape just what is appropriate and possible. Nonetheless, it is now clear that how service providers feel about themselves and their airline affects the way they serve customers, and is therefore an important competitive variable and potential source of competitive advantage that should not be ignored in liberalised markets.

Particularly during economic downturns and especially in the United States, single-minded attention to quarterly results appears on occasion to have led to pursuit of unfocused and poorly thought-out labour cost reduct-ions, cutting through the fat to the bone and giving insufficient prior consideration to the threat to product integrity posed by poor staff morale; Delta's mid-1990s drive to reduce unit costs to 7.5 cents/ASM is now often quoted as an example. Other threats arise from several different sources amongst staffing trends currently evident in some countries: one, for example, is the growing tendency to hire part-time and temporary staff, who may be difficult to acculturate to a particular airline's service ethos and who may not identify their own long-term interests with those of their employer; another is the outsourcing of customer service processes to organizations which might pay little attention to the impact of staff morale on the airlines they service unless closely monitored under the terms of a tightly drafted, performance-driven contract.

Other customers

Another important influence on any customer's perception of a service encounter is the presence and impact of other customers. The following points about customer-customer (C-C) interactions, how they differ in diff-erent circumstances, and why they can be problematic need to be apprec-iated by airline service design teams (Martin and Clark, 1996).

1. The volume of C-C interactions in any airline's service delivery system greatly exceeds the number of interactions between customers and employees. Furthermore, these interactions take place within the context of closer physical proximity to strangers than most people are accustomed to or comfortable with.
2. Whereas front-line staff can be trained to meet customers' expectations, are usually working off prescribed 'scripts' governing different types of service encounter, and are helped by tangible prompts such as uniforms and signage, customers often have limited awareness of (and some-times little concern for) the effect that their own 'unscripted' behaviour can have on other customers.
3. Whilst airlines can pay close attention to the attitudes, social skills, and service orientation of the front-line staff they consider hiring, 'select-ion' of customers goes no further than designing (and in some cases only loosely designing) certain service packages for certain segments of demand – packages in fact available not just to customers in those segments, but to anybody willing to pay for them. The more diverse the customer base targeted by any service concept and served by any service package, and the more overlap there is between the delivery of different services to different segments within the same delivery sys-

tem, the higher is the risk of C-C incompatibility attributable to conflicting expectations of the same service experience.

4. The roles that different customers perceive themselves to be playing (e.g., guest, member, passenger or even prisoner) will vary between individuals, social groups, nationalities, and members of different cultures and sub-cultures. They also vary over time and with usage. A top-tier FFP member, for example, might have views on his 'rights' that conflict with the expectations of other customers; an individual might also have different role perceptions when travelling alone on business compared to when part of a vacationing family group.

5. One customer's positive or negative comments about a service attribute or an incident can help shape the as-yet unformed perceptions of another, so ultimately influencing the latter's satisfaction level.

6. C-C interactions are inherently difficult to monitor, let alone control.

7. Whereas customer-employee encounters are usually task-driven and goal-oriented, C-C interactions may have little or nothing to do with the service being delivered.

Customer-customer conflict can result from different expectations of service or from crowded facilities or aircraft, for example. It is important that customers likely to encounter each other at key points in the service delivery system are as compatible as possible (Pranter and Martin, 1991). There are several steps that can be taken.

- **Step 1** Identify and target homogeneous market segments and, if choosing to serve more than one, blueprint to keep them apart as much as possible during service encounters in order to minimise the negative effects arising from conflicting expectations.
- **Step 2** Design facilities and processes that minimise contact between segments likely to have conflicting expectations. Where this cannot be done, there is often no real alternative other than to hope that past experiences serve to manage customers' expectations.
- **Step 3** Train employees to recognise and manage conflict between customers. Depending on the circumstances, thought might have to be given to higher staffing levels at critical points of contact to minimise the time available for conflict to develop.

The problem of C-C incompatibility is a difficult one for airlines to solve because of airport and cabin space constraints. This does not mean that it should be ignored – although often it is.

Designing service encounters

Peppard and Rowland (1995) suggest that each service encounter should be designed around the answers to three questions.

1. **The task** What needs to be done and what do customers expect?
2. **The process** How can the process of task performance itself help deliver what customers expect whilst at the same time getting the job done effectively?
3. **The purpose** What attitudinal, behavioural, and technical attributes do the airline's people need in order to get the job done and meet or exceed customers' expectations?

Zeithaml and Bitner (2000: 240-247) have suggested the following approach to developing customer-defined standards for service encounters.

1. Identify the existing or desired sequence of service encounters, using blueprinting and – wherever possible – asking customers for input regarding ways in which they would like to do business with the airline.
2. Translate customers' expectations into employee behaviours and actions required for each service encounter.
3. Design a metric which can be used to capture the performance of any important behaviours and actions that can realistically be measured.
4. Establish target performance levels for each metric.
5. Develop feedback mechanisms which monitor performance from the customers', rather than the airline's, point of view (e.g., surveys, observation, and complaints for 'soft' metrics, and objective data-gathering for 'hard' metrics).
6. Track actual against targeted performance.
7. Ensure that employees receive ongoing feedback to support continuous improvement efforts, and to trigger root-cause analysis of service failures or performance shortfalls.
8. Periodically update the system to ensure that what is being measured is still relevant to customers, that standards have been set high enough, and that feedback mechanisms are still adequate.

The problem is, of course, that not all elements of a service encounter can be routinised to the point where meaningful standards can be established, and attempts to over-standardise might become counterproductive (e.g., the 'have a nice day' syndrome). There are therefore two aspects to the monitoring of service encounters.

- **Hard standards** Some dimensions of a service encounter might involve tasks that can be monitored using objective data. Examples include holding times on reservations lines, web site availability, and time taken to resolve a complaint. The important point is that standards should be set on the basis of customers' expectations with regard to the type of encounter concerned, rather than being keyed-off what the airline thinks is acceptable.
- **Soft standards** The more subjective aspects of service encounters, such as courtesy, helpfulness, responsiveness, and empathy, can normally only be judged through the use of customer surveys. A complicating factor for international carriers is that people from different cultures may have very different evaluations of a given encounter (as, perhaps somewhat less frequently, may people from the same culture), and might also react differently to a survey instrument.

Scripts

Given the roles allocated to customers and service providers within the context of a particular service package and service delivery system, each is likely to have prescribed 'scripts' to follow – much like actors and actresses in a play. The concepts of 'role' (drawn from sociology) and 'script' (taken from psychology) are similar. Their main difference is that scripts tend to be more specific than roles; their principal similarity is that the outcome of acting out a role or a script is always to some extent dependent on the behaviour of others.

Hoffman and Bateson (1997: 144) have observed that,

> [o]btaining consumer and employee scripts is a potentially powerful technique for analyzing the service encounter. Scripts provide the dialogue from which consumer and employee perceptions of the encounter can be analyzed and potential or existing problems identified. Overall, scripts provide the basics for planning service encounters, setting goals and objectives, developing behavioral routines that maximize the opportunities for a successful exchange, and evaluating the effectiveness of current service delivery systems.

Scripts, which are derived from service blueprints, outline activities and behaviours expected of participants playing their roles in particular service encounters.

- The more familiar these participants – whether long-serving employees or repeat customers – are with a particular script, the smoother and less stressful an encounter is likely to be.

- The departure of a service encounter from a customer's anticipated version of the script can, depending on circumstances, generate customer satisfaction (e.g., a flight attendant's good-humoured spontaneity) or dissatisfaction (e.g., an unexpectedly long delay in getting beverage service). In other words, customer satisfaction levels can be affected by discrepancies between expectations of a 'script' and perceptions of how 'the play' was actually performed.

- In this context, it is important to ensure that both service providers and customers are 'working off the same script' – which is essentially to say that airlines should endeavour to understand customers' expectations, then meet them where they can or manage them into conformity with what the service package is actually designed to deliver. 'Convergent scripts' enhance the probability of customer satisfaction, whereas 'divergent scripts' suggest consumer expectations are not being met (ibid).

- The alteration of scripts can generate resistance amongst service providers and customers, and could affect perceptions of service quality. Major alterations therefore need to be carefully managed and, in significant cases, consideration also needs to be given to the possible impact of a planned change on the market positioning of the service-price offer.

(See Tansik and Smith (2000) for a comprehensive review of variables that can impact the scripting of service encounters.)

Individualism on both sides of the service encounter

There is growing research evidence – none yet from the airline industry – that employee discretion (if used, which is not inevitable) has the potential to enhance consumer satisfaction. This requires, above all else selection of front-office staff who have positive attitudes, well-developed interpersonal skills, and a service orientation, together with a willingness on the airline's part to invest heavily in training.

In the mid-1990s, both British Airways and Air France initiated major product re-launches in their premium cabins that shared the common theme of treating consumers as individuals and maximising spontaneous, unscripted interactions with staff. More recently, Air Canada and Delta have built marketing campaigns around the treatment of customers as individuals, the former focusing its television advertising on functional attributes such as on-demand meals in premium cabins and the latter making a more emotional appeal with the strap-line 'Millions of reasons to fly today, but only one that matters to you'.

iv. Servicescapes

> It can hardly be a coincidence that no language on earth
> has ever produced the expression 'as pretty as an airport'.
> Douglas Adams

The word 'servicescape' was coined by Bitner (1992) to describe a physical environment within which service encounters take place. This includes not only the physical settings within which services are delivered, but also the equipment and techniques used to deliver them. We touched on the idea of servicescapes earlier in the chapter, in the context of ground- and cabin-related service attributes.

Why servicescapes matter

Design of a servicescape, as with the design of most other things, needs to pay attention to both form and function. A servicescape not only conveys information and facilitates service delivery, it is a potentially distinctive part of the service itself – akin to the packaging of consumer goods (Zeithaml and Bitner, 2000). Servicescapes contribute meaningfully to customers' experiences, and therefore to their evaluation of service quality and ultimately to the image they hold of the airline's brand(s). Servicescapes shape customers' perceptions through their visual impact, through the nature of the social interactions to which they give rise, and through their impact on the effectiveness and efficiency of service delivery. Decor (particularly choice of colour and fabrics, and the purposeful use of design to influence perceptions of space), lighting, background noise, signage, symbols, quality of materials, and spatial configuration (sometimes together referred to as 'atmospherics') all provide clues which make more tangible the essentially intangible service that has been purchased and which – during delivery – is being evaluated against expectations by consumers. These are strong image-carriers for employees as well as consumers, and their symbolic effects inevitably influence employee motivation, productivity, and satisfaction. In summary:

- servicescapes help shape the expectations both of consumers entering them and prospective customers who see them;
- customers at ease within a servicescape appropriate to the level of service they expect are more likely to perceive favourably other attributes of the service delivered to them than would be the case were the servicescape inappropriate;

- employees are likely to respond positively to a pleasant servicescape consistent with the type of service they are expected to deliver;
- its servicescapes are significant contributors to each airline's visual identity and therefore to its brand-building efforts.

Bitner (1992) emphasises the power of a servicescape to affect both customers and employees (albeit subject to intervening variables such as personality, attitude, mood, situational factors, and cultural background). It does this in one or more of several ways.

1. **Cognitively** Servicescapes, as well as service encounters generally, influence people's knowledge structures and beliefs with regard to the airline concerned and what to expect from its services. They can have considerable symbolic meaning.
2. **Affectively** Servicescapes affect people's emotions, notably the level of pleasure they feel at being present in a particular environment.
3. **Physiologically** The conditions in a servicescape can stimulate physiological responses from those present, which feed through to cognitive and affective responses. For example, an overcrowded, disorderly check-in area might generate stress, which in turn leads to a feeling of displeasure and a downgrading of beliefs about the airline's service generally.

Cognitive, affective, and physiological responses to a servicescape may drive behaviour, notably the willingness of prospective customers to purchase, of current customers to repurchase, and of employees to engage positively in their work. However:

- different people respond differently to any given cognitive, affective, or physiological stimulus;
- behavioural outcomes may be moderated by variables such as mood (e.g., whether anxious or relaxed) and context (e.g., whether in a hurry or not) at the time a customer is present in the servicescape.

Bitner (ibid) suggests that the role of a servicescape is to:

- 'provide a visual metaphor for an organization's total offering' (ibid: 67);
- distinguish the organization, positioning it visually within its chosen market segment(s);

- facilitate customers and service providers in the playing of their respective roles in the service delivery system, at the same time shaping social interaction within and between groups.

The design elements in a servicescape

There are several, notably the following.

1. **Location** Processes requiring the physical presence of customers have 'tied locations', whereas others do not.
2. **Layout** Safety, functionality, and flexibility are major considerations. (For a full list, see Hope and Mühlemann (1997), p. 237.)
3. **Physical surroundings** These encompass external and internal appearances, including interior decor, furnishings, choice of fabrics, and aesthetics.
   - Appearance, decor, and furnishings should be consistent with the customer value and positioning required by the service concept.
   - Colours should reflect the corporate brand, but it might need to be borne in mind as far as interior surfaces and lighting are concerned that different colours do have distinct effects on mood – with blues and greens found to be more calming and restful than reds and oranges, for example (although this is not something that appears to trouble Virgin Atlantic).

   Some airlines do take a great deal of care in presenting themselves visually to customers. It nonetheless remains true that many aircraft interiors – particularly, but not only, in short-haul fleets – are bland and show little evidence of proactive intent with regard to creating or reinforcing a visual brand identity.
4. **Equipment**
   - Anthropomorphic factors affect staff (e.g., check-in positions) and customers (e.g., seats in lounges and aircraft).
     - Body dimensions vary widely between races, genders, and generations, as well as within each racial, gender, and age group.
     - In some countries anthropomorphic data does exist to guide design decisions, but the problem for long-haul international carriers in particular is that they serve many different anthropomorphic groups.

   Seat pitches on some European charter carriers exemplify in the extreme what happens when anthropomorphic considerations are traded-off within the context of a low-fare service concept requiring low production (i.e., seat-mile) costs. Throughout the 1990s many airlines were intent on cramming more seats into their economy/coach classes to ease unit cost pressures, and this trend – together with the fact that people on average are growing in size and weight in many countries – encouraged the UK Civil Aviation Authority to launch, at the turn of the decade, a study to investigate the implications that increased seating densities might hold for cabin evacuation. From a service design perspective, the move by American in 1999 to remove seats from across the fleet suggests that at least some airlines are taking another look at the cost/yield trade-off inherent in seating density decisions.

- Neurological factors influence equipment design because whenever an employee or customer uses equipment, learned behaviour will affect assumptions with regard to how, for example, knobs and switches should be manipulated or output on a dial or screen should be interpreted.

5. **Signage** Its purposes are to help orient, inform, or instruct customers, to communicate clues about the quality of the service being provided, and to contribute to the airline's visual identity.

- Key issues include: visibility, legibility, and intelligibility.
- Because international airlines carry passengers of many different nationalities, multilingual signs and the heavy use of symbols are essential.

6. **Ambient conditions** Variables could include noise, temperature, illumination, and air quality.

- Noise: turboprop aircraft are frequently – although not always correctly – perceived as having noisy servicescapes; neither departure lounges as a whole, club lounges in particular, nor cabins onboard long-haul aircraft generally have quiet areas for those who want them – although there are exceptions; cabin crew talking loudly in a galley close to sleeping passengers can also be an annoyance on night-flights.
- Temperature and humidity: these need to reflect the number of people present in the facility at a given time, together with their activity levels. For example, several hundred people manhandling cases in a baggage reclaim area need lower temperatures to be comfortable than half a dozen sitting in a first class lounge; on an aircraft, 250 people packed into the rear half of a fuselage will need more cooling than 60 people 'spread' through business and first class cabins in the front half; physically active staff may have different needs from the customers they are serving, and these should be reflected in their uniforms.

- Illumination.
  - Natural light: this is to be preferred if it is adequate for tasks and activities within the servicescape.
  - Artificial light: the level needs to be appropriate to the setting (e.g., it is not uncommon for cabin lights to be fully on at times during a night flight for the convenience of flight attendants delivering food and beverage service to passengers who are awake, ignoring the preferences of those who are trying to sleep). The participation of specialised lighting consultants in design teams remodelling long-haul cabins is not widespread, but is growing; British Airways, for example, has teamed with specialists to develop patented technology that uses lighting to transform cabin appearance – and thus affect customers' perceptions of their environments – as each flight progresses.
- Air quality: some smells – such as those associated with air freshener and fresh coffee – are thought to be widely appealing, but in general odours should be kept to a minimum. There are two particular issues:
  - smoking in flight: this is increasingly being forbidden;
  - cabin air quality: airlines operating modern equipment have considerable control over air recirculation and exchange rates and fresh air supply. Some opt for standards lower than would be permissible for public buildings in many countries.
7. **Interpersonal conditions** Variables here include the physical organization of interactions between staff and customers as well as between different customers, the degree of crowding, and the appearance and behaviour of staff.
   - People have 'personal spaces' which, when breached, can be a source of stress. However:
     - personal space concepts vary not only between individuals, but also between cultures;
     - the economics of the airline industry make it inevitable that, with the possible exception of first class passengers or those travelling at off-peak times, most customers will have their personal spaces penetrated.
   - The only answer is staff training to raise awareness of this unseen source of stress, and therefore of potentially negative perceptions of service quality.

Design criteria for a servicescape

A servicescape should promote favourable cognitive, affective, and physiological responses from employees and customers, and it should also reinforce both desired behaviour and the airline's corporate brand image. Whereas back-office settings (the 'hidden organization') can be designed to maximise process efficiency and employee satisfaction, front-office settings – 'servicescapes' – must also be designed with reference to their effect on consumers' perceptions. Servicescapes should therefore reflect an airline's service concept and the positioning of the service-price offer being delivered. The problem faced by a lot of airlines is that they have limited control over many of the environments within which their services are delivered, notably the common-use areas of airports. This is one reason why, wherever possible, carriers offering highly differentiated first and business class services in particular try to create their own spaces – check-in areas and lounges being primary examples – within which they have some measure of control over the identity projected to consumers by the environment.

There may be a conflict between the needs of the airline (e.g., for minimisation of costs or maximisation of productivity), of employees (e.g., for a congenial working environment), and of customers (for whatever it is they expect out of a particular service). In principle, the needs of customers should prevail; in practice, life may not always be this simple. The guide in resolving any conflict must be the airline's service concept, the positioning of its particular service-price offer(s), and the operating strategy that flow from these starting points.

Large carriers are increasingly using either long-term or project-specific design alliances with external consultancies to help in both designing individual servicescapes and ensuring consistency across all areas of visual brand identity. Design Acumen, for example, has been responsible for revolutionary cabin concepts in partnership with British Airways – the first class 'flying bed' introduced in the mid-1990s – and American Airlines – the Flagship Suite introduced in 2000. In the latter case, the design team also included other specialist firms responsible for seats, component ergonomics, and overall cabin styling; in both cases the design briefs were based on in-depth market research, which was used to help understand customers' expectations in general and also to arrive at a satisfactory balance between the sometimes dissimilar expectations of passengers from different parts of the world (Dryburgh, 2000).

Modern technologies, notably virtual reality, offer the prospect of airline managers being able to bring alternative servicescapes to life during the design phase, before resources are committed to implementation, and also being able to simulate the performance of alternative service environments under different demand loading conditions. Low-cost/low-fare carriers live in a different world in terms of design resources, and in most cases do not feel the need to place anything like as much emphasis on servicescape attributes as full-service airlines do. It would nonetheless be foolhardy to believe that because a particular segment of customers buys largely on the basis of low fares it will continue to tolerate, say, tatty and unclean cabins if a better and equally low-priced alternative should become available.

v. Conclusion

Having outlined the service concept in chapter 3 and related it to more specific issues of service design in chapter 4, this chapter has dug deeper into the field of services management by looking at the menu of service attributes available for airlines to design into their service-price offers, at service blueprinting, at the importance of service encounters, and at the significance of servicescapes. After a service-price offer has been designed, the customer value and market position embodied in it have to be communicated both to the segments of demand being targeted and to the staff who will deliver the service; an airline also communicates – through its servicescapes, its people, and its systems – during the course of service encounters. Communication is the subject of the next chapter.

6 Managing Communications

Have regard for your name,
since it will remain for you longer than a great store of gold.
The Bible

Having settled on a service-price offer consistent with our service concept and the market position chosen for it, the next task is to communicate information about the airline and its offer to targeted segments. This chapter takes a broad view of the communication task, and draws heavily on the brand management literature. It opens by reconsidering brand identity and brand image. Possible communications objectives are summarised, and the importance of strategic consistency is stressed. Finally, the challenges involved in communicating with people both outside and inside the airline are considered. Figure 6.1 illustrates how the present chapter fits into the discussion in preceding chapters.

i. Brand identity and image revisited

A brand is a promise, and in the end you have to keep your promises.
A product is the artefact of the truth of a promise.
Watts Wacker

In chapter 3 (page 105) I introduced an initial definition of a brand. This section will broaden that definition before then turning to matters of identity and image, and ending with a review of the elements that comprise a brand.

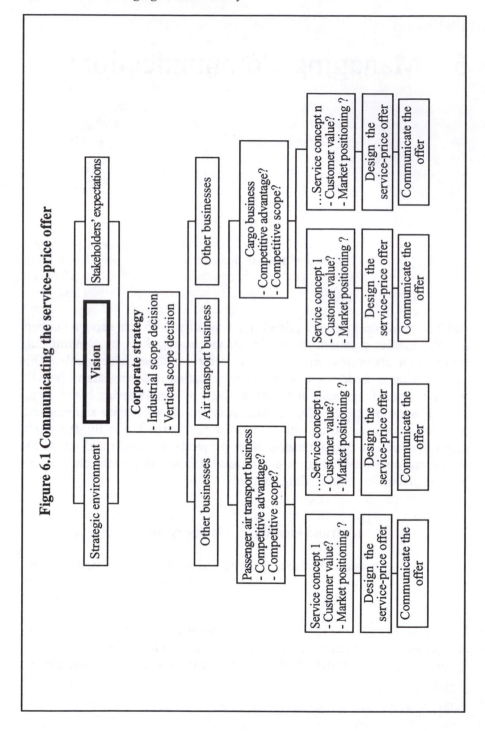

Figure 6.1 Communicating the service-price offer

Brands defined

There is an argument that what separates a brand on the one hand from a product name or 'label' on the other is nothing more than the ability to sell a branded product for a higher price than a functionally equivalent competitor (Kay, 1993). An effectively branded service might indeed sell at a premium over similar competing services. For example, it has been established by research carried out on routes between the United Kingdom and Europe that in the early 1990s the British Airways brand name was generating a three per cent price premium (Cronshaw and Thompson, 1991). However, it is questionable whether a price premium alone is enough to distinguish a brand from a product name or label; price, particularly in a revenue-managed network industry, is too volatile a criterion by which to judge the distinction between a name and a brand.

The notion that a brand can only exist when customers are willing to pay more for it than for an 'unbranded' competitor is an economist's perspective; the argument is that a brand creates a situation of imperfect competition – in effect, a mini-monopoly is fashioned by a producer able to create a demand for something (whether emotional or tangible) that *only* it can offer and that customers are willing to pay a premium to obtain. This ignores the fact that a brand is in effect nothing more than an image held in a customer's mind, and that the more favourable image of one airline compared to the image of a competitor may influence a purchase decision in a situation of price and product parity – that is, without the winning brand being able to command a price premium. To argue that a brand only exists where there is premium pricing implies that Southwest is not a brand. This is clearly not a plausible argument.

There are quite a few alternative definitions of 'brand' in the literature. My preference draws on the distinction made in chapter 4 between the functional/performance attributes of a service package and the emotional/symbolic attributes:

- whereas a *product* is capable of delivering only functional benefits,
- a *brand* is able to deliver emotional/symbolic benefits as well.

Furthermore, a brand is associated with reliable, consistent delivery of both functional and emotional benefits. A brand tells us what to expect from the underlying product.

People's relationships with a brand stand on two pillars: cognitive and emotional (Kapferer, 1997). Potential customers learn through various forms of communication that an airline is serving one or more markets in which they are interested, and over time satisfactory service usage leads from this situation of prompted brand awareness to one of spontaneous awareness built on favourable emotions towards the carrier. Research suggests that people tend to be most spontaneously aware of their preferred brands (ibid).

Favourable emotions towards a brand will sustain preference in the absence of other meaningful points of difference vis a vis competitors. However, should a competitor begin offering benefits which provide valuable distinctiveness sufficient to undermine the attractions of familiarity and emotional attachment, that competitor might be able to build on the cognitive pillar to generate trial and ultimately perhaps a new emotional attachment to its brand.

Particularly when service-price offers targeted at the same segment provide very similar functional benefits, it is the emotional/symbolic benefits associated with its brand that allow an airline to position the underlying service concept firmly in people's minds. A 'strong' brand is one that offers and clearly communicates augmented benefits in addition to the core and expected benefits associated with the service concept(s) concerned (all of which we met in chapter 4); it comes readily to the minds of customers thinking about a particular product class, it conjures vivid and positive images, and it is considered dependable – its story is believable. This applies whether the story being told is of intercontinental luxury – such as British Airways First – or low-fare, high-frequency, reliable, cheerful, short-haul functionality – such as Southwest; both have strong identities which powerfully convey their own distinct messages to targeted segments.

However, a brand is not just something that marketing executives create – it is something individuals hold in their minds. It is in fact a bundle of perceptions (de Chernatony and McDonald, 1998); a brand is 'strong' wherever perceptions are consistent and positive. Not every individual holds the same image of any airline; there will be different levels of individual awareness, different histories of exposure, different experiences, and different perceptions. Because we are here talking about multiple individuals who arrive at interpretations of what any brand means to them on the basis of their own experiences of actual service and predictive clues and also under the influence of other people's interpretations, we can argue that a brand is in fact a 'social construction'; this is much like the idea of organizations as social constructions that we met in chapter 1. This 'social construction' is sometimes referred to as 'reputation'; where this word is used, a distinction is often drawn between image as a relatively short-term and individualised construct based on a single image-holder's experiences with the organization and strongly influenced by the most recent experience, and reputation as a more stable construct that is widely held by people as a whole. To say that British Airways, for example, has a reputation for 'professionalism' does not mean that every individual holds this image, but that in general most external audiences do. Reputation and image clearly feed-off each other over time.

Complicating matters further is the fact that the airline business is truly international in scope, with the result that the images of a particular brand held in one market or cultural milieu are unlikely ever to be precisely the same as those held in other areas. Image fragmentation is something that international carriers in particular need to address. British Airways, for example, might have one image widespread in the UK, a somewhat different image in Italy, and a very different image in Japan. It is therefore necessary to have a singular identity, but to manage it differently wherever this is required in order to have it translated into desirable and marketable images in different milieux. Modes of communication have to be flexible, but this flexibility should not compromise the carrier's fundamental identity.

A brand is therefore a complex entity linking an airline's activities on the one hand – activities that together create an 'identity' – with customers' perceptions on the other (de Chernatony and Dall'Olmo Riley, 1997). It is not a name or a logo, but an interpretation and evaluation of everything a customer sees, hears, and experiences with regard to a particular airline. It is not a tactical variable in the marketing mix, but something fundamental that needs to be strategically planned and consistently implemented.

This, however, leaves us with a problem insofar as if the consistent delivery of emotional/symbolic (i.e., psycho-social) benefits is taken as a key determinant of brand strength, there are arguably few strong brands in the airline industry as a whole. There are certainly strong corporate names with, in some cases, well-defined ranges of products associated with them, but many of these names are only just beginning to move beyond the provision of fairly standard functional benefits to the delivery of emotional/ symbolic benefits. The delivery of these latter types of benefit can contribute greatly to building 'points-of-difference' in the minds of customers; in this book I am assuming that more airline management teams will in future be thinking about how they manage their brand identities – as opposed to just the functional attributes of their products.

We have an identity, others hold an image

Why does Coke continue to outsell Pepsi despite blind taste tests regularly confirming that, on the whole, consumers prefer the taste of Pepsi (Piercy, 1997)? Closer to home, why did second-tier regional and charter carrier Dan-Air fail to attract business travellers (and subsequently go under) despite launching what at the beginning of the 1990s was the best (i.e., most spacious) intra-European business class cabin by some margin? The answer lies in the power of brand image.

A brand is an intangible asset. Like every other asset it has a job to do, the primary task in this case being to communicate with and build loyalty amongst a target group of customers – although, as we will see, brands also communicate to constituencies other than customers. A strong brand is a unique source of competitive advantage because it is an essentially inimitable resource; other brands – perhaps strong in their own separate ways – can compete with it, but they cannot clone its distinct personality.

A competence in brand management is essentially all about building and projecting an identity which successfully positions the airline and its service-price offers. Identity is path dependent (see chapter 2). It owes much to history, as well as to the currently prevailing values, beliefs, and goals of the airline's people. Because each identity is a unique manifestation of shared experiences over time – experiences that have created often unquestioned core assumptions about how to behave – it is not easy to change (Ind, 1997).

The importance of the emotional dimension in service-price offers makes it possible to 'personify' brands by thinking about them in terms of their *personality*: the Virgin brand personality, for example, brings to mind fun, flair, innovation, choice, and nonconformist individualism. Underlying a brand's personality are its *values* – in Virgin's case belief in being competitive and in championing consumers against the vested interests of 'the establishment'. Brand personality is a metaphor on brand values and a shorthand device that can curtail customers' information search activities prior to making a purchase decision (Aaker, 1996). Personality and positioning clearly need to be consistent. The perceived personalities of some airline brands are intertwined with those of their founders (e.g., Virgin and Southwest).

Brand image is identity mediated by the perceptions of people both inside and outside the airline; a brand's image in the minds of customers and its market positioning are very closely related concepts – some would argue they are essentially the same. The image of an airline held by a particular person or audience is the summation of all their experiences, beliefs, feelings, impressions, and knowledge regarding the company up to that point in time (Worcester, 1997). Communications (especially, but not only, marketing communications) help translate identity into image. Actions taken or not taken also convey an impression, contributing to the formation of a holistic mental representation of what an airline is and what it stands for. An image is the sum of perceptions an airline manages to create of itself in the minds of individual stakeholders. Image shapes people's attitudes and behaviours towards an airline, contributing to purchase decisions by customers and to decisions by other stakeholders about whether or not to provide resources to the airline – resources such as capital, labour, and support in respect of regulatory and other issues. Box 6.1 defines 'perception'.

Box 6.1: Perception

People react not to some concrete, immutable reality but to what they each perceive to be reality (Boulding, 1956). Every individual makes sense of the world in different ways. Perception is concerned with how different individuals come to understand their environments. They do this by using processes of selection, organization, and interpretation (Fill, 1995).

- Selection *Individuals are bombarded with stimuli from marketing and other sources, most of which they filter out. 'Attention' is the process through which some information is absorbed whilst other information is ignored. Which stimuli are selected for attention will depend on the nature of the stimulus (e.g., whether an advertisement grabs the attention in some way), the context (e.g., whether the individual is in fact planning a trip), and the person's predispositions (e.g., whether a particular stimulus – a claim in an advertisement perhaps, or a surly member of staff – is consistent with prior beliefs about what to expect from the airline concerned). A forgettable advertisement that is seen by a customer who has no plans to travel and which makes claims in respect of services offered that the individual concerned feels based on past experience are exaggerated will not be strongly or favourably received.*

- Organization *Stimuli absorbed by individuals who receive them are organized in memory. This is achieved through a process of 'pattern recognition'. One example of use in marketing communications is the grouping of related stimuli into patterns of association. A key objective of branding is to associate an airline and its services with something positive – smiling cabin attendants (e.g., Singapore Airlines), appealing national culture (e.g., Thai International), or a particular set of clearly defined brand values (e.g., Virgin Atlantic).*

- Interpretation *Once selected and organized into a category, each stimulus is interpreted to give it meaning. How a stimulus is interpreted will depend in part upon expectations driven by past experience.*

An airline's ability to build a consistent, credible, and feasible brand image will depend to a considerable extent on understanding how stakeholders –

particularly customers – select, organize, and interpret stimuli relevant to the airline concerned and its service-price offers. Everything from advertisements through promotional literature, servicescapes through staff behaviour provides stimuli that customers and others select, organize, and interpret into perceptions of who we are and what we are capable of delivering.

Images are formed in part around the attitudes and behaviours of staff (who, in turn, have their own images of their employer), and around the physical appearance of tangible resources. They transmit information about corporate culture to both internal and external stakeholders. Image and corporate culture are closely intertwined. Corporate culture will affect how an airline presents itself to stakeholders verbally (e.g., telephone manner), visually (e.g., offices, check-in areas, lounges, aircraft cabins, signage, and both written and media communications), and attitudinally (e.g., the approach staff adopt towards each other, towards external actors such as customers and suppliers, and towards their tasks). In turn, each of these communicates various impressions which people receiving the communications use to help form an image of the airline.

Image is therefore a product of both appearance and action (Ind, 1997); the appearance of an airline's facilities, equipment, and people and the actions taken by its people all help to create an image. People hold images because images help order an overwhelmingly complex flow of information. They seek out information in that flow which corresponds with their existing images, and will rarely accept at first pass anything other than the most categorical information that contradicts their image. Over time, contradictory information could change the image.

Properly nurtured, a brand may engender sufficient trust that it can long outlast the functional product form at the heart of any service-price offer. Whereas the functional attributes of a service package might be 'refreshed' every few years, and even the emotional/symbolic attributes will occasionally be reworked in response to changing social values and lifestyles for example, a brand image can outlive all of them. Figure 6.2 illustrates some of these points.

This is the theory. In practice, few airlines appear to have a clear idea of their brand's identity, what it stands for, and how it fits with long-term strategy. Individual marketing communications campaigns may indeed be linked to current strategic objectives, but it is still rare for either to be explicitly linked to an articulated brand charter – a statement outlining the brand's vision and values, the needs it is to satisfy, what makes it different, what sustains that difference, and what makes it recognisable (Kapferer,

Figure 6.2 Identity and image

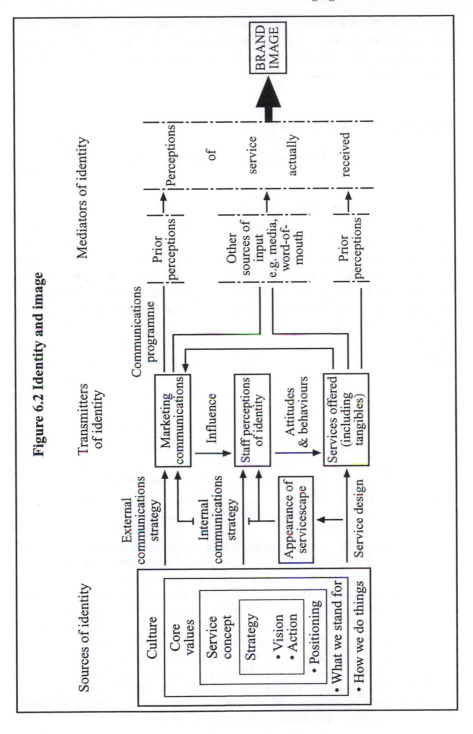

1997). Too often a brand – whether a corporate brand or a service sub-brand – is taken to be something visual that is synonymous with a name or a logo rather than something broader and intangible which has its own image in the minds of customers.

Managing identity and image

> The block of marble contains an image. I have to set it free.
> Michelangelo

Our communications objectives with regard to identity and image are fairly straightforward, even if implementation of the strategies required to attain them might not be. We want to build an overall image for ourselves in the minds of stakeholders – particularly customers – which accords as closely as possible with the type of company we are and what we hope to achieve for each stakeholder group, and which also supports our service concept(s). At a macro-level we do this through marketing communications and the careful management of brand elements – a topic we will turn to in a moment. At the micro-level, we do it by performing up to – ideally beyond – the expectations of individual stakeholders. The latter in particular is not easy, because any stakeholder's direct experience of an airline will depend upon variables such as mood (on both sides of the encounter), context, and the sub-culture of the particular part of the airline that is being dealt with. Customers, suppliers, competitors, journalists, shareholders, analysts, and lenders might each as a group see very different sides of any one airline's 'personality'. The more consistent that personality is, the more it is bound together by a set of core values, the more universal and stable the overall image is likely to be. It is worth quoting at length the view of one practitioner and writer regarding the breadth of the challenge.

> The problem for many organisations is that communications are compartmentalised: corporate affairs talks to financial audiences; marketing talks to consumers; and human relations talks to employees. Even within marketing in large organisations people will commission direct marketing activity, public relations, design and advertising. Unless there is a powerful integrative force, the possibilities for fragmentation are enormous. It needs glue to hold it all together. That can come only through structures and systems that encourage convergence, and most importantly through a powerful, shared vision that helps to achieve a degree of uniformity in attitudes and behaviour....[T]he organisation has to try to build a set of values that creates consistency. This is the problem of variability of performance that service industries all have to confront in their relationships with consumers (Ind, 1997: 10).

Brand identity and image therefore need to be actively managed. The following questions can help.

- What is the airline's vision, how is this reflected in its service concept(s) and in the organization's values and culture, what is the competitive advantage underpinning the service concept(s), and what would targeted customers be missing if the airline ceased to exist?
- Who precisely are we addressing when we communicate? Do we understand the images they hold of us?
- Is it known why customers in a particular segment buy one brand rather than another and, if so, what role brand image plays in the decision process relative to functional benefits?
- How is our image perceived by employees, customers, members of the media, suppliers (especially financial institutions), shareholders, the communities we serve, governments, and opinion-formers generally? With regard to customers and prospective customers, questions can be asked such as, 'What is the first thing that comes to mind when X Airlines is mentioned?' 'When you use X Airlines [or one of its sub-branded products], what type of message do you send to yourself and to others whose opinions you value?'
- In what way is the airline's image distinct from those of its competitors?
- What is its image in respect of: quality, price, and value; technical capabilities; customer orientation; overall professionalism; financial condition; and labour relations?
- Are these aspects of the airline's image appropriate to its corporate objectives and consistent with the positioning of its service concept?
- If not why not, what should be done, and by whom?
- Does the airline have a formal objective and programme for the development of its identity and the tracking of its image?
- If so, who is responsible?
- What is that objective, and is it relevant to prevailing business conditions? In what way does it build on inimitable resources, leverage distinctive competencies, and exploit competitive advantages?
- Is there an integrated communications programme based on formal research into various constituencies' attitudes towards the airline, and designed explicitly to bridge any identified gap between the chosen identity and the image(s) these constituencies actually hold?
- What is the extent of sensitivity to image, throughout the airline generally and in particular amongst customer-contact staff and in respect of

those parts of the carrier (e.g., aircraft, premises, vehicles, and printed materials) that interface with stakeholders?

It is important to note that no matter how well thought-out our identity-management programme might be, image is not something that can be managed according to our own preferred time-scale or with any real precision. Marketing communications initiatives are not the only things that shape image. It is being formed and re-formed daily in media comments and analyses, and by the minute in service encounters between staff and customers. Image cannot be controlled, only influenced. Whatever influence we have should be used to ensure as far as possible that our image is: appropriate to the airline's vision and service concept(s), consistent with the strategies adopted, relevant and agreeable to customers and other stakeholders, and both clearly and consistently held. Only in this way can we be reasonably sure that the image – of the airline as a whole or of any particular sub-brand – is really a positive service attribute capable of delivering emotional benefits to customers.

> ....by comparing the organisational 'reality' – or the identity – with perceptions – or image – we begin to see whether the corporate brand is being accurately represented: whether communications are supporting the organisational strategy, are culturally credible and relevant to all the brand's stakeholders. If the image and identity are misaligned, dissonance is created and corrective action, either in organisational performance or communication or both, needs to be taken (ibid: 64).

Alignment

It has been suggested that the closer the match between the values of a brand and the rational and emotional needs of targeted customers, the more successful that brand is likely to be (de Chernatony and Dall'Olmo Riley, 1997). If an airline's image is unappealing to a particular customer, there will be a lack of alignment (Holloway, 1998b). Virgin Atlantic's image is inherently less appealing to some than is the British Airways image; for others the reverse is true. This, of course, takes us back to market segmentation.

Alternatively, if there is customer appeal but expectations are not fulfilled, there will be a different type of misalignment. As we saw in chapter 4, expectations are the baseline against which customers' perceptions of service actually received will be measured during and after service delivery; any shortfall of perceived service below expectations will trigger dissatisfaction. A shortfall demands attention either to the management of whatever expectations are being created (e.g., by advertising) or to the effectiveness of service delivery processes – or possibly to both. Effective delivery of benefits expected by significant numbers of consumers within target segments, on the other hand, can build not only a positive image but with it also a degree of customer loyalty – a bond between producer and consumer – capable of creating a market entry barrier competitors could find expensive, difficult, and time-consuming to overcome. The goal should be alignment of identity, image, and service strategies with the expectations of targeted customers.

Alliance issues

An emerging challenge is the management of brand identity across networks of allied entities that could include a core airline, special-purpose units or subsidiaries, franchisees, and code-sharing partners. A particularly interesting question over the next few years surrounds the blending of multiple corporate images within emerging alliance structures. In cases where there is a long-term commitment to merging services, efforts to blend successfully will be essential. In the Northwest/KLM partnership, for example, the problems inherent in having two separate images with different strengths in different parts of the globe were addressed by launching a shared sub-brand: 'World Business Class'. The role of image in less broadly based, more transactional arrangements such as route-specific code-sharing poses something of a conundrum.

Airlines are selling not just locational transformation, but also an experience which has psychological and social dimensions; this raises challenging issues in the context of global alliance strategies. Although alliance partners might each offer high quality in their own separate ways, the emotional benefits arising from flying on Delta as opposed to Air France, on United as opposed to Lufthansa, Varig or Thai, or on British Airways as opposed to Qantas or Cathay Pacific are fundamentally different; they are likely to remain different unless the partners merge their identities and people into new entities capable of having their own distinct images. Until this probably distant time, airlines committed to alliances are faced with the task of, on the one hand, paying rightful homage to the growing significance of individual corporate images in increasingly competitive markets yet, on the other hand, allowing these expensively crafted images to become blurred by what in some cases are kaleidoscopes of alliance affiliations (ibid).

The communications challenge therefore lies in nurturing the distinct images of individual partners, whilst at the same time selling the added benefits offered by the alliance – primarily a large, well-integrated network providing greater convenience (e.g., higher frequencies, through-check-ins, 'seamless' transfers), the opportunity to 'earn and burn' miles on any of the partners' routes, access to any partner's front-line staff for other partners' customers who have a problem that needs solving, and mutual recognition of each partner's high-value customers. At the moment, alliances are weakly branded in most customers' minds, and they are likely to stay that way for as long as the actual service they purport to offer – consistent delivery of similar benefits throughout a seamlessly interconnected network – is actually delivered to customers by strongly and separately branded members. Alliances have limited visual presence, no identifiable 'points of difference', no distinct culture, and they rely on members to deliver services to customers. Turning alliance names into alliance brands will not be an easy task, and it has only just begun.

Brand elements: the building blocks of identity and image

> If anyone can build a brand, it is the customer. The
> marketer can only create favourable conditions for a
> brand image to develop in customers' minds.
> Christian Grönroos

A brand is a holistic amalgam of elements which together communicate an identity that customers then interpret into an image and, perhaps, a personality. Its purpose is to communicate emotional/symbolic benefits as well as information about the standards and consistency of functional benefits, so distinguishing the airline from competitors and simplifying consumer choice. Brand elements are particularly important in the context of a service industry because together they can create around an essentially intangible service delivery process an image which has at least quasi-tangible qualities; in this sense, they can help edge what is basically an 'experience product' closer to being a 'search product' – two concepts we will look at shortly. Brands communicate value and values. It is vital that all their elements are managed consistently as part of an integrated communications management effort, and that a coherent house style is used. Brand elements include the following.

Brand name

A name is little more than a label attached to a company or a product. A brand name, on the other hand, has four particular qualities.

1. A brand name is a *prompt* which triggers associations and stimulates images of the value and service on offer, based on one or a combination of past experience, word-of-mouth comments from others, or exposure to previous marketing communications. The more consistent these experiences, comments, and communications, the better formed the image is likely to be.

2. A brand name is a *short-cut* into the different parts of their memories where customers have stored information about competing service-price offers in the product category concerned. People tend to filter information and organize it in mental 'pigeon-holes'. A brand-name provides rapid access to information that might be stored randomly in a product category 'pigeon-hole', as well as a link to other associations that a particular individual might hold in memory as a result of past experience of the brand or exposure to its marketing.

3. A brand name is a *shorthand device* carrying a mass of stored information – an image – that is often sufficient in itself to curtail a pre-purchase search for further information about competing offers. When a brand name conveys information which leads to a purchase decision, it helps create expectations of service.

4. A brand name makes an *emotional appeal* in respect of product benefits, supplementing purely rational attempts at persuasion that might get lost in the noise of competing claims and counterclaims being generated in increasingly competitive markets. Metaphor and symbol sometimes carry stronger messages than bald facts. The most important emotional drivers are trust and loyalty, built-up over a history of satisfactory experiences.

The brand management challenge as far as names are concerned varies depending upon whether we are dealing with an existing or new brand name.

Existing brand names The issue here is whether or not *brand equity* has been built-up around the name and, if so, how it can best be maintained and leveraged. We will look at brand equity in chapter 8.

A name with positive brand equity attached to it is a resource which needs careful managing. 'Southwest' is a name that no longer accurately conveys information about the airline's geographic scope, whilst Midwest Express has a name more appropriate to a regional than to a coast-to-coast operator of (albeit small) mainline jets; but the brand equity tied up in both is significant. British Midland recognised that its name was both largely unknown in the United States and unhelpfully limiting in descriptive power when it re-entered the North Atlantic market in 2001, but the brand equity it carried in existing markets was such that its rebranding included only a limited name-change – to 'bmi british midland international'. The power of a brand name is evidenced by the recognition still afforded 'Pan Am', despite the different uses to which the name has been put since the original carrier was liquidated. On the other hand, when a name yields negative brand equity the time has come to leave it behind – as was the case with ValuJet.

'Brand new' names Zero-based brand-building can be an expensive business, and the chosen brand name is an asset that should be turned into a resource purposefully deployed to convey a message about the positioning of the service concept to which it is attached. British Airways' business class sub-brands Club World and Club Europe have names which were chosen in part to convey messages about the type of service being offered; US low-fare carrier ValuJet had a name which, before it became tarnished and had to be changed, conveyed a clear sense of market positioning; UK low-fare carriers easyJet and Go convey to their targeted segments a message that they are straightforward, hassle-free brands to deal with.

Whether done internally or with the help of consultants, the naming process involves several steps.

- Consider the brand's position and the competencies that sustain it.
- Decide the sense of identity the name should convey, and the image it should help to evoke.
- Establish criteria based on the desired positioning and identity.
- Generate alternatives. These should be: simple; distinctive; and meaningful in the context of both the service concerned and the message being conveyed about the service.
- Screen alternatives. This should involve: market research; a check on the ease of pronunciation and range of meanings and associations in different languages and cultures; and verification that the name is available and legally protectable. The potential pitfalls in this area are exemplified by the early-1990s Aeroflot spin-off Touch and Go Airlines – a name with two very different implications in English.

For any company, introducing a significantly new name – as opposed to a minor change, such as from USAir to US Airways – is a risky step. Specifically, it puts at risk accumulated brand equity and, perhaps, also the loyalty of staff. For airlines, however, there is an additional conundrum: whereas some are happy to trade on the associations inherent in the 'national champion'/'flag carrier' names inherited from a different era in commercial aviation, any that want to take their brand identities truly global will suffer from having an overtly parochial brand name such as Air X or Y Airlines. Yet it is still not clear that customers in some countries are ready to see (at least the largest) carriers lose their national identities – as British Airways found out in the late 1990s. In due course this will almost certainly change, but perhaps in stages; so, just as British Telecom became BT and British Airports Authority became BAA, British Airways might eventually – if perhaps temporarily – become BA.

Logos and symbols

Most airlines have logos and symbols that are used both as shorthand for the brand name, and to reinforce the contribution of the brand name to brand identity. Sometimes these are lettered abbreviations such as those used by American Airlines and Northwest, sometimes they are stylised elaborations of the corporate name such as the Arabic calligraphy used in the Emirates logo, and sometimes they are non-vocalised symbols such as the British Airways 'speedmarque', KLM's crown, or Japan Airlines' crane.

Characters

The creation of an artificial character to personify a brand is a technique still largely restricted to fast-moving consumer-goods and a few other types of tangible products (e.g., the Michelin man). Although airlines in general have not taken this road, some have used members of staff to add a 'personal touch' to particular advertising messages. This is usually done in consumer advertising, with perhaps the best example being the decades-old presentation of 'Singapore Girl' – a presentation around which the entire corporate identity projected into consumer markets has been built. Swissair's advertising has used 'authentic passenger statements' to endorse its service. Air France Industries and Swissair have both recently been running campaigns to sell their engineering services into industrial markets using identified members of staff to add tangibility to an essentially intangible offer.

Visual clues

An airline's visual (or 'graphic') identity can help position the corporate brand; for example, the change of livery introduced by British Airways in the 1990s – which led to 'world art' appearing on aircraft tail-fins, met with mixed reactions, and was eventually terminated – was part of a wider effort to reposition the carrier's identity as less British and more global. The most potent visual clues to an airline's brand identity are:

- the appearance (including the uniforms) of staff, together with their attitudes during service encounters and the manner in which they are seen to behave (particularly, but not only, during the service delivery process);
- the appearance of servicescapes – notably facilities and equipment (including aircraft livery, and lounge and cabin decor), and signage – and their standard of upkeep;
- the feel and presentation (e.g., typeface, colour, accuracy, tone) of written communications, including letters, promotional material, and the web site as well as press releases, and briefing materials;
- the tone and presentation of advertisements.

That visual identity has a role building brand awareness as well as conveying brand image is borne out by Southwest. Until its recent modification, the carrier's livery was widely acknowledged, inside as well as outside the company, to be visually unappealing – but it was indisputably noticeable. Brand recall clearly won-out over style.

Strap-lines

Slogans, catch-phrases and strap-lines, such as 'The World's Favourite Airline', are widely used to reinforce the positioning of brand identity alongside any other message that a particular advertisement (or other form of communication) might be conveying. Only in the 1990s did United drop its 'Friendly Skies' line, after some 30 years; the decision was in part a response to research showing that many consumers in US domestic markets no longer thought of travelling by air – on United or most of its competitors – as a friendly experience. The line remains powerfully associated with United, however, and can be expected to reappear – perhaps in modified form – at some point in time.

Claims need to be believable. Having said that, it is true that when British Airways first told the world that it was their 'favourite airline' in the 1980s, nothing could have been further from the truth. The claim was aspirational – intended more to motivate staff and declare 'strategic intent' (Hamel and Prahalad, 1989) than to reflect reality at the time.

Claims also need to be unambiguous. Cyprus Airways' claim to be 'Up there with the best' leaves open the question as to whether the airline sees itself as being one of their number, or simply an outsider rubbing shoulders with 'the best' – whoever they might be.

Oral clues

The most important oral clues are the telephone manner of staff, the clarity and professionalism of gate and cabin announcements, and the tone and content of radio advertisements. (See Murley (1997) for coverage on the importance of telephone technique as a communication medium, as well as for insight into the technology and management of call centres.) Some carriers consistently use a musical theme in both television and radio advertisements and in aircraft cabins to augment name and logo in building brand identity. TWA started doing this in the 1960s with 'Up, up, and away', and Cathay Pacific managed to associate its corporate identity with a consistently used theme-tune introduced in the early 1980s.

Physical (or 'tangible') evidence

The packaging and quality of tangible service attributes such as ticket wallets, meals, and inflight amenities communicate identity. This is why whatever is offered should be well-presented; if cost is an issue and, particularly, if an attribute is not critical to the delivery of customer value in the segment concerned, it is better to offer nothing than to offer something that sends a message of cheapness or indifference.

Some airlines have contracted with manufacturers of branded food and beverage products and amenity kits. Particularly where a carrier is able to negotiate a rate below industry terms in return for a commitment to purchase branded products from manufacturers who perceive a benefit in gaining exposure for their products in an airline environment (notably in premium cabins), a mutually beneficial arrangement is possible. Many carriers, on the other hand, either do not bother with branded goods or rotate them regularly. In addition to whether the branded item is what customers actually want, there is the question of whether its image is compatible with the perceptions of its own image that the airline is trying to create.

Secondary associations

Despite all the talk of globalisation, the airline industry remains predominantly based on national identities, and the style with which services are delivered by individual carriers almost invariably has a strong national flavour. Indeed, national reputations are often deliberately leveraged into corporate brand and sub-brand identities. By 'leveraging' I mean that the airline in question consciously associates itself with certain attributes that are believed to characterise the country's 'brand' and which are relevant to the positioning of the carrier's own brand. Other sources of secondary association include alliance partners – which may include airlines, financial institutions with which a co-branded credit card is offered, and other companies associated with a carrier's FFP; alliance partners need to have similar price/quality positions in their markets – and, where possible, similar brand values – if the association is to build the respective brands as well as provide whatever extra functional benefits are on offer to customers.

Service capabilities

Consistent delivery of functional and emotional/symbolic benefits appropriate to the service concept and chosen positioning of the brand is clearly a significant brand element and a major contributor to identity and image. This element is, in turn, driven by competencies and culture.

Summary

Seat-departures might have become 'commoditised', but airline service-price offers have not. One of the reasons this is the case is that each offer embodies unique emotional benefits associated with the image of the airline concerned. Image is driven by perception. Perception is reality as far as customers are concerned. No matter how good you as an airline manager reckon your carrier's service to be, what matters most is how customers perceive it – and customers' perceptions are fashioned by a wide range of impressions. Service management is not just about designing and delivering services that look good on paper. It is about orchestrating the many different sources of these impressions – described above – into a coherent, consistent strategic theme. There are two critical strands that can be used to pull all this together.

1. **Design** Design – mentioned in chapter 4 in the context of servicescapes (e.g., aircraft cabins, airport lounges, and city ticket offices) and the more tangible aspects of service delivery – underpins external communications. All of the elements described above are, in however small a way, contributors to the manner in which customers perceive an airline. Design makes competitive strategy visible. It needs to be carefully managed, possibly in co-operation with an external consultancy.
2. **Corporate culture** Because corporate culture affects the behaviour and attitudes of staff, it is a source of the dynamics that give life to design efforts. The two must work in unison; there is no point in designing an identity which says one thing to customers and other stakeholders, and

then allowing a corporate culture to exist that says something complet-ely different. We will look at corporate culture in chapter 8.

ii. Communication objectives

> Sincerity is the key to success. If you can fake that, you got it made.
> Groucho Marx

Although we will see later in the chapter that corporate communications can have a number of objectives, our interest at this point lies primarily with its role in ensuring that the brand identity being projected is consistent with the chosen service concept(s).

Strategic and tactical messaging

> One cannot not communicate.
> Paul Watzlawick

This section will assume a distinction between strategic and tactical comm-unications that has certain practical merit but can be dangerous if taken too far. All forms of communication – even those whose immediate objectives are avowedly tactical – have the potential to affect a brand's image and positioning. Without distinguishing between the strategic and the tactical, we can say that the principal objective of communications is likely to be one or more of the following (Bradley, 1995).

- Building confidence in the brand.
- Deterring aggressive behaviour from competitors by demonstrating a determination to sustain long-term support for the brand.
- Encouraging enquiries and stimulating sales.
- Increasing frequency of purchase.

That said, we will now draw a finer-grained distinction between strategic and tactical communications.

Strategic messaging

From a strategic perspective, communications have several objectives. Each of these might relate either to the corporate brand identity or to the identity of an individual sub-brand.

1. **To build awareness** Do targeted customers know who we are, what we offer, and what we stand for?
2. **To help fashion a desired brand image** What comes to customers' minds when they think of us – particularly in terms of market positioning (quality and value) and brand personality?
3. **To promote recognition** Having been exposed to our message(s) in the past, can target customers remember the exposure?
4. **To promote brand recall** If given a product category stimulus relevant to the segment concerned (e.g., 'airline offering service between X and Y', 'low-fare airline', or 'premium quality airline'), do target customers recall us? If so, how high up their listing of recalled brands do we come?

In other words, a primary objective of communications from a strategic point of view is to build 'brand knowledge'. Brand knowledge – awareness, image, recognition, and recall – is a critical marketing resource. It strongly influences another key marketing resource: customer loyalty. Investment in the building and maintenance of these resources needs to be evaluated as rationally as investment in tangible resources. They are, after all, the resources that actually generate customers for an airline; aircraft are simply the tools that are necessary to get the job done. Expenditures and revenues associated with brand knowledge can, and should, be modelled as rationally as those arising from any other investment. They rarely are.

Tactical messaging

The purposes of tactical messaging are as follows.

1. **To inform** It is easy to assume that because we as managers know how good some aspect of our service is, everybody else knows as well.
2. **To stimulate purchase** It is not enough to tell people how good we are at doing something; it is vital that they are made aware of why what we are offering should matter to them.
3. **To provide reassurance** Particularly because services are intangible, we need to actively reassure potential customers of our ability to meet their expectations, reassure consumers about the wisdom of a purchase already made, and also hopefully promote 'customer retention'. There are few better sources of reassurance than service delivery that meets or exceeds consumers' expectations. Service delivery plays a vital part in the marketing communications mix, and is in fact the opening shot in the next 'campaign' to stimulate a purchase decision.

Every brand element has a role to play in both strategic and tactical communications. Each is a predictive clue; as with any investigation – an 'investigation' which in this case is being conducted, perhaps subconsciously, by targeted customers – the more clues there are pointing consistently in the same direction, the stronger the customer's conclusion is going to be regarding whether or not a particular brand offers the type of value he or she is looking for. Clues are not all perceived to be equally predictive, but together they build a 'case'. In the short run, an esteemed brand name is perhaps the strongest predictive clue to brand performance – but it is potentially a wasting resource in the absence of constant care and attention. 'Care and attention' mean ensuring that all brand elements are integrated so that they tell a consistent story to targeted customers, and are periodically refreshed or re-launched as the market changes.

Leveraging consistency

A strong brand can be 'extended' within a 'brand hierarchy'. We will look briefly at both these concepts.

Brand extension

An airline wanting to brand a new service-price offer has broadly two choices.

1. Create an identity around a new brand name. This can be expensive given high and rising media costs and the absence of the communication economies of scale that can arise when a single, existing brand identity is being supported by every message. On the other hand, a start-up has no choice other than to follow this route, and several in the low-cost/low-fare segment have managed to establish brand identities by relying more on astute public relations than paid advertising.
2. Create an identity by leveraging into new markets the goodwill embodied in an existing brand name. This is 'brand extension'. It can take two forms.
    *   *Line or range extension* Line extension occurs when a new segment is entered within a product-market domain already served by the existing brand (e.g., introducing a new class of onboard service). This type of extension might pursue new sources of revenue in their own right, or it might be part of a competitive strategy intended either to attack or pre-empt competitors.

- *Category extension* In this case a different product-market domain is entered (e.g., launching a branded consultancy service trading off the airline's expertise and name recognition). This is often part of a corporate strategy of diversification. An interesting example of category extension is provided by the Virgin brand name, which has been stretched from music publishing to airlines (four at the time of writing), and on to retailing, cola, financial services, and various other ventures in a wide range of product-market domains. Virgin stretches its brand not by deploying specific technical competencies, but by leveraging its key corporate resource: an image of youth, dynamism, innovation, and value for money (Ind, 1997). The owner of mid-1990s UK low-fare start-up easyJet is also engaged in brand extension, having moved into car rental and subsequently into other service categories.

Full-service network carriers have taken different approaches on entering low-fare/no-frills markets. Delta and United, for instance, opted for line extension by branding internal units as 'Delta Express' and 'Shuttle by United'. British Airways, on the other hand, opted to launch a similar venture as an ostensibly stand-alone subsidiary called 'Go', and KLMuk followed the same route with Buzz.

Arguments in favour of brand extension include the following.

- Because brand awareness already exists, customers might perceive purchase risk to be substantially lower.
- Economies of scale and scope could be available (Holloway, 1997).
- Risk of early post-launch failure is probably reduced by direct association with an existing master-brand which the airline would not want damaged.

Brand extensions are not risk-free, however.

- It is possible that the new service will gain little from association with the master-brand or, worse, that the association will generate confusion and alienation amongst customers and staff alike.
- Failure could weaken the image of the master-brand. Continental Lite comes to mind as an example of both this and the previous point.
- Even if total failure is avoided, the extension may struggle to establish a separate identity. Low-fare units in particular might come to be seen as little more than a de-tuned version of the master-brand sold at deeply discounted prices.
- Master-brand sales could be cannibalised.

There is no 'correct' answer. Extensions need to be judged with regard to what benefits the master-brand can bring to the new product in terms of salience and favourable associations in consumers' minds within the targeted segment, and also what impact association with that product might have on the master-brand. Two forms of brand extension that have become increasingly popular in the airline business over the last decade are code-sharing and franchising (see Holloway, 1997, 1998b).

Brand architecture

Brand architecture generally takes one of two forms in the airline industry: the stand-alone corporate brand, or the brand hierarchy. Choices tie in closely with the alternative approaches to service concepts we met in chapter 3.

Stand-alone corporate brand This might be an independent carrier (e.g., Southwest), or it might be a subsidiary of an airline parent which does not directly 'endorse' it by tying the parent's name to that of the subsidiary (e.g., Buzz). In either case, it is the stand-alone corporate identity which is projected to customers – albeit perhaps with some implicit 'halo effect' if the entity concerned has a widely recognised parent. In most service industries, and the airline business is no exception, it is the corporate brand rather than individually branded services that stands out. Many 'branded' services are in fact little more than product labels, offering customers no additional benefits over and above the product's functional benefits together with any psycho-social benefits associated with the corporate brand. Individual services – such as a named business or first class – are in this case just components of a single corporate brand (Berry et al, 1988).

Corporate master-brand heading a hierarchy of sub-brands with master-brand endorsement In this case, the corporate brand identity is extended to a hierarchy of sub-brands. The approach might be appropriate when there is a diversity of businesses within the corporate portfolio, or when market segmentation and/or operating economics argue for making a clearly distinct offer separate from the main corporate brand. Communication economies of scale available to a large corporate brand can still be available in this sub-branded structure provided that the sub-brands are clearly endorsed, so raising awareness, recognition, and recall of the master-brand. For this type of brand hierarchy to work well, the core values of the master-brand should permeate the entire portfolio of different service concepts, providing a platform off which sub-brands can be developed. Unless these core values can be transmitted to each sub-brand in a way that makes sense to the segment of demand the sub-brand is targeting, the logic of brand extension and the particular hierarchy itself are open to question.

At most small airlines and quite a few large ones as well, the question of sub-branding is moot. Many rely on their corporate brand alone to identify both different categories of air transport service (with names given to classes of inflight service being just labels), and also any related services they offer – such as ground handling, catering, and third-party engineering.

Where sub-brands do exist, they can cover different service concepts within the passenger air transport business; these concepts might encompass service delivery within the same aircraft (e.g., BA's Club World and World Traveller sub-brands) or by different fleets (e.g., American Eagle). Sub-brands might also be extended to cargo operations (e.g., British Airways World Cargo), and to businesses other than air transport (e.g., Lufthansa Technik). Each sub-brand needs to make a clearly distinct value proposition, delivered to equally distinct specifications. Part of each value proposition should be an emotional appeal relevant to targeted segments of demand which exists over and above the functional benefits offered and whatever appeal is conveyed by the corporate master-brand; without this additional value, we are dealing not with a sub-brand but with a product name. It is, of course, not always easy to distinguish the two: is a distribution channel such as Lufthansa's online 'InfoFlyway', an ongoing promotional medium such as British Airways' 'World Offers', or a hub such as Crossair's Basle 'EuroCross' a name or a brand? Some marketers might like to think of these as sub-brands, but this must be open to doubt.

iii. External communications: customers

> Half the money I spend on advertising is wasted.
> The problem is that I don't know which half.
> Lord Lever

External communications have a variety of objectives and come in a variety of forms. Although the elements of the marketing communications mix (advertising, PR, sales promotion, etc.) are the most commonly recognised forms of external communications, everything an airline does to present itself visually (e.g., marketing communications, facilities and equipment, correspondence, web sites, staff appearance and behaviour) and orally (e.g., telephone manner, tone of encounters between staff and customers or other external stakeholders) is part of the external communications effort. This effort needs to be managed with consistency and constancy of purpose. Consistency means, for example, not that every message is the same but that there is a recognisable thread to the presentation and tone of messages; readers of certain print media, for instance, sub-consciously recognise that an advertisement featuring a large block of blue containing a short, white-lettered message and supplemented by explanatory text is a message from British Airways. This type of design-influenced consistency in the way the corporate identity is presented is particularly relevant to an airline because service companies need to use every lever available to make their offers as tangible as possible in the minds of customers.

External communications are targeted at three groups in particular: customers; intermediaries in distribution channels; and other stakeholders. Our interest in this section lies with customers. We need here to bear in mind the distinction already drawn between customers (the people who make pre-purchase assessments of competing service-price offers, experience delivery of pre-purchase services such as reservations, and make purchase decisions) and consumers (the people who experience delivery of post-purchase services – most notably the air transportation service). Whereas we have been largely treating the two as synonymous and using the single catch-all 'customers', in the current section of the chapter these words need to be used more precisely.

This leads us to another distinction which should be borne in mind. Purchase decision processes by end-consumers – individuals or families travelling on vacation, for example – usually involve fewer people than decision processes within organizations. In the latter case it is necessary to identify the individuals concerned; sometimes referred to in aggregate as a 'buying centre', 'decision centre' or 'decision-making unit', their roles and respective influence need to be established so that communications can be properly targeted. There is in fact a substantial literature contrasting consumer and organizational (or 'industrial') decision processes, but this lies outside the scope of the present book.

Purchase behaviour

Clearly, the development of both a brand identity and a marketing communications programme should to a significant extent be keyed-off what it is that stimulates customers in the targeted market or segment to purchase particular services. This takes us back to the importance of customer understanding, touched on in chapter 3.

Broadly speaking, there are two generic models of consumer purchase decision-making (Tidd et al, 1997).

1. **Rational/utilitarian model** This describes a rational process involving: information search, evaluation of alternatives, followed by purchase. Marketing communications might, for example, be used to inform and/ or to stress benefits known to be significant as part of a particular segment's evaluation process.
2. **Behavioural model** This describes a process of attitudinal change leading to a behavioural outcome: awareness changes to interest, then (perhaps via improved understanding and a developing conviction regarding the service) to desire, and finally leads to action – that is, to purchase. (This is commonly known as the AIDA model.) Marketing communications can be targeted at different points in the chain, depending upon their purpose.

The balance between rational and behavioural influences is likely to be shaped by the level of consumer 'involvement' in a particular purchase. The level of involvement in a purchase decision depends upon:

*   the knowledge and experience of the buyer;
*   the 'social visibility' of the decision – that is, the extent to which the choice is visible to others whose opinions matter to the purchaser;
*   the financial and other risks perceived to be potentially present.

'High involvement' purchase decisions require greater information search and deliberation than 'low involvement' decisions.

Bateson (1995) has proposed a three-stage model of service purchase behaviour which contains elements of both the rational/utilitarian and behavioural approaches.

1. The **pre-purchase stage**: Why do customers buy?
    *   What are the needs and wants they are trying to satisfy?
    *   How do they search for information about alternative means for satisfying these needs and wants – for information about alternative benefits? In other words, how do they develop an 'awareness set' of alternatives (Howard and Sheth, 1969)?
    *   How do they arrive at a shortlist of potential brand alternatives about which they have positive feelings (i.e., 'the evoked set' or 'consideration set')?
    *   How do they make their final choice?
    Are we in their awareness set? If not, we need to focus communications on building awareness. The components of brand awareness are brand recognition (a consumer's ability to confirm prior exposure to the brand when given a brand element – often a name – as a cue) and brand

recall (a consumer's ability to retrieve the brand from memory when given a cue that relates either to product category – such as 'low-fare airlines' – or need satisfaction – such as 'business class service from London to Sydney' – but does not specifically identify the brand concerned). Together, brand awareness and brand image comprise a consumer's 'brand knowledge'; one of the fundamental tasks of external communications is to ensure that target customers have the desired brand knowledge structure – that is, to ensure that brand knowledge is appropriate to the intended positioning of the service and is likely to encourage purchase (ibid). A primary purpose of any properly managed package of brand elements is to stimulate recognition and recall.

Are we in the evoked set? If not, we need to find out whether their feelings towards us are neutral or negative, and in either case address the problem with appropriate communications (e.g., stressing benefits). If we are in the evoked set, communications should reinforce the perceptions that put us there (and integrated management of service design, communications, and delivery should reinforce and build on the reality underlying these perceptions).

2. The **consumption stage**: How do consumers react to the service delivery experience? In particular, which aspects of service delivery have the most impact on the 'post-choice' evaluation process (an early and important part of post-purchase evaluation)?

3. The **post-purchase evaluation**: To what extent do consumers perceive that the service rendered has matched expectations? In other words, how satisfied or dissatisfied are they with the service outcome?

    *   What drives consumers' expectations?
    *   What drives their perceptions of service?
    *   Is the consumer going to be a positive or negative participant, through word-of-mouth comments, in the airline's future marketing efforts?

Communication in the pre-purchase stage

The characteristics of intangibility, inseparability, and variability we met in chapter 3 make the purchase of services a more complex process than buying goods. The following criteria can influence service purchase decisions: factors internal to the purchaser; perceptions of risk; and external factors.

Factors internal to the purchaser These include:

*   Individual needs, wants, and preferences.
*   Past experience with the airline concerned.

- Expectations with regard to alternative carriers.

Risk The issue here is the degree of confidence consumers can have that they know what they are buying – whether they are first-time users of an airline's services or repeat purchasers. The topic of consumer risk is often approached by categorising products according to whether or not they possess certain 'qualities'.

- **Search qualities** Products high in search qualities are those which have attributes that consumers can search out and assess before making a purchase decision (e.g., consumer durables).
- **Experience qualities** Products high in experience qualities are those with attributes that can only be properly assessed in use (e.g., a meal in a fine restaurant).
- **Credence qualities** Products high in credence qualities have attributes that can only be evaluated over time (e.g., surgical procedures, insurance).

Most products have elements of all three qualities, but a preponderance of one. Tangible goods, for example, tend to have more search qualities than services, while services are long on experience qualities and, in some cases, credence qualities. Airline service has all three: the physical appearance of a ticket office and the demeanour of its staff or the presentation of a web site can be 'searched' for clues; prospective customers, particularly those travelling on business, also must give 'credence' to the likelihood of a favourable airline response if things go wrong – flight delays, missed connections, or misdirected baggage, for example. In essence, however, airline service is more an 'experience product' than a 'search product' or a 'credence product'.

The purchase of airline services can be considered riskier than the purchase of tangible goods because their experiential quality makes the outcome particularly prone to 'variability', and because the simultaneity of production and consumption – that is, the presence of the consumer in the service delivery system – makes the consequences of an unexpected outcome more immediate.

There are several types of risk a service purchaser may face.

- **Performance risk** Because air transport services are intangible and experiential, they cannot be 'test-driven' or in some other way evaluated prior to purchase. It is therefore difficult to assess in advance the risk that the service might fail to offer expected performance benefits (e.g., flights might be delayed or baggage might be misrouted).

- **Financial risk** Whatever the actual level of performance, a service might not be considered worth the fare paid for it. This is a risk faced more by passengers travelling on 'full fares', particularly in premium classes, than by those using low or promotional fares.
- **Psychological risk** The service might fail to deliver expected psychological benefits (e.g., enhancement of self-image derived from flying with a particular airline or in a premium class).
- **Social risk** The service might fail to deliver expected social benefits (e.g., esteem within social reference groups derived from association with a particular airline or service).

Customers engage in several risk reduction strategies.

- They can rely on satisfactory past experience with an airline as an indicator of future satisfaction. This points to something we will be looking at in chapter 8: airlines able to nurture a large base of loyal customers can create a significant barrier against competitors. It is one of the primary objectives of brand building – that is, the consistent management of brand elements to create an image which is appealing to targeted customers and reduces their perception of purchase risk.
- They can accept word-of-mouth comments from others. This also underlines the importance of a loyal customer base: aside from their potential repeat purchases, loyal customers often play an important advocacy role on behalf of airlines.
- They can search out additional information, looking in particular at various brand elements for clues which might support an opinion about the service. This affords the airline an opportunity to provide appropriate predictive clues – with 'appropriate' meaning clues that are consistent with the level of service being provided, and which are both integrated across brand elements and able to convey information to prospective customers about what they should expect. If our advertising is poor in quality or credibility, if our people and facilities are scruffy, if our equipment is dirty, and if we send letters with spelling mistakes on company letterhead, we are inviting negative predictions about service quality; if we have some of these problems but not all of them or not all the time, we are at best sending an inconsistent message.

External factors The most important external factors influencing pre-purchase decisions are as follows.

- The availability and relative prices of alternatives.

- The context – for example, whether the planned trip is for business or pleasure.
- The efforts made by the particular airlines competing for business in a given segment to reduce perceived purchase risk. This goes back to the question of 'clues' mentioned above. Efforts made could encompass:
  - the conveying of an integrated, accurate, and consistent message about service levels using vehicles such as marketing communications, the appearance of facilities and equipment, and the knowledge, attitudes, and behaviour of employees;
  - the use of promotional offers to stimulate trial usage – often as part of a wider capacity management programme (e.g., a low-season 'two-for-the-price-of-one'/'companion flies free' ticket offer);
  - the use of service guarantees and quality certification (e.g., ISO 9000 and similar programmes) to reassure cargo customers.

Communicating during the pre-purchase stage   The following questions need to be answered when assessing both design of the service-price offer, and design of pre-purchase communication strategies.

1. What must we offer and do to **qualify** – that is, to get into a targeted customer's 'awareness set' of suppliers that come to mind when a purchase is being considered and 'evoked set' of acceptable choice alternatives (Howard and Sheth, 1969)?
2. What must we offer and do in order to **sell** to targeted customers?
3. What must we offer and do in order to be their carrier of **preference**?

There is a clear linkage between these questions and our consideration of resources, competencies, and competitive advantage in chapter 2. It can be expressed as an additional question.

4. Are we able to deliver at a profit whatever service-price offer is required to qualify, sell, and – particularly – build customer preference within the targeted segment(s)? In other words, can we *Manage to Make Money*?

Because airlines are asking themselves these questions in respect of perhaps tens of millions of individual customers, it is inevitable that the answers will represent a 'common denominator', making it equally inevitable that some of those many individuals will be dissatisfied with particular aspects of a service package addressed at 'average' customer expectations. An additional challenge arises from the fact that in a dynamic marketplace answers to each question will shift, perhaps fairly rapidly, over time. Nonetheless, unearthing answers should help an airline target its services at segments in which its competitive advantage is relevant, and also guide design of the service package and communications strategy.

Advertising, PR, sales promotion, and direct marketing will be amongst the communication tools used in the pre-purchase stage. Choice of medium will depend upon the specific audience and objectives.

1. **Existing customers**

- Remind them about the brand, and inform them about anything new in what it has to offer.
- Stimulate increased or earlier purchases.

Assuming segmentation has produced the required information, we might want to target our most valuable customers, our most loyal customers, those with good future revenue prospects, and customers most likely to respond favourably to the current campaign (based on their previous buying behaviour).

2. **New customers**

- Build brand awareness and interest (with 'top-of-mind' awareness being the ideal, but 'unaided' or even 'aided' awareness perhaps being more cost-effective to achieve).
- Reduce perceived purchase risk.
- Increase the probability of a purchase. An aggressive approach to stimulating trials from among competitors' high-value customers was Virgin Atlantic's mid-1990s offer of free companion tickets to any purchaser of Mid Class or Upper Class travel who was a member of BA's Executive Club FFP and had in excess of a certain mileage to their credit.
- Shape expectations about the type of service to be anticipated. A key role of marketing communications is to generate expectations amongst customers and potential customers and, by helping to manage expectations in this way, to mediate between expectations and perceptions of service. (The more focused a service, the more important it is to communicate the nature of the offer to avoid as far as possible 'the wrong' customers entering the system, becoming dissatisfied, and perhaps thereafter spreading negative word-of-mouth. For example, Southwest wants to avoid attracting customers who expect a gourmet meal and interline baggage transfers.)

Attaining focus with prospects is not as straightforward as targeting existing customers. One important variable is whether or not we have a good profile of prospects – perhaps based on knowledge of existing customers, where this is relevant to the markets under consideration.

3. **Both existing and new customers**

- Create/reinforce a competitive image attractive to targeted segments and clearly distinct from the images of competitors.
- Build brand loyalty and brand equity. There is – or at least should be – a great deal of symbolic value in marketing communications, and through its impact on socio-psychological attributes associated with the airline's corporate brand and its individual service concepts this symbolic value should contribute to brand equity. Consistency, timing, volume, style, and appropriateness to the target audience are all factors affecting whether communications will build brand equity; in the long term, however, brand equity can only be sustained by delivering service that meets or exceeds customers' expectations.

Marketing communications in the pre-purchase stage have to be balanced between the strategic generation of awareness and building of a brand on the one hand and tactical, shorter-term revenue stimulation on the other. Tactical communications tend to be oriented towards specific products (including destinations) and sub-brands. Potential customers need to be informed, persuaded that purchase risks are insubstantial, and reminded about the benefits specifically targeted at them and the merits of those benefits relative to what competitors are offering. This might involve single-benefit positioning (e.g., Cathay Pacific: 'Arrive in Better Shape'; KLM: 'The Reliable Airline'), double-benefit positioning (e.g., Thai: 'Centuries-old Tradition, State-of-the-Art Technology'), or even multiple-benefit positioning; but as more benefits are pushed, the scope for disbelief or confusion widens (Holloway, 1998b). People have limited cognitive capabilities, with the result that whatever information is presented to them should not be too complex and should focus in particular on those benefits most likely to lead to a favourable purchase decision in the segment being targeted.

The broader an airline's competitive scope (i.e., the more service concepts it has developed), the more different types of customer it has to target, and the more important it becomes to ensure that each message gets through to the right people. Attracting customers to a service-price offer from the wrong segments can cause a mismatch between experience and expectations, both for them and for customers actually targeted, leading to dissatisfaction amongst both groups. It can nonetheless be difficult to prevent segments receiving messages aimed at other segments. Thus, promotional pricing intended for the leisure segment might aggravate passengers travelling in the same class on full fares, whilst messages trumpeting quality improvements targeted primarily at business class travellers will probably come to the attention of those in the 'main cabin' and might raise their expectations. Compounding the problem is the fact that most people who travel on business are also leisure travellers at some time each year.

Communication during the consumption stage

As well as potential customers, marketing communications can also be addressed to consumers already participating in the service delivery system. Individual service encounters communicate messages about the airline. Routine encounters can be scripted, perhaps subject to as much latitude as the nature of a particular type of encounter allows; non-routine encounters will in many cases be unscripted, and staff might be empowered to make their own judgements about how to act within defined parameters. Low-fare/no-frills service concepts clearly allow less latitude for unscripted, empowered encounters than do more labour-intensive, attribute-rich concepts.

Service environments also convey messages. Encounters and environments are as much a part of the marketing communications effort as, say, advertising or public relations; they are strongly oriented towards generating repeat business.

Thus, key communications media during consumption are the facilities, equipment, processes, and staff of the airline itself. Communication tasks are:

- to reassure consumers that they have made a good choice;
- to influence consumers' perceptions of the service being delivered, in order to ensure that it matches or exceeds their expectations.

Communication in the post-consumption stage

A third category of customer to be communicated with is comprised of consumers who have already been through the service delivery system. Whether or not they become consumers again (assuming a future need to travel and the availability of a choice between alternative airlines) will depend in part upon how perceptions of their experiences measure up to prior expectations. Prior expectations will have been shaped by any earlier experiences with the airline, word-of-mouth endorsements, the activities of competitors, and – perhaps most importantly – by the airline's own marketing communications. Marketing communications are also a significant benchmark against which consumers make post-consumption evaluations of the service experience. There is clearly a natural tension between, on the one hand, the use of marketing communications to stimulate demand and, on the other, the need to moderate the message in order to restrain expectations and so create a higher probability of consumer satisfaction.

The communication objectives in the post-consumption stage are essentially the same as those in the consumption stage.

- To stimulate positive word-of-mouth: the best way to do this is to deliver service that is perceived by customers to meet or exceed their expectations.
- To stimulate repeat purchases: service delivery is, once again, the critical factor, although other forms of communication can also play a role in helping shape consumers' post-experience evaluation and so the likelihood of repurchase. At this point, the cycle returns to the pre-purchase stage.

Conclusion

The purpose of communicating with customers in general is to raise the percentages of people in each targeted segment who are aware of the airline's service-price offer, have tried it, have repeated the purchase, and are willing to do so again. This is not a simple challenge. Every time an airline's people, equipment or facilities impinge on a customer's perceptions, a communication is taking place just as much as when that customer sees an advertisement, a piece of PR, a web-site or a sponsored event or as when she is exposed to direct marketing or personal selling. We need to be thinking in terms of the image we want to create, how controllable each form of communication is both in the context of delivering a specific tactical message and reinforcing a consistent brand image, how best we can control it, what if anything it costs in aggregate and per contact, and how selective it is in targeting audiences. It is very easy to assume that marketing communications are simply a question of whether or not to spend a fortune on an advertising slot during the Superbowl. Important though this might be as a consideration in some carriers' marketing communications strategies, there is a lot more to communicating than just the 'Madison Avenue stuff'; whenever a reservations agent answers a call, a cabin attendant serves coffee, or a ramp worker washes a vehicle this is marketing communications in action. These 'touchpoints' need to be proactively and coherently managed.

iv. External communications: other stakeholders

Because the airline industry still relies heavily on intermediaries to distribute information about its services, and because these intermediaries can have a significant effect on customers' choice of carrier in some segments, communicating with travel agents is an important (and expensive) part of most airlines' marketing communications function – the exception being those low-cost carriers which only sell direct (e.g., easyJet). The same is true with regard to informing and training alliance partners' staff wherever they have taken over marketing activities for a carrier in the partner's home territory.

Looking at external stakeholders more generally, Kotler (1984) has suggested that two additional 'Ps' should be added to the 4Ps (or, in the case of services, the 7Ps) of the marketing mix: political power and public opinion. We saw in chapter 2 that the resource-based theory of competitive strategy argues the need for access to whatever resources are required by a particular choice of strategy (or, alternatively, that resource availability should dictate strategy). At any one time, some resources are likely to be held internally whilst others are in the hands of external parties. These external resource-holders include potential customers (resource: their spending power), potential lenders and investors (resource: finance), potential employees (resource: skills and commitment), central governments and their agencies (resource: the right to do business, either at all or in specific markets), and issue groups along with general public opinion (resource: legitimacy). Some of these audiences overlap. Box 6.2 describes a body of theory which tries to explain the significance of resource acquisition to the attainment of organizational goals.

Box 6.2: Resource-dependence theory

The basic premise of resource-dependence theory (Pfeffer and Salancik, 1979) is that because the external environment exerts such a powerful influence on their performance, organizations must attempt to actively manage it. They have to do this because it is necessary for them to draw resources (such as capital, labour, equipment, knowledge, access to distribution channels, and consumer markets) from their environments. This dependency on others for the provision of critical resources requires that outsiders be managed so as to insulate the organization as far as possible from any adverse effects of their demands (i.e., influence, negotiating strength, etc.). One form of insulation is to create 'counter-dependence'; another is to dilute overdependence by creating multiple dependencies (e.g., having alternative sources of supply for key inputs); a third is to regulate

dependencies contractually. Diversification, vertical and horizontal inte-
gration, joint ventures, interlocking directorships (e.g., linking the organiz-
ation with suppliers, partners, distributors, and/or customers), and lobby-
ing (to manage regulatory dependency) are amongst the phenomena that
have been examined using the resource-dependence framework.

Power can be expected to accrue to internal actors best able to take
advantage of opportunities that present themselves for coping with uncert-
ainties arising from whatever resource dependence contingencies apply to
a particular airline at a particular point in time.

Our concern in respect of external communications with parties other
than customers lies primarily in communicating the identity and values of
the corporate brand, and furthering its interests with regard to identified
issues. Individual sub-brands communicate primarily with consumers and
so do not generally have such a wide range of stakeholders to influence as
do their corporate master-brands – although they might.

Beneath any significant factor revealed by scanning an airline's internal
or external environments (perhaps as part of a formal planning process)
might lie an identifiable 'strategic issue', around which different groups of
stakeholders may coalesce (Joyce and Woods, 1996). A strategic issue can
be defined as, '….something which causes concern because of its expected
impact on the aims of the organization (expressed as goals, mandates, mission, values, etc.) and which requires urgent action if the organization is to
survive and prosper' (ibid: 58). Communications – including, but not limited to, marketing communications – can help secure required resources by
influencing stakeholders and the issues important to them.

'Environmental influencing' is a planned communications effort intended to shape or change both the general attitudes of influential stakeholders
and their expectations with regard to specific, targeted issues. Given the
range of vital issues which confront the industry, the need for proactive
influencing by individual airlines and by industry associations has never
been greater. Although messages to each constituency will have to be tailored to get the airline's particular point(s) across, this needs to be done
within the context of a single, credible, positioning and a consistently
adhered-to 'tone'. (See Heath (1997) for a detailed treatment of issues
management from a public policy perspective.)

Finally, it is worth noting that in addition to the inherent good they achieve, charitable support programmes can also be a source of positive PR
with external stakeholders – including customers. (Dasburg (1998a), for
example, provides a description of the Northwest AirCares programme.)

v. Internal communications

> I don't want any yes-men in this organization. I want people to speak
> their minds – even if it does cost them their jobs.
> Samuel Goldwyn

Internal communication channels – both vertical (up as well as down) and horizontal (between functions and/or teams) – need to be kept open. In particular, front-line personnel – the people whose actions contribute so much to the fashioning of brand image – need to understand an airline's service concept(s), and they need to be able to translate current strategies into workable tasks and activities. A fundamental objective of internal communications is therefore to help staff understand and maintain the airline's brand values and strategies – what it is trying to achieve for its customers – and the centrality of their role both in the successful delivery of these values, and in brand-building generally. Indeed, de Chernatony and McDonald (1998: xi) argue that in the service sector branding efforts should first be directed at employees, because unless they understand the vision for a brand, and its values, personality, and positioning they will not be able to convey any of these to customers and other stakeholders.

An equally fundamental objective of internal communications is to motivate staff to actually deliver brand values; the intention should be to leverage understanding into commitment and, ultimately, job satisfaction. The larger the airline, the more important it is likely to be that the service concepts and associated brand values need to be clearly communicated through a formal, sustained education programme. To help align actual behaviour with strategy, this type of internal communications effort should be reinforced by:

- the development of departmental, team, and personal goals consistent with both short- and long-term corporate objectives;
- focused training to help individuals and teams attain their goals;
- a compensation system that recognises and rewards goal attainment;
- senior executive behaviour that is at all times consistent with the airline's brand identity and underlying brand values;
- regular updates on performance via newsletters and bulletin boards (both paper and electronic), clearly linking what is being achieved to current strategic themes in terms that people can relate to as part of their daily work.

Ind (1997: 84) observes that, 'To sustain the corporate brand, employees need to be able to perform their jobs functionally and they need to understand and be motivated by the higher aspirations of the company. Both are required and both need consistent and effective communication.' Generating and sustaining commitment is not a task made easier when staff work semi-independently, as many do in airlines (e.g., flight crew, cabin attendants, and personnel at outstations), or when staff are part-time or employed on temporary contracts. The only solution is consistent communication of core values by a credible leadership – and even this might not be a complete solution.

Sources of internal communication

Staff are impacted by various types of corporate communication: external communications received internally; explicit internal communications; and implicit internal communications.

External communications received internally

The marketing communications to which they are exposed can affect the perceptions employees hold of their airline, and may influence how they see their role in the service delivery system. Whilst this can and should be motivational, it may in fact be demotivating for staff to observe being marketed a level of service they know cannot be delivered. There is, for example, no point in having communications promise, say, the highest standards of customer care while top management continuously reinforces the importance of cost-cutting over all other performance criteria. What happens in this case is that:

- uncertainty is created amongst staff as to the airline's true priorities;
- there is little likelihood that customers' expectations will be met.

Explicit internal communications

Internal communications can be 'broadcast' using memos, newsletters, and intranets, or 'narrowcast' to specific employee groups and (usually in a task context) to individuals; all should be consistent with the airline's core values. For example, broadcast communications promoting involvement and empowerment will only generate cynicism if the management style experienced every day by groups and individuals is secretive and control-oriented; 'broadcasts' from top management will do little good unless they are consistent with the corporate culture that guides everyday 'narrowcast' communications, both formal and informal.

An organized and focused internal communications programme can be an invaluable tool for motivating employees and keeping them centred on the customer. Airlines that believe the key to customer satisfaction lies in putting their people first might choose to adopt an 'internal marketing' approach. Two ideas underlie the internal marketing concept.

- Employees, if they are to deliver high quality service whether internally or externally, need to be 'sold' on what they are doing. This mirrors external marketing insofar as it requires the researching of employees' needs, wants, and preferences, the design of job specifications and reward packages to suit the requirements of different segments of the workforce, and the use of both internal and external communications to convey the values, culture, service strategy, and objectives of the organization to employees. Satisfied employees, it is believed, lead to satisfied customers; we will meet this argument again in chapter 8. Employees, like customers, are knowing and sceptical. They realise that the airline wants to influence, if not control, their behaviours and attitudes. They will look for substance beneath the motivating prose. Above all, if top management expects employees to respect customers, top management needs to respect employees. The recent history of labour relations at some airlines suggests this is not always the case: when senior managers award themselves multi-million dollar bonuses and stock options whilst at the same time forcing benefit cuts onto front-line employees – something that happened at more than one US major during the 1990s – the message being communicated to those employees is not one of openness, trust, teamwork, and shared commitment. It can then be no surprise that employees bargain aggressively when the economic cycle turns upwards.
- Everybody in the organization has a customer. Treating internal customers with the same consideration given by front-line staff to the expectations of the final consumer contributes greatly to the quality of the end-product. It can also consolidate a 'service culture' within an airline, built around a broadly understood and coherent sense of brand values and positioning.

As with external marketing, the purposes of internal marketing are to build awareness and affect behaviour. More specifically, internal marketing moves the focus of HRM away from administration and control towards achieving an alignment between human resource potential on the one hand and organizational objectives and strategies on the other (Collins and Payne, 1994) – and, importantly, towards gaining the commitment of employees to those objectives and strategies (Piercy, 1997). Grönroos

(2000: 335) proposes a definition which stresses that internal marketing is not simply a management tool, but a platform on which relationships between employees and organization are built. He argues that the objective of internal marketing is,

> ….to create, maintain and enhance internal relationships between people in the organization, regardless of their position as customer contact staff, support staff, team leaders, supervisors or managers, so that they first feel motivated to provide services to internal customers as well as to external customers in a customer-oriented and service-minded way, and second have the skills and knowledge required as well as the support needed from managers and supervisors, internal service providers, systems and technology to be able to perform in such a manner.

The design of an internal communications programme needs to address questions similar to those that must be addressed when communicating externally: What are the objectives of the communications strategy? Who are the target audiences? What is the key message for each target audience? What are the appropriate media for each target audience? What is the timeframe for each stage of the communications strategy? How will we know that the communications have been received? How can we evaluate their impact? Are we recognising that communication is a two-way process that involves listening as well as talking? In other words, are we engaged in internal *marketing* rather than internal *selling*? Evidence – not specific to the airline industry – suggests that internal marketing programmes have in fact had mixed results, and indicates that problems arise from insufficient top-management commitment and from expecting too much too soon (Mercer, 1997).

Implicit internal communications

The upkeep of equipment and facilities together with the choice of issues that top management gives attention to have high symbolic value, and are capable of communicating a great deal to staff (as well as other stakeholders) regarding an airline's core values. These variables are examples of implicit internal communications media. Another important medium is corporate culture, which we will be looking at in chapter 8.

The critical importance of internal communications to service delivery

Before moving on, I want to reproduce a quotation from a senior industry practitioner (Sue Moore from British Airways, quoted in Irons, 1997b: 20) which emphasises the critical importance of internal communications to successful service delivery.

> The big difference in the marketing of services is people. You are relying on them to execute the thinking. This adds even more importance to the need for communication, especially internal communication. They have got to understand what it is you are trying to achieve. Training in marketing of those outside of 'marketing' is, in this sense, vital. Motivation is also a key issue in this. In fact, I think that we have to put more effort into the internal aspects in the future and are already moving this way. So, the recent re-launch of Business Class has had more resources put behind internal marketing than ever before. For example, we have spent £7 million on cabin crew training alone. I would go so far as to say that I think we could even come to the conclusion that in a future change we could limit external communication to a targeted audience, via mailing for example, and concentrate the rest of the spend on internal development.

Whilst the major re-launch of a service is always likely to be accompanied by a significant external communications programme (as was, in fact, the case with regard to BA's re-launch of Club World in 2000/2001), the fundamental point in the quotation is absolutely sound: internal audiences are critical to external effectiveness.

Communications within alliances

Alliances pose several challenges to the corporate communications effort.

1. Internal communications within alliances have to be made relevant, meaningful, and non-threatening to staff. Unless this can be done, they will have little positive impact on customers.
2. They have to be made relevant and meaningful to customers.
3. A credible modus vivendi has to be found between the identity of the alliance and the corporate (as well as sub-brand) identities of its members.

Clear, consistent, timely internal communications are the key to building sound alliance relationships (Bleeke and Ernst, 1993), particularly in the early implementation stage when alliance-building activities are still likely to be more symbolic than real and uncertainties abound. Perspectives need to be understood from both (or all) sides. External communications are also important, because to varying degrees different stakeholder groups affected by an alliance will want to know where they stand.

As an alliance starts to communicate in its own right to build awareness and identity through advertising, shared sales outlets, and co-branding in partners' servicescapes, questions immediately arise about the relationship of this identity to, and its possible effect upon, the corporate identities and positioning of members' own brands. Both Star and **one**world, for example, have established clear visual identities; what neither they nor any other alliance has yet done is establish meaningful 'points of difference' that matter to customers and are separate from the various 'points of difference' already established by their members. There is clearly considerable scope for confusion and misunderstanding amongst staff – particularly while alliance relationships remain fluid; a major task for the internal communications effort has to be to tackle this problem.

vi. Development of an integrated communications programme: melding brand elements into a credible message

The essence of the communications challenge is to manage sometimes conflicting relationships with a variety of audiences. It is important to understand what each audience needs to know at a given point in time, establish clear communication objectives to guide the briefs given either internally or externally to those responsible for orchestrating communications, and then approach each audience in a way that is appropriate to them and yet consistent with what we want to achieve in respect of the other audiences.

Individual messages can have one or more of many different purposes, justifying their own particular communications mix, but the fundamental long-term purpose of an integrated communications programme is to build trust amongst stakeholders in the consistency of service and brand values. The more global an airline's operations become, the more difficult this is to achieve because the number of stakeholders increases, as does the complexity involved in recognising and managing their perceptions. The fact that air transport involves consumers who might be quite cosmopolitan in their outlooks and tastes means that segments can increasingly be targeted for communication with regard to lifestyle, self-image, and worldview rather than national or cultural origins; whilst this is far from being a universal truth, the existence and growth of transnational segments does make the task of integrating communications internationally a lot easier than it was. On the other hand, in dealing with the media and governments, a local agenda needs to be stressed if interest is to be stimulated.

Clearly, communication is a multi-dimensional endeavour. Its primary target is usually, and quite correctly, taken to be customers and consumers;

however, intermediaries, other stakeholders, and – particularly – staff also need to be communicated with. Often, communications aimed at one target will have 'collateral impact' on others; hence the need for communications to be purposefully focused, and yet also highly integrated. Different management functions will continue to address different stakeholder groups – customers, suppliers, community activists, environmental lobbyists, regulators, investors, lenders, and employees, for example – but it is vital that there is consistency in what they each are saying insofar as it affects the corporate identity. Advertising, press releases, media interviews, staff newsletters and other internal 'broadcasts', presentations to financial analysts, and liaison with government departments all need to be integrated. To achieve integration, some carriers use communication audits to examine what it is that they say, to whom, and how, to establish whether or not a consistent 'tone of voice' is used, and to find out whether internal and external audiences are being listened to. (Hargie and Tourish (2000) provide a comprehensive treatment of communication audits.)

Although our focus in this section is on *marketing* communications, in reality addressing the market is only one part of the wider communications task. The marketing communications effort should respond to changes in external environments – particularly, but not only, the competitive environment. Just as communications as a whole need to be integrated into a coherent approach to stakeholders, so marketing communications also need to be integrated. The idea of *integrated* marketing communications is broader than the range of traditional marketing communications. It has been defined as follows (Grönroos and Lindberg-Repo, 1998: 10).

> Integrated marketing communications is a strategy that integrates traditional media marketing, direct marketing, public relations and other distinct marketing communications media as well as communications aspects of the delivery and consumption of goods and services, of customer service, and of other customer encounters.

Whilst it is essential that a *consistent* set of core brand values is communicated *consistently* over time, it is also essential that communications are kept 'fresh'. Also, whenever an element of the service-price offer to a particular segment is being changed, an effort must be made to communicate the (presumably enhanced) value being offered. Because service-price offers are now changing more frequently and competition is intensifying in most markets, clarity in communications becomes both more important and more difficult. The proliferation of code-sharing can make it especially challenging for marketing communications to mediate successfully between expectations and perceptions of service.

One of the barriers to integrated communications is that every exposure to or experience of an airline contributes to a stakeholder's image, yet different exposures and experiences are frequently controlled by different departments or divisions. A marketing department might successfully integrate all marketing communications efforts to produce a coherent, consistent, presentation, but if this is not reinforced by the attitudes and behaviours of the airline's people – whose training, development, and performance might be under the 'control' of human resources and one or more operations functions, with the latter also perhaps responsible for different servicescapes – then coherence and consistency will be lost. Marketing, human resources, and operations have to speak with a single voice: this is the essence of Lovelock's (1996) 'services management trinity', first mentioned in chapter 2. Ensuring communications are integrated, and that they promise something the airline's culture, resources, competencies, and external circumstances allow it to deliver, is very much a team effort.

Extending the last point, it is vital that marketing communications are used not only to influence and to sell, but also to manage purchasers' expectations. We saw in chapter 4 that gaps between expectations and perceptions of service received are key drivers of customer satisfaction and service quality evaluation; it is therefore critical not to overpromise. Many airlines have a problem with this, and several highly regarded international carriers still regularly overpromise through the images they use in their advertising.

Ind (1997) has suggested that an integrated communications strategy should be:

- consistent and long-lasting, presenting the airline's strategic position in a way that overarches short-term, tactical messages;
- distinctive, based on real points of difference (tangible or intangible) that matter to consumers, rather than on flights of fantasy;
- single-minded and all-encompassing, yet flexible enough to address different audiences with separately relevant messages.

Box 6.3 illustrates an integrated tactical marketing communications programme initiated by Southwest to support route entry.

Box 6.3: Integrated communications for market entry

(The description below has been reproduced from Kurtz and Clow (1998: 422-423), drawing on original work by Lawrence (1993). Note that whilst not all of the specific initiatives mentioned here would necessarily be appropriate in other countries or situations, this example does nonetheless

amply illustrate the integrated nature of a tactical marketing communic-
ations effort. It also illustrates the importance of 'below-the-line' (BTL)
communications – such as event marketing, sales promotions, and direct
marketing – relative to paid advertising.)

'The importance of integrating the communications program is illustrated
by Southwest Airlines' expansion to the East Coast. Their low fares and
integrated marketing programs have pushed Southwest to the number-
seven position amongst U.S. carriers. Because of Southwest's low-cost
philosophy, it was essential they develop an effective integrated commun-
ications program. Their communications mix includes advertising, sales
promotions, community-relations, and special events marketing. Advertis-
ing expenditures are the lowest percentage of this mix.

When Southwest expanded to Baltimore, the marketing process began
with two months of research. This research indicated Southwest had a low
level of awareness in the Baltimore area. The research also indicated that
baseball was an important component of the Baltimore community. Before
Southwest arrived in Baltimore, the marketing team worked on integrating
government affairs, service announcements, special events, advertising,
and promotions. Five weeks prior to arriving in Baltimore, Southwest
Chairman Herb Kelleher and the Governor of Maryland announced South-
west's planned expansion to Baltimore.

To launch a $49 fare from Baltimore to Cleveland, Southwest took 49
elementary students for a day to the Rain Forest at the Cleveland Metro-
parks Zoo. Prior to the trip, Boog Powell, a former Baltimore Orioles
baseball player, gave hitting lessons to the youngsters. Four weeks prior to
the inauguration, Southwest conducted a direct mail campaign aimed at
frequent, short-haul travelers in the Baltimore area. The direct mail piece
offered a special promotion to join Southwest's frequent-flier program,
called the Company Club. The last marketing effort was a street campaign.
To reinforce the direct mail, the public relations effort, and the advertising,
employees handed out fliers promoting Southwest Airlines. Selected busy
street corners were chosen for this part of the campaign.

Advertising in Baltimore used the theme "Just Plane Smart". The ad
credited the city of Baltimore and its people for being smart enough to
invite Southwest to come to the city. Advertisements in Cleveland and Chic-
ago had used presidential themes in their launches. Each new launch by
Southwest uses a different theme designed to maximize the impact for
Southwest. Once Southwest is launched in a city, a marketing office is
opened in that city. An area marketing manager works on local promotions
and events to maximize marketing resources for the area.'

(See also Dasburg (1998b) for a description of how Northwest used inte-grated marketing communications to re-launch its Memphis hub in the mid-1990s.)

vii. Conclusion

There are three broad approaches to external communications: 'pull' communications targeted at customers and consumers; 'push' communicat-ions targeted at distribution channels (primarily travel agencies); and environmental influencing, which targets all stakeholders (including cust-omers and channel intermediaries) exposed to it, but tends to be issue-oriented and therefore focus more on policy-makers and opinion-leaders. Internal communications are an important adjunct insofar as an airline's people need to understand its strategy, its brand values, and the role each individual plays in delivering on the expectations created by external communications. Different communications mixes (i.e., advertising, PR, personal selling, direct marketing, web sites, lobbying, etc.) will be used to communicate with different audiences, but these mixes should nonetheless be managed in an integrated and consistent manner. A leading practitioner in the field of identity management has this to say (Wolff Olins, 1995: 10).

> The fundamental idea behind an identity programme is that in everything the organization does, everything it owns, and everything it produces it should project a clear idea of what it is and what its aims are. The most significant way in which this can be done is by making everything in and around the organization – its products, buildings, communications and behaviour – consistent in purpose and performance and, where this is appropriate, in appearance too.
>
> Outward consistency of this kind will only be achieved, and for that matter is only appropriate, if it is the manifestation of an inward consistency – a consistency of purpose. This consistency of purpose derives from the vision or the central idea and is almost always the base from which a successful identity programme can be developed.
>
> The central idea or the vision is the force that drives the organization. It is what the organization is about, what it stands for, and what it believes in.

In the final analysis, however, the best form of communication as far as consumers are concerned is delivering a service that meets or, preferably, exceeds expectations. It is to service delivery that we turn in the next chapter.

7 Managing Service Delivery

You ponce in expecting to be waited on hand and foot. Well I'm trying to run a hotel here. Have you any idea how much there is to do? Of course not, you're all too busy sticking your noses into every corner, poking around for things to complain about, aren't you?

John Cleese (aka Basil Fawlty)

Having designed and communicated a service-price offer that is consistent with the service concept and its positioning, the offer now has to be transformed into a 'service outcome' by delivering the service package to targeted customers. Figure 7.1 extends the model introduced in chapter 1. Note that service delivery is 'about the totality of the way in which the service is *accessed* before, during and after a sale' (Irons, 1997b). A clear understanding of the relevant service concept is critical to effective service delivery: 'If well-defined and easily understood service concepts are lacking, chaos will reign in the organization, and managers and customer contact and support employees alike will be uncertain about how to act in specific situations, in planning as well as in implementing plans' (Grönroos, 2000: 384).

The absence of truly unique competitive strategies to distinguish many competing airlines means that real distinctiveness frequently boils down to implementation – specifically, to the effectiveness and efficiency with which services are delivered. It also lends weight to the critical importance of doing even the routine, apparently low-impact things well.

Service delivery happens as a result of the processes an airline uses to transform inputs into outputs (e.g., passenger enplanements, flight departures, ASMs/ASKs flown, RPMs/RPKs sold) and outcomes (e.g., regulatory compliance, or satisfied consumers). The first part of this chapter will look at the concept of process, and the second section will discuss the resources,

233

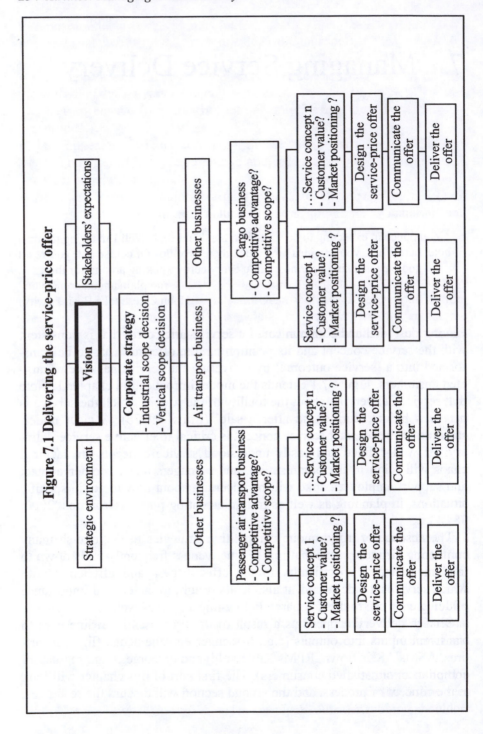

Figure 7.1 Delivering the service-price offer

tasks, and activities which together comprise each process. We will then briefly touch on the question of organization structure.

i. Processes

Processes defined

Processes are comprised of linked activities, and every activity is comprised of various tasks, each of which involves the use of resources. A process is 'a structured, measured set of activities designed to produce a specified output for a particular customer or market....a specific ordering of work activities across time and place with a beginning, an end, and clearly identified inputs: a structure for action' (Davenport, 1993: 5). Whereas functions are aggregates of broadly similar tasks (e.g., marketing, finance, etc.), processes are networks of activities related by the outputs and inputs they exchange (Gattorna and Walters, 1996). Traditionally structured on the basis of tasks grouped into functional departments or product- or market-oriented units, many airlines are now becoming more process-oriented – looking at how tasks and activities can best be grouped to produce the desired value for customers whilst minimising the cost of delivering that value.

We are not concerned with process details because, as I pointed out in the opening chapter, this is a book primarily oriented to service strategy rather than to detailed operational matters; nonetheless, we have seen throughout the text that the simultaneity of production and consumption of airline service makes the operating strategy and its constituent processes very much a part of the service package. In service businesses, the processes used to serve customers are important attributes of the product with the result that strategic and marketing issues cannot be separated from operational issues, which in turn cannot ignore behavioural issues arising from contact between customers and staff (Fitzsimmons and Fitzsimmons, 1998). Indeed, there is an argument that in a service business, 'the operation itself is the product' (Hoffman and Bateson, 1997: 127).

Processes vary in scope (e.g., whether or not they cross the boundaries of functional units and perhaps even organizational boundaries) and scale (e.g., the breadth and complexity of the tasks that they embody). Three basic types of process can be identified (Peppard and Rowland, 1995).

1. **Strategic processes** Oriented to the medium- and long-term future, these include all aspects of strategy formulation and implementation that do not fall into either of the following two categories.
2. **Service delivery processes** Day-to-day processes aimed at acquiring, satisfying, and retaining customers. We will look at these shortly.
3. **Enabling processes** This is a broad category which could, for example, include routine human resource, financial, and partner relationship management processes.

Depending upon how detailed we want the level of analysis to be, we might identify up to 25-30 'meta-processes' in any airline, each comprised of a number of constituent sub-processes. Every task, activity, and process involves a combination of resources which may be cognitive (i.e., involving employees) or non-cognitive; cognitive resources are usually intangible (e.g., knowledge), whereas non-cognitive resources might be intangible (e.g., brand image or slots at a congested hub) or tangible (e.g., the fleet, airport counter and lounge space, or gate facilities). Organizational culture (looked at in the next chapter) is so important in high-contact service industries that it qualifies as a resource in its own right. Figure 7.2 relates these points in a general way to the structure of the present book, and figure 7.3 provides a detailed example drawn from a maintenance process. For a comprehensive introduction to process and sub-process documentation based on an approach developed by the International Benchmarking Clearinghouse at the American Productivity and Quality Center (APQC), see Tenner and De Toro (1997).

In chapter 2 we identified the possession of firm-specific (in addition to industry-specific and strategy-specific) competencies as one possible source of competitive advantage. It is worth pausing briefly to consider the difference between competencies and processes.

- **Competencies** Competencies are generally taken to refer to the way people communicate, co-operate, and work together to apply resources in a competitively advantageous way. As originally defined by Prahalad and Hamel (1990), they describe the application of technological and production expertise across intra-organizational boundaries in a way that allows an organization to leverage itself into – perhaps even create – new markets. In manufacturing industry, Honda's core competence in engine technology and Canon's in optics are widely cited examples; in the airline business, we can think in terms of Southwest having a competence in rapid gate turnarounds, and British Airways having competencies in cabin product innovation and also brand management.

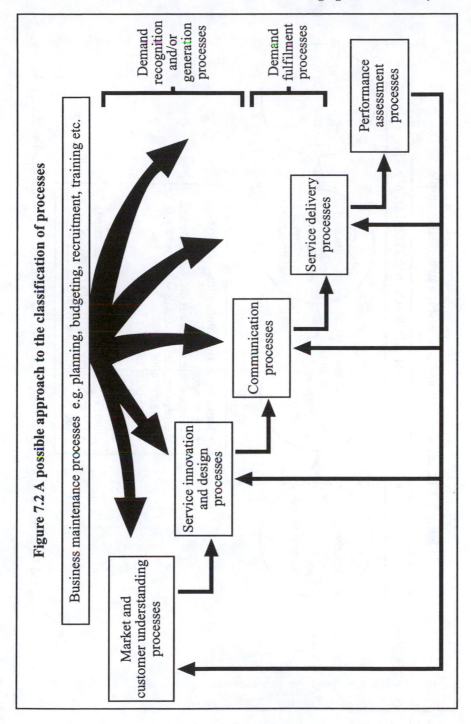

Figure 7.2 A possible approach to the classification of processes

Business maintenance processes e.g. planning, budgeting, recruitment, training etc.

Demand recognition and/or generation processes

Demand fulfilment processes

Performance assessment processes

Service delivery processes

Communication processes

Service innovation and design processes

Market and customer understanding processes

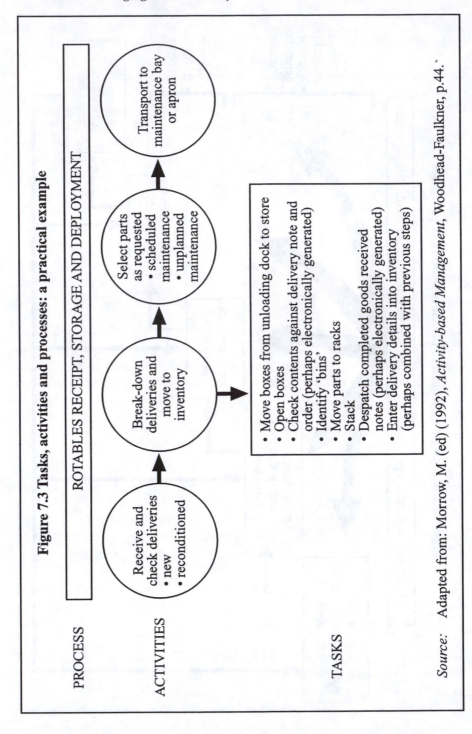

Figure 7.3 Tasks, activities and processes: a practical example

ROTABLES RECEIPT, STORAGE AND DEPLOYMENT

PROCESS

ACTIVITIES

Receive and check deliveries
• new
• reconditioned

Break-down deliveries and move to inventory

Select parts as requested
• scheduled maintenance
• unplanned maintenance

Transport to maintenance bay or apron

TASKS

• Move boxes from unloading dock to store
• Open boxes
• Check contents against delivery note and order (perhaps electronically generated)
• Identify 'bins'
• Move parts to racks
• Stack
• Despatch completed goods received notes (perhaps electronically generated)
• Enter delivery details into inventory (perhaps combined with previous steps)

Source: Adapted from: Morrow, M. (ed) (1992), *Activity-based Management*, Woodhead-Faulkner, p.44. `

- **Processes** These are the accumulations of tasks and activities which together 'get the job done' from a customer's perspective. We saw in chapter 2 that there is a strand in the literature, distinct from the competence-based approach to competitive strategy, which argues that a business able to identify the processes central to delivery of customer value and manage them better than competitors are able to do possesses a strategic 'capability'. A capability according to this definition is a set of business processes that has been understood in their strategic context. Every company has business processes that deliver value to the customer, but few think of them as the primary object of strategy. Capability-based competitors 'identify their key business processes, manage them centrally and invest in them heavily, looking for long-term payback' (Stalk et al, 1992: 62).

    The reality, of course, is that most capabilities are not managed as integrated processes, but as piecemeal activities still locked into vertical silos and fiefdoms. The fact that the world's airlines safely fly large numbers of passengers around the world each year suggests that this approach to their business works fine; the question is whether it works as well as alternative approaches could. A fundamental tenet of systems theory is that making individual subsystems (e.g., departments) as efficient or effective as possible will not necessarily optimise the overall system (e.g., the process). Greater focus on better integrating strategic capabilities, and less on optimising activities within departments or divisions, might lead to surprising gains in system efficiency and effectiveness. It is processes rather than departments or functions that get the job done.

Both competence- and capability-based approaches are drawn from the resource-based theory of competitive advantage we met in chapter 2. In either case, competitive advantage is likely to arise only if performance is causally ambiguous (i.e., not easily understood and imitated by competitors) or is based on tacit (i.e., uncodified) knowledge and 'ways of doing' that cannot be readily transferred. If a business model can be copied in its entirety by others, it is not one based on unique resources and distinctive competencies and the sustainability of any competitive advantage is therefore open to question.

Each process has only one role: to satisfy a customer or group of customers, internal or external, as efficiently as possible given a clear understanding of what 'satisfy' actually means. Service delivery processes are designed to satisfy external customers.

Service delivery processes

We established in chapter 4 that one of the most important factors distinguishing service industries from manufacturing enterprises is that external customers are present throughout some of the most important service delivery processes, and indeed are expected to participate in many of them. This has given rise in the services management literature to descriptive if somewhat inelegant new words such as 'prosumer' to emphasise that consumers co-produce at least some of the services they experience, and 'servuction system' to draw attention to the fact that service production and consumption happen simultaneously.

The important point is that consumers evaluate delivery processes as part of the service itself. In chapter 5 I introduced the concept of service blueprinting and stressed that those service delivery processes actually experienced by consumers are as much a part of the service package as any tangible attribute such as seat pitch or comfort. Like other service attributes, processes with which consumers are involved can have both functional and emotional dimensions. Process configuration accordingly involves choices which, because of their direct impact on consumers, are integral to an airline's service package. Processes carried out with consumers present are sometimes referred to as 'front office', 'front stage', 'front line', or 'customer-facing', whilst those which external customers neither participate in nor witness are 'back office' or 'back stage'; clearly, the two have to work tightly in unison.

- **The front office** This is where customers' expectations and perceptions of service will start coming together to shape outcomes which can range from satisfaction through dissatisfaction. It involves both active service encounters with staff and also passive experience of servicescapes, stretching throughout the customer activity cycle from first enquiry to the post-flight resolution of any outstanding problems. The configuration of front- and back-office processes, the trade-off between resource allocation and customer service which has been decided upon (particularly during periods of peak demand), the use of technology, and the attitudes and empowerment levels of employees will all affect satisfaction and perceived quality levels. More generally, the presence of customers affects the choice of operations management techniques that can be adopted for front-office processes.
- **The back office** Behind the 'line of visibility' separating processes that customers experience directly from those that they do not, the back office is where much of the effort takes place which ensures safe performance of published schedules and lays foundations for successful

service encounters in the front office. Some airlines are now trying actively to ensure that back-office staff look upon those in the front office as 'internal customers' and stay focused on the impact back-office decisions and actions will have on the ultimate paying customers. The absence of direct customer contact nonetheless does allow more latitude in the choice of process design, with the result that back-office managers in service businesses such as airlines can adopt many of the same techniques used in manufacturing industries (e.g., ERP).

In practice, the neat distinction between front and back offices which is drawn in the literature and referred to at various points in this book is not always as clear-cut as it might seem. It is in fact possible to identify:

- **front-office processes**, within which service encounters take place (e.g., check-in and many aspects of cabin service);
- **visible back-office processes**, which, because they are at least to some extent seen by customers, might have a direct impact on customers' perceptions arising from the way they are performed – irrespective of the functional result of their performance (e.g., some ground handling activities);
- **hidden back-office processes**, which customers cannot see and therefore evaluate only in terms of their functional results (e.g., aircraft maintenance, scheduling, and other fleet and capacity management processes);
- **hybrid processes**, which take place in both back- and front-offices (e.g., flight catering – a process which involves initial preparation (hidden back-office), delivery to aircraft galleys (either hidden or visible back-office, depending on the circumstances of the flight), galley preparation (front-office), delivery to passengers, and consumption (both front-office)).

Box 7.1 takes a brief look at how one airline manages a hybrid, cross-functional process.

Box 7.1: The departure control process at Southwest

The management of aircraft turnarounds can have a profound impact on costs because the longer aircraft are on the ground, the less utilisation the airline is getting out of these expensive fixed assets, the gates at which they are parked, and the ground staff handling them; it has an equally profound impact on customer satisfaction through its effect on service attributes such as baggage handling, ontime departure, and proper provisioning of inflight service processes. The departure control process is a complex exercise in cross-functional co-ordination because people from several different functional specialisms and organizations (e.g., reservations, gate agents, baggage and cargo handlers, fuellers, despatchers, cabin attendants, pilots, caterers, engineeers/mechanics, cleaners, flight operations control) are engaged in a number of highly interdependent tasks which build into several activities and one process.

In a study of four US majors, Gittell (1999) found that Southwest's average aircraft turnaround time was 37 minutes against 61 minutes for the overall sample, and its staffing ratio was 43 station employees per 1,000 departing passengers against the sample average of 77. Southwest's ontime performance, baggage handling, and customer satisfaction ratings were nonetheless significantly higher than those of the other three carriers. Part of the explanation undoubtedly lies in the fact that Southwest offers a relatively simple service package which does not involve extensive hubbing, baggage interlining, or complex catering services, and it offers this across a single-type fleet operating on predominantly short- and medium-haul sectors. But Gittell does ascribe a significant contribution to this superior performance to sound cross-functional co-ordination, which she puts down to three factors.

1. Co-ordination mechanisms *The heart of co-ordination is purposeful management of information. The 'information' hub for each departing Southwest flight is a single operations agent who has no other responsibility than to co-ordinate everybody involved in handling that flight. Because these agents handle only one flight at a time and deal face-to-face with gate, ramp, and onboard personnel rather than handling multiple flights from a distant operations control centre and relying heavily on information technology, this approach is staff-intensive. Southwest appears to find high levels of staffing in this co-ordination function pay off in terms of overall process efficiency and effectiveness.*

2. Control mechanisms *Whereas performance reviews at many airlines ascribe blame for controllable departure delays to individual functional areas (such as catering, line maintenance, cargo handling, etc.), Southwest ascribes any delays to the entire team involved in a particular departure. This cross-functional accountability appears to encourage efforts to keep communications and information flowing between different functions. Another control mechanism Gittell found to be important was Southwest's high ratio of supervisors to front-line employees, which came in at around 10 per 100 and gave supervisors much smaller spans of control than at the other sampled airlines. She argued that the higher ratio contributes both to improved information flows*

and better opportunities for giving positive feedback to staff; in contrast, at airlines that have cut supervisory staff numbers, supervisors tend to be so tied-up with problem-solving that they have insufficient time to support their staff with information and feedback.

3. Human resource practices *Employee selection, flexible work rules, and conflict resolution were identified by Gittell as human resource practices contributing significantly to effective cross-functional coordination of Southwest's departure control process. Selection processes look not just for functional expertise, but for positive attitudes and an ability to work co-operatively in teams. Despite Southwest's high rate of unionisation, its contracts do not include restrictive work rules; the result is a considerable degree of flexibility allowing people to work across functional boundaries in order to get the job done. Conflict resolution procedures can be important when a potentially stressful, time-constrained process such as aircraft turnaround is dependent on the co-operation of different functional groups who have a history within the industry of insularity and well-developed status consciousness. Whereas conflict resolution at many carriers is limited to 'grievance procedures' for addressing problems arising between different levels of a functional hierarchy, Southwest proactively addresses horizontal conflicts between front-line personnel and different employee groups through the use of cross-functional 'information gathering meetings' at which problems are confronted and solved.*

The message here is that when service delivery depends upon the coordination of several different functions, focus on the employee/customer interface is not enough. To realise the potential source of competitive advantage that employees offer, an airline must also find ways to manage functional interdependencies within cross-functional processes. What needs to be managed in particular is the quality of relationships and the effectiveness of communications between different employee groups (ibid).

Rather than talk in detail about specific operational processes, what I will do in this section is concentrate on their relevance to strategic services management. The remainder of the section will therefore look first at operating strategy, and then briefly at process design.

Operating strategy

> High expectations are the key to everything.
> Sam Walton

In chapter 2 we met the concept of 'strategic logic' – a belief system linking resource deployment to targeted outcomes. In chapter 3 this was translated into the idea of a 'service concept' – a clearly articulated view about the value we intend offering to customers, who we intend serving, and how we will serve them; in chapters 4 and 5 we further translated strategic logic and the service concept into the more specifically market-oriented 'service-price offer'. The final link in the chain is to translate all three into the actual delivery of services to customers, and in order to achieve this we need an 'operating strategy'. An operating strategy should not be seen as something in isolation – as just the 'implementation' stage in a strategy-making process – but as an integral part of the service package that operations people must deliver.

We saw above that whether producing goods, services or both, all businesses are in essence a bundle of processes designed to transform inputs (e.g., materials, information, passengers, and cargo) into outputs (e.g., ATKs, RTKs, etc. – which are proxies for output or sold output respectively) and outcomes (e.g., satisfied customers); these processes provide value by satisfying the expectations of targeted customers. Transformation processes apply certain technologies (including IS/IT and know-how as well as facilities and equipment), and these technologies tend to be used to help categorise industries. The management of transformation processes is 'operations management' – a discipline with an extensive literature of its own. Its function is to design and manage an operating system – comprised of tasks, activities, and processes using firm-specific and firm-addressable resources – capable of delivering services to customers as designed and on specification.

The characteristics of services in general that were outlined in chapter 4 (intangibility, perishability, inseparability of production and consumption, and variability in delivery) make operations management in a service business such as the airline industry a complex task. Customers' direct experiences of the production processes in which they participate are very much part of the overall service experience, and therefore contribute to the service outcome (i.e., satisfaction or dissatisfaction) just as much as any tangible attribute designed into a service package. Indeed, the substance and style of service delivery are themselves the carriers of important service benefits – especially emotional/symbolic benefits. The design of service packages and the processes through which they are delivered, particularly the front-office processes, are entirely symbiotic.

Operating and marketing strategies must therefore be tightly co-ordinated, along with human resource strategy – the 'services management trinity' (Lovelock, 1996). A production orientation, focused internally on airline requirements rather than externally on customers' expectations, is not the currency of competition in liberalised air transport markets; on the other hand, the best marketing programme will yield nothing sustainable if operational processes cannot deliver what customers in targeted segments are expecting. Whereas marketing delivers promises, operations delivers *on* promises (Holloway, 1998b).

We saw in chapter 3 that every service concept implies a particular approach to the management of an airline's cost and revenue streams. This translates into two broad objectives for any operating strategy.

1. It must support the choice and positioning of the service concept by delivering the type of customer value embodied in that concept and in the service-price offers that flow from it. In other words, service delivery needs to be *effective* within its chosen context.
2. It must be capable of delivering desired service outcomes at a cost which is the lowest possible consistent with the particular service concept. That is, service delivery needs to be *efficient* within its particular context.

Operating strategy is the science – sometimes the art – of delivering at a profit the value expected by targeted customers. Every task and activity in every process needs to be identified as value-adding or non-value-adding – with value defined by the customer. Anything that does not add value should go if at all possible. Anything that does add value needs to be subjected to two further tests: Does it deliver a type of value that targeted customers expect, and is value delivered to expected standards as efficiently as possible?

The fundamental challenge of operating strategy is to get costs into line with prices that targeted customers are prepared to pay in return for the level of service embodied in the airline's service package(s). The correct approach is to identify what the customers in each target segment want, provide it to them at a price they are willing to pay, and then ensure that production costs allow this to be done at a profit. At least, that is the theory.

In practice, airline costs can be extraordinarily difficult to manage (see Holloway, 1997). Depending upon the time-scale adopted, a high proportion of them can be considered fixed. Capacity management is a major operational challenge in the industry, both at the macro-level (i.e., maximising revenues and optimising load factors) and the micro-level (i.e., managing queues at various stages in the service delivery process). Furthermore, several important variable costs are either prone to sudden and sizeable swings (e.g., fuel prices) or are set by monopoly suppliers such as providers of airway and airport facilities. Historically thin operating margins leave airline profitability exposed to the impact of the industry's typically high financial and operating leverage (ibid).

Without wanting to trivialise the difficulties facing airline operations managers working under constant pressure to keep expenditures under tight control, I do think it can be helpful to look at costs not so much as absolute numbers that must inevitably be minimised, but as revenue-generators that need to be proactively *managed* within the context of the particular type of value embedded in each service concept. (This links through to the argument in chapter 9 that a useful, if still rarely used, productivity metric is revenue generated per unit of cost – taking cost in aggregate, by function, and by category.) Cost 'management' implies cutting controllable costs with a purpose, rather than slashing them across the board, and sometimes even increasing them if incremental revenues more than compensate for incremental costs. In other words, the supply side (i.e., production costs) should not be considered in isolation from the demand side (i.e., revenue generation). Short-term cost minimisation and long-term profit maximisation do not inevitably equate, particularly when serving premium segments; the attacks launched on customer value by several US majors during the 1990s suggest that there is an influential body of opinion within the industry which does not share this view.

Easier said than done though it might be, operating strategy can in principle be reduced to two prescriptions.

- Costs are affected by the nature of the demand an airline's management chooses to serve (e.g., service requirements, traffic density and mix, and peaking characteristics), by management's ability to balance capacity and demand to ensure that capacity is adequately utilised, and by the attributes designed into whatever service package is necessary to serve targeted demand. An airline should not be incurring any costs other than those that are essential to the delivery of services, as designed, to targeted segments.
- Cost management should be about cutting waste not customer value – minimising absolute input costs and maximising resource productivity, subject to what is required by the service package that has been designed. How frequently an aircraft gets deep-cleaned and how rapidly minor cabin defects are fixed should not be arbitrary decisions; the answers should be 'often' and 'quickly', but just what these two words

mean in practice needs to be determined within the context of a particular service concept. Note that I am not implying that low-cost/no-frills carriers, for example, should ignore this type of service attribute; at the end of the day, dirty aircraft and broken lights or tray tables will not build the brand loyalty that even low-fare carriers need if they are to establish customer preference against other, equally low-fare airlines. These decisions nonetheless need to be made with one eye firmly fixed on the expectations and the 'zones of tolerance' (see chapter 4) of targeted customers.

Some service packages permit considerable efficiency in their delivery – for example, inclusive tour charters operated with high seating densities, load factors, and aircraft utilisation, and low seat accessibility and marketing costs; low-fare/no-frills scheduled operations also qualify in this regard. Delivery efficiency can be reflected in low prices, leading to a balanced and effective service-price offer providing good value to targeted segments. Other service packages will carry appreciably higher production costs because they do not permit as much efficiency in delivery processes – for example, high-frequency short-haul flights serving business segments with relatively small aircraft, high seat accessibility and marketing costs, and lower seating densities, load factors, and aircraft utilisation. Again, these costs can be reflected in prices – higher in this case, but still allowing a balanced and effective service-price offer to be made. In both cases, intensifying competition as markets liberalise encourages airlines to be as efficient as possible at achieving required levels of effectiveness – however 'effectiveness' might be defined by particular targeted segments.

Process design

Types of process

Processes can fall within 'project', 'job', 'batch', or 'flow' structures. All four can be found in an airline's service delivery system.

- **Project** This is a single, complex, multi-process undertaking with a defined beginning and end. The initial introduction of a new fleet would be an example, as would aircraft heavy maintenance, route introduction, and the major redesign of an inflight product.
- **Job** A 'job' is an element of a larger project (and under some circumstances could be characterised as a small project in its own right).

- **Batch** A 'batch' is characterised by the grouping together and more or less simultaneous processing of inputs. Much passenger processing is effected in batches corresponding to flight departures.
- **Flow** In this case, inputs are processed in a continuous flow. For example, at large hubs, many airlines have check-in desks which service more than one flight at a time, the intention being to reduce the customer queuing often associated with batch processing and also to raise employee productivity by smoothing the rate of customer arrivals.

The design process

Designing and blueprinting a process is itself a process. It starts with a set of objectives, which in the case of service delivery processes would be expressed in terms of service specifications established early in the service design (or redesign) effort (see chapter 4). Different delivery process design options are then assessed along three dimensions (Slack et al, 1998).

1. **Feasibility** Do we have the required quality and quantity of resources (including financial resources) to pursue this design option?
2. **Acceptability** Can the design option satisfy performance criteria specified for the service package, and can it do this at a satisfactory profit?
3. **Vulnerability** Do we understand the implications of each design option, its potential fail-points, what can be done to minimise the risk of service failure, and what the consequences are if we get it wrong?

The design process initially involves asking some very simple questions: With regard to a new process, who are the customers, what do we need to do in order to meet or exceed their expectations, and how can we do this in the most direct way and at the cheapest cost consistent with required service standards? With regard to existing processes, what problems need solving and how can we make the process more efficient and, ideally, more flexible? With regard to all processes, how can we embed continuous improvement and performance goals that 'stretch us'?

Complexity and divergence

Two important variables in service process design are 'complexity' and 'divergence'.

- **Complexity** is a function of the number of activities and sequences of activities involved in a given process. The fewer sequences and activities there are, the lower the complexity of a process.

- **Divergence** reflects the degree of latitude allowed for the varying of an activity or the reordering of a sequence. The less latitude permitted, the lower the 'divergence' in a process and the greater the level of standardisation (of activities, policies, and procedures, for example).

Airlines must as far as possible ensure that the complexity and divergence designed into their processes reflect the choices made with regard to service concept and operating strategy. Both should be as low as possible for a low-cost/low-fare carrier; a full-service airline might want to introduce a higher level of divergence into its front-office (i.e., customer-contact) processes, although both economic feasibility and possible threats to service consistency need to be borne in mind.

ii. Resources, tasks, and activities

> You can duplicate airplanes. You can duplicate the gate facilities. You can duplicate all the hard things, the tangible things you can get your hands on. But it's the intangibles that determine success. They're the hardest to duplicate, if you can do it at all. We've got the right intangibles.
> Herb Kelleher

We saw earlier in the chapter that resources are applied to tasks, that linked tasks comprise distinct activities, and that linked activities comprise individual processes. The last section introduced the concept of process. In this section I will briefly look at aspects of resources, tasks, and activities that are relevant to the subject of strategic services management.

Resources

In chapter 2 we defined resources as tangible or intangible assets deployed in pursuit of some objective; a competence is a sustained, successful deployment of particular resources consistent with the strategic logic underlying what the airline is and what it is trying to achieve for its customers. Resources can be either firm-specific (i.e., internally controlled) or firm-addressable (i.e., controlled by external parties but accessible to the airline). An obvious example of firm-addressable resources is the industry infrastructure of airways and airports; as congestion increases, some of these resources are becoming steadily less accessible. Part of the logic of alliances is to extend access to firm-addressable resources – particularly resources such as fleet, facilities, slots, route authorities, and market presence.

I do not have sufficient space to discuss resources in any great depth, so what I will do is briefly categorise them in order to help organize what is a very broad concept .

Non-cognitive resources

These are resources that are impersonal rather than derived from human capabilities. They can be tangible or intangible.

1. **Tangible resources** An airline's physical infrastructure, its facilities, and its equipment are the most obvious of its many tangible resources.
2. **Intangible resources** Intangible resources include assets as important as slots at congested hubs and route authorities in regulated markets – which can be deployed to deliver the 'schedule benefits' in a service package – and brand image – which can be consciously influenced to deliver the emotional/symbolic benefits in an offer. Once well established, an airline's core network is a critical intangible resource because it is part of the service offer and, more particularly, because of the market presence it creates. Systems are also a vital resource, and arguably the most important system in any modern airline is its information infrastructure. This links it to suppliers, distributors, and customers, integrates internal processes (an ideal not all airlines have yet achieved), provides input into executive information and decision support subsystems, and in some cases enables the development of information-based services that might be saleable outside the airline. Through the use of 'middleware' to avoid the expense of moving to a common platform, members of leading global alliances are using links between their information systems to deliver services to each other's customers (e.g., Star's StarNet).

Cognitive resources

> All genuine knowledge comes from direct experience.
> Mao Tse-Tung

Since the 1980s, people in organizational settings have been looked upon less as individuals who need to be supervised and controlled through the functional instrumentalities of 'personnel management', and more as a major potential source of competitive advantage – a 'human resource' to be nurtured and developed (Storey, 1992). In itself, process design cannot deliver customer value or other desirable performance outcomes. 'In the long run the quality of an organization's people is a key determinant of whether it succeeds or fails. Process design alone is not enough. As more companies learn how to create state-of-the-art processes, the advantage will belong to those with an institutionalised capacity for staffing those processes with well-selected and well-trained people' (Hammer, 1996: 118). People are a critical resource.

A clear linkage between strategy and people has been forged. Advantage derived from human resources is based on cognitive capabilities and on values, which together underpin the attitudes and behaviours that are brought to bear on designing, communicating, and – perhaps most importantly in the present context – delivering air transport services. We will look at values and organizational culture in chapter 8. With regard to an airline's cognitive resources, it can be helpful to distinguish between organizational knowledge and individual knowledge.

Organizational knowledge Stewart (1997: ix) uses the term 'intellectual capital', which he defines as 'everything everybody in a company knows that gives it a competitive edge'. Too frequently, strategic services management is characterised as a process that involves managers formulating strategies and employees implementing them. In fact, viable strategies often emerge from front-line experience. Indeed, there is a now widely accepted view that modern corporations are repositories of intellectual capital that needs to be unlocked if creativity and emergent initiatives are to flourish. Intellectual capital can be used for broadly two purposes: improvement – doing the same things better; and innovation – doing new things. A way must be found to translate its potential into relevant action. Normann and Ramírez (1994: 100-101) note that,

> The effectiveness of persons in a knowledge-creation system depends on the team they are involved with; the tools and the network they have access to; the form of management structure and other corporate support systems they are a part of; the human resources and professional development programmes that they have participated in; the information, 'theory', and 'world-view', values, ethics, and codes of conduct that guide them.

Using a distinction that closely parallels the line between declarative and procedural knowledge drawn in computer science (particularly in work on artificial intelligence), Kogut and Zander (1997) suggest that organizational knowledge be categorised into two linked types of resource: information (a content variable) and know-how (a process variable). This differs from the usual categorisation, which sees data as a first step in the development of information, then knowledge, and perhaps ultimately wisdom.

1. **Information** is a resource that has been treated from two perspectives in the academic literature (Sveiby, 1997).

    *   Information as a stand-alone resource: in this view, information exists in the form of identifiable 'objects' that can be managed in information systems. According to Fitzsimmons and Fitzsimmons (1998), the underlying objectives of managing information are to: create barriers to entry (e.g., FFPs); generate revenues (e.g., revenue management systems); build a database asset (e.g., for sale, or for use in developing services and customised marketing programmes); and enhance productivity (e.g., inventory management, ERP, data envelopment analysis, and scheduling).

    *   Information as a resource embedded in people: from this perspective, knowledge exists in people's stores of experience and their capabilities, and it can only be managed by capturing the benefits of learning.

    Both angles have merit. For example, Wayland and Cole (1997: 45) define customer knowledge as something that flows from, '….the effective leveraging of information *and* experience in the acquisition, development, and retention of a profitable customer portfolio'. They go on to argue that '[e]ffective customer knowledge management puts to work both the surface-level, explicit knowledge resulting from direct exchanges with customers, and the deeply embedded knowledge of the customer that resides tacitly in the heads of a company's customer-serving personnel….' (ibid: 50). Airlines need to identify strategic knowledge assets – particularly, in the context of this chapter, those assets that contribute to service delivery – and actively manage (i.e., deploy, sustain, and enhance) them. One way of doing this is to look for knowledge in the foundations of core competencies and strategic capabilities.

2. **Know-how** is procedural knowledge that is reflected in current practices within an airline. In chapter 2 we met the concept of 'organizational routines' (Nelson and Winter, 1982) and 'ways of doing', and noted that when outcomes are causally ambiguous it is possible for competitors to observe them without understanding precisely how they are achieved. When these outcomes are relevant and valuable to customers, inimitable, and resistant to substitution, the know-how that produces them is a source of competitive advantage.

Every airline has a store of knowledge or 'intellectual capital'. What is done with it will depend in part on how it is distributed, how its use is co-ordinated, and how co-operative people are in sharing and utilising it – in other words, how efficiently the firm is organized to recognise and deploy it. Knowledge-based theory of competitive strategy argues that a firm can create an advantage by accumulating, distributing, and co-ordinating learning from both internal and external sources and being more efficient and co-operative in its use than competitors; this is something Foss (1997) refers to as a firm's 'combinative capability'. More than this, how well an airline responds to its rapidly changing marketplaces depends in large measure upon whether or not it can unleash the creativity and intelligence available within its people; the more knowledge that people are able to accumulate, the more difficult it becomes for them to avoid taking responsibility and acting (Fitzsimmons and Fitzsimmons, 1998).

Organizational knowledge is relatively valueless outside the context of the organization concerned. If acquired knowledge is valuable outside the organization, it is individual knowledge that the individual concerned can take with her – knowledge that may indeed be useful to the organization, but is not specific to it in the sense that it belongs to the collectivity.

The source of organizational knowledge is 'learning'. Organizational learning is something that '*sustains and develops distinctive competencies which belong to the organization*' (Eden and Ackermann, 1998: 75, italics in the original). But 'organizational learning' refers to more than just knowledge acquisition.

> Learning....is seen as not just the acquisition of new knowledge. It also relates to how those within a firm collectively change their values and share mental models of their company and markets....Indeed it is the ability to shed outmoded knowledge, techniques and beliefs, as well as to learn and deploy new ones, which enables firms to carry out given strategies (Pettigrew and Whipp, 1991: 238).

What is done with organizational knowledge – specifically, whether it can be turned into the industry-, strategy-, and firm-specific competencies we first met in chapter 2 – will depend upon the effectiveness of organizational routines (which we also met in that chapter). 'Routines' (Nelson and Winter, 1982) are shaped both by formal rules, procedures, technologies, and structures, and by an informal structure of beliefs, frameworks, paradigms, codes, and culture (Levitt and March, 1988; Mabey et al, 1998). They can be likened to an individual's skills (Sanchez et al, 1996).

> Just as the individual's skills are carried out semi-automatically, without conscious coordination, so organizational routines involve a large component of tacit knowledge, which implies limits on the extent to which the organization's capabilities can be articulated (Grant, 1991: 110).

From a resource-based perspective on competitive advantage, the embedding of learning into routine activities is potentially a 'resource mobility barrier' because competitors find this type of development much more difficult to imitate than episodic training programmes (Kamoche, 1996). Resource mobility barriers can be particularly important when the development of human resources is linked in some way to the development of other unique strategic resources; from a services management perspective, for example, development of both human potential and the airline's brand image or style and tone of service delivery are likely to be highly significant. Of course, this opaque learning can only be strategically relevant – other than in a haphazard, fortuitous way – if it is explicitly recognised and tapped as part of strategy formulation and/or implementation processes (Burgoyne, 1988).

The management of organizational learning and knowledge accumulation is not easy because the 'raw material' is intangible. According to Mabey et al (1998: 325),

> The learning organization is a term that has been used to characterize an enterprise where learning is open-ended, takes place at all levels and is self-questioning. Here there is an emerging interplay between individual ideals and action, and company policy and collective operations….[Unfortunately], the literature has been more successful at describing the learning organization and how it might be experienced than providing examples of it happening; although, by definition, there is no blueprint that can be transposed from one organization to another.

Airlines – like most other organizations – are akin to icebergs, and people find it easier to focus on the small fraction visible above the waterline; knowledge is part of the invisible two-thirds. The following framework can help.

1. Think first of strategy, then of the tasks, activities, and processes required to implement strategy.
   - What information and know-how relevant to these do we have and how can they best be drawn out?
   - What information and know-how do we not have, where can they be found, and/or how can they be developed?
   - How can we make relevant information and know-how available where they are needed and when they are needed?
2. Then think of knowledge itself, and ask what we have that our current strategies are not leveraging and that could be the foundation either for fundamentally new approaches to those current strategies or for fundamentally new strategies.

3. Finally, get really abstract and ask what we already do to define, promote, and measure learning and how we could do more.

It is common for the literature to talk about management of organizational knowledge in terms of 'stocks' and 'flows' (Stewart, 1997).

- **Stocks of knowledge** The places to look for potentially valuable knowledge are an airline's people, processes, information systems, and external relationships (particularly customer relationships). The challenge lies not so much in codifying those stocks into 'knowledge databases'; this can be done, notwithstanding that knowledge is often tacit or contextual. The real challenge, especially for large airlines, lies in ensuring that the wheel is not continuously reinvented – that lessons learned are absorbed not just by the people concerned, but into the airline as a whole. One approach is to build corporate knowledge maps – not lists of who knows what in detail, but signposts to who has worked on particular types of problem or issue, to who has particular types of skill, to research undertaken by or for the airline in the past, to customer, competitor, and other market information (formal and informal), and to analytical documents and project papers prepared in the past that could be of use now. 'Islands of knowledge' need to be pulled together just as much as do 'islands of automation'.
- **Flows of knowledge** The management challenge in this case is to ensure that available knowledge is integrated into practice, and that further learning ensues. Sometimes this can be done using procedures manuals and rules; often in an airline these are mandatory. But they should not be the only way of transmitting knowledge. 'Communities of practice' can evolve amongst people who share common work contexts and common problems; bulletin boards and other network media might be available to transmit information and knowledge from people who have it to others who need it. This is where functional hierarchies (which pass knowledge up and down rather than horizontally) can be a hindrance, but modern IT can be a blessing. A major challenge, of course, is to create a culture in which people willingly share knowledge they believe to be proprietary to career advancement.

The big questions to ask are, 'What knowledge drives the business, who has it, who needs it, and how do we get what is needed to the people who need it?'

Individual knowledge Social knowledge within an airline is underpinned by individual knowledge, which can be categorised into information and skills.

1. **Information** One of the by-products of individually-held information is that it is usually accompanied by a set of beliefs regarding causal relationships among phenomena (Sanchez et al, 1996). These beliefs are the building blocks of managers' mental models – themselves a potentially valuable source of competitive advantage. 'Organizational mindsets' arise when a group of individuals share the same beliefs about causality (von Krogh et al, 1994).

2. **Skills** Changes in the industry's competitive environment are imposing on more carriers the need for a new breed of commercially attuned managers. The individual skills required in future will include updated variants of established requirements, such as network management, capacity and revenue management, and cost and productivity management. In addition, skills that have had only limited application in the airline industry until relatively recently will also be required, such as those necessary to deal with new forms of competition as markets are deregulated, to manage alliances and strategic supplier relationships, and to manage both corporate and service brands. The skills to understand important signals hidden within a deluge of information about constantly changing markets, to manage customer loyalty, to accommodate complexity and turbulence in external environments generally, and to respond sensitively to different cultural milieux will be required. The airline industry is in transition from an industry which manages fleets of aircraft and sells the output they generate, to a multi-billion dollar global service business that responds to the expectations of targeted customers and depends for its financial health upon skills developed to meet and exceed those expectations. This is a transition which inevitably demands new and sometimes innovative skills (Holloway, 1998a). Skills can be categorised in the same way that we categorised competencies in chapter 2: industry-specific (i.e., skills that enable us to run an airline); strategy-specific (i.e., skills that enable us to pursue a certain strategy); and firm-specific (i.e., skills that allow us to do valuable things that no competitor can do).

Types of organizational and individual knowledge The concept of knowledge is central to both the knowledge-based and the competence-based approaches to competitive strategy. We have said that organizational knowledge is a key resource comprised of information and know-how, and identified organizational learning as its source; individual knowledge has been broken into 'information' and 'skills'. Whether we are talking about individual or collective knowledge, two types can be distinguished (de Chernatony, 1999b).

1. **Explicit/non-tacit knowledge** This is knowledge that can be articulated, codified, and communicated – perhaps in manuals, checklists, application software or in the course of formal training programmes.
2. **Tacit knowledge** This is knowledge held within an airline by individual employees or employee groups, derived from their own experiences – of particular activities, processes, alliance partners or customers, for example – and their understandings of these experiences, which is not easy to articulate or communicate but which can nonetheless be tapped. It is often context-specific, embedded in opaque and taken-for-granted 'ways of doing', and nurtured by organizational culture (ibid). It may be positive if it contributes in some way to competitive advantage, but it can also be negative if, say, inaccurate tacit 'knowledge' (e.g., 'our customers care only about price, not about how they get treated') drives imprudent actions. The utility of tacit knowledge can also be overtaken by change.

The concept of tacit knowledge is grounded in the fact that individuals appear to know more than they can explain (Polanyi, 1966). Tacit knowledge can distinguish one competitor from another in a service industry and can also underpin competitive advantage. Tacit knowledge might be consciously surfaced through mechanisms such as staff shadowing each other in teams or across organizational boundaries, through workshops, and perhaps through the creative use of metaphor to unearth what people do and how this relates to their perception of brand identity. However, not all tacit knowledge can be surfaced, and neither is it inevitably sound from a competitive standpoint that it should be; indeed, the positive side of having competencies underpinned by tacit knowledge and outcomes cloaked in causal ambiguity (see chapter 2) is that they are not readily imitable. The negative side, on the other hand, is that they are not easily manageable.

The importance of human 'resources' in service delivery

> We hire great attitudes, and teach them any functionality they need.
> Herb Kelleher

Market access is opening up as a result of regulatory liberalisation, technology is more or less uniformly available to those with sufficient financial resources, and functional service innovations can in most cases be readily imitated. This makes the quality of an airline's people – in particular, the appropriateness of their values, attitudes, and behaviour to the airline's brand values and service package(s) – a vital source of distinctiveness. Grönroos (2000: 374-375) puts it as follows.

> In spite of automated service systems, the increased use of information technology and the Internet, the creativity, motivation and skills of people are still the drivers behind successful development of new services, the implementation of service concepts and recovery of service failures....

In everyday language and in organizational documents such as annual reports, it is common to talk of employees working hard *for* the company, being loyal and dedicated *to* it, overcoming challenges faced *by* it, and being *part of* it (Gowler and Legge, 1986: 10-11). These pictures conjure an image of a unitary 'thing' called a company that is variously served or hindered by its employees. But we saw in chapter 1 that there is a strong argument for believing that employees do not simply work for, at, in or against their organizations, but that through the meanings given to their language, actions, and relationships they actually create – and over time re-create – those organizations. Certainly, for the customers of high-contact service businesses such as airlines, front-line staff to a considerable extent *are* the organization. It is therefore essential that all employees, but particularly those at the customer interface, share a common understanding of their airline's service concept(s) and ascribe common meanings to what are often vague ideas such as service, customer satisfaction, service failure, and service recovery.

Because customers are present when front-office employees are doing much of their work, the skills, attitudes and behaviours of these people – as well as the co-operation and focus of back-office employees – have a profound effect on each customer's service experience. Design of the service package and of the processes used to deliver it, together with excellent infrastructure, equipment, and logistics can easily be undone by front-line staff who lack the technical skills, the interpersonal skills or simply the right attitudes to interact as required with customers.

The basic 'what' element of airline service – safe, timely transportation – is now more or less a given. It is certainly still the core attribute in any service package, but it is simply a qualifying variable in customers' purchase decisions. In competitive markets, and particularly in less price-sensitive segments of these markets, heavy emphasis must be placed on the 'how' of service delivery. The technical/functional effectiveness of service delivery is vital, but so now is its 'personality'.

The personality of service delivery depends upon two factors:

- people: their selection, training, motivation, and development;
- corporate culture: the values and beliefs which underlie action. (Culture and values will be discussed in the next chapter.)

If we take job design as a given, and consider selection, training, and motivation (including empowerment), we will find broadly two approaches in the literature (Mabey et al, 1998). One follows traditional contingency theory by arguing that for every strategy there is a single correct approach to the management of human resources which will ensure alignment between that strategy on the one hand and employees' attitudes, behaviours, and competences on the other; thus, a low-cost/low-fare service concept will require a different – more cost-oriented and mechanistic – approach than a differentiation strategy. The second view, and the one I personally prefer, is that in a high-contact service business employees are an absolutely critical asset, that there is no inevitable linkage between poorly trained, demotivated, and badly remunerated staff on the one hand and low unit costs on the other, and that every airline should be trying to hire the best people it can, to develop their talents, and to unlock their potential for consistent, creative contribution – irrespective of its chosen product strategy. One of the central themes of the services management literature is that service companies need to move away from the industrial model in which employees are seen as costs in need of close control and towards a new model which treats them as partners, contributors, and revenue generators (Vandermerwe, 1993). Additional reasons for preferring the second view are that:

- strategy is better identified as a theme or pattern rather than a specific 'thing' to which other 'things' – such as HRM – can be rationally, explicitly linked;
- strategy-making is assumed by many textbooks to be a rational, episodic event, but in practice it is incremental, uneven, and negotiated – the implication of this being that human resource needs are not fixed once-and-for-all over the defined lifetime of a plan, but evolve as strategy evolves;
- HRM practices need not simply be reactive to strategy, but can actually lead strategy through their impact on employee development and organization culture (Hendry and Pettigrew, 1990).

The first view above is broadly consistent with Porter's (1980, 1985) standpoint: human resource strategies should 'fit' the competitive strategy an airline has chosen in response to environmental forces. The second view is consistent with the resource-based and competence-based approaches to competitive strategy: employees (and, incidentally, their culture) represent a unique and potentially valuable source of competitive advantage off which strategy can be keyed, and their selection, training, development, motivation, empowerment (where appropriate), and retention are keys to superior performance (Bowman and Ambrosini, 1998).

The literature in recent years has pointed conclusively to the importance of having a committed workforce. McCarthy (1997) makes the following observations.

- Simply satisfying customers is no longer enough. To have any chance of winning and retaining their loyalty, it is necessary to *exceed* their expectations.
- To exceed expectations, employees are needed who are willing to put in 'discretionary effort' – that is, effort over and above the minimum they are obliged to make.
- Employees have to be motivated to put in discretionary effort, provided with the tools, training, and cultural environment necessary to support their efforts, and treated with consideration and respect. This is an ideal some large airlines continue to have difficulty achieving, at least with respect to some if not all of their labour groups.

One of the key factors determining whether a particular carrier is a service business or an operation that moves aircraft around a route network is the attitudes of its people – including people who do not have customer-contact roles. Many airline managers still see themselves as being in the business of producing a transportation product, and it is not unusual to see this product referred to as a commodity; a smaller number see themselves as producers of a transportation *experience*. Often, the difference between these two perspectives will hinge on whether an airline's people believe in what they are doing, are proud of the service they have been trained to deliver, and actually look for opportunities to improve that service, or whether they are just on duty to qualify for their 'appearance money'. Staff do not simply deliver service, they are part of it. Inevitably, any airline will have people who sit on both sides of this divide as well as some who sit on the fence. It is easy to write about the merit of having staff who are passionate about ontime departures, exceeding customers' expectations and so on, but not at all easy to get perhaps tens of thousands of people genuinely committed; this is why staff attitudes appropriate to the service concept can be such an important strategic resource and a distinctive source of competitive advantage – and why the few chief executives who successfully orchestrate it (e.g., messrs Bethune, Carlzon, Kelleher, and Marshall) reach 'hero-manager' status in services management textbooks.

Tasks

> "Keep up the good work, whatever it is, whoever you are."
> *New Yorker* cartoon

In the scheme adopted in this chapter, resources of various types are applied to tasks, which when linked together comprise the separate activities from which individual processes are built-up. Tasks therefore contribute to one or more transformation processes. They are the subject of a voluminous work-study and job-design literature in the field of operations management, and have also been extensively analysed by psychologists, industrial psychologists, and organization theorists interested in exploring their links to topics as broad as motivation and organization structure.

The strategic implications of job design lie in the dichotomy between early management theories such as Taylorism, Fordism, and scientific management, which dictate extreme job specialisation in pursuit of cost and productivity advantages, and later approaches, such as the Quality of Working Life Movement and the 'softer' admonitions of recent strategic HRM theory, which advocate a broadening of job design. The benefits of broadening task responsibilities are argued to lie in the stimulus to creativity and commitment that come from engaging people's full potential by allowing them to develop beyond the constraints of a mechanistic work regime.

Although the shifting attitude towards job design – evident in the rhetoric of 'multi-skilling' and 'flexibility' – has had its most profound impact on manufacturing industries, it is not absent from service businesses. The formation of cross-functional (sometimes self-managing) teams, the movement of some technical personnel such as pilots and engineers into positions where they spend part of their time attending to commercial or at least non-technical issues, and the spread of empowerment are all evidence that at some airlines this trend has been taken seriously. As a whole, however, it does not appear to have made significant inroads into the airline business – perhaps because relatively few tasks involve the sole-destroying mindlessness of the manufacturing production line. Another reason might be that the industry's traditional command-and-control approach to management has found it difficult to let go of the idea that the role of management is to move ideas from managers' heads to employees' hands, rather than nurture and tap the initiative, creative potential, and resourcefulness of employees. Finally, many airlines remain shackled by union contracts which adhere to strict job demarcation and eschew multi-tasking; one of the keys to Southwest's success has been the staff flexibility delivered both by contract and by culture.

Activities

Tasks build into activities. Activities are sometimes categorised as 'primary' when they contribute directly to organizational or departmental purpose (e.g., inflight service activities), or 'secondary' when they support primary activities (e.g., training). Where a process is comprised of activities that are each carried out in different functional areas or departments of an airline, traditional cost accounting – which allocates expenditures to functional or departmental cost centres – is likely to be less helpful than activity-based costing (Holloway, 1998b).

However activities are analysed, the following questions at the very minimum need to be asked about each (Hope and Mühlemann, 1997: 233).

1. **Purpose** What is being done? Why is it being done? What else could be done? What else should be done?
2. **Place** Where is it being done? Why there? Where else could it be done? Where should it be done?
3. **Sequence** When is it done? Why then? When else could it be done? When should it be done?
4. **Person** Who does it? Why that person (or those people)? Who else might do it? Who should do it?
5. **Means** How is it done? Why that way? How else can it be done? How should it be done?

We saw earlier in the book that customer value is produced by delivering bundles of attributes capable of providing the benefits that customers value. These benefits are created by performing various activities. In chapter 2 we noted Porter's (1991) argument that activities are the ultimate source of any differentiation advantage, and that the economics of performing them determine a firm's relative cost. Very often, therefore, it is the choice of activities and/or the manner in which they are performed that provides the basis for competitive advantage.

Distinct strategies are frequently based on performing activities that competitors either do not perform or perform in a different way or, alternatively, on choosing not to engage in activities which competitors do perform. Differences between full-service network carriers and low-cost/no-frills airlines provide many examples of these alternative choices. But what is likely to make a competitive advantage unique and sustainable is not so much whether or how *individual* activities are performed, as the manner in which whatever activities are in fact performed are melded into what Porter (1996) refers to as an 'activity system'. According to Porter, competitive strategy is about being different. It means deliberately choosing a different set of activities to deliver a unique mix of value. Some of these activities will be performed by the airline itself and some will be outsourced, but the airline is responsible for orchestrating them to deliver customer value. A potentially unique source of competitive advantage, an airline's activity system links strategic logic, service concept, brand positioning, service-price offers, and competencies on the one hand to service delivery on the other. (See Holloway, 1998b, for an example of an activity system at Southwest.)

iii. Organizational architecture

> Before I built a wall, I'd ask to know what I was walling in or walling out.
> Robert Frost

Organizational architecture is a term now commonly used to describe the totality of an organization's internal design or structure and its external linkages (vertical and horizontal). It can have a profound impact on the efficiency and effectiveness of service delivery. We will consider first some of the popular theory on the subject, and then some of the practical issues.

The theory: value chains and value constellations

The 'value chain' is a concept popularised by Porter (1980, 1985) and used to describe all of the activities which come together within an organization to provide the final customer – the passenger, in this case – with 'value'. The concern here is not with organizational structures as represented in charts and hierarchies, but with what is actually done to transform tangible and intangible resources into outputs (e.g., ASKs/ASMs) and outcomes (e.g., satisfied customers). The logic is as follows:

- an airline's service concept helps determine the market segment(s) it chooses to serve and the services it will deliver to them;
- activities must be undertaken in order to design, communicate, and deliver services to customers, and these activities can be grouped into separate processes;
- considered as a whole, processes form a 'value chain' – an interlinked complex of activities which transform tangible and intangible inputs from outside the organization into the services sold to customers. The more vertically integrated an airline is, the more of these transformation activities and processes it conducts inhouse for itself;

- value is added at each stage of the chain and, inevitably, a cost is associated with this. As we saw when defining customer value in chapter 3, profit is a function of the cumulative cost of inputs on the one hand and the price paid by the final customer on the other;

- processes and activities must be coherently managed for effectiveness and efficiency within the context of the value they are intended to deliver to targeted customers. Firms must also manage linkages between their own, inhouse, value chains and those of their suppliers, alliance partners, distributors, and customers;

- 'management' of this 'value system' (or 'value constellation') of processes, activities, and external linkages – 'operations management' – should follow an 'operating strategy' appropriate to the airline's strategic positioning. Competitive advantage can reside in what is done, how it is done, or how what is done is co-ordinated, both internally and with external parties;

- thus, at the end of every airline value chain is a service. The fundamental questions are whether this service offers value desired by targeted customers at a price which both recovers the costs involved in producing it and matches the willingness of buyers to pay, and whether there is something distinctive, valuable, and difficult to imitate about the manner in which it is produced.

We met value chain analysis in chapter 2 in the context of the 'strategic positioning' approach to competitive advantage. In the language of its root discipline, microeconomics, thinking in terms of the value chain encourages airlines to identify and exploit the non-tradable, proprietary resources that allow them to perform activities (i.e., production functions) which competitors cannot perform, or cannot perform as cost-effectively, and to earn economic rent from doing this (Hergert and Morris, 1989). Clearly, the value chain concept moves the strategic positioning approach closer to the more inward-looking perspective of resource-based theory. Porter argues that thinking in terms of value chains can help understand potential sources of competitive advantage, and how each activity adds value for customers. Figure 7.4 illustrates the concept at a very general level.

There are those who suggest that because the value chain concept is based on the metaphor of the assembly line, it is too constraining and we would do better to think about organizations as players in multi-party 'value constellations' – technology-enabled co-operative networks (Normann and Ramírez, 1994). I will briefly look at network organizations in a moment.

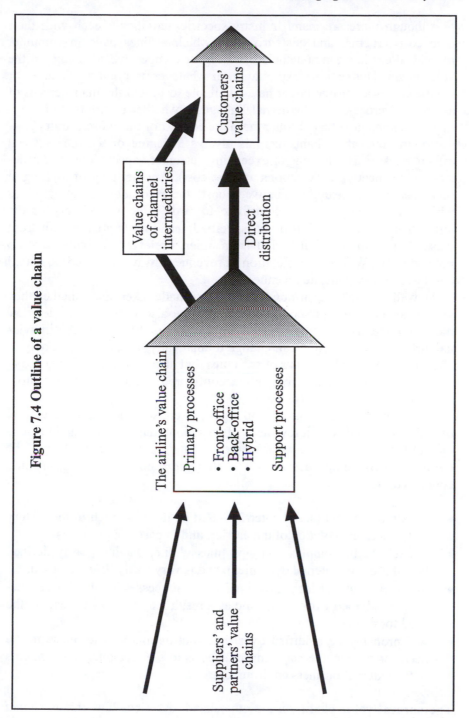

Figure 7.4 Outline of a value chain

Although there are many industry-specific activities – each with their own cost structure and cost drivers – which airlines have in common, individual carriers can nonetheless search for competitive advantage in the value chain. This requires exploitation of whatever proprietary resources or competencies an airline might have available to it, and the management of all internal processes and external linkages – whether proprietary or not – in a holistic manner that is coherent in the context of the chosen strategy.

Within any value chain, there is always a degree of tension between effectiveness (i.e., satisfying or exceeding customer expectations) and efficiency (i.e., meeting expectations at least cost). Another way of looking at this tension is to distinguish between costs incurred undertaking activities which add value – that is, contribute towards effective delivery of the airline's services as designed and specified – and costs arising both from these value-adding activities and from other, irrelevant, activities that do not add value. Whilst the generation of revenues always incurs costs, not all costs necessarily generate revenues.

As well as analysing *which* activities are undertaken and whether they are consistent with our service concept(s), we also need to consider *how* they are undertaken. Airlines each combine inputs differently. An individual airline's cost structure can change dramatically in response not only to changes in the cost behaviour of activities, but also as a result of changes in the way in which such activities are configured within the various processes comprising its value chain.

Value chain analysis is a challenging exercise when applied to real organizations, and what it reveals is often suboptimal. O'Sullivan and Geringer (1993) distinguish between 'contrived' and 'natural' value chains. The **contrived value chain** describes how things *are* done in the organization concerned. It:

- is path-dependent (see chapter 2) – that is, it owes much to the history and structural evolution of the carrier, and to past compromises;
- is likely to be complex, perhaps 'messy' (i.e., having poorly defined boundaries and internal dynamics), and is very likely ill-understood;
- may well contain a lot of positions and/or processes involved in reconciling misaligned work flows, and as a result may be slow to react to the need for change;
- will probably be modified over time, but as much in response to the need for further internal compromises as to the changing requirements of the external business environment.

The **natural value chain**, on the other hand, describes how things *should be* done. It:

- is focused entirely on the value-adding activities needed to meet objectives, and the resources required to give effect to these activities;
- limits complexity by defining only interrelationships and dependencies necessary to achieve objectives in an optimal manner;
- needs few reconciliation positions and/or processes, and so tends to react more rapidly to change;
- exists in only one ideal form;
- is stable over time, but does get modified – although more in response to changing business needs than to fresh internal compromises.

It might never be possible in practice to pin down the ideal of the 'natural value chain' for an organization. Despite almost two decades of interest in value chains and activity-based costing, 'the general irrelevance of traditional accounting data for strategic decision-making' remains a significant impediment (Hergert and Morris, 1989: 175). Nonetheless, the concept can help to keep strategic managers focused on the search for inadequacies in the 'contrived value chain' within which they work.

The practice: internal structure and external linkages

We saw above that service delivery takes place as a result of the 'horizontal' processes which connect inputs of goods and services from outside the airline to the final output of a service valued by the customer. Some of these processes are invisible to the customer, some are visible, some are directly experienced, and some are hybrids. However, the resources, tasks, and activities of which any one process is comprised are not necessarily managed on a process basis; frequently they are allocated to vertically oriented functional 'silos' – such as marketing, human resources, customer service, flight operations, and so on.

Organizational structure is essentially a reflection of the manner in which an airline breaks down what it does into different activities in order to deliver (or support the delivery of) service, and then integrates them for co-ordination (and control) purposes. The concepts underlying formal structuring of any organization are therefore 'differentiation' and 'integration'.

- **Differentiation** Tracing its origins back to Adam Smith's notion of the division of labour, the idea of differentiation is that the complex tasks undertaken by an organization in pursuit of its goals – too complex for any one individual to perform alone, hence the formation of the organization in the first place – are broken down to be performed by *different* people who each assume defined tasks. The division of labour is a child of the Industrial Revolution, and a reversal of the pre-existing heritage of craft-worker responsibility for an entire product from start to finish. 'Responsibility' – who is supposed to do what – came to be defined by task differentiation. Degrees of horizontal and vertical differentiation vary between organizations, and are partly path dependent. Similar or related tasks are usually grouped into departments, either on the basis of activity (i.e., function), product, or geographical market (Mabey et al, 1998). Teams (ad hoc or permanent, and sometimes cross-functional) have become increasingly important differentiation mechanisms in some airlines over the past decade.

- **Integration** This refers to the steps taken to co-ordinate differentiated activities – perhaps informal at first in a small carrier, but growing more complex as the number of people and activities concerned both multiply. The more differentiated an organization's activities are, the more elaborate its integrating structures and processes must be (although the need for elaboration can flow from environmental complexity as well as intensive differentiation). Policies, practices, and culture are sources of integration. Another is an airline's formal authority structure. 'Authority' is power attaching to an organizational position (and is therefore different from power an individual might have as a result of charisma, expertise or other traits). Typically, authority has been distributed hierarchically; other forms of authority distribution – matrix organization, for example – are now more widespread in many industries, although not particularly so amongst airlines. Where authority is broadly distributed the organization is considered 'decentralised', whereas concentrations of authority lead to 'centralisation' – often at the top of a hierarchy. (Bear in mind that there is a distinction between physical dispersion of an airline's activities and decentralisation of its decision-making.) 'Span of control' is a measure of the number of subordinates reporting to each position in a hierarchical organization; it correlates with the degree of vertical differentiation, because the fewer layers below a position – particularly a managerial position – the higher is likely to be the number of people reporting to that position.

We saw above that when cross-functional teams are used to perform tasks, activities, or processes in preference to functional units, they are a form of differentiation; when used to co-ordinate the work already done or being done by other units, however, they are a form of integration (and as such a perhaps expensive way of compensating for inefficient organization design). Finally, the communication channels through which information flows are an important integration mechanism, and the explosion of distributed information-processing power has the potential – not always realised – to de-couple these channels from pre-existing authority structures.

Chandler (1962) was the first to argue the now popular position that structure should be aligned with strategy, because it is the sole purpose of structure to translate strategic decisions into action in the marketplace. The danger is that strong functional departments can impose themselves upon, rather than facilitate, wider organizational strategies. Another problem is that if we take the view that strategy is an emergent theme derived from organizational learning rather than a minutely planned script, the admonition for structure to follow strategy becomes somewhat tautological.

One of the hotter topics in the recent literature is new forms such as network organizations. The network metaphor embraces two ideas.

- **Internal networks** The picture here is no longer of a highly different-iated organization integrated by hierarchical flows of responsibility and authority, but instead a collage of horizontal partnerships and teams (e.g., design teams, engineering teams, marketing teams, customer service teams, etc.), all focused on serving internal or external customers and integrated by instantaneous flows of information. Because the use of teams presupposes a shift from direction and control to objectives and trust, these flows allow near real-time adjustments, without the need for intervention from above. In the past, one of the key justifications for centralising decisions within a hierarchy was that the corporate database was in the form of paper files, accessible only to decision-makers present where those files were located – almost invariably corporate, divisional, or regional headquarters. Development of IS/IT in general, and of distributed networks and certain other tools in partic-ular, has removed this rationale. Furthermore, '[t]ools like e-mail, teleconferencing, and groupware let people work together despite dist-ance and almost regardless of departmental and corporate bound-aries....' (Stewart, 1997: 184).
- **External networks** The concept in this case is similar, except that the teams are situated in different organizations (i.e., different legal entit-ies) and so constitute a 'virtual' rather than a 'real' organization. The goal is to build 'collaborative advantage' on the basis of business relationships which competitors might be able to see, but cannot imitate precisely. We saw in chapter 2 that the competence to organize itself and its unique 'constellation' of relationships with external parties can be the source of competitive advantage for an airline. Although there has been a lot of imprecise talk about 'network organizations' and 'virtual airlines' in recent years, there is a very real issue here. The

issue is the manner in which, given a choice, managers choose to mix vertical, partnership, and market relationships when structuring the creation and delivery of services. We will look briefly at external architecture later in the chapter, and then return to the topic of external relationships in chapter 8.

Internal structure

Doyle (1994), quoted in Gattorna and Walters (1996: 290), has described recent efforts to change traditional hierarchies in the following terms.

> Today's leading companies are attempting to change dramatically by turning the pyramid upside down and flattening it. By flattening it they aim to take out layers of management and so slash overhead cost. By turning it upside down they seek to create a customer-led business with front-line employees motivated and empowered to satisfy customers. These new organizations recognize, first, that everything should start from a customer perspective. Second, those employees closest to the customer are at the top of the organization. They should be empowered to exercise their freedom to act within their areas of competence – to take responsibility, to accept accountability, to exercise initiative and to deliver results…[to] see themselves as owner operators….Third…[these organizations] see the primary role of staff, middle and senior management as helping the front line by providing the right products and resources and removing obstacles.

There has been a widespread historical tendency for airlines to be structured as highly centralised single-unit enterprises, often functionally oriented. This is not necessarily inappropriate for small carriers, or even for larger airlines operating in relatively stable competitive environments. As markets are liberalised and environmental turbulence intensifies, it risks becoming anachronistic, particularly if a policy of related diversification has produced a portfolio containing businesses linked to air transport but operating in their own third-party markets according to their own strategic logic, and facing distinct competitive conditions; in this latter case, a multidivisional or holding company structure is more appropriate than a functional structure. Changes at some airlines in recent years have indeed resulted in decision-making authority and the accountabilities which should go with it being increasingly pushed out of the corporate centre and down into geographical or product-oriented units closer to the marketplace. Nonetheless, quite a few of the world's larger airlines remain unusually centralised in comparison with companies of similar size (as measured by revenues and asset bases).

A combination of market instability, accelerating IS/IT capabilities (which can both democratise access to information by distributing it widely yet at the same time help centralise control over decision-making), changes in the tenor and scope of relationships with key suppliers, and the advent of alliances has stimulated much discussion of new metaphors – such as 'network', 'virtual', and 'tightly-coupled' organizations. Process-oriented structures are generally believed to lead to higher and more consistent levels of customer satisfaction in service industries, but airlines sometimes have to work hard to get people in pockets of highly specialised functional expertise to perceive their work in terms of wider, customer-serving processes. Functional hierarchies are anyway not going to disappear. Their primacy might be threatened by new concepts of organization, but the centres of professional excellence many of them house will always need to be nurtured. Process-oriented management should not be seen as a substitute for functional structures, but as a stage on which team-minded specialists can bring their various talents to bear in a non-hierarchical framework.

Finally, with regard to functional organizations, it might sound anachronistic to warn about the dangers inherent in having marketing departments in service businesses. Large airlines in particular will need specialists in functional marketing disciplines such as market research, service design, and marketing communications – and I am certainly not arguing against having a marketing department. The danger is, however, that the existence of such a department can and often does divert attention from the fact that in a service business everybody who has any sort of contact with customers and potential customers is a marketer. (The Nordic school of service marketing long-ago coined the expression 'part-time marketer' to reinforce this point; Grönroos (2000) in fact devotes an entire chapter of his textbook to explaining how to avoid the pitfalls of thinking that only the marketing department is responsible for marketing.)

There is not the space here to discuss different forms of airline organization. I will therefore make a number of generally applicable observations.

1. As mentioned in chapter 1, there are people who see organization structures not as real, immutable 'things' but as 'social constructions' created by the meanings people give to their experiences within the organization. Whether or not we accept this as an argument, there is merit in accepting it as a warning – a warning not to be 'hemmed-in' by organization charts to the detriment of the value-adding, customer-serving processes that actually get the work done. Organization charts do not represent real, tangible 'things': the offices and people they 'map' are real enough, but the idea of an organization 'structure' is simply another of the metaphors that the field of organization studies

relies so heavily upon. What we are actually interested in is the internal infra*structure* (another metaphor) through which communications (e.g., information, decisions), power, authority, and influence flow; although lines on an organization chart might map the 'formal organization', a large proportion of important flows tend to take place through the (socially constructed) 'informal organization'.

2. Two of the central concepts put forward in this book – competencies (assumed to be critical to competitive advantage) and service delivery (assumed to be critical to customer satisfaction) – both intuitively sit more comfortably in a horizontal, process-oriented framework than a vertical, command-and-control structure. There is a danger that both competencies and sight of the end customer might be 'locked away' in functional silos, inaccessible to others in the organization (Prahalad and Hamel, 1990).

3. When organizing anything, a good starting point is to specify just what it is you are trying to achieve. Tradition, inertia, and organization politics make life more complex than this suggests, but keeping the service concept and desired service outcomes firmly in mind must be a good starting-point. This is logical, but it is also important insofar as structures not only *reflect* ways of thinking, they also *generate* them – and this can have a profound impact on the perception and possibility of future organizational change (Mabey et al, 1998).

4. Structures need to be sufficiently 'crisp' to minimise decision-making costs by promoting clear roles and decision processes, yet at the same time sufficiently 'fuzzy' to accommodate the greater discretion and adaptability demanded in complex environments with ambiguous cause-effect relationships. Different parts of an airline's structure might show evidence of each, with operational functions tending towards the 'crisp' and structures housing strategy-making and commercial processes being somewhat more 'fuzzy'. This in turn has implications for sub-cultures, insofar as 'fuzzy' structures are more likely to accept iconoclastic views and welcome experimentation than would more purposeful and accountable 'crisp' structures (Butler, 1991).

5. Structure can either promote or hinder learning and change.

> Potential problems of learning are often….compounded by the routine processes of operational control. Hierarchies typically reinforce the values of conformity; to contradict a superior can be seen as a challenge to their authority, and it can seem wiser and safer to discard one's own experience and defer. This is just one of the ways in which vital knowledge is censored out of the organization. In times of rapid change these processes are often intensified, with insecurity serving to heighten individual and group defensiveness, thereby further restricting the flow of information

within the company. If at this stage the hierarchy is used to impose ill-informed strategic change, then one has created a recipe for disaster (Roberts, 1992: 10, quoted in Mabey et al, 1998: 347).

6. Not all structural forms are necessarily transferable with ease across national or cultural boundaries – something which is of interest in the context of global alliances. In a study documenting the failure to transfer teamworking, Salaman (1996) emphasises the need for the local context to be supportive of new structural forms if their potential benefits are to be acquired.

7. Whether or not we want to buy into the populist imagery of the inverted organization pyramid with customers on top being served by front-line staff, who in turn benefit from supportive back-office staff and a responsive senior management (at the bottom) brought closer to the customer by organizational de-layering, the fact remains that in a service business the organization should be designed to support and effect the delivery of service. In reality, of course, this is seldom the case in the airline business – but things will change.

One of the interesting things about the upper echelons of management hierarchies is that below the CEO there is rarely any single person with a clear responsibility for either revenue generation or cost management. (Over a decade ago British Airways appointed a director with responsibility for *both* marketing and operations, but this scope of responsibility made the position so all-encompassing that it was arguably equivalent to deputy CEO.) Were an airline's internal structure being (re)designed on a blank piece of paper, there might be merit in establishing a tripartite executive office comprised of the CEO, a Chief Revenue Officer (CRO), and a Chief Cost Management Officer (CCMO). Below this triumvirate could be a matrix structure of directors or vice presidents with specific functional and/or processual responsibilities – each accountable to the CRO and CCMO for the revenue and cost implications of what is done in their departments or divisions; this matrix could embody titles that fit with the approach adopted in this book and are unusual but certainly not unique in the industry – such as director of service delivery and director of innov-ation. There would be considerable overlap in responsibilities, and this would be quite deliberate: tightly drawn boundaries encourage a silo ment-ality, whereas fuzzy edges require negotiation, compromise, and – most importantly – teamwork. The overarching importance given to revenue and cost management by this structure takes us back to a point made in chapter 3: each service concept implies a revenue generation strategy and a cost management strategy which need to be managed holistically if a coherent value proposition is to be made and profitably delivered to the marketplace.

External linkages

Certain tasks and activities have to be performed in order to deliver air transport services to customers. Vertical integration reflects decisions taken regarding which of those tasks and activities will be performed inhouse and which will not; outsourcing occurs when a task or activity previously performed inhouse is moved outside the organization – although in colloquial usage it has come to be equated with any task or activity not undertaken internally, irrespective of whether or not it ever was inhouse. As we saw in chapter 1, economics has a theory to explain decisions affecting vertical integration and outsourcing: transaction cost theory argues that these decisions are driven by a comparison of the costs inherent in internalising a process within the organization, relative to the information search, contract negotiation, performance monitoring and purchase costs involved when buying-in from the market or entering into a partnership. Appealing though this might sound, it seems likely that path dependency, power, compromise, fad, and non-rational senior management choice criteria have as much to do with vertical integration decisions as any purely rational analysis of transaction costs.

There are five vertical scope options, with the word 'vertical' here being loosely defined to apply to any activity or process contributing ultimately to the delivery of customer value (Holloway, 1998b).

1. **Inhouse supply by an internal cost centre** The traditional – monopoly supplier – approach adopted in many large, highly integrated airlines.
2. **Inhouse supply by an internal profit centre or subsidiary** The traditional approach modified by infusion of a more entrepreneurial mindset, greater cost transparency, and – perhaps – a desire to tap into third-party markets.
3. **'Inhouse' supply by a joint venture** When airlines choose to joint venture activities, they usually do so either to access third-party markets, access expertise, and/or reduce future investment costs. Many of the joint ventures between airlines and powerplant OEMs established over the last few years, for example, share all these motivations. The realisation in cash of unrecognised shareholder value hidden in the airline's balance sheet might also motivate spinning an inhouse department or wholly-owned subsidiary out into a joint venture (or, alternatively, floating its equity).

4. **Tapered integration** This involves retaining inhouse some of the work done in respect of a certain activity or process, and outsourcing the rest. Possible advantages include the first-hand knowledge the airline retains in respect of costs and achievable efficiency levels against which to benchmark outsourced work, the avoidance of total reliance on external suppliers, and the flexibility it provides to outsource work during periods of peak loading whilst retaining a baseline inhouse capability to cope with normal operations. Some carriers, particularly in North America, have not been expanding their MRO capacities as rapidly as their fleets in recent years; the inevitable result is that more MRO work is being outsourced than in the past, and 'tapered integration' is thereore growing.

5. **Outsourcing** This involves contracting with external suppliers to undertake certain activities or processes. Outsourcing can encompass individual activities (e.g., aircraft cleaning), processes (e.g., payroll administration), or entire functions (e.g., IS/IT). Any activity or task that is 'separable' – that is, can be done independently of other activities and tasks in the value chain – is a potential candidate for external sourcing. Not a new phenomenon, the scale of external sourcing has increased significantly in the airline industry as start-ups have outsourced as many processes and activities as possible (including, in some cases, even flight operations) and established carriers have taken a closer look at what constitutes a 'core' activity and what is a candidate for outsourcing. Many outsourcing decisions are accompanied by declarations of 'partnership' between supplier and airline, particularly when the process concerned is significant to the outsourcing carrier's cost base, profits, and/or service quality without being a source of real competitive advantage worth retaining inhouse and investing in; whether this talk of 'partnership' is in fact hyperbole or a new way of transacting business varies from case to case.

There is an extensive literature to explain the behaviour of organizations faced with a choice between internal provision or external supply of required goods and services (Elfring and Baven, 1996). For a discussion of arguments in favour and against outsourcing, see Holloway (1998b). If all or part of a process is to be outsourced, several conditions have to be met:

- an external market must exist;
- what is to be outsourced must be measurable;
- interdependencies with retained activities and processes must not be so close as to make outsourcing impractical.

Once again, there is no single 'correct' answer. Much depends upon the specific circumstances of each carrier. The 'path dependency' concept we met in chapter 2 highlighted the importance of an organization's history in defining what it is and what it does today. There is a continuum of possibilities (Holloway, 1998a).

- At one extreme might be a traditional flag carrier – vertically integrated, dealing with suppliers largely on a transactional basis, and moving at best hesitantly towards adoption of outsourcing and partnering concepts.
- At the other extreme might be an airline which sees processes and accompanying competencies falling into one of two distinct categories:
    - core processes that should be retained inhouse: these could embrace control over the service concept, market positioning, service design, network management, brand management (including marketing communications and certain other aspects of the marketing mix), quality assurance, and management of ongoing customer relationships (through frequent flyer programmes and customer information systems, for example);
    - processes that might be externalised: these could include capacity provision in certain markets, many back-office processes, and (subject to tightly drawn service level agreements) even some front-office processes.

As noted in chapter 1, decisions with regard to vertical integration and outsourcing are clearly both strategic and competitive in nature. They are strategic because they affect business scope and scale; they are competitive because they affect the cost and/or quality of service delivery. These decisions should in principle be driven by a detailed analysis of the value chain, and by firm opinions on where it is possible to add value internally and where it is not.

iv. Conclusion

I will end the chapter with a quotation which links what we have been talking about to the content of preceding chapters.

> The heart of distinctive competence and competitive advantage may lie not in possession of specific organizational resources and skills; these can usually be imitated or purchased by others. Rather, competitive advantage may reside in the orchestrating theme and integrative mechanisms that ensure complement-

arity among a firm's various aspects: its market domain, its skills, resources and routines, its technologies, its departments, and its decision-making processes. Indeed, organizations may be viewed as systems of interdependency among these components, all of which must be coordinated to compete in the marketplace. It is the complexity and ambiguity of these relationships that give some organizations unique capacities that are all but impossible to copy. Configuration, in short, is likely to be a far greater source of competitive advantage than any single aspect of strategy (Miller, 1996: 509-510).

In a sense, the end of this chapter marks a natural break in the book. Adopting a process approach, we have looked first at what is 'strategic' about strategic services management, before then turning to the service concept, service design and pricing, communications, and – in this chapter – service delivery. In the remaining chapters we will consider three topics that are relevant to each stage in the process: the management of relationships; the monitoring of performance; and the management of innovation and change.

8   Managing Relationships

Any business arrangement that is not profitable to the other fellow will in the end prove unprofitable for you. The bargain that yields mutual satisfaction is the only one that is apt to be repeated.

B.C. Forbes

One of the most influential metaphors in the contemporary literature conceptualises organizations as systems embedded in a complex web of relationships with external environments and actors within those environments. In this chapter we will be taking a look at some of the more important of these relationships.

The ability to develop and maintain beneficial relationships with an increasingly wide range of stakeholders is an important competence in the airline business. The traditional view of an airline has been as a portfolio of routes and aircraft – a system through which customers are moved. A better view is that an airline is a portfolio of relationships – with customers, suppliers, regulators, employees, and various other stakeholders. Relationships are organizational resources, and as such need to be professionally managed. This chapter will look first at stakeholder networks in general, before focusing in turn on employee relationships, customer relationships, and collaborative relationships.

i. Stakeholder networks

Airlines have a wide range of audiences watching their activities: local and national governments, industry and other regulatory bodies, communities and special interest groups, stockholders, lenders and financial analysts, members of the media, suppliers, alliance partners, distribution channel intermediaries, customers, and competitors. As we saw in chapter 6, these audiences provide the context within which issues have to be managed and, in particular, internal and external communications have to be framed. It is vital that communications with stakeholders be as open as possible and bi-directional: every stakeholder relationship needs to be based on listening to and understanding the audience as well as addressing it.

In this chapter we will focus on relationships with a small number of important stakeholder groups. Although we will look at each separately, implying that they all have their own isolated positions and roles within a linear value chain, contemporary theories portray a much more complex world. Rather than being relatively simple dyadic (i.e., two-party) exchanges, stakeholder relationships in fact form interlocking networks of influence and impact; these networks can be characterised as systems, such that a change in behaviour or relationship at one point in the network can have perhaps unforeseeable consequences elsewhere. If we think just in terms of the supply chain, we can conceptualise our airline as an integrator, standing at the centre of an interdependent network of goods and services providers (each of which has its own unique stakeholder network), all being co-ordinated for the purpose of delivering satisfaction to the airline's customers. Such networks can be mapped; their scope will be in part dependent on the vertical integration and outsourcing decisions touched upon in chapters 1 and 7. Some couplings between organizations within these networks are 'tight', others looser and more transactional.

The network just described might be called a 'performance network', its primary objective being to 'perform' from a service delivery standpoint. This performance network is, however, only part of the story because it is inevitably enmeshed in a wider network of stakeholders, and the issues which concern these groups may have little to do directly with serving airline customers – although their indirect influence can be considerable (e.g., environmentalist lobbies). Managing dynamic stakeholder relationships is a difficult balancing act – one that requires consummate skills in the arts of listening, understanding, and articulating. These networks are complex and dynamic social systems with their own roles, conventions, expectations, behaviour patterns, conflicts, rewards, and sanctions.

We touched briefly on the management of stakeholder relationships in chapter 6 – the context there being the pivotal role of communications and brand image in addressing different audiences. In this chapter we will look just at employees, customers and performance networks (i.e., supplier partnerships and alliance relationships). This is not to imply that investor relations or government and industry relations, for example, are unimportant; we do not have the space to look at them here. Another set of relationships I will not be looking ar is those between airlines and intermediaries in distribution channels. Butler and Keller (1998) cover relationships between airlines and travel agencies (chapter 35) and freight forwarders (chapter 36); readers interested in cargo markets will also find the latter a useful adjunct to the discussion of alliance relationships in the present chapter.

Finally, it is worth mentioning that a topic I will not be exploring in any depth but which is gaining prominence in the literature is 'trust'. Berry (1999) devotes a chapter to the role of trust in underpinning relationships with employees, partners, and customers; Child and Faulkner (1998) take a comprehensive look at the concept in the context of alliances. Trust between employees and organization is often referred to as a 'psychological contract' – a contract that is stronger in some national cultures than others and that is brittle in the face of downsizing, de-layering, rightsizing, and the like (as Delta discovered, to the detriment of its reputation for high standards of service, in the mid-1990s).

ii. Employee relationships

> How come when I want a pair of hands I get a human being as well?
> Henry Ford

Employee relationships could be looked at from the perspective of modern strategic HRM theory (see Mabey et al, 1998), or given a more practical slant by examining them from an industrial relations standpoint. Another practical issue in the contemporary airline industry is the impact on attitudes and performance of employee stock ownership (see Holloway, 1998a). What I want to do instead is look at the wider context of corporate culture, which is a powerful influence not only on employee relationships but also on customers' experiences in the service delivery system. Later in this section of the chapter we will also briefly consider industrial relations and the importance of employee satisfaction to customer satisfaction.

We have already touched upon the importance of employees when looking at internal communications in chapter 6 and the role of resources – in this case, human resources – in service delivery in chapter 7. The reason I want to focus on culture in this chapter is to balance any implication in chapters 6 or 7 that employees are simply resources to be manipulated. As we will shortly see, there is an argument that – particularly in service businesses – employees and their culture *are* the organization.

Culture

> It is the dedication of the people in it that has made this airline a success.
> It is only through them that we will continue to have success in the future.
>
> Herb Kelleher

Culture is a shared pattern of meanings, understandings, attitudes and behaviours learned through socialisation – through a process of internalising values, expectations, and norms (i.e., unwritten rules of behaviour). It is a shared way of thinking and doing which is driven by certain basic assumptions and beliefs that may operate unconsciously. The assumptions, attitudes, beliefs, and values held by an airline's staff influence consumers' brand perceptions as much as do technical skills (de Chernatony, 1999a). They do this through their impact on commitment, enthusiasm, and consensus – alternatives to compliance and conflict that can be a vital ingredient in distinguishing one airline's service from the service delivered by competitors. Senior management needs to be confident dealing with issues of corporate culture, and able to clearly communicate core values to staff; the more this is so, the less likely it is that inconsistent service delivery will lead to disparate perceptions amongst customers (Kotter and Heskett, 1992).

Levels at which culture operates

It is usually sufficient for strategy-makers to be aware of the following.

National and regional cultures Seminal work examining the influence of national cultures on organizational cultures has been undertaken by Hofstede (1980). His central thesis was that organization cultures are to a large extent manifestations of the national cultures in which they are embedded. Hofstede explained differences in national cultures using four dimensions.

- **Power distance** Members of cultures with low power distances are less accepting of inequities (in authority, for example) than members of cultures with high power distances.
- **Uncertainty avoidance** Members of cultures with low uncertainty avoidance are more open to things that are unfamiliar or innovative and to ambiguous, unstructured situations or relationships than members of cultures with high uncertainty avoidance.
- **Individualism** Members of individualistic cultures are happy with loose and shifting relationships, whereas members of collectivist cult-

ures seek the support of collectivities (e.g., family, tribe or company) and are prepared to offer loyalty in return for that support.

• **Masculinity** Members of masculine cultures accept distinct gender roles and expect men to be assertive whilst women are nurturing, whereas in feminine cultures gender roles are not as pronounced.

In later work, Hofstede added a fifth dimension:

• **Perceptions of time** Different constructs of time and different time-scale emphases can lead cultures into very different outlooks on such things as strategy formulation (e.g., long-term versus short-term orientation) and the operational importance of time (Hofstede and Bond, 1988).

Hofstede's work has the practical advantage of focusing our attention on the difficulties an airline with a strong existing culture might face establishing itself in a country with markedly different cultural traits along these dimensions. In particular, it underlines the challenges facing ethnocentric airlines as they attempt to globalise in one way or another and adopt more polycentric enterprise cultures. It also highlights the separate contributions made by different national cultural traits to the lattice-work of meanings which underlies the social construction of organization cultures; culture plays a highly significant role in the processes through which people ascribe meanings to what happens in their organizations – and we saw in chapter 2 that individual creation of meaning can be taken as a central contributor to the social construction of organizational (and brand) identity. Finally, it draws attention to the fact that organizations – particularly 'national champion' flag-carriers – might still themselves be characterised as artefacts of a wider culture. What Hofstede's seminal work does not do is offer an explicit link between the values underpinning different dimensions of national culture on the one hand, and actual behaviour on the other. Cray and Mallory (1998) have provided this link by arguing that individual and organization-level cognitive frameworks interpose themselves between the effects of national culture and behavioural outcomes. (See Holloway (1998a) for a summary of the impact national culture can have on airline strategy, service design, and service delivery.)

Cray and Mallory (1998: 85-86) summarise the influence of national culture on strategy as follows.

> Formulating and executing strategy, more than other management functions, relies on the perceptions and judgements of the managers involved. Strategic decisions require that estimates are made about the future operations of

markets, competitors, suppliers and regulators, as well as the reactions of employees to any necessary changes. The ambiguity of information and the limited definition of alternatives mean that biases and predilections, including those provided by national culture, may hold greater sway than in other, more structured functions. The greater scope for choice, the larger number of alternatives available to the global firm, also expands the arena for the operation of cultural influences.

Industry culture In chapter 2 I referred to industry recipes and mindsets. These can manifest themselves in shared beliefs about what customers value, how to deal with issues, how and where to compete, what to do and not to do. Industry culture is most vividly thrown into relief for all to see when an outsider comes along and breaks with established norms. (See Smith et al (1991) for an analysis of recipes and mindsets in the US domestic airline industry.)

Organization culture National culture inevitably influences organization culture – which itself can affect strategic choice, service design, and service delivery (Wong-Rieger and Rieger, 1989; Holloway, 1998a). Beginning in the early 1980s and given particular momentum by Peters and Waterman (1982), the study of culture in an organizational context has gained considerable currency. We will return to this shortly.

Professional, departmental, and other subcultures Although some researchers conceptualise organizational cultures as unitary (Schein, 1985), others see them as multi-faceted (Siehl and Martin, 1984; Van Maanen and Barley, 1984). In the same organization there might, for example, be both a market-oriented or customer-oriented culture on the one hand and a strong power culture (Handy, 1985) built around a particular leader on the other. There will also be different managerial, occupational, professional, work group, departmental, and/or functional subcultures – ramp workers as distinct from customer service personnel, for example, and pilots as distinct from flight attendants. One of these might be dominant. If the different subcultures are not pulling in the same direction – if, for example, there is 'goal incongruence' with regard to whose interests the organization should be serving – friction is likely. Realistically, the presence of multiple subcultures must at the very least add complexity both to the airline and to the tasks involved in managing service delivery.

Subcultures can vary enormously between the same professional groups in different airlines. One US major is particularly well-known for a flight-deck subculture marked by supreme arrogance, for example, whilst a close competitor deliberately avoids hiring pilots unable to fit into a service-oriented team culture.

Organization culture

Consideration of organizational culture is not introspective indulgence. When a customer enters 'our world' (Irons, 1997b), they experience our culture as surely as a tourist entering a foreign country. An airline's culture is in this sense a major part of the 'destination product' a customer buys into when purchasing that carrier's service. An airline's culture is a key part of its service-price offer, which in turn implies that we need to look at it in terms of its relevance and appeal to targeted customers. More broadly than this, however, any airline operating in truly competitive markets must have a 'service culture' – something Grönroos (2000: 360) defines as,

> ….a culture where an appreciation for good service exists, and where giving good service to internal as well as ultimate, external customers is considered by everyone a natural way of life and one of the most important values.

Organizational culture is defined in many different ways in the literature, but a common theme is the sharing of perceptions and definitions of reality (Marion, 1999). Brown (1998: 9) defines it as 'the pattern of beliefs, values and learned ways of coping with experience that have developed during the course of an organization's history, and which tend to be manifested in its material arrangements and in the behaviours of its members'. A hallmark of culture is the nature of behaviour that is rewarded and behaviour that is discouraged. Culture both generates and legitimises ways of thinking and doing.

However strong or weak it might be in any given case, culture is always present whenever people gather together in a social system such as an airline or any other type of organization. (Not all academics would agree with this statement – some, such as Morgan (1997), arguing that culture is not a real phenomenon but just one of several metaphors (alongside 'system' and 'structure', for example) that we use in order to help us make sense of organizations.) Its culture embodies each organization's shared memory of what has happened and what has worked in the past; it therefore drives people's perceptions of what will work in response to emerging or potential issues in the future. Culture is a lens through which the world is viewed; by shaping people's perceptions of external environments, it helps to create what passes as 'reality'. The stronger it is the more stable it is likely to be, because it will be more easily transmitted from one 'generation' of the airline's people to the next. A strongly embedded culture might be a welcome source of stability, or it might shelter inertia; everything depends upon the relevance of the attitudes and behaviours it promotes to the needs of the airline and, specifically, the expectations held by targeted customers.

The following three approaches have been adopted for the study of organizational culture (Martin, 1992).

1. **Integration approach** This, dominant, view conceptualises culture as a 'thing' that organizations 'have' – an independent variable that strategic managers must shape into homogeneity so that it is a positive influence capable of *integrating* everybody's goal-oriented efforts. Schein (1985) has proposed a three-level model of the content of culture that has been particularly influential within the integration paradigm.

   • *Artefacts* Symbols (including brand logos), rituals, myths, apocryphal stories about founders, heroes, or great leaders, ceremonies, rites and rituals, the design of corporate spaces (e.g., welcoming and accessible, or assertive and forbidding), mission statements, and other symptoms of culture which are visible on the surface but often difficult to decipher provide cultures with a superficial layer of artefacts. Schein suggests that artefacts might be manifested physically (e.g., office decor and business attire), behaviourally (e.g., communication patterns and punishment/reward systems), and verbally (e.g., language usage, myths and metaphors). When United – to name just one of many possible examples – dropped use of the word 'passengers' in its premium class lounges and adopted 'customers' instead, cynics could have interpreted the change as a superficial nod in the direction of the latest management fad; alternatively, it could be read as a deliberate piece of symbolism targeted as much at staff as at customers.

     Artefacts are important communicators of underlying values, norms, beliefs, and assumptions, and these are closely linked to the brand elements discussed in chapter 5; they need to be regularly audited, and changed when necessary. Through their emotional appeal they can sometimes engage loyalty and influence behaviour in ways that rational strategies and formal structures cannot (Barley et al, 1988).

   • *Values, beliefs, attitudes, and norms* These are respectively, the principles which bind members of the culture together (i.e., which define what they *value*), what people think is and is not true (e.g., about cause-effect relationships linking action and outcome), people's learned pre-dispositions (i.e., evaluations based on feelings which influence beliefs), and the unwritten rules through which expectations of behaviour are imposed (i.e., expectations of what is considered *normal*). It is behaviour in conformity with values, beliefs, attitudes, and norms that creates the cultural artefacts used to reify and reinforce the culture. Box 8.1 looks at values.

- *Basic assumptions* The invisible 'subterranean' heart of an organization's culture and the third level in Schein's integrationist model, these are the unconscious, taken-for-granted truths and realities that drive how an airline's people perceive their experiences and act in response to them. According to Schein (op cit), core assumptions shape the manner in which organizations:
  - adapt to their external environments, by developing a consensus on mission, goals, strategies, and performance measures;
  - integrate internally, by developing a consensus on common language and concepts, criteria for inclusion within the group and disposition of status, power and authority, and means for managing intra-group relationships (e.g., rewards, punishment, and friendship).

Box 8.1: Values

Those are my principles. If you don't like them, I have others.
Groucho Marx

Shared values are a significant ingredient in the glue that binds people into an organizational culture, and are a major contributor to service consistency. Values, alongside beliefs and other dimensions of culture, are also a significant ingredient in the identity of an airline as constructed by people – particularly staff – who experience it (Durand, 1997).

They define what is considered important in individual, and therefore organizational, behaviour. They also contribute to the definition of organizational purpose. More open communications and ready accessibility of information are making it increasingly difficult to sustain different sets of values in relation to different stakeholders; it is therefore now more necessary than in the past to ensure that one set of values is applied to dealings with employees, suppliers, customers, creditors, and investors, for example. There needs to be congruence between corporate values and the 'brand values' we met in chapter 6. Readers who reckon this is fairly fuzzy stuff should reflect on the different brand identities of Virgin Atlantic and British Airways, or Southwest and American; these identities are underlain by very different value systems – value systems that have a profound impact on service delivery.

Airlines with multiple subcultures have a particular need for a set of core values which can serve to define a consensus, or at least an accommodation, about what the organization is, and about what it is striving to achieve and to become. A widespread consensus regarding core values normally translates into what can be described as a 'strong' corporate culture.

Not all values are equally significant. In any airline, some – 'core' – values will be central to the culture and widely shared, whereas others will be marginal. However, unless values are recognised and the important ones identified, they cannot be managed; some writers believe the central task of chief executives is nothing more or less than to manage values (Peters and Waterman, 1982). Once the shared values that predominate in an airline have been recognised they can – according to integrationist theory – be managed through recruitment and socialisation processes and, as the need arises, changed to accord with new organizational circumstances.

It can in fact sometimes be very difficult to manage strategies without managing values. For example, if an airline has an objective which calls for decentralisation of decision-making authority to empower front-line staff so they have greater latitude to act without upward referral, the people to be empowered must be comfortable with the new freedom and their managers must have values which support the practical implementation of the approach. In other words, the necessary values must be widely shared. New strategies often demand adoption of new values. Conversely, it is important that new values are backed by credible action; a credibility gap is inevitable, for example, if a management preaches empowerment but practises tightly centralised control.

Values frequently programme the manner in which people respond to problems. If a carrier is losing market share on a route, should it discount fares, advertise more aggressively, launch a promotion, or reallocate capacity elsewhere in its system? Or should it probe deeper to find the root cause(s) of the loss, looking for problems with the service-price offer being made to customers or with the service delivery system?

But most significantly, values relevant to the needs of target market segments are a potential source of competitive advantage. Because the services airlines deliver are largely intangible and experiential, values can be an important tool for 'programming' quality into service delivery processes. Employees who do not know what their airline stands for, and what its point of view is on the marketplace, have no consistent framework within which to interact with customers. Values must therefore be clearly established and nurtured so that each airline is able to offer targeted customers a clear proposition about itself around which brand loyalty can be built.

Alliances may pose problems in this latter respect. It is difficult enough to fashion and communicate within a single carrier values consistent with that airline's service concept(s) and operating strategy. To achieve this within a wide-ranging global alliance will be challenging. Yet if partners do not share core values, it is somewhere between likely and inevitable that their ways of serving customers will be different. And if their approaches to customers are different, what purpose does a comprehensive alliance uniting two or more networks serve that market-by-market agreements with a constellation of different partners could not achieve?

Having said all that, there are nonetheless two alternative views on the merit of shared values.

- *There is a widely held view that organizations benefit when their people share core values (Peters and Waterman, 1982).*
- *A different view is that organizations are frequently too large for all their people to share even core values, but this does not matter because diversity in fact helps them cope better with complex change and avoid 'group-think'.*

2. **Differentiation approach** This second perspective on the nature of organizational culture accommodates the idea of professional, departmental, and other subcultures, whereas the integration paradigm does not. An important implication is that conscious efforts need to be made by senior managers to understand different subcultures, and members of these subcultures need to understand the significance of what they do within the context of the wider service delivery system. This is important because every subculture has the potential to frame in a different way the manner in which staff interpret, and therefore project, brand identity to stakeholders, particularly customers.

   An alternative approach to cultural differentiation might be to look for different cultures not just in functional units, but in a 'candy metaphor'. Whilst it *might* be plausible to think in terms of a small carrier having a single culture, the industry giants are inevitably more complex than this – akin to a candy with a hard, bureaucratic inner core (which customers only 'bite into' in the event of a major service failure) surrounded by a sweeter, service-oriented outer coating or subculture. Managing two such different subcultures, and in particular keeping the outer coating from 'melting away', can be a formidable challenge.

3. **Fragmentation approach** The view from this perspective is that culture is neither an integrated whole within an organization, nor a differentiated set. Instead, it is seen as a fluid series of consensuses built

around specific issues. Culture is therefore uncertain, ambiguous, and in constant flux (Brown, 1998).

Some of the academic interest in culture has used the concept as a new paradigmatic lens through which to analyse organizations – to describe the shared meanings employees give to their experiences within the organization and also to stand for their negotiated understanding of meanings imparted by symbols, events, and behaviours. From this perspective, organizations are seen *as* cultures, rather than as instrumental or mechanistic entities that *have* cultures (de Chernatony, 1999b). Its culture defines what an organization *is*; its members continually construct and reconstruct the meaning they give to their experiences, and in the process imbue actions with a particular understanding that separates the culture of which they are a part from any other culture.

An alternative standpoint, particularly popular in the practitioner literature, is to see culture as an attribute that organizations *have* and which can be proactively managed in pursuit of improved performance (Barley et al, 1988). The following subsections largely adopt this second theme, because it is intuitively appealing – despite the lack of generalisable empirical support – to believe that culture can have a profound impact on the style, tone, and outcome of service encounters and so should be consciously managed, and because this reflects the most widespread paradigm. Managers tend to prefer this approach because they recognise that culture affects the implementation of service strategy, and by nature they like the thought of having at least some measure of control over implementation variables. However, in treating culture as something an organization *has* and as a manageable 'design variable' we are making an assumption about reality that is no better grounded in fact than the contrary view that culture is what an airline *is* and that its evolution can be nudged in one direction or another by events or by astute leadership but cannot be fine-tuned as though it were, say, an inflight product.

How organization culture is created The best single explanation is 'values'. The size, history, and ownership of an airline will also affect its culture, as will the various external environments within which it operates. Organization design, systems, procedures, and HRM policies – notably recruitment and reward policies – are important mechanisms for embedding culture. This is rather simplistic, however. From a resource-based perspective on competitive strategy, any airline's culture is part of a deeply embedded social architecture that develops slowly over time and which may be a source of competitive advantage as a result of its particular capacity to learn and the accumulation of tacit knowledge (Mueller, 1996). Downsizing, de-layering, process re-engineering and outsourcing may or may not be 'rationally' justifiable in particular cases, but one of their costs is erosion of this social architecture.

A significant contributor to the culture of any airline is its people, particularly the dominant person or group, because the flow of influence between individuals and organizational culture is very much a two-way affair: people are socialised by the culture which envelops them, but over time they in turn can also shape that culture if they have sufficient power. Much of an airline's culture comes from within its people, and this is what makes it so hard to blueprint, manage, or imitate. That said, what leaders pay attention to, their use of language, and how they react to critical events can be primary carriers of culture; particularly in a power culture, how leaders behave, what they do, and what they reward are amongst the most important drivers of airline culture.

The literature draws attention to dangers in permitting inconsistencies to develop between 'espoused culture' and 'culture-in-practice': the former represents an ideal state espoused in documents such as the annual report, in senior management urgings, and perhaps in training programmes, whilst the latter is the actual culture experienced by employees (Brown, 1998). de Chernatony (1999b) has identified three types of inconsistency that can cause gaps between the type of culture senior management might want an airline to have and the type of culture employees perceive it to have.

1. **Action inconsistency** Senior managers who talk extensively about the importance of consistent service delivery but reduce the staff training budgets necessary to help improve it are guilty of action inconsistency.
2. **Symbolic inconsistency** Senior managers who talk about high-quality service but pay no attention to the outward appearance of the airline's facilities and equipment are guilty of symbolic inconsistency.
3. **Ideological inconsistency** Senior managers who espouse certain values, say the importance of people to the organization, but who do not live by those values – perhaps because they do not listen to staff or they give little attention to staff development – are guilty of ideological inconsistency.

Senior managers clearly need to be aware of these types of inconsistency and the impact they can have on both corporate culture and service delivery.

Links between organizational culture and performance Writers linking organizational culture to performance (such as Tom Peters and others in the 'excellence' genre) argue that:

- organizations *have* cultures that can be identified and assessed;
- organizations perform more effectively when they develop cultures that are both 'right' and 'strong';
- such cultures create consensus, unity, and commitment and motivate staff more efficiently than traditional approaches using structures, procedures, and rules;
- in these and other ways, culture can affect corporate performance through its impact on attitudes and behaviours;
- cultures should be actively managed and, where necessary, should be changed by manipulating cultural artefacts and altering employees' values, beliefs, attitudes, norms, and basic assumptions;
- it is the responsibility of senior managers to monitor and where necessary change organizational culture (Mabey et al, 1998: 462).

There are, however, problems with this view of culture as an essentially positive, integrative, shared carrier of organizational intent. First, even without empirical evidence it is fairly obvious that in any large airline widely shared values will be overpowered when they conflict with the values of the daily experienced work group: people who work together develop a strong system of meanings which drives their interpretation of what they are doing, why they are doing it, and how they should relate to each other and the organization (Pettigrew, 1979). Many of these group value systems and subcultures are clearly manifest in labour contract negotiations. Second, although culture is widely written about as a force for the good, there is no objective reason why this should be so. If culture is not unitary, consensual, and consistent (ibid), there is clearly scope for it to be fragmented, ideological, and divisive.

As noted above, no incontrovertible link has been established between culture and performance (Brown, 1998). Nonetheless, it is intuitively appealing to follow the integrationist approach and conclude that culture can have an influential effect on processes that are important to strategy generally and service delivery in particular. Holloway (1998b) has suggested the following.

- **Organizational culture can affect decision-making** Culture guides decision-making both at the strategic level and throughout an airline, simply because decisions – and particularly strategic decisions relying on extensive information gathering, analysis, and interpretation – are rarely value-free. Culture can either foster or suppress emergent strategies, and it strongly influences the manner in which intended strategies are implemented. It affects how people perform their tasks, manage resources, respond to environmental stimuli, handle conflict, and cope with uncertainty and change. It can motivate or discourage different types of action. It is capable of providing the sense of identity that many people look for from their working environment, and so can generate consensus, loyalty and commitment, which are believed in turn to feed through to higher levels of customer service and satisfaction. A culture which encourages service providers to internalise service-oriented, customer-focused norms can be a powerful resource in any service delivery process.

- **Organizational culture can affect people's understanding of what needs to be done** 'Excellence', 'quality', and 'good service' are not objective, measurable facts but abstractions which can mean different things to different people in different organizations or different parts of the same organization (Schein, 1985). Culture has the potential to influence people's understanding of these and other aspects of language usage to create a shared realm of meaning. Culturally based misunderstandings can disrupt organizational life when different parts of an airline or different parts of a supply network do not share common definitions of the language they use – as when what one input producer (e.g., a contract cleaner) considers acceptable is not what their immediate customers (e.g., the cabin crew taking over a flight) consider acceptable.

- **Organizational culture can affect learning** In fact, the relationship between culture and learning is interdependent: what, how, and how quickly airlines learn depends on the attitudes and behaviours promoted by their cultures, whilst cultures are inevitably influenced by the outcome of collective learning, how it is stored in organizational memory, and how it is accessed and retrieved when needed (Schein, 1985; Brown, 1998).

- **Organizational culture can affect the balance between control and autonomy** Culture shapes management's willingness to listen and grant autonomy to front-line staff, and its commitment to delivery of the value that customers want rather than what the airline thinks they ought to want. It defines the airline's attitudes towards people – customers, suppliers, partners, and employees; it can affect recruitment criteria, rewards and compensation, with those working in tune with the culture benefiting both materially and also from additional freedoms in carrying out their tasks. It drives conformity and the willingness to accept nonconformity, the propensity to take risks, and the desire to seek out root causes of identified problems in order to improve processes. Organizational learning is accomplished best by 'doing', and managers 'do' in response to a corporate culture which reinforces certain types of risk-taking, which encourages them to act in new ways without empirical evidence of the likely outcome, and which rewards them for taking the responsibility this imposes.

Culture is a medium of control because people internalise the values and norms prevalent in an airline and act in accordance with those norms, much as they internalise the rules and norms of the wider societies in which they live. Internalised beliefs are capable of motivating people to extraordinary performance levels. People are a vital resource; it is one of the tasks of organizational culture to engage them and draw out their full potential.

- **Organizational culture can help communicate and reinforce an airline's image** Culture is a major contributor to the brand image which every airline builds either explicitly or implicitly in the minds of its customers and other stakeholders. Particularly – but not uniquely – in the case of service industries, it is a significant part of what is being sold.

  Culture embodies an airline's approach to the identification and satisfaction of customers' needs, and it tells the customer sufficient for her to recognise things she likes, with which she can identify, and around which she can build loyalty. It is a significant element in market positioning. Barney (1986a) concluded that culture is an organizational resource that can generate sustainable competitive advantage provided it reinforces activities that contribute to achievement of specific performance objectives keyed off the organization's service concept(s), it is unusual, and it cannot easily be imitated.

- **Culture can be important to service consistency** People can be trained to deliver high-quality service, but they cannot be trained to deliver it at every service encounter. Attitude is a key driver underlying what actually happens at the customer interface, and attitudes are strongly influenced by – as well as themselves being influences on – corporate culture. It is very difficult to get consistent behaviour out of people through use of rules alone. It is far better that attitudes and behaviours are shaped by values. Whereas rules prescribe what should and should not be done, values guide both how to do things and what to do in situations where there are no rules.

The danger in any organizational culture, not just one that is weak or badly aligned, is that there is a tendency for it to be rooted in what happened in the past rather than what needs to happen in the future. There is a risk of fighting the last war. Repetition and rigidity may drive out innovation. This danger aside, culture is a powerful ingredient in competitive advantage – particularly for a high-contact service business such as an airline.

Nonetheless, few airlines take the monitoring of culture as seriously as Southwest, which has a standing committee charged with the task. This committee comprises 108 employees who serve staggered two-year terms and meet twice a year to pool ideas and feedback received at various face-to-face meetings with peers around the system that each gets time off to attend (McCarthy, 1997).

Alliances There are two issues regarding alliances and culture. First, airline alliances in many cases involve managing relationships across national cultural boundaries. Inevitably, managers 'are faced with integrating the actions and attitudes of individuals and organizations operating in contexts quite different from their own. They must negotiate with groups that have not only different goals, but different methods of reaching them and different expectations of their counterparts' behaviour' (Cray and Mallory, 1998: 2). As and if airline alliances develop further along the road to closer integration, the challenge will be one of integrating complex, intercultural organizations which span cultural milieux separated by the five dimensions of national culture referred to earlier (Hofstede, 1980; Hofstede and Bond, 1988) – a separation tellingly referred to by Shenkar and Zeira (1992) as 'cultural distance'; cultural distance will inevitably manifest itself in different approaches to the gathering, interpretation, and marshalling of information, different decision-making styles, different approaches to the management of human resources, different expectations associated with the role of leaders (e.g., 'great man', administrator, consensus-builder, etc.), and different degrees of willingness to adapt to new ways of thinking and doing.

Second, culture has a direct impact on the tone and style of service delivery. Culture usually shapes the way things are done in an airline or any other type of organization. Unless and until an alliance can establish a culture of its own, whose 'ways of doing' are to be followed? And there is a deeper question. If people, their values, and the influence their organization's culture has on the style and tone of service delivery really are important foundations of competitive advantage for any airline unprotected from competitors by regulatory and/or infrastructural barriers to entry, if tacit knowledge and inimitable, embedded routines within individual airlines do lead to causally ambiguous but competitively valuable outcomes (see chapter 2) – how can alliances establish competitive advantage and compete in their own right? Network scope, advertising spend, and customer recognition can all be imitated. In a high-contact service industry, what matters at the end of the day is the culture underlying delivery of actual services to actual customers; for the foreseeable future this is likely to be in the hands of individual alliance members – each of whom inevitably has different cultures and values, no matter how many press releases argue the contrary.

Industrial relations

Industrial relations often involve a juxtaposition of conflict and collaboration. The arena in which these forces play out is to some extent shaped by path dependency (i.e., the history of a particular airline and its employment relations), and to some extent by the nature of current issues and dominant personalities; particularly influential are the culture, legal system, accepted industry practices, and labour market characteristics of the airline's home country. Herein lies another challenge awaiting global alliances if they are ever to mature into the much-hyped global mega-carriers.

Industrial relations is a very broad subject that can be treated in a variety of ways, but looking at it as an adjunct of culture is appealing insofar as the tone and quality of industrial relations are both influenced by, and profoundly influential upon, organizational culture. Two points need to be made from a strategic services management perspective.

1. The right approach for managements to take is to want to offer their people as much as they feasibly can, in return for the highest possible levels of productivity consistent with the service concept(s) being pursued. We need to focus on people's value as well as their cost.
2. The objective of the exercise should not be to gain employee acquiescence or compliance, but to set the stage for a real commitment to delivering the customer value that the airline's service concept(s) aim to deliver.

These are not ideals that have yet been widely fulfilled across the airline industry as a whole. In particular, getting commitment from people is not an easy task in some national cultures (especially those that are more individualistic) because whether we are prepared to recognise it explicitly or not, airlines are like most other forms of organization insofar as they are on one level systems of control – so what we are in fact arguing here is that people should be committed to the purposes of a system designed inter alia to control them (Collins, 1998).

Nonetheless, given the significance of employee morale to standards of customer service, it is astounding how long contract negotiations are permitted to drag on at some airlines – particularly in the United States. It is often difficult for outsiders to escape the conclusion that neither internal communications nor levels of mutual respect are all they should be when bargaining is allowed to stretch over several years. Adversarial employee relations may or may not save some dollars in the short term, but any saving has to be weighed against the immediate revenue impact of industrial action on the airline concerned and its alliance partners – as in the case of disputes at Northwest in 1998 and United in 2000. In the long term, adversarial labour relations can cost serious money; the reason lies in the linkage, long intuitively appealing but now empirically supported, between employee satisfaction and customer satisfaction.

The importance of employee satisfaction to customer satisfaction

> "I've half a mind to be apathetic."
> Banx cartoon, *Financial Times*

Like most employees, airline staff tend to treat customers in much the same way that their managers treat them. If corporate values fail to recognise the importance of people and their inner needs, it is unlikely that front-line staff will recognise the importance of customers and what it is that they in their turn need and expect. Research has indicated that a clear correlation exists between employee satisfaction and customer satisfaction. Heskett et al (1994, 1997) have popularised the concept of a 'service-profit chain' built around three central relationships that need to be understood and managed.

1. Employee satisfaction and customer satisfaction feed off each other.
2. Employee loyalty and customer loyalty feed off each other.
3. Customer loyalty generates higher, sustainable profits.

Specifically, the logic of the chain is as follows.

- **Internal service quality** is driven by variables such as work-place design, job design, employee selection and development, employee rewards and recognition, the availability of appropriate equipment and systems for serving customers, and positive feedback from service delivery.
- **Employee satisfaction** is driven by internal service quality, and in turn influences employee productivity, turnover, and retention. These feed through to **external service value** – which in essence means the benefits delivered to customers.
- **Customer satisfaction** is driven by experience of a service that was designed to meet their particular needs and expectations, and which

    succeeds in doing this – in part through the efforts and commitment of satisfied employees.

- **Customer loyalty** is triggered by satisfaction (an argument which, as we will see later in the chapter, has been opened to debate by recent empirical findings). Loyalty is manifested in **customer retention** and positive **word-of-mouth** referrals.
- The end of this chain is enhanced **revenue growth** and **profitability,** which can then be fed back into sustaining or upgrading internal and external service – and so on around this 'virtuous circle'.

Heskett (1995: 453) has this to say about the linkage between employee loyalty and customer loyalty.

> Market share quality often results directly from efforts to build the satisfaction and loyalty of service workers who are in direct contact with customers. Employee satisfaction results from initiatives to match attitudes and skills with jobs, train and recognise people, rethink work, and provide technological support to increase the capability to deliver results to customers. It clearly requires attention to both operating and human resource management issues, once again a bridging of functions.

    The alternative is a 'cycle of failure'. Empirically identified in a number of service industries and certainly no stranger to the airline business, this often appears in reaction to economic downturns or corporate underperformance: in an effort to cut costs the product is compromised by eliminating customer value, reducing staff training, downsizing front-line staff, and generally ignoring the linkages that turn satisfied, loyal employees into satisfied, loyal customers. Paring costs without paring value to avoid slipping into a cycle of failure is not an easy challenge for managers under bottom-line pressure. This is why, as mentioned several times already, cost management strategy and revenue management strategy should be treated as symbiotic within the context of a given service concept rather than as distant cousins.

    It is vital that the linkages between employee satisfaction, customer satisfaction, and shareholder value are understood by top management – especially the board. Some managements, particularly in the United States, seem to have lost sight of these linkages and over-focused on shareholder value alone. In the absence of a real – as opposed to simply espoused – understanding of the critical importance to long-term shareholder value of investments in people, attention to culture, and obsession with what customers expect from their service experiences, it is all too easy for top managers' gaze to revert to the bottom of the next quarterly report. Maximising short-term earnings at the risk of breaking the service-profit chain poses a threat to long-term shareholder value (Hallowell and Schlesinger, 2000).

iii. Customer relationships

Profit in business comes from repeat customers, customers that boast about your product and service, and that bring friends with them.

W. Edwards Demming

In this section of the chapter we will first draw a distinction between transactional and relationship exchanges in marketing, and then outline the philosophy behind relationship marketing. After that we will examine the important services management concepts of customer loyalty, customer retention, and customer defection.

Managing customer relationships

The concept of 'exchange' is central to marketing theory. Exchange occurs when two or more parties offer something of value to each other and enter freely into the exchange process. Several types of exchange have been identified in the literature, amongst which the two most significant for our purposes are 'transactional' and 'relationship'.

- A **transactional** exchange occurs independently of any previous or subsequent exchanges. The vast majority by number of most airlines' exchanges with their customers remain primarily transactional – although whenever a strong brand imposes itself favourably on the perceptions of a customer, even if subconsciously, what appears to be a series of unconnected transactions might in fact be driven by an implicit relationship between customer and brand.

- A **relationship** exchange occurs when the parties concerned develop a commitment to engaging in further exchanges in the future. As just mentioned, this commitment might not be consciously arrived at by the customer. Furthermore, the airline concerned might be targeting its brand image at segments or markets as a whole rather than at specific individuals. On the other hand, many airlines do try to build explicit relationships with their core, high-value frequent flyers and corporate accounts in particular.

The two approaches represent distinct marketing paradigms, one focused on customer acquisition followed by a single marketing transaction ('conquest marketing') and the other on customer retention and multiple transactions over the lifetime of a relationship hallmarked by loyalty. Philosophically, transactional and relationship approaches are very different. Transactional exchanges are driven by the 4Ps of traditional marketing – product, price, promotion, and place – augmented to 7Ps by the more recent arrival in the services management literature of people, processes, and physical evidence. The relationship approach, on the other hand, looks beyond individual exchanges to the development of sustained social interactions fuelled by a collage of brand elements, past impressions of service quality, and various types of communication – all encapsulated in the airline's brand image (Dierickx and Cool, 1988; Tapp, 1997). Although in practice there is always a degree of overlap in the implementation of the two philosophies, there is one core difference between them that has considerable practical importance: relationship marketing is founded on the premise that customer retention rates are a significant driver of shareholder value.

The relationships in an 'installed' customer base can be seen as a core strategic resource that needs proactive maintenance, just like any other. They are a source of future cash flows, and the foundation of future increases in shareholder value.

Relationship marketing

A number of airlines – particularly carriers targeting premium segments – are now directing greater efforts than in the past to customer retention, aiming to satisfy the most important of their existing customers and build longer term relationships with them. The basis of a relationship is likely to depend upon which benefits predominate in a customer's choice of brand. For example, a customer strongly attracted by the emotional benefits of a brand will retain a relationship with that brand for as long as it continues to provide those benefits. On the other hand, a customer might be attracted to a carrier largely by the functional benefits it offers (e.g., network and schedule); as long as these remain on offer at the requisite level of quality, perhaps through flying to the right places at the right times and with reliable punctuality, the relationship will continue – unless a competitor can offer a compelling reason to defect. Clearly, it would be helpful for airline managers to know what it is that *their* customers – particularly their most loyal, revenue-rich customers – look for out of the relationship.

Bateson (1995: 457) has defined relationship marketing as:

...the union of customer service, quality, and marketing. Relationship marketing emphasizes the importance of customer retention, product benefits, establishing long-term relationships with customers, customer service, increased commitment to the customer, increased levels of customer contact, and a concern for quality that transcends departmental boundaries and is the responsibility of everyone throughout the organization.

Payne (1995) sees the principal elements of relationship marketing as:

- a deliberate emphasis on maximising the lifetime value of profitable customers and segments;
- recognition that service quality is the key to customer retention, that quality is defined by reference to customers' expectations and perceptions, and that delivering quality service is the responsibility of everybody in the airline;
- willingness to enter into a dialogue with customers (either individually or, more frequently, by sampling within segments) to ensure that their expectations are understood;
- a 'network' perspective, which sees the maintenance of relationships with other stakeholders as important to provision of the quality of service required to maintain relationships with customers.

When talking about customer relationships we can, as implied above, be referring to one or both of two ideas.

1. **General brand relationships** Many airlines, perhaps most, rely on brand image and customer self-selection as the foundation of relationships with their customers. Whether they are aware of it or not, once customers' brand recall and recognition reach certain points they begin to develop a relationship with the brand concerned. The nature and intensity of the relationship will depend upon usage rate, exposure to brand elements, and in particular experiences of service delivery. A frequent flyer will develop a relationship based on more deeply held perceptions than an occasional traveller. One of the principal objectives of branding is to build preference amongst customers. This does not mean that customers will buy at any price (although lower price elasticity is indeed sometimes correlated to brand loyalty); it does, however, imply that other important criteria being equal, those with a choice will prefer (i.e., remain loyal to) the brand as a result of the relationship that has been established. The preferences driving brand loyalty flow from many different sources, but at their heart lie a service concept relevant to the targeted segment, clear marketing communications, effective

service delivery, and a perception of good value in the minds of targeted customers.

A key objective of any airline should be to attract and retain targeted customers – those for whom a service-price offer has been designed and who, presumably, should value it the most. If a service has been effectively branded it will develop a 'franchise' in the minds of target customers such that whenever they want a product in a particular market (e.g., business class out of London) they will recall a specific brand or sub-brand (e.g., British Airways' Club World or Club Europe). This applies as readily to a low-fare/no-frills carrier, although in this segment brand preference will most probably kick-in only if prices are at least as low as those offered by competitors.

According to Schultz and Barnes (1999), a brand relationship develops over a series of 'brand contacts'. A brand contact is any information-bearing and/or image-altering exposure to an airline experienced by a customer or potential customer – irrespective of its source. Some brand contacts – servicescapes and advertising, for example – can be closely managed; others cannot – the most significant of these being unscripted service encounters, and also word-of-mouth comments passed on to others by customers.

2. **Individualised brand relationships** A few airlines, particularly full-service network carriers with a sophisticated approach to marketing, are developing dialogues with certain of their customers. Only occasionally does this extend to the 'segment-of-one' dialogue we read so much about in the business press, but technology will increasingly allow connections to identifiable – in most cases high-value – customers. What dialogue relationships mean more commonly at the moment is attempts – through research, modelling, marketing initiatives, and response evaluations – to find out more about typical customer characteristics in increasingly fine-grained segments, and to 'individualise' relationships with members of each segment on the basis of what is learned from such statistical profiling. Because establishing and maintaining individualised relationships – often using direct and database marketing techniques – is expensive, many low-cost/low-fare carriers do not go down this route; others – British Airways being a prime example – devote large percentages of their marketing budgets to direct marketing for the explicit purpose of building relationships with high-value customers.

Ongoing customer relationships are assets; they do not appear on an airline's balance sheet, but in highly competitive markets they can be as important to earning power as any tangible resource and they need to be actively managed. Customer relationships have been aptly likened to the opening of an emotional bank account, from which withdrawals in the form of tolerance can be made in the event of service failure and into which deposits are placed in the form of customer satisfaction with each successful transaction or recovery (Band, 1991: 119). Another way of looking at this is to characterise every service encounter or each journey in its entirety as an 'episode' (Ravald and Grönroos, 1996) set within a wider relationship; the stronger that relationship, the more resilient it will be to individual unsatisfactory episodes.

Particularly as far as high lifetime-value customers are concerned, full-service airlines are increasingly interested in marketing themselves into long-term relationships rather than simply marketing on a transactional basis. The objective of relationship-building is to strengthen customer loyalty, raise the likelihood of repeat purchases, and access a higher share of the customer's potentially accessible lifetime spending. To do this, the airline needs to know the depth of targeted customers' feelings about the company and the source of those feelings, their perceptions of its brand personality and how they are formed, the relative importance of different brand elements in forming perceptions, the degree of trust placed in the airline's brand(s), and whether customers feel sufficiently strongly to recommend the airline to others (Ind, 1997). The challenge is to estimate the potential of each targeted customer, assess what percentage of that potential you are consistently winning, find ways to fill this 'potential gap' by winning a greater share of their business, then estimate the ROI on whatever investments are necessary to achieve all this. The purpose of the effort is to turn:

- high-value prospects into customers;
- customers into satisfied, repeat-purchasing loyalists;
- loyalists into advocates.

Managing, the customer portfolio means making decisions about how to invest in the acquisition, development, and retention of customers. Investments in relationships involve cash outlays – on direct marketing and service upgrades, for example – that it is hoped will stimulate sustained or, better yet, increased revenues; with cash outlays and revenues aggregated by market segment, these investments need analysing just as much as investments in aircraft or other tangible assets. Although there are some notable exceptions, very few even amongst airlines that think in terms of customer relationships yet analyse their relationship investments in this way.

In summary, we can see that the basis of any relationship is:

- the airline's understanding of the benefits that its targeted customers expect from the air transport services they are buying;
- customers' perceptions of service actually received relative to prior expectations of service;
- the airline's understanding of customers' perceptions, and of any gaps between perceptions and expectations.

We met these variables in chapter 4 in the context of service design, and we will be looking at them again in chapter 9 in the context of service quality assessment.

Brand equity

We saw in chapter 6 that brands are sometimes said to have 'personalities', and that this – often implicit – personification of brand image is the basis on which they build relationships with customers. The idea is that if a brand has a well-defined personality underpinned by values with which most customers in the targeted segment feel comfortable, those customers will over time build a relationship with the brand much as they would with an individual. It might seem 'academic' and naive to imply that passengers on a high-density charter flight, on a low-cost/no-frills scheduled carrier, or in the 'main cabin' of a full-service operator are going to build any meaningful kind of relationship with those airlines' brands. My view is this:

- if and when these customers purchase air travel services again, their purchase decisions are indeed likely to be price-driven. However, price considerations being more or less equal, it is reasonable to assume that perceptions of their past service experiences will influence choice;
- whilst low-cost, high- or relatively high-density products are always going to lack the 'personal touch' that staffing ratios in the premium cabins allow for, it is not inevitable that their service delivery processes must treat consumers as 'self-loading cargo' (an expression coined in the 'Straight and Level' column of *Flight International*). Ongoing relationships with high-yield frequent flyers are inevitably easier to build, and for most full-service carriers more important, than relationships with more price-sensitive segments; this does not mean that travellers amongst the latter do not have perceptions of what different carriers stand for and how they treat their customers. It is out of these perceptions that implicit relationships with different brands very often emerge.

Positive relationships between a brand and its customers contribute to a store of goodwill which the literature refers to as 'brand equity'. One of the reasons behind recent interest in brand equity has been to develop methods for quantifying its contribution to shareholder value. Some of the methods advanced have been highly complex, but for our purpose it is sufficient to think in terms of brand equity as the discounted value of future net cash flows anticipated from customers whose purchase decisions are attributable to some degree of brand loyalty. At the price-driven, highly transactional end of any air transport market brand loyalty might be weak to non-existent, but on occasions when two or more carriers are offering similar prices it is possible that more favourable perceptions of one might tip the balance of the purchase decision; at the less price-sensitive, premium end of the market, perceptions of different brands will almost certainly come into play – although, again, other variables might intervene, such as schedule or FFP benefits for example. Relating all this esoteric imagery to future cash flows is pretty fuzzy stuff, but the fact remains that people's – conscious and subconscious – relationships with brands have been shown to influence purchase decisions under certain circumstances, and that purchase decisions drive cash flows and shareholder value. Brand equity is therefore a potentially valuable concept to keep in mind, even if actual numbers merit healthy scepticism.

Customer loyalty

A customer's loyalty to, say, British Airways is not founded on a relationship with the public limited company that defines the airline as a legal entity, but on a relationship with the image held of the corporate brand – an image built on all the elements we have been talking about in the last several chapters. Similarly, her loyalty to Club World is not a relationship with a particular cabin design, but with the totality of what that sub-brand name embodies for her – a totality of which cabin design is only a part.

The objective of relationship marketing is to build and retain customer loyalty. Determinants of customer loyalty include:

- an airline's corporate brand image and, where relevant, its sub-brand images;
- levels of satisfaction with past service experiences, and particularly with the last experience;
- relative perceived performances of competitors;
- extent of customer inertia;
- membership of an FFP.

I want to look briefly at the roles played by customer satisfaction and by loyalty programmes.

Linkages between customer satisfaction and customer loyalty

The view that customer satisfaction is a key driver of shareholder value has hit the headlines over the last ten years, but in fact has its roots almost half a century ago in the idea of the 'marketing concept' – the idea that 'the firm should base all its activities on the needs and desires of customers in selected target markets' (Grönroos, 2000: 233). Advanced by writers such as Drucker and Levitt, this was an argument – revolutionary at the time – that businesses should not simply be producing what they felt inclined to produce and then trying to sell it, but should instead be producing what customers actually want. After 50 years of development, the argument now proposes that if we satisfy customers by meeting their expectations, profit and growth in shareholder value will follow. Profit is seen here not as an objective with an autonomous life of its own, but as a vital consequence of producing value for customers (Reichheld, 1996). This of course leaves out 'minor' details such as how to identify which customers can be profitably served, how much to invest in acquiring and retaining them given their lifetime value to the airline, and how to keep the costs arising from service delivery below what customers are prepared to pay for that service; the argument is nonetheless still fundamentally sound.

The primary way to investigate loyalty is to use customer satisfaction surveys which incorporate 'loyalty questions' regarding repeat purchase intentions. Going one step further, customer satisfaction indices (CSIs) can contribute anecdotal evidence, based on the assumption that high levels of satisfaction imply high levels of loyalty. Comparison of loyalty questions and a CSI can be interesting: if repurchase intentions remain stable while the CSI edges down, 'loyalty' is likely based more on inertia (or the 'chains' of an FFP) than on preference, and can be vulnerable to what are perceived as better value propositions from competitors; if repurchase intentions decline while a CSI remains stable or climbs, one reason could be that a competitor has indeed made a preferable value proposition.

Communications and promotional initiatives in particular can benefit from sub-segmenting customers on the basis of loyalty and value. A six-cell matrix can be constructed by dividing low-value and high-value customers into three loyalty categories:

- **Committed** Loyalty should be rewarded and any service failures strongly recovered. Requests should be listened to carefully and accommodated wherever physically and economically feasible, particularly in the case of the 'high-value committed' sub-segment.

- **Vulnerable** Attention should be given to the sources of vulnerability, and improvements actively communicated.
- **Uncommitted** The relative costs and benefits of winning over this segment will need to be carefully weighed, with the high-value uncommitted segment taking priority.

(These categories are far from being definitive. For example, one airline identifies five loyalty segments: advocates; loyalists; occasionals; lapsed; and prospects. These are sub-segmented into high-value and low-value, with marketing efforts prioritised from advocate down to prospect for high-value customers, and then advocate down to prospect for low-value customers.)

Whereas customer satisfaction surveys can be used for feedback from our own customers, wider surveys of the market as a whole – often known as 'market standing surveys' – can be used to help isolate vulnerable and uncommitted segments of competitors' customer bases and understand the reasons why their loyalty is wavering. Clearly, there is overlap between customer bases – with 'our' customers and 'their' customers being to some extent synonymous, other than perhaps in cases of the most extreme brand loyalty. These types of survey can be used to evaluate what service improvements are required to win over the waverers and how benefits might be better communicated – particularly where we are perceived, incorrectly, to be under-performing the competition. Possessing finely-tuned skills at measuring customer satisfaction, segmenting by loyalty, and responding to what is learned about segment needs is part of the 'customer understanding' that we met in chapter 3.

However, it is now widely argued that to ensure customer loyalty it is no longer enough to simply 'satisfy' customers by meeting their expectations; it is necessary to exceed expectations or – as the literature puts it – 'delight' them (McCarthy, 1997). It is reasonably apparent from both anecdotal and survey evidence that there are some fairly sizeable airlines – particularly, but certainly not only – in the United States that are some way from providing the majority of their customers with 'delightful' service experiences. In a world where only totally satisfied customers – those whose reasonable expectations of what they will get from a service-price offer have been exceeded – are likely to be truly loyal and yet customer loyalty is the bedrock of future shareholder value, this should be disturbing to anybody looking further ahead than the next financial quarter. (Of course an alternative to building shareholder value by satisfying customers and winning their loyalty is to buy competitors and reduce choice in the market-place; some argue that this is what airline consolidation is really all about.)

Customers who are satisfied are more likely to be loyal than those who are not – although satisfaction is certainly not, in itself, sufficient to ensure retention. There is a caveat, however. Although intuitively appealing, the empirical evidence for a direct causal relationship between customer satis-faction and customer retention is not yet totally convincing. A satisfied customer might switch to a competitor offering price or promotional entice-ments, for example. Furthermore, because the relationship between satis-faction and loyalty is not linear, a satisfied customer is several times more likely to switch than one who is 'highly satisfied'.

This last insight, much cited in the services management literature, was originally uncovered by Xerox; in the course of polling customers using a five-point scale ranging from 'extremely dissatisfied' to 'very satisfied' it was found that 'very satisfied' customers were six times more likely to repurchase Xerox equipment than those who were simply 'satisfied'. Whilst taking this as yet unproven hypothesis and then transferring it along with the Xerox findings into the airline industry is not very 'scientific', it would be unwise to ignore the point entirely and assume that 'satisfied' customers are 'in the bag'. One lesson from the Xerox finding might be that differing interpretations of the word 'satisfied' are in use: whilst the assum-ption of many questionnaire designers using the word seems to be that it has positive implications, customers completing questionnaires might use the word in the sense of 'O.K.', 'nothing negative', or even 'nothing *too* negative'.

Even if we accept the requirement to distinguish between 'satisfied' and 'highly satisfied' or 'delighted' customers for relationship-building purpos-es, there is a need for caution in handling vague concepts such as 'total customer satisfaction' which emanate from the evangelical end of popular management literature. 'Total customer satisfaction' is simply impossible; no airline carrying millions of people every year can satisfy all of them all of the time. Even efforts aimed at 'maximising customer satisfaction' need to be approached with careful forethought. There should perhaps be two thrusts.

1. Service packages and service delivery systems should be designed in such a way that as many targeted customers as possible (but inevitably not all) are consistently satisfied by their experiences.
2. Particular attention should be paid to maximising the satisfaction of high lifetime value segments:
    *   satisfaction levels in these segments need to be monitored as often as is practically and economically feasible;

- investments aimed at raising customer satisfaction should in particular be targeted at, first, boosting, and then maintaining levels of satisfaction in these segments;
- defections from these segments need to be minimised to ensure that the airline (or alliance) maximises its share of their accessible travel expenditures (and in so doing maintains the *quality* of its market share).

(A recent development in the literature has in fact moved beyond the idea of lifetime value to look at customers' 'full profit potential' (Hallowell and Schlesinger, 2000). Whereas transactional marketing considers one exchange at a time and lifetime value looks at a series of exchanges over the life of a customer's relationship with the firm, 'full profit potential' is realised by taking positive action to increase lifetime value by proactively influencing each targeted customer's purchase behaviour – by encouraging them to buy more, to buy more often, or to buy higher-margin services, for example.)

The only way to secure long-term customer loyalty is to try to ensure that as many customers as possible have exceptionally good experiences at every point of contact with the airline – by which I mean experiences that exceed expectations, albeit subject to what is reasonable within the context of the particular service-price offer concerned. In other words, design, communicate, and deliver services capable of meeting and exceeding customers' expectations. Clearly, this is a challenge that relies heavily on having the right people working in the right culture and giving them the right tools for the job – including customer information. This may not be easy or cheap and it will need to be a sustained long-term commitment, but in the long run it can be cheaper than losing customers who have a potentially high lifetime value.

Loyalty programmes

Airlines need to build loyalty amongst both their end-users and intermediaries such as travel agents and freight forwarders. Close attention has long been paid to intermediaries, who – despite recent assaults by some airlines on their distribution costs – are in many markets still plied with incentives in addition to 'standard' commissions. One source of loyalty in either case is the imposition of switching costs; airlines have used volume-based commission overrides to impose these on travel agencies and encourage them to move market share in the airline's favour, for example, whilst express package companies have used proprietary hardware and software to the same effect. The imposition of switching costs on the vast number of passengers present in competitive air transport markets is less easy, but over the last few years more airlines have been trying. Two of the most important techniques used are frequent flyer programmes (both individual and corporate) and corporate rebates. (See Holloway, 1997, 1998a, 1998b.)

Generating loyalty amongst hard-core travellers is clearly important both in revenue terms and, particularly, to the establishment of any serious relationship marketing effort. The problem is that FFP membership on the one hand and loyalty in the sense of a bond of preference with an airline's brand on the other are not always synonymous. Stewart (1997: 142-143) has written a very readable book on intellectual capital; he begins a chapter on what he calls 'customer capital' with the following tale.

> Every hour on the hour, a United Airlines flight leaves La Guardia Airport in New York bound for O'Hare Field in Chicago. Just behind or just in front of it is an American Airlines flight, likewise headed for O'Hare. At five o'clock P.M. a week from Friday (as I am writing these words), I will be on one of those planes, en route to my mother's seventy-fifth birthday party. The two aircraft will probably be equally crowded; they will arrive as they depart, within minutes of one another; they will serve meals of identical inedibility; they will have, in their seatback pockets on board, inflight magazines with crossword puzzles of approximately equal difficulty and divertisement. I could have bought the ticket from either airline for the same price. I will be on the American flight. My sister, who is leaving New York the next day, will fly United.
>
> You know why one of us chose American and the other United? Several years ago we made different choices about which frequent-flyer plans to feed. Other things being equal (which they usually are), I ask my travel agent to book me on an airline in whose frequent-flyer programme I chose to build up miles. For reasons I no longer remember, I made American's plan one of my "core holdings" but not United's. In both 1995 and 1996, that preference was worth about $55,000 to Bob Crandall's company. If the creek don't rise, it will be worth similar amounts in 1997, 1998...
>
> My behaviour makes me an asset to American Airlines – not as valuable an asset as a neighbour who logs more than 100,000 miles on American each year, but an asset nevertheless, the kind no company can have too many of: a steady customer. American makes a few investments to preserve the value of me-as-an-asset. It gives me a small return on my capital in the form of free trips; it sees to it that Citibank, MCI, and various other companies invite me to buy credit or telephone service that will add to my account and, perhaps, make me more loyal to American than I am; it makes partnership arrangements with hotel and car-rental companies and other airlines; it sometimes (rarely, alas) gives me an upgrade to first or business class if I remember to ask, if there's room, and if a more valuable asset isn't in the same departure lounge. It invests enough to maintain my allegiance, though not enough to

deepen it to the point where I'd fly American even if other things were un-equal.

Although presented as programmes for rewarding loyalty, FFPs can also be characterised as bribes carefully structured to mutate into blackmail. Many observers would disagree with this characterisation, of course. It is nonetheless difficult to dispute that most FFPs reward activity (i.e., miles flown) rather than loyalty (i.e., 'share of wallet'), and that miles flown can at times be a poor proxy for customer profitability. The problem for many airlines at the moment is that their FFP, reservations, revenue management, and revenue accounting systems have difficulty sharing information about customers; this is gradually being addressed by new customer relationship management systems and approaches such as data warehousing and data mining, but these are not yet widespread in the industry as a whole.

What is beyond doubt is that loyalty driven *solely* by FFP membership is less stable than loyalty driven by a genuine brand preference – of which the FFP programme might well be a part, but only one of several attractions. Furthermore, FFPs are not themselves unitary service attributes. Each FFP needs to be based on a thorough understanding of what targeted customers expect from it, and these expectations should be reflected in conscious design decisions regarding variables such as accrual drivers (e.g., distance travelled, class of travel, eligibility of discount fares, or ticket revenue), accrual partnerships (e.g., with other airlines and non-airline service partners), rewards (e.g., free flights, upgrades, lounge access, wait-list priority, other air transport-related benefits, redemption opportunities on partners' networks or with non-airline partners), seat availability for redemption purposes, black-out periods, and the efficiency of FFP customer service.

The message is that as well as seeing its FFP as a marketing database and a source of incremental revenues earned from selling award points or miles to third parties, an airline should see it as a service attribute that needs to be as carefully designed (and regularly re-designed) as every other attribute flowing from the underlying service concept. In other words, it is important to know what the FFP is supposed to achieve (e.g., customer acquisition as well as customer retention?), for whom (e.g., just high-yield frequent travellers or everybody who flies regularly on the airline?), how (e.g., in what way does each programme feature contribute to meeting objectives?), with what impact on purchase behaviour (e.g., do we actually understand customers' purchase behaviour – because if not, an FFP is essentially a shot in the dark), and in what way all this is relevant to the service concept. (For more comprehensive coverage of the issues raised in this section, see Butler and Keller (1998), chapters 43 to 45.)

Conclusion

Customer loyalty, a prerequisite for customer retention in truly competitive markets, does not just happen; it is something that has to be worked at systematically. In this context, 'working at' customer loyalty means making superior value propositions to targeted customers, and being perceived to deliver consistently on these propositions in a way that at least matches customer expectations.

However, we need to be cautious. Research has yet to confirm that loyalty is a simple unidimensional construct stretching from, say, brand avoidance to passionate advocacy. It is at the moment no more than a reasonable working assumption that satisfaction and loyalty are indeed unidimensional constructs that are causally linked insofar as increasing satisfaction raises the likelihood of loyalty, and that customer loyalty can be gauged by customer retention and defection rates. The services management literature has introduced these useful constructs and they help order our approach to customers, but their precise dimensions and linkages are still under investigation.

Finally, there is one further reason for caution. Whereas in Europe over half of business travellers are believed to be free to choose the carriers on which they fly, the figure is thought to be as low as 20 per cent in the United States (*Aviation Week*, December 11, 2000: 38). Nobody can be sure what the true figures are, but this is a consideration which raises the interesting prospect that airlines need to be trying to satisfy the high-value consumers who travel with them and at the same time building relationships with the 'buying centres' that set corporate travel policies and negotiate the deals.

Customer retention

Promises – expressed or implied, written or spoken – attract customers; the fulfilment of promises and the building of trust in the brand is what will retain them – until something palpably better comes along. A key objective of relationship marketing is to maximise retention of profitable customers; the same objective looked at from the reverse angle is to minimise defection of profitable customers. We will look at customer retention here and customer defection in the next section; the two are clearly linked, and so should be their management.

The common core of all customer retention strategies must be doing best those things that matter most to customers (Hill, 1996). The key to customer retention is creating superior value for customers (Reichheld, 1996;

Tapp, 1998). Retention is not, therefore, a periodic marketing initiative. It is the essence of everything that we discussed in the first seven chapters of the book; get the basics right – vision, service concept, service-price offers, delivery, culture, and values – and retention will not be the challenge it will be if you get them wrong and simply try to bolt-on a customer retention strategy as a retro-fit option.

Retention defined

The 'retention rate' is the percentage of customers with an airline at the start of an analysis period – say, a year – who remain with it at the end of the period. A commonly used metaphor is the leaky bucket: a customer portfolio in any one period is comprised of new customers 'poured' into the bucket in addition to those already there (i.e., those that have been retained), less defections 'draining' out through leaks in the bottom. Stem the leaks – that is, retain more of your customers – and the portfolio will grow very much more quickly, and so will profits. Indeed, research has indicated that even small increases in retention rate (e.g., just five per cent) can lead to considerably larger increases in profits over the medium term (Reichheld, 1996).

'Customer retention' is the product of an ongoing relationship with a loyal customer. It yields a revenue stream beginning with the first purchase and boosted by subsequent purchases. However, repurchase is not in itself evidence of customer retention because there are two reasons why repurchase might occur.

1. Opportunistic or contextual repurchase (e.g., in response to a price promotion or because there is on one particular occasion no reasonable alternative to the airline concerned).
2. Preference-driven repurchase (i.e., the customer is loyal to the airline concerned and will purchase its services whenever feasible). It is this type of loyalty which evidences 'retention' of a customer.

Retention is not a once-and-for-all phenomenon. Not only can persistent service failures alienate a previously-loyal customer, but customers' preferences and buying patterns might change over time – with increasing age, for example, or as a result of raised expectations flowing from new, competing alternative services. As with most relationships, airlines have to work at retaining the loyalty of those customers they particularly want to retain. Customer relationships can no longer be taken for granted: customers as a whole are more knowledgeable, demanding, and proactive in their response to perceptions of poor service than in the past, and in many markets there are now more alternative offers to tempt them to defect.

Why customer retention matters

Customer retention has an impact on both the cost and revenue sides of an airline's income statement.

Lower costs Customer retention can lower costs in several ways.

1. Loyal customers do not need as many marketing dollars spent on them to induce a purchase as do prospects. It is generally believed to be cheaper to market to existing satisfied customers than to mass market for new customers. American Airlines has estimated the cost of attracting new customers at up to five times the cost of retaining existing ones (Martin, 1995; Reichheld, 1996). The important word, however, is 'satisfied'. A satisfying service experience is often used by customers as a predictor of future satisfaction, and therefore a driver of repurchase decisions.
2. Marketing dollars that are spent on retaining customers can be better targeted than more general marketing expenditures, provided that through an actively updated database the airline makes a serious effort to keep track of and understand the expectations of these customers.
3. Existing customers are often cheaper to serve once they enter the service delivery system because they 'know the ropes' and are less likely to require non-standard attention. Existing customers are familiar with the practices and procedures of the airline concerned – that is, with its 'script'; they therefore tend to require less special handling than would an infrequent traveller buying the same class of service. (This does not mean that, say, frequent flyers do not require personalised attention; however, such attention should be designed into service packages and delivery systems, and is something very different from the help a new and infrequent customer might require – particularly at those potential fail-points where customers themselves are expected to participate in service delivery.)
4. Loyal customers *may* over time show a greater propensity than first-time or infrequent users to deal directly with the airline and so cut-out expensive intermediaries such as travel agencies and GDSs. (Some carriers are in fact none too subtle about encouraging their FFP members to do precisely this.)

5. Loyal customers – especially those who are highly satisfied – contribute to lower acquisition costs through word-of-mouth advocacy, leading to cheaply acquired referral business.

The argument is not quite as simple as this, of course, because airlines do not just stop acquiring new customers in order to spend money on retaining existing customers. Furthermore, some new customers arrive simply as a result of a carrier's market presence. As far as spending in order to acquire specifically targeted new customers is concerned, the real issue is not so much what it costs to acquire them as it is acquisition cost relative to lifetime value.

Higher revenues For Wayland and Cole (1997: 4), 'the value of a firm is ultimately equal to the sum of the values of its customer relationships, and this sum can grow only through the acquisition, development, and retention of profitable customer relationships'. The argument is that an airline can usefully be seen as a bundle of customer relationships rather than a portfolio of services; services are simply one tool used to nurture customer relationships (alongside communications, for example); the primary goal is maximisation of the lifetime value of customers to the airline.

The potential lifetime value of a customer (or segment) is the total revenue (or better yet, if meaningfully calculable, the total operating profit) that a given customer (or segment) could be expected to generate over a period of sustained loyalty to the particular airline. The following procedure can be used to calculate it (Stewart, 1997).

- **Select a time horizon** This is a matter of preference, but ten years is a fairly common choice (Jenkins, 1992).
- **Calculate an average annual revenue figure for each customer segment** This can be done using surveys and by sampling FFP databases. We need to consider average transaction value, average number of transactions per year, additional revenue earned (e.g., from duty-free purchases), and the revenue attributable to word-of-mouth referrals. (Ideally, a contribution figure should be arrived at by subtracting the marketing costs of acquiring first-time customers and retaining existing customers in each segment, as well as the costs of serving all of them; any positive balance is that segment's contribution to the airline's fixed costs including its cost of capital, whilst a negative balance implies that serving the segment destroys shareholder value. In practice, relatively few airlines yet have the accounting capability to deliver activity-based costs in this amount of detail.)

- **Estimate the customer defection rate** This will tell us approximately what percentage of customers will defect over ten years.
- **Discount the ten-year cash flow** Selecting a discount rate equivalent to the target rate of return on assets (bearing in mind that an 'installed customer base' is an intangible asset), the ten-year revenue stream adjusted for defections can be discounted to its present value (or net present value, if costs are also calculated and included).

Wayland and Cole (1997) refer to the figure derived above as 'customer equity' and see it as the principal driver of growth in shareholder value. They go on to characterise as the 'customer portfolio' the aggregate value of customer relationships across all segments. It is used as a framework within which to make choices about the acquisition, development, and retention of customer relationships. These choices are in fact investment strategies, just as much as a fleet plan is an investment strategy. Customer portfolios can be managed at three levels: market (i.e., the portfolio structure is representative of the market as a whole), segment (i.e., one or more segments within the market are separately managed), or individual. Explicit individual relationships (as opposed to implicit brand relationships) tend to be formed only with their highest-value customers by the relatively few airlines that have invested in technologies enabling 'segment-of-one' approaches.

The essence of customer portfolio management lies in bringing to bear the customer understanding that we discussed in chapter 3 so that decisions can be taken regarding the economic attractions of serving particular segments given their service expectations and the particular airline's capabilities. No matter that the figures might be very approximate, they serve to emphasise the importance of retaining high-value customers and to provide a rational framework within which to make decisions about how much to spend on customer retention initiatives such as direct marketing and FFPs.

This discussion tends towards the frame of analysis likely to be adopted by a marketing-oriented full-service carrier. Low-cost/low-fare carriers might prefer the 'field of dreams' approach to customer knowledge: build it (i.e., capacity) and they'll come (if the price is right, of course). Some of them would argue that they use price to keep their customers loyal, and their cost base cannot justifiably absorb the expense of this type of analysis – even were the data required for steps 2 and 3 readily available, which often it is not; they would also argue that because they do little direct marketing and have only fairly basic loyalty programmes if they have one at all, insight into justifiable levels of expenditure for customer acquisition and retention is not a priority. This is a reasonable argument, provided it is not taken too far. There are potentially loyal frequent flyers even in the segments targeted by this type of carrier; the lifetime value of their business will hardly be comparable with that of a frequent traveller in long-haul premium classes, but is worth having nonetheless. They should not be ignored. There is merit in the view that investing some effort in understanding what customers expect alongside low prices and how they identify value in a service-price offer is worthwhile even for carriers offering the most basic levels of service. Customer attachments can be formed in this segment of the market as well.

It is worth highlighting the significant role believed to be played by positive word-of-mouth endorsements arising over the lifetime of a loyal customer. These endorsements do not, however, take the form of simple linear flows from a single satisfied customer to, say, five or ten contacts. First, the social structure of a particular customer's network of friends and contacts will have a bearing – how dense or close that network is, for example, and whether people within it have their own dense networks through which a positive endorsement might ripple. Another factor is the propensity of people within the social network to fly, to fly in markets where the airline concerned offers service, and to want the particular type of service that airline offers. The message here is that whilst single dyadic (i.e., one-to-one) relationships are vital media through which endorsements flow, the full significance of these endorsements can only be evaluated within the context of the wider networks in which each is embedded. Researching such networks is neither a cheap nor a precise science; the importance of word-of-mouth endorsement is nonetheless something that all staff need to understand, even though in most cases airlines make few explicit efforts to quantify it.

Average lifetime value per customer in a segment can be used to guide spending on segment-oriented marketing efforts for both customer acquisition and retention. It can be a useful guide to the development of relationship marketing programmes, and of tools to assist in managing service recovery.

Developing a lifetime value for each customer is accomplished by a combination of data mining [in customer data warehouses] and algorithms designed to suit [a] particular airline. [Typical inputs include] frequency, recency and some financial component such as revenue or net profit. When this value is developed, service personnel can make far better decisions on how to react and reduce the impact of travel incidents [i.e., service failures]. Ideally, [what is wanted is] to spend as little as possible – [whilst doing] as much as is necessary to make the customer delighted, to maintain their loyalty and hopefully to increase lifetime value (Thornett, 1997).

Conclusion Work by Reichheld and Sasser (1990) outside the air transport industry suggests that profits are more closely correlated to customer loyalty than to market share. This underlines the importance of the *quality* of market share. There is an argument that market share quality, which might be defined as the proportion of revenues attributable to repeat purchases by loyal customers, should be given as much attention as market share itself. The issue in this case is no longer simply how to sell services, but how to retain customers – particularly high-value customers. The life-time revenue figures involved are likely to be very much lower when a low-cost/no-frills carrier considers customer loyalty than when a full-service airline thinks about its full-fare frequent flyers, but this does not mean that customer retention is irrelevant.

A few words of caution are necessary, however. First, airline service in some markets falls so far short of most customers' expectations that loyalty is not on those customers' agendas. What the airlines concerned might want to think of as loyalty is in many cases likely to be lack of alternative, inertia precluding the search for alternatives, or the blackmail of the FFP. Loyalty has to be earned – it cannot be bought (Reichheld, 1996).

Second, even where customers are in fact loyal insofar as they have bought into the general brand image and specific service-price offers of one carrier over and above others, they still might see the relationship more as 'steady dating' than the 'lifelong marriage' that some marketing people read into it. Most loyal customers will 'see other people', either because the preferred airline is unavailable – flights are booked or there is no service to the destination in question – or because a competitor makes a particularly seductive offer.

When we talk about customer loyalty we need therefore to bear in mind that whilst we are after the biggest chunk of a customer's air transport spend that we can get, this is rarely ever going to be 100 per cent. We should certainly be striving for a relationship between the brand and the customer – particularly if a high lifetime value customer – such that whenever our offer goes head-to-head with a competitor's offer it is ours that will be chosen. Exclusive brand loyalty is, however, a marketer's dream rather than an actual reality in most markets (Ehrenberg, 1972).

Customer defections

The primary purpose of any retention effort is to limit customer defections. Several possible reasons to defect can be identified (DeSouza, 1992; Keaveney, 1995).

1. Price – which might have risen and/or be too high relative to what new competitors are charging in the market.
2. Inconvenience – perhaps arising from schedule incompatibility, for example.
3. Preference for a competitor's newly available alternative product, which is perceived to offer superior value.
4. Poor service, which could stem from failure of a tangible service attribute, a service encounter, or an attempted service recovery. Important variables here might include:
   - the level of a customer's prior conviction about overall service quality;
   - the seriousness of the failure giving rise to dissatisfaction with the latest experience;
   - switching costs (e.g., loss of FFP benefits);
   - the availability of more attractive alternatives.
5. Exit of the defector from the market.
6. Switching to an alternative technology offered by a competing industry (e.g., train, telecommunications or fractional ownership of business jets).
7. Ethical reasons.

Why do defections matter? A customer retention rate of 90 per cent might sound reasonable. However, if ten per cent of an airline's existing customers defect each year, getting on for half the people who pay for today's salaries and dividends will not be doing business with the carrier in five years' time. In a growing market many of them can be replaced; but acquiring new customers is not only expensive, it also masks the significant loss of potential revenue arising from defections. Losing ten first-year customers, each with an annual revenue potential of just $2,000 and possible loyalty periods of ten years leads to an aggregate lifetime value loss of $200,000; add a couple of zeroes here or there and these figures begin to get serious. Subjective and simplistic though this type of calculation is, it does point to the importance of customer retention, and also to the importance of the other side of the coin: defections management.

'Defections management' is the process of identifying and reducing defections. The following general guidelines apply.

1. Do not try to prevent all defections – this would be too expensive and is anyway likely to be impossible.
2. Ensure that employees understand the lifetime value concept and are alert to the importance of reducing defections.

3. Train employees, and where possible use technology, to identify potential and actual defections. For example:
   - declining sales to corporate accounts or FFP members;
   - accumulation of FFP miles credited for hotel and rental car usage at online locations but at times that do not tally with flight usage (Zakreski, 1998);
   - specific instances of service failure involving a high-value customer;
   - complaints;
   - improved service-price offers launched by direct competitors.

4. Find out why customers are defecting. Possible reasons were listed above, but pay particular attention to the following.
   - Dissatisfaction: Were expectations unfulfilled? Were they too high? Why were perceptions of the service received below expectations? Was there a service failure? Was service recovery mishandled? Does design of the service package and/or delivery system need reconsidering?
   - Heightened competition: What is attractive about the competitor's new service-price offer?

5. Above all, engender an organization-wide commitment to raising customer satisfaction levels. (I personally find this more plausible than rallying cries to achieve 'zero defections' – something that is just as improbable in a service business as zero defects. However, there are respected writers in the field, such as Hoffman and Bateson (1997: 376), who take the more aspirational approach of arguing for a 'zero defections culture'.)

Some customer defections are in my view inevitable. The key skills in defection management involve finding out approximately how many customers are being lost, understanding why, identifying where they are going, deciding which ones matter (because some invariably do not), and remedying the situation. Understanding and dealing with the root causes behind defections of the highest value customers and defection trends across segments is fundamental. All this is not as easy to achieve in the airline business as in some other service industries, because airlines are network operations serving (in many cases) multitudes of discrete geographical markets as well as customers who are to a considerable extent still anonymous. Nonetheless, those investing in extensive customer information systems will be increasingly able to monitor changes in tracked usage patterns and rates amongst their more important customers and across segments; they will also be able to integrate product creation and tailored distribution into 'segment of one' marketing efforts. For others, surveys might have to suffice.

Complaints can be useful sources of information. Although a particular complaint might not lead to loss of the complainant's business, uncounted silent defections could be attributable to the same problem were it to be systemic. It is necessary to dig beneath superficial reasons for defections to identify their root causes: long lines at check-in counters, for example, could result from inadequate staffing, inefficient employees, poor systems support, unreliable baggage belts, or space constraints inhibiting provision of sufficient service points. If the problem is staff inefficiency, the root cause might be found in recruitment, training, motivation, or overall morale.

That simple example is sufficient to illustrate the interdependencies between many of the ideas and constructs discussed in this book: the service concept, service design, service delivery, communications, customers' expectations and perceptions of service, culture, employee satisfaction, customer loyalty and retention, and customer defection. All have a direct impact on costs and revenues, and all feed through to long-term shareholder value – although precisely how these linkages create value is still more intuitively than empirically understood.

One thing of which we can be reasonably sure is that a loyal, profitable customer base can be a source of competitive advantage – because its loyalty represents a barrier to switching that competitors will have to invest in order to overcome, and its profitability means that funds should be available to work on retention initiatives or fend-off short-term price competition. We will look next at another potential source of competitive advantage: relationships with external suppliers and service partners.

iv. Collaborative relationships

> Choose your friends carefully. Your enemies will choose you.
>
> Yasser Arafat

We saw in chapter 2 that perhaps the most influential theory of competitive advantage and competitive strategy over the last two decades has been Porter's (1980, 1985) 'five forces' model and his argument that an organization's financial performance is determined in large measure by the profit potential of the industry(ies) in which it chooses to operate, the strategic position it adopts (i.e., differentiation, cost focus, etc.), and the consistency with which it pursues the operational implications of that chosen position. The theory sees competitive advantage arising from successful management of essentially adversarial value chain relationships with competitors, suppliers, distributors, and customers. Since the early 1990s, however, researchers have been exploring the notion that competitive advantage can also accrue from co-operative relationships between erstwhile adversaries. This development in the literature has left us with two new concepts to conjure with.

- **Co-operative strategy** This is 'the attempt by organizations to realise their objectives through co-operation with other organizations, rather than in competition with them' (Child and Faulkner, 1998: 1). Co-operative strategy can be used as a tool of corporate strategy insofar as co-operation can help gain access into an industry, and it can be an adjunct to competitive strategy when it is used as a means to compete within an industry.
- **Collaborative advantage** From the perspective of resource-based theory, collaborative advantage (Kanter, 1994) can be said to exist where:
  - a co-operative relationship gives one or more of the partners an advantage over competitors;
  - an individual airline has a competence in forming and productively managing competitively useful partnerships. This might be called an 'integrative competence'.

Types of co-operative strategy

It can be argued that collaborative advantage is a result of decisions to embark on co-operative strategies alongside the chosen competitive strategy (differentiation or cost leadership, for example). Barney (1997) recognises two broad categories of co-operative strategy.

1. **Tacit collusion** Collusive strategies involve airlines co-operating on output and pricing decisions – usually constraining output to help raise prices above competitive levels; collusion might be explicit or tacit. Although explicit collusion through open communications is still prevalent in many markets, it is broadly illegal in the United States, the European Union, and several countries with well-developed bodies of competition law (Holloway, 1998a); an exception to this generalisation is the highly questionable US practice of granting anti-trust immunity to US carriers and their partners from countries that have signed open skies bilaterals with the United States.

Tacit collusion exists where output and/or pricing decisions are co-ordinated other than through direct communication; the usual means is through forms of signalling, which might be recognised within the industry but not easily spotted by outsiders. Signalling could, for example, involve advance notice of fare or capacity plans giving time for competitors to indicate how they will react; where competing networks overlap and there is 'multi-market contact', an airline might signal its displeasure at a competitor's initiative in one market by responding aggressively in another, with the intention of getting the initiator to make a connection and reverse the initiative. Drawing on Barney's analysis (ibid), the airline industry offers many conditions that encourage tacit collusion: a small number of firms competing (which remains true in most air transport markets); product and cost homegeneity (both of which are widespread across markets, although there are of course notable exceptions); the presence of price leaders (which is the case in many international markets in particular); an industry social structure with behavioural norms receptive to co-operation; a large number of small purchasers; and the presence of barriers to market entry (see Holloway, 1997).

Tacit collusion is often a fragile strategy in the long term: first, it is open to cheating (the subject of mathematical analyses for over a century, and of much game-theoretic work in recent years); second, any market accessible by a competitor prepared to exploit differentiation or cost advantages will in all likelihood eventually attract just such a competitor. That the airline industry has periodic difficulty balancing capacity with demand and also faces perennial pressure to dispose of a perishable inventory makes tacit collusion a difficult strategy to maintain; Internet seat auctions, should they spread globally, will probably not make it any easier (unless there is collusion over 'reserve prices').

2. **Strategic alliances** This second type of co-operative strategy exists when firms explicitly and formally collaborate. Their purposes could include collusion on pricing and output decisions where this is legal, but are usually much broader – covering a range of initiatives on both the cost and revenue sides of their income statements (Barney, 1997; Dussauge and Garrette, 1999). Whereas collusion tends to be a horizonal strategy within a single industry, strategic alliances can also occur vertically within a value chain and across industry boundaries. They cover forms such as equity and non-equity alliances (e.g., airlines investing in other airlines or airlines entering into long-term supply agreements with third-party MRO providers), joint ventures (e.g., the cargo co-operation between Lufthansa, SAS, and Singapore Airlines), and franchising, for example. Separately incorporated joint ventures are

the exception rather than the rule in the airline industry (SAS being a particularly noteworthy exception); however, they are becoming increasingly common frameworks for co-operative relationships between airlines and other types of organization (e.g., engine OEMs entering the aftermarket business). Most alliances between airlines are based on contractual agreements of one form or another; sometimes a hybrid approach is adopted, wherein certain clearly defined activities are housed in a separately constituted joint venture whilst the rest of the alliance relationship is structured around contract law rather than company law. In economic terms, airlines 'have an incentive to co-operate in strategic alliances when the value of their resources and assets combined is greater than the value of their resources and assets separately' (Barney, 1997: 386). Specific motivations for entering into a strategic alliance include the exploitation of economies of scope or scale, the sharing of costs and complementary resources and capabilities, the opportunity to learn from partners, the management of risk and uncertainty, to facilitate legally permissible collusive practices, and to enter new markets or segments that otherwise could not be served either at all or cost-effectively.

Looked at from a resource-based perspective on competitive strategy, the advantage derived from tacit collusion is founded in its inclusiveness and in barriers to market entry: if most airlines in a market that is not easily contestable choose to collude, their co-operation automatically passes the tests of rarity and inimitability that we saw in chapter 2 are characteristic of strategically important resources. In the case of strategic alliances, rarity can arise from the uniqueness of the partners' particular combination of resources (e.g., brand images, market presence, slots, route authorities, etc.), and inimitability is based on trust and the socially complex relationships and ways of co-operating that alliance partners build up together over time and which transcend contractual agreements (ibid); their people, organizational culture, and experience with alliances make some airlines better at managing alliance relationships than others. Internal growth and/or acquisitions can in principle be substitutes for strategic alliances it is impossible to duplicate, but in the airline industry these alternative strategies can be difficult to implement because of one or more of cost, infrastructural, or legal constraints.

The nature and scope of partnership relations

Lamming (1993) defines partnership as a sharing of risks and rewards, of technology and innovation leading to a reduction in costs, improvements in service delivery and quality, and the creation of sustainable competitive advantage. Enduring rather than transactional, it is an investment in future potential as much as immediate gain. Partnership does not lead to a loss of identity, but a blurring of organizational boundaries is inevitable as ties become stronger and flows of ideas, information, services, and/or goods become more transparent and better integrated. A partnership is 'strategic' when it is intended to improve the medium- and long-term futures of the parties involved in a significant way (Håkansson and Sharma, 1996).

It can be analytically useful to distinguish between three types of partnership: vertical, horizontal, and complementary. Note that I use the terms 'partnership' and 'alliance' interchangeably, whereas some writers (such as Gattorna and Walters, 1996) limit the former to vertical relationships and the latter to horizontal and complementary relationships.

Vertical partnerships

Sometimes called 'value chain', 'supply chain', or 'link' relationships, but perhaps better thought of in terms of the performance networks mentioned earlier in the chapter, these are partnerships of a close and enduring nature between companies at different points in an industry's value chain. Looked at from an airline's perspective, they would cover relationships with other companies which supply critical goods and, particularly, services to support the carrier, or with companies that in some way facilitate the distribution of its services. Their scope will reflect decisions made with regard to vertical integration and outsourcing, and their intensity will reflect the airline's approach to relationship management. We are not only talking here about the more obvious relationships with, for example, MRO suppliers, caterers, or ramp or passenger handling agents; close, enduring relationships can also be formed with external specialists responsible for elements of service design (e.g., the design alliances discussed in chapter 4), communications (e.g., advertising, PR, and communications agencies), distribution (e.g., e-commerce ventures), and service delivery (e.g., software houses – which are having an increasing influence over back-office processes).

What is the difference between a 'vertical partnership' on the one hand and a 'supplier agreement' or simple outsourcing on the other? Whereas a vertical partnership involves mutual adaptation and – importantly – mutual learning, the other two are contractually based substitutions of external skills and capabilities an airline never had or no longer wants to retain inhouse. As with most concepts in strategy, examples of each are clear at the extremes and more fuzzy where they overlap.

Vertical alliances can move an airline upstream or downstream; an example of the latter is alliances with partners able to facilitate direct distribution and e-ticketing. The alliances between powerplant OEMs and certain of their leading airline customers to create regional centres for the maintenance of particular engine types is an example of a vertical alliance which does not diversify the carrier away from the business concerned (in this case powerplant maintenance), but expands growth opportunities within that business.

Supply chain management is already in its third IT era: the first generation was marked by 'one-to-one' EDI between airlines and suppliers, the second by 'one-to-many' information links between individual suppliers and their airline customers over the Internet (e.g., Boeing's GAIN system – Global Airline Inventory Network), and the third by portals offering 'many (suppliers) to many (airlines)' architecture. It remains to be seen how the unfolding of the current generation of B2B commerce will affect supply chain relationships in the long run. At present, there are several different types of player in the B2B marketplace: portals primarily driven by single or multiple OEMs and focusing in particular on their own partners' supply chains, but also looking downstream towards the airlines that buy from them; portals driven primarily by airlines and aimed upstream at their own supply chains; and independent portals. The stated objective of these initiatives is invariably to strip out inventory costs and transaction processing time; a possible subtext is market control – something which may or may not be feasible using these vehicles, but which competition authorities have anyway been examining. As these words are being written, the anticipated consolidation of airline-led and supplier-driven portals appears to be beginning, and a shake-out amongst independents seems imminent.

Horizontal alliances

Sometimes called 'scale alliances', these are relationships at the same stage of the value chain. Relationships between airlines might range from route-specific code-sharing or cost-saving co-operation at a single station to more comprehensive strategic alliances combining route networks and a range of operational and support activities. Economies of scale, scope, and density and the elimination of duplicated activities can contribute to cost savings (Holloway, 1997); integration of route networks, and the combining of market presence, marketing communications, and FFP coverage can contribute to revenue growth.

Complementary alliances

These are links with suppliers of complementary services such as hotels, car rental agencies, or credit card companies. Such linkages are frequently given effect through FFPs, and involve equity interests less commonly than in the past. At the time of writing, for example, British Airways lists 19 hotel groups, three car rental firms, a bureau de change, three mobile phone companies, and an airport car park concession amongst its 'Executive Club Business Partners' (as different from its 14 'Airline Partners'); by the time this book is read, the cast will inevitably have changed.

Affinity cards co-branded with a financial institution are a multi-purpose tool that is being adopted by a growing number of carriers. They can be used to target infrequent travellers, the objective being to bind them to the airline concerned to an extent that – given their low usage of air travel services – an FFP itself would be unlikely to do. They are also used to extend the breadth of relationships between the airline and high-value customers.

Management of collaborative relationships

There are several stages in the relationship management process, beginning with identification of the motive for establishing an alliance in the first place.

Motivations for entering into an alliance

Several streams of literature examine the benefits that draw alliance partners together. Most tend to approach the alliance phenomenon from an economic perspective, sometimes giving relatively little consideration to psychological, social, or cultural influences on decision-making. These 'rational choice models' are notably drawn from transaction cost economics and game theory. There are exceptions. Sociology has contributed resource dependence theory (which we briefly met in chapter 6) and network theory. The latter, having in recent years drawn-in contributions from economics and several other disciplines, is gradually encouraging researchers and practitioners to think in terms of the interrelatedness of actors within complex clusters of firms; not all these relationships will necessarily qualify as 'strategic alliances', but where such alliances do exist, it can be helpful to consider them as part of the wider network of both loose and tightly coupled relationships within which each partner is embedded. Another exception is institutional theory, which argues that alliances may come about not only as a rational response to the environment but sometimes as a result of internal organizational variables such as culture and the disposition of power.

The strategic management literature has also looked at a number of alliance-related topics: the rationale underlying formation of alliances; criteria for partner selection; and how to secure a cultural fit between partners, for example. Unlike the deterministic positions taken by most economic theories of co-operation, the strategic management literature takes a more contingent view – making strategic choice a capacity endowed in human actors responding to the nuances of particular contexts, rather than a fait accompli predetermined by environmental circumstances. There is as yet, however, no unified theory or approach to the understanding of alliance formation (Child and Faulkner, 1998).

Decisions to enter into alliances are nonetheless usually assumed to be rational or boundedly rational, based on a systematic search for information on options in response to an identifiable stimulus. Market share protection or gain are widely believed to be the most powerful motivation behind airline alliances, and some carriers might take an even finer-grained approach in this respect by looking specifically for incremental performance in respect of high-value, premium traffic (Garvett and Avery, 1998). Sutton (1998) lists a number of possible benefits that are sought from alliances in general.

1. By broadening its information base, alliances can help an airline anticipate trends, and identify emerging opportunities, threats, and issues.
2. Alliances can help airlines gain access to strategically important external (i.e., firm-addressable) resources and competencies.
3. By combining only the complementary areas of their operations, alliance partners can achieve revenue or cost objectives without suffering the disadvantages of combining entire companies in a merger or acquisition.
4. Selective alliance-building can quickly fashion a global presence through myriad local presences.
5. Risks associated with internal growth or, more particularly, acquisitions can be reduced by building alliances, as can the investments required.

To this list we might add the defensive merits of co-operation amongst small competitors trying to resist the dominant presence in their markets of one or more larger airlines (the motive for building the ill-fated Swissair-led Qualiflyer Group and the more enduring TACA Group), and amongst carriers choosing to ally themselves with larger airlines' brands through franchising. Depending on the circumstances, alliances can be used both to overcome and to erect barriers to market entry. Finally, alliances offer the opportunity to learn both from and with the other parties involved. Learning can be of an operational or strategic nature and, importantly, alliances provide valuable opportunities for honing the skills necessary to build other alliances as the need arises (i.e., to build an 'integrative competence').

Focusing in particular on the airline industry and taking a somewhat more operational perspective, Bissessur and Alamdari (1998: 335) have summarised the following alliance goals.

- Increase the level of traffic through access to new markets/traffic feed....
- Ability to code-share, which has the effect of upgrading an interline connection to on-line status....
- Greater market power through increased joint market share, frequent flyer programme combination, ease of baggage transfer, single check-in for multiple-sector trips and shared airport lounges.
- Increases in load factors through improved traffic feed.
- Joint scheduling and hub co-ordination to increase operational efficiency.
- Cost reductions through the operation of joint services and rationalisation of schedules, reciprocal sales arrangements, joint ventures such as catering and maintenance, and joint purchasing of supplies.
- Enhancing the benefit of FFPs by offering a wide range of destinations.

However, given the uncertainty surrounding the course and outcome of most airline alliances to date, it is perhaps naive to suppose that they are formed entirely because two or more organizations – each acting in a unitary way – do their economic and strategic 'sums' and come to broadly the same conclusion that an alliance would suit their (perhaps differing) purposes. The reality is that few organizations, including airlines, act in a unitary way; their actions are negotiated between individuals and/or common-interest coalitions, and so are in one important sense a reflection of internal power distribution. Furthermore, alliances need at least one powerful champion in each partner to provide the momentum required to get the ball rolling and keep it mobile. Those champions, as well as others, need to bond in the first instance and then be able to work together. When champions depart, an alliance might rightly or wrongly be called into question – as happened when the two men behind the American Airlines-British Airways alliance left their respective organizations within two years of each other. Alliances are social, as well as rational strategic and economic, phenomena.

Selecting 'the right' partners

Potential partners inevitably need to be judged in the context of the motivation that has led to consideration of an alliance in the first place. There are broadly two questions each partner should ask itself about the other: first, does an alliance with the other party hold out a reasonable chance of success in achieving its objectives (e.g., increased market presence and/or network scope, meaningful cost savings, deterrence of competitors and competing alliances) and, second, what are the potential deal-breakers (e.g., incompatible cultures) and what risks do they carry?

Negotiating the terms of the relationship

As Child and Faulkner (1998) point out, negotiating to combine parts of two or more parties' value chains in an atmosphere of give-and-take complicated by the imprecision surrounding valuation of the resources and skills being contributed is a very different proposition to negotiating an acquisition. The key art in negotiating the formation of an alliance is to balance the urge of each partner to get the best possible deal for itself against the need to arrive at a jointly agreed solution that achieves what each wants out of the arrangement, forms a solid foundation for future working relationships, and builds collaborative advantage.

Establishing the structure

The structure of an alliance – whether a separately incorporated joint venture or a project-driven collaboration for example, and the means by which tasks are differentiated and integrated, communications are effected, and decisions are taken – will depend on the objectives of the deal and the preferences of key players. Economics has a theory to explain this as well. The central theme of 'agency theory' is the ability of 'principals' to ensure that their 'agents' pursue the principals' objectives; there is an assumed absence of common interests and mutual trust. Whilst the principal-agent relationship most widely studied in the literature as a whole has been that between directors and managements, the research stream has been extended to corporate strategy. Most obviously, parties to a joint venture might be cast as principals, and the venture's managers as agents; of more relevance in the airline industry, it is possible to see in any form of alliance a 'mutual agency' situation wherein each party is both principal and agent in respect of the other. The challenge then becomes one of crafting a governance structure capable of monitoring and incentivising a win-win performance whilst mutual trust is being developed.

Star for example, arguably the front-runner amongst the handful of emerging global alliances, encompasses a wide variety of structures: the alliance as a whole concentrates on revenue-generating and cost-saving initiatives on the passenger side of the business and has put in place a number of multilateral agreements covering matters as diverse as recognition of high-value customers, lounge access, and shared sales offices; a web of bilateral code-shares has been created, some as part of quite an intense co-operation effort between two or three members of the alliance on a particular set of routes; outside the mainstream of the alliance but nonetheless proximate are a number of ventures involving just some of the partners, notably in cargo and purchasing. Not all of every partner's operations are actively involved in the alliance, but most are affected in one way or another. This collage of linkages, some of which could truly be described as 'emergent' strategy-making (see chapter 1), has led to a complex and fluid set of overlapping governance structures.

Managing an alliance

Whilst game theory, agency theory, and resource-dependence theory all have something to say about the ongoing management of alliances, the literature on this topic is sparse compared with what has been written about alliance formation. A notable exception is Child and Faulkner (1998).

The successful management of an alliance requires a broader range of skills than is required in managing a single airline, the reason being a need to accommodate different cultures and management styles in colleagues, balance the needs of all the alliance principals, and nurture the relationship itself whilst at the same time coping with the internal and external challenges that any individual carrier might face. Alliance management is essentially management by consensus. At operational levels, employees need a willingness to co-operate – and in order to help develop this they require an understanding of why it is necessary to co-operate, what the limits of co-operation are, and how they can contribute to building a sound relationship between the partners. At general management level there is a real need for broad strategic awareness and an understanding of each partner's objectives; cultural sensitivity and skills in negotiating and bringing about adaptation are as or more important than traditional command-and-control skills. An openness to learning is important at all levels, as is the ability to work in teams.

Child and Faulkner (1998: 181-182) identify three key factors associated with successful alliance management.

1. Most importantly, a close relationship based on commitment, trust, and flexibility is essential. Commitment and trust can be present either in isolation or together; ideally, they should both be present. Managers with alliance responsibilities need not just to 'manage' in an operational sense, they need to spend time both developing this close relationship and helping others in their organization make sense of the alliance and understand what it should mean to them.
2. A second factor is efficient and effective arrangements for sharing information, resolving disputes, making decisions, monitoring outcomes, and generally 'getting the job done'.
3. Finally, partners need to set about proactively learning from each other, rather than simply looking for ways in which one partner's resources and skills can be used to overcome deficiencies elsewhere in the alliance and leaving it at that.

Much will depend on the organizational structure built into the alliance. As noted above, a few separately incorporated joint ventures and majority equity shareholdings have been established within the industry, but most strategic alliances involving airlines are best characterised as 'collaborations' governed to some degree by contract. Long-term vertical relationships with suppliers often develop around a contractual core, whereas horizontal collaborations with other airlines more frequently develop around issue-specific project teams – whose work may result in formalised contracts (e.g., code-sharing, FFP co-operation, and other marketing agreements), less formal arrangements, or just mutual understandings about what is to be done. The management and control of each of these mechanisms will differ, with project teams in particular lacking the stability and longevity of more traditional hierarchical structures. Whatever the architecture chosen, success is likely to be founded only on openness, commitment, and trust.

Problems in alliance management Alliances in general – not just in the airline industry – are fundamentally unstable forms of industrial organization (Harrigan, 1988; Bleeke and Ernst, 1993; Arino and de la Torre, 1998). This is not necessarily bad insofar as one advantage alliances have over mergers and acquisitions is that they can be reversed if the parties discover they have made a mistake or if circumstances change (Dussauge and Garrette, 1999); there has been no shortage of 'reverse thrust' on the airline alliance scene over the last few years, and doubtless we have not yet seen the last divorce. Nonetheless, assuming termination is not an objective (which sometimes, of course, it is in a fixed-term alliance formed for a specific purpose), we need to consider what can in fact get in the way of achieving goals. Sutton (1998) lists some possible problems.

1. The alliance might disproportionately benefit just one party.
2. Weak partners might debilitate others.
3. Environmental complexity and turbulence can make the maintenance of common objectives, or shared views on how to achieve common objectives, difficult to sustain.
4. Governance issues might delay decision-making.
5. Confidentiality can be compromised when sensitive information is shared by several organizations.
6. Taking the tough decisions sometimes necessary in a harshly competitive environment can be difficult in an alliance context, where compromise is frequently required.

Beyond this list, there are in practice two broad areas that need highlighting: cognition, and the international dimension.

1. **Cognition**
   - *Internal challenges: socio-cognitive complications* It can be argued that the competencies of individual airlines are embedded both in the beliefs of individuals and in shared beliefs about *what* needs to be done and *how* it should be done. Many of the dimensions of culture that we met earlier in the chapter will be 'carriers' of shared beliefs – dimensions such as symbols, myths, apocryphal stories, and the particular use of language within the organization; they will also be carried in established rules (both formal and informal) and in organizational routines (such as how information is collected, selected, distributed, and evaluated as part of the decision-making process). Not all of these beliefs will necessarily be consistent with the organization's 'strategic logic', although in principle they should be (Stein, 1997). If the recognition, leveraging, and building of competencies *within* a single airline is fundamentally affected by that organization's socio-cognitive dynamics, it is clear that recognising, leveraging, and building competencies within an alliance will require people not simply to do the same thing in different ways or to do new things, but to alter their beliefs and discard many of the social representations which embody the multiple belief systems that exist within any one organization.
   - *External challenges: the blurring of image* We saw in the early chapters of the book that an airline's image is a holistic set of perceptions held in the minds of stakeholders, particularly customers. The question arises as to whether alliances themselves are in the process of trying to create their own images and, if so, how these are going to sit with the separate images of their members – which,

after all, are the actual deliverers of service to image-holding customers. The scope for cognitive confusion among customers and employees is clearly immense.

2. **The international dimension** One of the problems sometimes encountered in managing international alliances is the very different approaches to HRM found in different national cultures. There is a significant body of research (usefully summarised in Mabey et al, 1998) which clearly identifies different cultural 'clusters' (e.g., North American, European, Confucian, for example or Anglo-Saxon, Nordic, Latin, Japanese, etc.), each of which tends to give rise to distinct approaches to HRM. Some take a task-oriented perspective of people as resources to be managed, whilst others take a more inclusive, participative view which emphasises dialogue and learning. Attitudes to the provision of training also vary widely between countries and cultures. Other industries cope adequately, but it can be a particular challenge in a high-contact service business such as the airline industry when partners disagree on the development of front-line staff. However, the problem will only become acute when cross-border mergers between airlines go further than they have yet gone.

In the meantime, several issue areas identified by research as affecting HRM within international companies can equally be expected to present themselves within cross-border strategic alliances between airlines (ibid).

- *Managing international diversity and multicultural teams* One possible danger with multicultural teams is that difficulties in communication and comprehension provoke tension, conflict, and confusion. In the longer term, such teams can be a resource insofar as they might not only move the alliance forward but also, as a result of their diversity and lack of 'group-think', contribute new ideas and perspectives. To get to this stage, team members need to display both cultural self-awareness and cross-cultural sensitivity. Nonetheless, ongoing decision-making within a multi-cultural team context requires constant sensitivity to different behavioural norms if it is not to become dysfunctional.

- *International recruitment and selection* The more global the airline industry becomes and the more complex its alliance interrelationships, the stronger is the argument for international recruitment strategies. Yet most carriers remain predominantly ethnocentric when judged by the constitution of their senior decision-makers at corporate headquarters.

- *International training and development* Few airlines yet seem to be actively engaged in the international and inter-cultural development of their people (e.g., through training and international job rotation) with a specific view to enabling them to better handle alliance relationships.
- *Performance management* In due course, airlines will have to develop explicit performance appraisal and evaluation techniques to help assess (and reward) individual successes in assignments involving the management of alliance relationships. This will become more important when these relationships move out of the multi-tiered working party/liaison group stage of management and adopt more formalised structures. The development of mutually satisfactory performance management systems in such an ambiguous, multi-faceted, negotiated context will not be straightforward. Not only might some airlines prefer to dodge this particular bullet, those that do address the issue might look to opposing criteria – one partner using process-oriented criteria (e.g., *whether* things are done), for example, while another adopts a performance orientation (e.g., *what* is achieved).

Extension and deepening of the co-operation

It has become a cliche to say that airline alliances are in flux. Observers have been waiting for over a decade to see the final pieces fall into place, and each time this appears to be happening an event comes along to disturb the assumption. There are simply too many idiosyncratic pressures on each alliance to link a definitive list of factors to a particular likelihood of success. Although much will depend upon the breadth and purpose of any given collaboration, it can nonetheless be plausibly argued that to have any chance of extending and deepening an alliance – assuming this to be the objective – it is necessary for it to have a good number of the following features (Holloway, 1998b): strategic symmetry; complementary competencies; plausible and shared expectations; sustained imperatives; image and reputation compatibility; strategic, operational, and marketing fit; cultural compatibility; commitment throughout both organizations (particularly at the top); appropriate alliance architecture; shared (or at least compatible) metrics; trust; and patience.

v. Conclusion

The fact that this chapter is so long and yet covers only three sets of relationships – internal relationships mediated by culture, relationships with customers, and collaborative relationships with external parties – amply illustrates just how important the management of relationships now is to airline performance. It is to performance that we turn next.

9 Managing Performance

> In God we trust; everybody else has to bring data.
>
> Roger Milliken

Having in previous chapters looked at the service concept, service design, communication, and delivery, and then considered the importance of relationships with customers, suppliers, and service partners, this chapter turns to the outcome of all that effort: business performance. We *measure* performance to check and communicate what has been, or is now being, accomplished; we use performance measurements to help *manage* current and future performance by highlighting what needs to be continued and what needs to be changed.

i. Performance management systems

> I don't try jumping over seven-foot bars.
> I look around for one-foot bars I can step over.
>
> Warren Buffett

What gets measured gets managed, particularly when individual appraisals are performance-based. The design of a performance management system is therefore an important communicator of the metrics that senior management thinks matter. This opening section of the chapter will look in very general terms at the design of performance management systems, considering first the choice of metric and then the uses to which performance information may be put. Subsequent sections will consider performance at the micro-level of the individual service encounter, and at the macro-level of the organization as a whole.

Design of a performance management system

> There are four things that hold back human progress:
> ignorance, stupidity, committees, and accountants.
> Anon

The design of a performance management system is essentially a matter of deciding which metrics will be tracked and what will be done with the information gathered.

The metrics: what is to be measured

There are some knotty issues here, notably how to decide what needs tracking, who to involve in the decision, how information should be gathered, and how to ensure that the entire system is not only measuring what matters but is doing it cost-effectively. These issues are addressed in the appropriate sections of most course textbooks on strategic management. What I want to emphasise here is the following two distinctions which are sometimes not brought out in textbooks.

Leading versus lagging indicators Lagging indicators such as profit describe performance outcomes – what has already happened; leading indicators or 'performance drivers' also describe what has happened, but because of their lagged linkages to other indicators which they influence they can also provide an insight into future outcomes. Current levels of customer satisfaction are now widely believed to be a leading indicator of future profits, for example. But if customer satisfaction is a performance driver that leads eventually to certain financial outcomes, it is also in itself a performance outcome which has its own drivers – particularly in the operations area.

When we take a performance outcome and ask 'Why?', the answer will help define relevant performance drivers. These may be: strategy-related – that is, a function of what the airline is trying to achieve for its customers; activity-related – a function of which activities are undertaken and how they are organized; process-related – a function of how processes are organized and managed within the wider context of organization structure; and/or environment-related – a function of the airline's social, regulatory, economic, or technological circumstances.

Strategic versus diagnostic indicators People have limited cognitive capabilities. Senior managers will therefore focus on a relatively small number of performance indicators related to major strategic objectives and critical success factors. Beneath strategic metrics can be a myriad of diagnostic measurements which keep more detailed track of how an airline is doing. Diagnostic metrics can include perhaps hundreds of measurements – often day-to-day operating variables – used to ensure that a business is under control, that nothing unusual is happening, and that it is functioning normally (Kaplan and Norton, 1996). Some of what can be seen as diagnostic from the perspective of top management (e.g., customer satisfaction with passenger services at a particular hub) is strategic to line managers (e.g., to those responsible for ground operations and customer service at that hub).

However, the idea that strategic performance can be measured takes an essentially rationalist view of organizations as 'things' that can be steered between goal-posts. It makes some important, albeit implicit, assumptions (Mabey et al, 1998).

1. Strategy can be reduced to a set of clearly articulated and ascertainable objectives. (Counterpoint: Strategies often emerge over time rather than being periodically planned, meaning that specific objectives are not a sine qua non of strategy and may anyway be overtaken by events.)
2. We can determine beyond doubt whether or not objectives have been achieved. (Counterpoint: This year we lengthened the depreciation period applied to our fleet and increased assumed end-of-life residual values, thereby lowering the depreciation charge in our income statement – so if we hit a profit target set without taking those adjustments into prior consideration, have we really achieved what we set out to achieve?)
3. We can know why objectives have or have not been achieved and, specifically, who or what has contributed to the outcome. (Counterpoint: Did we reach our yield target in the North Atlantic market because of our great new business class product, or because competitors reduced their advertising budgets – or was it a little of both?)
4. We can fully understand the cause-effect relationship underlying why objectives have or have not been met. (Counterpoint: We might see revenue or cost figures missing objectives and delve deeper to find out why, but can we ever really know with certainty what impact ill-tempered labour negotiations or the CEO awarding himself millions of dollars worth of stock options had on these outcomes? More generally, cause and effect can be widely separated in both time and space, and effects are very often the result of multiple complex causes which feed off each other in ways that are difficult to predict in advance and to unravel in retrospect – a central tenet of 'complexity theory'.)

5. We can 'manage' the cause-effect chain by responding to feedback. (Counterpoint: Whereas traditional models of performance control rely on the 'negative feedback' of the thermostat metaphor – that is, we sense divergence from targets and in response make adjustments to move the system back to its equilibrium state – more recent thinking sees organizations as complex socio-technical systems that cannot be managed in this way. The argument is that they are subject to 'positive feedback' – a loop of self-reinforcing changes which snowball until their origins become lost in a Gordian knot of cause-effect relationships. Moreover, much of what goes on in airlines and other complex organizations is based on the meanings and interpretations people give to events – and the management of meanings and interpretations is very much more difficult than the management of events.)

Despite doubts expressed in the literature about how realistic these assumptions are, there is nonetheless a widely accepted performance management model based on iterating through a five-stage cycle of: objective-setting; outcome measurement; feedback of results; linking rewards to results; and amending objectives and activities (ibid). Indeed, a performance management system is considered by some to be a potential source of advantage if it provides unique insights unavailable to competitors.

The outcome: what is done with performance information

According to the 'rational planning' model of strategic management that we met in chapter 1, strategies are formulated in order to reach broad, long-term objectives and more specific short- and medium-term goals; these strategies are implemented through detailed action planning and the purposeful allocation of resources. Performance measurement is used to assess the extent to which objectives have been met and strategies successfully implemented, and beyond that to help frame corrective action. Objectives inevitably reflect the value system(s) of top managers, and might represent a negotiated consensus within this group; to be tenable over time, they need also to incorporate the views of other important stakeholders.

These days, customers represent a critical stakeholder group. The implication of this is that significant attention must be given to aspects of performance that matter most to customers. First, we need to understand what does matter to customers in our targeted segment(s) so that the right things get measured. This should, of course, have been uncovered at the service design stage. Then, depending upon the size of the airline concerned, there is an argument for having an independent unit empowered to delve into service-related issues surfaced by the performance management system.

This type of proactive approach is philosophically very different from the more typical airline customer relations function charged with reacting to individual complaints. Establishing a unit of this type was one of the first steps taken by the new management brought in to turn British Airways around in the mid-1980s: its role was to act as the customers' advocate within the airline, and it was given ready access to senior management. Twenty years on, the approach has yet to be widely imitated.

In this chapter we will look at performance on two levels: the micro-level of the service encounter, and the macro-level of organizational performance as a whole. At the micro-level we will consider performance from the perspective of individual customers engaged in individual service encounters, focusing in particular on service failure and recovery. At the macro-level, we will look first at the 'strategy-performance pyramid' – a framework within which overall performance can be assessed – and then in some detail at customer satisfaction and, in particular, service quality.

ii. The micro-level: service failure and recovery

> The customer is frequently wrong. We don't carry those sorts of customer. We write them and say, 'Fly somebody else. Don't abuse our people.'
> Herb Kelleher

Service failure

Service failure occurs when a service attribute, which might include a service encounter, falls short of a customer's expectations. What matters is the customer's perception; only a customer can decide whether a service failure has occurred and, if so, how serious it has been. Because the air transport service is comprised of numerous functional and emotional attributes, it is quite possible for failure in respect of just one attribute to negatively affect consumers' perceptions of the entire experience. Indeed, failure in an 'augmented' attribute (see chapter 4) can tarnish the effect of successful delivery of the safe, timely locational transformation service that lies at the core of each airline's offer to its markets. A passenger who has had to queue for what is considered an excessive time in order to check-in, for example, will quite probably board the aircraft with a very different attitude compared with what would have been the case had the check-in process been smoother. This attitude could affect perceptions of inflight service – particularly if the flight is relatively short, so providing less time to forget the ground experience; it may also reduce satisfaction gained from ontime arrival or other successfully delivered benefits.

Because of the complexity of the airline industry and the millions of service encounters in which even a moderately sized carrier engages every year, the number of potential fail-points is very large. Those involving human interactions are difficult to monitor, and even the more 'mechanical' aspects of service delivery might fail for some reason from a consumer's standpoint notwithstanding that they appear to the airline concerned to be performing in conformance with expectations. 'Zero defects' – a concept at the heart of total quality management – is not a model that works particularly well in the service sector, where there are as many possible defects as customers in aggregate are able to perceive. There are no 'zero defects' employees, and neither can 'six-sigma quality' be engineered into a service delivery process. The logic of this becomes apparent if we bear in mind that service quality – and therefore service failure – is something that is judged not by any metric of functional performance, but through the perceptions of literally millions of individual customers.

Service failures arise when an expected attribute is not delivered or is delivered at a level below a customer's expectations. They happen for reasons which may or may not be within the control of the airline or its employees. Cost-cutting in one process, as opposed to cost management with the likely impact on customers' perceptions kept clearly in mind, can easily lead to a service failure that reflects badly on the entire airline. Hence the value of systems thinking. Sometimes service failures happen because of the behaviour of customers themselves – seeking special treatment, perhaps, or making errors when playing their roles in participative service delivery processes.

We will look at a categorisation of the generic reasons for service failure later in the chapter, where a model widely used for investigating service quality is applied to identify different types of performance 'gap'. At this point in the discussion, we need only think of service failures as being attributable to the following.

1. **Design failure** The service package, including delivery processes, was not designed in a way that meets the expectations of targeted customers.
2. **Delivery failure** One or more attributes, including perhaps processes, within the service delivery system is not operating the way it should. This could be attributable to:
   - facility failure (e.g., inability of facilities to cope with foreseeable peak demand);
   - equipment failure (e.g., aircraft reliability problems);

- staff failure (e.g., errors of judgement or procedural violations – perhaps attributable to inadequate training for the task, inadequate support systems, and/or poor awareness of customers' expectations);
- supplier failure (e.g., airport or airway congestion, or the failure of outsourced service providers);
- customer failure (e.g., late arrival at a departure gate).

It might be useful to reflect upon the following four certainties.

1. The 'bar' keeps getting higher. Customers who now have greater choice, higher expectations, more affluence, and less time than in the past are simply more demanding than they used to be.
2. Service failures will occur.
3. Service failures cause customer dissatisfaction, the effect of which may be a lower likelihood of repurchase. Failure attribution can be significant in determining the level of dissatisfaction felt by a consumer experiencing a service failure. If a flight is delayed or cancelled as a result of bad weather, for example, the airline is likely to be subject to lower dissatisfaction than if it had been directly responsible – provided its response to the failure meets customers' expectations. The problem is that in less clear-cut cases than this, consumers will vary considerably in their individual propensities to blame a carrier – some attributing blame where it does not justifiably lie.
4. Dissatisfied customers will tell many more people about their experiences than they would have done had those experiences been positive.

Given both the certainty that service failures will occur and the potential severity of their negative impact on customer satisfaction, every service management system should have in place sub-systems designed to:

- detect service failures;
- analyse failures and act to improve performance reliability;
- recover when things do go wrong.

Detecting service failures

> It isn't that they can't see the solution.
> It's that they can't see the problem.
> Grover Cleveland

When an AOG situation leads to a long flight delay, it does not take a passenger survey to conclude that a service failure has occurred. More often, however, service failures arising out of less dramatic happenings – often routine unmonitored service encounters – go completely undetected. One way of uncovering them is to ask customers directly (in focus groups) or sample the customer base for common problems (using survey instruments). Another way is to listen carefully to complaints.

Complaints Complaints are a valuable source of information on service failure and a potentially invaluable learning resource; they should be facilitated. Research shows that the majority of dissatisfied customers never complain, preferring instead simply to take their business elsewhere. On the other hand, complaints that are dealt with in a timely, positive (i.e., not defensive), and responsive manner tend in the majority of cases not to lead to customer defections.

The problem with complaints is that airlines, like most other organizations, do not get enough of them. Consider the following.

1. It is widely believed that fewer than five per cent of dissatisfied customers complain. Many of the 'silent majority' simply switch to other airlines – assuming acceptable alternatives exist and the loss of FFP benefits is not an overriding consideration; they also talk to as many as ten other people about their negative experience. If true, this suggests that one complaint masks:
    *   at least 19 unidentified service failures;
    *   approximately 200 (i.e., 20 x 10) potential customers exposed to negative word-of-mouth publicity.
2. Research by British Airways some years ago discovered that approximately one-third of its passengers felt dissatisfied in some way, and that of these dissatisfied customers:
    *   8 per cent contacted Customer Relations;
    *   23 per cent spoke only to the nearest BA employee;
    *   69 per cent did not talk to anybody (Sasser and Klein, 1994).

This begs the question of why people tend not to complain when dissatisfied. The literature suggests the following possible reasons: they do not see any payoff in complaining; they prefer to avoid conflict; and/or they do not blame the particular service provider involved for what they perceive to be an organizational problem, and do not want to risk getting that person into trouble.

Clearly, the manner in which complaints are handled can affect not only an airline's ability to learn from what customers are telling it, but also the likelihood that a complainant's future business will be retained. The probability of retaining a dissatisfied customer's business will rise through the following stages.

- No complaint registered.
- Complaint registered, but not resolved to the customer's satisfaction (although this might, depending on the circumstances, carry a higher risk of customer defection than the 'no complaint registered' situation).
- Complaint resolved to the customer's satisfaction.
- Complaint resolved *quickly* to the customer's satisfaction.

An effective complaint management system will most probably therefore be one with the following capabilities.

1. It ensures that front-line employees are trained to:
   - identify and resolve unarticulated dissatisfaction;
   - handle different types of complaint.
2. It ensures that there is a well-organized complaint-handling system away from the front line capable of accommodating:
   - customers' complaints;
   - information and suggestions from employees arising from customers' informal comments or their own observations.
3. It encourages the 'silent majority' amongst those customers who are dissatisfied to register their complaints, because this gives the airline an opportunity to:
   - learn how service might be improved;
   - attempt service recovery.

Commonly used methods include inflight survey forms, interactive terminals in club lounges, direct contact with high-value accounts (e.g., during sales calls on corporate customers), toll-free numbers prominent in inflight magazines and FFP literature, and opportunities to comment provided on an airline's web site.

It is absolutely vital that customers as a whole, but particularly customers with a problem, perceive the airline as approachable and responsive and that they do not perceive it to be defensive. Some airlines nonetheless still hide from this potentially valuable source of feedback, making it difficult to complain and frequently using their internal procedures to turn dissatisfied customers into transgressors. It remains relatively rare to find on ticket wallets or on tickets themselves (if airline, rather than IATA, stock) the invitations to comment about the product that are found on the packaging of consumer goods in many countries.

On the other hand, a growing number of airlines do now have systematised procedures for logging, coding, responding to, and learning from complaints. According to Sasser and Klein (1994), British Airways found that complainants want: to be taken seriously; to receive an apology or recognition that the problem exists; to have input into the solution or, at least, an explanation of what went wrong and what has been done to lower the risk of it happening again; and to see a quick resolution – ideally by telephone and with a single point of contact (i.e., a single 'owner' of the problem). Research suggests that customers expect 'fairness' of three types when their complaints are being dealt with (Tax and Brown, 1998): outcome fairness – a response which recognises their problem and offers redress proportional to their perception of its seriousness (e.g., vouchers to purchase duty-free goods in the event of an IFE equipment failure on a long-haul flight); procedural fairness – hassle-free access to a clear complaint-handling mechanism on the ground if a problem gets that far without being resolved on the front line; and interactional fairness – courtesy, concern, and signs of a palpable effort to deal efficiently and effectively with the problem.

This suggests that customer relations staff:

- should: sympathise, explain if explanation is possible, rectify, and where necessary compensate;
- should not: avoid, delay, deny, or justify;
- need: training in conflict management, paraphrasing problems, negotiating, and decision-making; latitude, within clear limits, to rectify and compensate; credibility within the organization to act as the customers' advocate; and information systems which:
  - allow instant access to each complainant's file, charting progress in resolving the complaint;
  - permit cataloguing of the root causes of complaints so that recurring problems in the service delivery system can be addressed.

Finally, we need to be aware that articulated complaints these days may not be sent directly to the airline concerned. Internet chat-rooms and even special-purpose web-sites need to be monitored by an airline actively interested in improving its service and protecting its image.

Failure analysis and reliability improvement

Whatever the failure, there is likely to be a 'root cause' hidden below the immediately apparent reason(s). For example, the root causes(s) of poor punctuality could be airport or airway congestion, an ageing and mechanically unreliable fleet, a new fleet with 'teething' problems, tight scheduling of aircraft, crews, gates, and/or connections, or inefficient turnaround procedures. Below each of these problems might lie a further layer of 'root causes' that need investigating. Figure 9.1 illustrates use of the Ishikawa/fishbone/cause-and-effect technique to assist with the learning process.

Developing Ishikawa's work, Lovelock (1996: 478) has proposed that factors which might cause a specific problem should be identified (e.g., in brainstorming sessions) and categorised into one of eight groupings: facilities and equipment; materials and supplies; front-stage personnel; back-stage personnel; procedures; information; customers; and other causes.

Fault-tree analysis is similar in principle to the Ishikawa approach, except that it starts with an actual or potential failure and works backwards to one or more causes. Ask why a problem is occurring, then apply a further 'Why?' to the answer and to each subsequent answer through, say, five iterations (i.e., 'the five whys') and the root cause of any problem is likely to become clear. Other approaches to the analysis of failures include focus groups and the critical incident technique. The latter requires customers (or staff) to give accounts of specific incidents in the course of service delivery that caused (or are believed by staff to have caused) dissatisfaction; reasons for dissatisfaction can then be categorised and linked to specific service failures and their causes.

Having analysed why service failures are occurring or could occur in future, efforts will need to be made to prevent them or make them less probable. The reliability of an airline's service delivery system can be improved by one or more of the following: designing-out fail-points (e.g., improve gate allocations at a hub to help passengers make tight connections more easily); build redundancy into the system (e.g., add more standby staff and aircraft); fail-safe critical points of the delivery system; improve system maintenance – which includes staff training as well as the maintenance of facilities and equipment. None of this is necessarily cheap. As always in services management, there is a trade-off between effectiveness and efficiency to be arrived at; the context within which resolution should take place is the particular airline's service concept(s) – the type(s) of customer value it is offering and the market positioning of the offer(s).

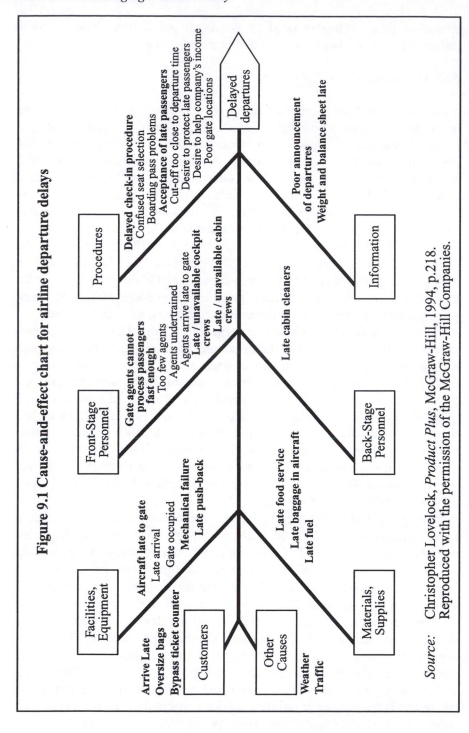

Figure 9.1 Cause-and-effect chart for airline departure delays

Source: Christopher Lovelock, *Product Plus*, McGraw-Hill, 1994, p.218. Reproduced with the permission of the McGraw-Hill Companies.

Service recovery

> A problem is a chance for you to do your best.
> Duke Ellington

Service recovery efforts might range in scale from an operations control centre trying to get aircraft and crews back onto the published schedule after a major weather disruption, down to a customer service representative dealing with a single passenger's missed connection. Service recovery is an integral part of defections management. The manner in which service failures are to be identified and handled and how recovery procedures can be used proactively to avoid customer defections should be considered as part of the service design process. Different recovery procedures will be needed to meet different types of failure, but they should all share the same basic elements: information about the problem, resources to deal with the problem, and the right attitudes on the part of suitably trained and empowered, service-oriented employees. Service recovery is not just a matter of procedures, it is also a question of commitment and culture (Pai and Trefzger, 1998).

Whilst a service failure cannot be recalled to the factory, recovery is nonetheless often possible. Indeed, because production and consumption of the air transport service are simultaneous, it is sometimes feasible to identify failures as they develop and initiate service recovery immediately. Although unsatisfactory service is inherently more difficult to 'replace' than a bad product, if correctly handled a service failure need not lead inevitably to a customer defection; indeed, there is some research evidence suggesting that a successful service recovery can actually heighten loyalty – perhaps because, for the customer concerned, advertising slogans claiming high standards of service have been transformed into action focused specifically on him or her (Goodman, 1999).

Conversely, research has shown that between one third and a half of unsatisfactory service encounters can be attributed to the inability or unwillingness of employees to respond appropriately to service failure – what is called 'double deviation' from customer expectations (Bitner at al, 1990). There is also evidence that expectations of successful service recovery grow with the quality of the service-price offer that has been 'bought into', with the reputation of the airline, and with the loyalty that a particular customer feels she gives to the carrier concerned.

Service failure can come to an airline's attention at any stage from initial enquiry through post-purchase evaluation. How efficiently and effectively the problem is dealt with will determine whether or not the airline can recover any of the customer satisfaction dissipated as a result of the failure.

It is generally believed that an effective service recovery will have more impact on a customer's future purchase intentions than dissatisfaction felt as a result of the original service failure (Spreng et al, 1995).

Appropriate levels of service recovery How far an airline should go in its recovery efforts ought to reflect:

- the importance of the affected customer(s) in terms of current and potential business;
- the severity of the error in terms of its future impact on the relationship.

Many airlines have in place graduated responses to deal with 'whole-plane' service failures such as delayed flights: these might range from honest explanations and apology, complimentary drinks during onboard delays, meal vouchers during in-terminal delays, through accommodation and alternative bookings if required. Our concern here is less with 'whole-plane' service recoveries dealt with using pre-formulated recovery procedures than with recovery from a more individualised failure.

Particularly with regard to response deadlines and scope of redress, recovery efforts directed at an individual customer who has experienced service failure and subsequently complained should be guided by the nature of the service failure and the estimated lifetime value of the customer concerned. For example, a serious service failure involving a high-value customer must be prioritised for recovery and follow-up. Similarly, whereas a minor failure affecting a low-value customer might not warrant recovery efforts beyond the norm, the same failure involving a high-value customer could justify more focused service recovery and follow-up.

What makes this prescription difficult to operationalise for many airlines is their inability to put a monetary value on customer relationships. A few carriers are now beginning to build databases capable of capturing information that allows them to arrive at approximate valuations of customer relationships and detect drop-offs in service usage over time; drop-offs might be indicative of either or both specific, unreported service failures or a general decline in the airline's competitiveness.

Many airlines nonetheless still have reservations, marketing, check-in and FFP systems that cannot communicate, and are only just beginning to think about how best to get customer-specific information about preferences, service failures (on previous journeys or the present trip), FFP standing, and projected lifetime value to the front-line staff who could actually use it in order to help prioritise and better manage service recovery efforts.

Structured approaches to service recovery These require the following.

1. Development of an explicit and clearly understood service recovery programme which addresses all reasonably foreseeable 'fail points'. Value chain analysis and flow-charting can help here, but perhaps the most important step is to train employees to quickly recognise and recover from service failures. A key variable is the extent to which employees are *empowered* to respond.
2. Facilitation of complaints, comments, and suggestions – which are important sources of learning – and the keeping of a database of root causes.
3. Looking both at actual sources of failure and at what it takes to facilitate recovery, and seeing if what is learned can be factored into a redesigned service package or service delivery system.
4. Ensuring that management and employees are totally committed to service recovery as an important revenue generation tool, and that adequate resources are allocated to the effort.

Some airlines are now addressing a wider range of potential service failures than in the past (although the 'Airline Customer Service Report' released by the Transportation Department Office of The Inspector-General in February 2001 suggested that most US majors still had plenty of room for improvement). Some have responded to their more intensely competitive circumstances by initiating structured approaches to service recovery. An interesting issue is the compatibility of recovery responses within alliances. Where these are incompatible, however justified the reasons, customer dissatisfaction in the event of service failure could be heightened by a recovery response that falls short of expectations. An example might be different policies regarding the treatment of delayed passengers.

In the final analysis, the primary objective of any well-designed service recovery programme should be to overcome a customer's feelings of dissatisfaction arising from a service failure with a stronger feeling of satisfaction arising from the recovery; at its best, service recovery can be an opportunity not just to transform a potential customer defection into successful customer retention, but to build loyalty by being responsive and empathetic. Another objective is to learn why a failure occurred and how similar incidents can be avoided. A final objective should be to learn about service recovery itself – to find out what works and what does not in dealing with particular types of failure in particular types of circumstance.

Pitfalls in service recovery In general, customers' expectations in respect of service recovery will be higher than expectations in respect of the service attribute or encounter that failed (Zeithaml and Bitner, 2000). The literature suggests that a failed service recovery, no matter how genuine and well-meaning the effort, is likely to lead to even greater consumer dissatisfaction than had no recovery been attempted. And even when service recovery is well-executed, if service failures – either of the same or different types – keep coming to the attention of the customer concerned, the 'authority' with which the service is provided is undermined, raising that customer's perception of service risk and heightening the likelihood of defection.

Figure 9.2 illustrates linkages between the concepts discussed in this section of the chapter.

iii. The macro-level: organizational performance as a whole

> Not everything that can be counted counts,
> and not everything that counts can be counted.
> Albert Einstein

In this section of the chapter I will first briefly introduce the 'strategy-performance pyramid', before going on to look in more detail at the concepts of customer satisfaction and, in particular, service quality.

The strategy-performance pyramid

> Money doesn't talk, it swears.
> Bob Dylan

Until relatively recently, 'performance' was shorthand for 'financial performance'. Since the mid-1990s, however, many businesses – and airlines are no exception – have been adopting a broader perspective. Kaplan and Norton's (1996) widely popular concept of the balanced scorecard has been a powerful stimulus, providing a simple yet potentially rich alternative by urging attention to customers, internal processes, and innovation and learning in addition to financial performance. (Olve et al (1999) provide an interesting example of British Airways' use of the balanced scorecard to manage London Heathrow ground operations.) The strategy-performance pyramid illustrated in figure 9.3, also adopts a balanced approach to performance measurement; the advantage I have found it to have in practice over other scorecard approaches is that it is more explicit in linking different aspects of achieved performance to strategic thinking.

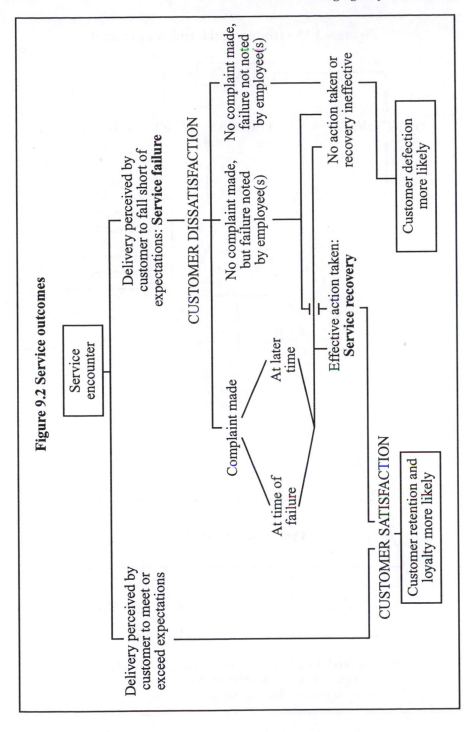

Figure 9.2 Service outcomes

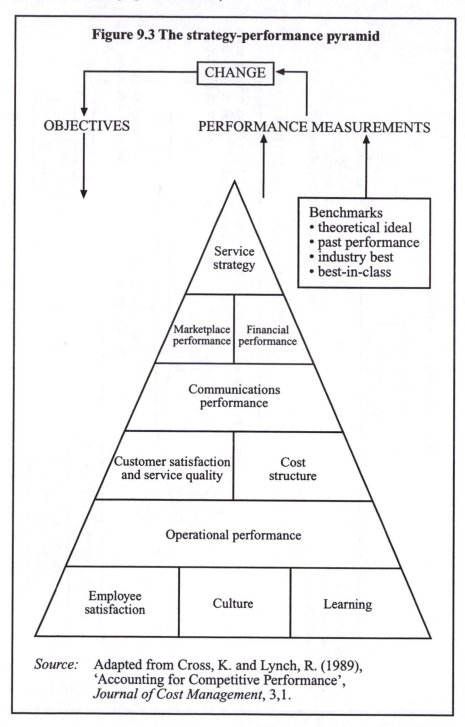

Figure 9.3 The strategy-performance pyramid

CHANGE

OBJECTIVES

PERFORMANCE MEASUREMENTS

Service strategy

Benchmarks
• theoretical ideal
• past performance
• industry best
• best-in-class

Marketplace performance | Financial performance

Communications performance

Customer satisfaction and service quality | Cost structure

Operational performance

Employee satisfaction | Culture | Learning

Source: Adapted from Cross, K. and Lynch, R. (1989), 'Accounting for Competitive Performance', *Journal of Cost Management*, 3,1.

The logic of the pyramid is that its foundation layers – employee satisfaction, culture, learning, and operational performance – underpin service quality, cost structure, marketplace performance, and financial performance. Guiding everything from the top is the airline's strategy.

One of the advantages of the strategy-performance pyramid is that it can be used as just the surface layer of a performance 'drill-down' designed to suit the strategy and circumstances of any particular airline. For example, if we take 'customer satisfaction' in figure 9.3 as Level I and identify a decline, drilling-down to Level II might reveal amongst the metrics chosen as underlying drivers of customer satisfaction a decline in punctuality at a key hub; further drilling-down to Level III might isolate passenger processing at check-in or security, non-adjacent gates for connecting passengers, crew scheduling, or ramp handling as a source of the problem. Level I metrics in some areas of the pyramid (e.g., operational performance) may well be drill-down (i.e., Level II or Level III) drivers of metrics in other areas (e.g., cost structure or customer satisfaction); similarly, some Level III and Level II metrics inevitably drive more than one Level I metric – perhaps in the same or different areas. This serves to emphasise and help isolate critical system interdependencies; for example, aircraft utilisation problems might drive declines in Level I metrics for operational performance, cost structure, customer satisfaction, and/or financial performance.

Mention of system interdependencies underlines the related point that objectives are means rather than ends. To an engineering manager, completing a heavy check on time might be an achieved end; to a scheduling manager it is simply a means to deliver the schedule as published; to a marketing manager, delivering the schedule is just one (albeit vital) aspect of delivering an overall service package; to a financial manager, these are all just means to generate a positive financial outcome; to the engineering manager, a healthy financial outcome might be a means to motivate staff with performance-related bonuses. Performance of any sort within a complex system is therefore a means as well as an end. A major responsibility of strategic managers is to bring coherence to this means-ends loop and to incentivise performance.

The next few paragraphs will briefly introduce the main elements of the model. Whether it is suitable for use in a particular situation and, if so, what type of performance information will need to be gathered is something that must inevitably depend upon the circumstances of the airline concerned and – importantly – the nature of its strategy.

The human dimension: employee satisfaction, culture, and learning

Employee satisfaction Raw data on absenteeism, retention rates, and both the time and money spent on staff training and development are easily collected. In recent years increasing attention has also been given to staff attitudes, motivation levels, and satisfaction in general – the belief being that profitability and growth flow from customer satisfaction and loyalty, which are driven by employee performance levels that are in their own turn dependent upon employee satisfaction and loyalty (Heskett et al, 1994).

Culture Although several writers have argued that a strong culture can help corporate performance because shared values lend commitment and consistency to employee behaviour (Deal and Kennedy, 1982; Peters and Waterman, 1982), research has failed to establish an incontrovertible link between the two (Brown, 1998). As I argued in the last chapter, it is nonetheless intuitively appealing to believe that culture can have an impact on processes that are important to strategy implementation in general and service delivery in particular. Although survey instruments have been developed (see Brown, 1998), few airlines appear to pay any formal attention to their culture in the sense that they actively monitor it. Southwest is a notable exception, having established a committee tasked with protecting the unique corporate culture that is believed to be one of the key foundations of the carrier's commercial success.

Learning 'A learning enterprise is one skilled at acquiring, creating, storing, and transferring knowledge, and using it to change the way work is done' (Martin, 1995: 407). 'All organizations are learning most of the time. The question is to what extent the learning is repetitive and unconscious, or co-ordinated and channelled in a synergistic and progressive manner' (Mabey et al, 1998: 325). The importance of learning is that it unleashes an airline's human talent by equipping people to constructively question and better contribute to organizational purpose. We should be concerned with two types of learning.

1. **Individual learning** This is a process with three overlapping stages: cognitive change, leading to behavioural change, culminating in changed performance outcomes (Martin, op cit). Cognitive change begins with new knowledge gained either from learning-by-doing, or from observing the experiences of others. Learning can be 'adaptive' or 'generative' (Senge, 1990).

- *Adaptive learning* requires analysis of what did and did not work well in the past, and then adapting practice in order to help cope with new challenges.
- *Generative learning* is more speculative and in many ways more fundamental, looking for new options and possibilities in the future and at how to change established mental models and possibly even values.

2. **Organizational learning** When new knowledge is transferred from an individual or group into an organizational record independent of that individual or group, organizational learning has occurred. New behaviour in response to unchanged stimuli is evidence of learning (Argyris, 1990). (This can be contrasted with what happens when new stimuli produce the same behaviour because past success has created a 'defence routine'.) Airlines themselves may or may not 'learn', but they do have knowledge storage capabilities such as information systems, routines and procedures, and even cultural artefacts such as myths and symbols. The more tacit individual or group knowledge is, the more likely it is to be transformed into organizational knowledge in the form of opaque routines and 'ways-of-doing' rather than clearly codified practices or knowledge bases. A 'learning organization' is one that has institutionalised the capacity to tap individual learning at all levels in its structure, and transmit the knowledge gained to where it can best be used to change the way the organization acts; there is an argument that in turbulent and increasingly complex environments, only organizations able to develop their collective capability to learn and then exploit that capability more rapidly than competitors will survive in the long term (Senge, 1990).

Learning, whether individual or organizational, can occur at two levels within any airline.

- **Operational level** Learning at this level leads to error detection and correction and to improvement generally, but not to significant changes in objectives or strategies.
- **Strategic level** Learning plays a significant role in strategic management from two perspectives.
  - *Learning as a mode of strategy-making* As we saw in chapter 1, some researchers and practitioners characterise strategy-making not as a process of planned strategic action preceded by rational analysis, but as an emergent process defined less by intent than by what is learned from 'doing'.

- *Learning as a foundation of competitive advantage* Strategic learning has been at the heart of the competence-based approach to competitive strategy since theory-building in the area began in the early 1990s. Indeed, in their seminal article on the subject, Prahalad and Hamel (1990) equate an organization's 'core competence' to its 'collective learning'. Learning contributes to strategic flexibility (Sanchez, 1995) and is critical to the building, leveraging, and maintenance of competencies (Sanchez and Heene, 1997). Some researchers have argued that an organization's only source of sustainable competitive advantage in the long run is the ability to learn faster than competitors (deGeus, 1988) by reconstructing and adapting its knowledge base – and, from time-to-time, perhaps also its value system and the strategic logic of the business. Learning from customers is obviously a critical facet of learning as a whole, and airplanes – where customers are 'trapped' for long periods – are excellent places in which to learn.

Strategic learning can come from experience and experimentation (learning-by-doing), observation of others, or what is widely referred to in the literature as 'strategic thinking'. Strategic thinking implies stepping outside the strait-jacket of sometimes linear experience, using scenario planning to develop and test new hypotheses and to create new mental models of possible futures, and to have sufficient foresight to detect the need to build new competencies for the future.

It is fairly clear that internal communication is an important lubricant in the learning process. One of its primary objectives must be to help staff understand what the airline is trying to achieve for its customers and to gain their commitment. Another is to facilitate the transformation of new individual knowledge into organizational knowledge, and the dissemination of new organizational knowledge to other individuals who need to have access to it. Communications surveys can therefore be a useful metric, as can the availability and usage rates of IT and other tools provided specifically to enable co-operative work and group learning. If formal organization-wide learning initiatives exist, their progress can be tracked. Metrics derived from staff training and development programmes – hours, days, dollars spent on training, together with delegate satisfaction levels, for example, and percentage of staff with individual development plans – can be used as proxies for the dissemination of codifiable knowledge (although training is only one medium of many available to promote and facilitate organizational learning). Because innovation is usually based on experiential or observational learning (and only occasionally on pure inspiration), new service concepts, service attributes, and methods of communicating with new or established markets and segments can also provide measurable evidence of learning. Examples of questions that could be used to assess service innovation include the following.

- What have we done to improve customer value, and what evidence do we have that the effort was successful? How recently have we done a customer value analysis?
- What service innovations have we introduced since the last performance review?
- How rapidly were the innovations introduced? (Some airlines do a great deal of market research before innovating, whereas others prefer 'expeditionary marketing' – frequently launching unresearched, but often relatively minor, innovations and seeing how well they are accepted in the marketplace.)
- Have the 'points of difference' which distinguish our offers from those of competitors been expanded upon or eroded?
- What redundant service attributes have been dropped?

Cultural metrics can provide evidence of whether or not receptivity to learning has been embedded into an airline, and survey instruments have been developed for the purpose (Pearn et al, 1995). This is important because it is individuals, albeit socialised by a particular airline's culture, who make decisions that have a profound effect on the acquisition and use of knowledge and on the adoption of organizational routines; the role of human agency in organizational learning cannot be overlooked.

External environments are now too complex for most airlines to rely just on a gifted strategist or a team of strategists at the top of the organization, making decisions based on supposed omniscience – and perhaps omnipotence. The better way to cope with complexity and change is to encourage and motivate everybody to make a commitment to organizational learning – a commitment to questioning assumptions and mental models, to experimentation, to involvement, and to improvement. This is not easy in airlines which have strong 'power cultures' or subscribe unbendingly to the idea that there is 'one best way' to do everything, because these are not arenas in which people are rewarded for challenging the established mindset or debating alternative models of the business, its environment, and its future. Some national and organizational cultures promote more readily than others the questioning and openness to change which underpin learning; this is just one of the many barriers that will have to be overcome if the emerging global alliances are going to move beyond their still largely superficial relationships.

Operational performance

> An expert is a person who has made all the mistakes
> which can be made in a very narrow field.
> Niels Bohrs

This is the area of the strategy-performance pyramid that will have the most drill-down levels, reaching from basic Level 1 metrics of front-office and back-office performance such as holding time on reservations lines and the number of failed calls, flight completion rate, punctuality, denied boarding, involuntary downgrades, and IFE availability statistics, for example, down to measures of supplier performance and detailed metrics for individual stations such as check-in queuing times, servicescape appearance, baggage mishandling rate, time to arrival in the baggage hall of the first and last bags off an incoming flight, and staff injury and equipment damage events. Airlines are fortunate insofar as quite a lot of their operational activities can be subjected to statistical analysis.

Most airlines already compile detailed operational performance measurements – indeed, some still compile nothing other than operational performance metrics. The key issue is whether the right ones are being addressed. A good approach is to think about the particular benefits that a given airline's service concept requires it to offer targeted customers, question how these have been translated into service attributes, ensure that each attribute has a measurable specification (even if this is qualitative and only subjectively measurable, such as 'cleanliness' of equipment or 'appearance' of cabins and other servicescapes), and then measure whether specifications have been met. Meeting service specifications will not necessarily ensure that customers are satisfied, but it will help narrow down the reason for any dissatisfaction: perhaps the specification is being met but is too low for a targeted segment given what a competitor is now offering, or perhaps passengers simply do not perceive the airline to be meeting a particular service specification even though in fact it is. As far as customers are concerned, perception *is* reality; it nonetheless helps an airline move ahead if its performance measurement system has a grip on both.

Any airline functions through a considerable number of processes other than those that can properly be called 'service delivery processes'. Some are obviously not connected directly to service delivery – such as strategic planning and budgeting processes – notwithstanding that they may ultimately have a profound effect on the specification of services. In other cases it might be possible to argue about whether a particular process is or is not a 'back-office' service delivery process. My rule of thumb is that if a process has a direct and proximate impact on service delivery – such as aircraft maintenance, for example – it is a service delivery process (back-office in this case). The semantics are far less important than ensuring that every significant process is measured at one level or another in the strategy-performance drill-down.

Our concern is with process efficiency and outcome effectiveness. There are many different tools available for assessing process performance, with the choice of what is appropriate often depending upon the nature of a particular process. Different departments and divisions will evidently have their own metrics (and, in some cases, quality control/quality assurance programmes – such as flight operations quality assurance). For example, amongst many other metrics, an MRO division will track airframe maintenance cost/flight-hour, engine maintenance cost/flight-hour (unless a power-by-the-hour outsourcing arrangement has been agreed), inflight shutdown rate, unscheduled shop visit rate, engine removal rate/1000 flight-hours, achieved check intervals, elapsed time per check, cost (manhours, materials, and overhead) per check, and productivity of each hangar, line, and shop. Another example is the revenue management department, which will have metrics (such as spoilage, dilution costs, unit revenue, yield, load factor, and oversales) that can be used for comparison with optimal flight performance and for uncovering improvement opportunities (Cross, 1998).

Partner and supplier performance External organizations contribute to a greater or lesser extent to the performance of most internal processes. These might range from other airlines in horizontal alliances, through external suppliers with whom a close, long-term strategic partnership has been formed, to more transactional relationships. The performance of all these partners and suppliers needs to be assessed in the context of the contribution they make to the airline's own operational performance.

As far as horizontal alliances are concerned, O and D traffic flows and profitability need to be monitored, for example. With regard to suppliers, formal assessment procedures are now commonly in place. The purpose of formal assessment and accreditation programmes for suppliers (whether done individually, or globally through insistence on ISO9000 or similar certification) is to raise quality and reduce both costs and risks in the supply chain. Specific measures of performance could include:

- total acquisition cost of inputs (purchase price, together with delivery, inspection, inventory, and administration costs);
- quality (with much of what goes onto aircraft having to be certificated for the purpose at hand);
- dependability;
- speed and flexibility of response to airline needs;

- tone of the overall relationship between the airline and the supplier.

The more critical a good or service input is to an airline's own performance, the more closely supplier performance should be monitored – and the more merit there is likely to be in developing a close working relationship with the supplier concerned.

Cost structure

The Level 1 cost performance outcome metric that gains most attention is cost per unit of output (i.e., cost per ASM/ASK or ATM/ATK, irrespective of whether or not the output is actually sold). Whether an activity-based costing system or a more traditional approach is used, there is a wide variety of drill-down metrics that can be adopted to get to the root of an airline's cost structure. I have the space here to go down only two levels, keeping the discussion fairly general.

Unit cost is influenced by two fundamental performance drivers: absolute costs and productivity.

Absolute costs These reflect the prices an airline is either obliged to pay or able to negotiate for purchased inputs, ranging from aircraft to paper clips. Particular attention is needed in the following areas: human resources; fuel; airport and airway charges; distribution; and maintenance. Location of an airline's home base and major operational centres can be an important lower level cost driver; a small number of carriers based in high-cost countries have responded to cost pressures by relocating potentially foot-loose back-office functions (such as IS, reservations, and aircraft maintenance) to cheaper locations or by outsourcing.

Another important cost performance driver is the purchasing process itself. Over the last decade or so a number of airlines have focused on this by appointing a director of purchasing rather than diffusing responsibility throughout the company. Combining the purchasing power of alliance partners, either station-by-station or more formally through a joint venture such as AirLiance Materials (United, Lufthansa, and Air Canada) is also increasingly popular.

Productivity Productivity is a ratio of outputs to inputs – either all inputs in aggregate, or just a single category of input such as labour. Whilst in principle the maximisation of productivity is desirable, this is a metric which involves balancing two sometimes (although not always) contradictory objectives within the context of the airline's particular operating strategy.

- **Efficiency** Efficiency is a measure of productivity, with maximum efficiency being the production of maximum possible output at a given level of input (e.g., ASMs/ASKs produced per aircraft or per employee, revenue and operating profit generated per employee, revenue generated per line item of expenditure, passengers processed per unit of station cost, enplaned passengers per employee, employees per aircraft). The most important, but often overlooked, efficiency measure is revenue earned per dollar of cost (looking at cost both in aggregate across the airline as a whole and by reference to separate functions and, where possible, processes); another is operating profit per ASM/ASK.

  We saw in chapter 7 that whereas some service concepts permit considerable efficiency in their delivery – for example, low-fare/no-frills services operated with high seating densities, load factors, and aircraft utilisation, and low marketing costs – others carry much higher production costs because they do not permit as much efficiency in delivery processes – for example, high-frequency short-haul flights serving business segments with relatively small aircraft, high seat accessibility and marketing costs, and lower seating densities, load factors, and aircraft utilisation. We also noted that in both cases, intensifying competition as markets liberalise encourages airlines to be as efficient as possible at achieving required levels of effectiveness – however 'effectiveness' might be defined by the segment(s) of demand being targeted.

- **Effectiveness** The issue here is whether or not a desired outcome is achieved. The key metric is customer satisfaction – with the airline as a whole, or with some aspect of service delivery such as inflight service or ground service at a particular station.

Efficiency and effectiveness can often be improved simultaneously – for example by investing in more efficient capital equipment such as aircraft or information technology or by re-engineering processes. On the other hand, trade-offs sometimes have to be arrived at (e.g., with regard to staffing levels at check-in and in aircraft cabins); the challenge is to maximise efficiency subject to the particular type of effectiveness required by the customer value, market position, and operating strategy implied by a given service concept.

The fundamental economics of the industry – the impact of economies of scale, scope, and density, for example – inevitably generate important low-level cost drivers, as do many of the discretionary choices made by managers with regard to network design (including alliance strategy), fleet structure, service design, process design, and outsourcing (Holloway, 1997).

A key lower level driver with a profound impact on system productivity is **utilisation** – a measure of the percentage of available time that a given resource (e.g., an aircraft, a gate, or a maintenance bay) is being used to generate output. Production capacity carries with it certain fixed costs that do not vary within a given range of output. If output is low relative to what existing capacity is capable of producing, fixed costs per unit of output will be high; as output rises within the range of existing capacity, the fixed costs associated with that capacity are being spread across the greater output and so should be falling on a per-unit basis. Of course, what really matters is whether the incremental output can be sold – and sold at a profit.

Customer satisfaction and service quality

Satisfaction drivers are broadly similar for most carriers, but their relative importance can vary depending upon the requirements of a particular segment and the nature of the service concept. Detailed research can reveal the relative importance of different satisfaction-drivers to members of the targeted segments served by a given airline. Knowledge of satisfaction-drivers can help understand customer satisfaction data.

Customer satisfaction data should, from whatever source, converge on a common point within the airline. It can then be organized and distributed to the people ultimately responsible for design of the service package and service delivery system, and for recruitment and training of appropriate staff.

Because of their significance to the services management approach around which this book has been structured, we will look at customer satisfaction and service quality in more depth later in the chapter.

Communications performance

Our interest here is in external communications, because internal communications performance will have been audited in the context of either or both learning and employee satisfaction.

Communications performance outcomes The two most important Level I communications outcomes are brand positioning and brand image. Both can be tracked using 'market standing surveys' (Hill, 1996), drawing on the perceptions of a representative sample of both customers (past and present) and non-customers.

1. **Positioning** The fundamental question is whether we are achieving the desired positioning for our service(s). A related issue is whether or not

our brand is maintaining its 'points of difference' vis-a-vis competitors. As noted in chapter 3, positioning is very much a relative concept. Relativities can usefully be illustrated using a positioning map, showing price on the vertical axis and customers' perceptions of service quality on the horizontal. Clearly, detailed market research is necessary to generate a meaningful position map. If position mapping reveals a gap between intended and actual positioning, there needs to be an assessment of whether this is due to: service delivery inconsistent with the intended positioning; ineffective communication of the intended positioning; changes in the evaluation criteria used by customers to position competing offers; or competitors' activities.

2. **Image** What comes into the minds of customers, prospective customers, and other stakeholders when presented with the stimulus of our brand or sub-brand name(s)? Gaps between the composite image held by targeted customers (sometimes referred to as 'reputation') and the identity we are trying to project need to be identified through market research. Profile studies are being used more frequently than in the past to track the images held of particular airlines by their key stakeholders, notably customers. Focus groups and surveys are amongst the techniques used to track customers' image evaluation criteria, as well as the actual images they hold of individual airlines and their competitors.

The concept of brand equity was introduced in chapter 8. Useful though it is for highlighting the financial implications of brand loyalty, it does suffer from having multiple definitions. At its heart, however, lies a simple notion: if a brand's image has a favourable impact on customers' purchase decisions, 'brand equity' can be said to exist. Brand equity is therefore an intangible asset created by all of the brand-building activities that we have been discussing in this book. The performance of an asset as important as brand equity clearly needs to be monitored. The problem is that the existence of nuances in its definition lead inevitably to different ideas regarding how best to measure and track it. Some writers measure brand equity as incremental cash flow that arises from associating a product with a brand name (Farquhar, 1989), some see it as any income earned above the average for the sector (de Chernatony and McDonald, 1998), some characterise it in terms of the added value customers receive over and above the value they would otherwise get from an unbranded, generic product (Aaker and Biel, 1993), whilst others link it to brand knowledge and specific consumer purchase behaviours arising from such knowledge (Keller, 1993).

Given that brand equity is in essence a set of mental associations triggered by a brand name and having some effect on the purchasing behaviour of possibly millions of customers, measuring it is clearly going to be a highly subjective exercise. So subjective, some observers argue, that it is pointless. On the other hand, a growing number of companies have risen to the challenge of valuing their brands for financial accounting purposes. Although this is not a trend that has taken off in the airline industry, it has merits.

- By drawing attention to the value of brand equity we are also drawing attention to the long-term impact of marketing initiatives and brand management strategies – particularly communications strategies (in the broadest sense of the word 'communications', as used in chapter 6).
- Paying attention to brand equity might help counter any pressures to curtail sound brand management strategies in pursuit of short-term profit gains (or loss minimisation).

Space precludes explanation of alternative brand equity valuation techniques, but the books cited above provide plenty of examples.

Communications performance drivers Communications outcomes are driven by a wide range of stimuli that can be conveniently grouped under two headings: brand elements in general and marketing communications.

1. **Brand elements in general** We saw in chapter 6 that a brand is a holistic amalgam of elements that together communicate an identity which customers then interpret into an image. The 'performance' of brand elements – such as visual clues hinting at service quality, for example – can be evaluated with regard to whether or not they are communicating brand benefits to customers and making a positive contribution to the desired brand image.
2. **Marketing communications** Whilst every element of an airline's brand identity communicates something to customers and other stakeholders and so needs to be closely monitored, our interest here is in the performance of more 'traditional' forms of marketing communications – such as advertising, PR, and promotions. There are many different measures of marketing communications performance, which most good textbooks on the subject fully explain (see for example Fill, 1996). In essence, the purpose of the exercise is to assess the effectiveness of marketing communications in building 'brand knowledge' amongst customers. Strategic performance criteria include the success of marketing communications in:
   - building *brand awareness*: Do targeted customers know who we are, what we stand for (i.e., what our values are), and what we are offering?

- promoting *brand recognition*: Having been exposed to our brand in the past, can target customers remember the exposure?
- promoting *brand recall*: If given a product category stimulus relevant to the segment concerned (e.g., 'airlines offering service between points A and B', 'low-fare airlines', or 'premium quality airlines'), do target customers recall us? If so, how high up their listing of recalled brands do we come?

In addition to these strategic criteria, the performance of marketing communications needs to be assessed at a tactical level. This means tracking their success at: informing; reducing perceptions of purchase risk; stimulating purchase; and providing reassurance about the wisdom of a purchase already made. In particular, airline advertising intended to inform and to stimulate purchase should draw attention to benefits which rank highly as purchase criteria amongst target customers. On the other hand, the risks associated with miscommunication can be high:

> Virgin Atlantic....found at one time that the results of their research among Japanese passengers into reactions to the service they had received (Virgin always measures customer reactions in both absolute terms and in comparison with expectations) showed that there was a worrying discrepancy between perceptions of service and expectations among these passengers. Further investigation showed that in translating their advertising into Japanese, some unrealistic expectations were being created. The advertising was changed and the reactions of passengers to the service they received 'improved' – they now had realistic expectations, which could be reasonably met.
>
> Virgin Atlantic use extremely sophisticated research to track customer experiences against expectations, so they were able to recognise this imbalance early on and correct it. Other organizations without such clear links between 'service brand' and communications have not been so lucky (Irons, 1997a: 111-112).

We saw in chapter 6 that the purpose of communicating with customers is to raise the percentages of people in each targeted segment who are aware of the airline's service-price offer, have tried it, have repeated the purchase, and are willing to do so again. More generally, external communications should create a positive image of the airline in the minds of all external stakeholders, rather than just customers alone. It is against these purposes that the performance of external communications needs to be judged.

Marketplace performance

> It is not enough to succeed. Other must fail.
> Gore Vidal

Sooner or later, all the performance drivers and outcomes considered so far in this chapter feed through either directly or indirectly to marketplace performance and financial performance. We will look at financial performance shortly. With regard to marketplace performance, key outcomes include output produced (ASMs/ASKs and ATMs/ATKs – all of which can also be considered as operational performance outcomes), output sold (RPMs/RPKs and RTMs/RTKs), load factor (the percentage of output produced that has been sold), passenger enplanements, and market share. These performance outcomes can be monitored on a systemwide, route, or market basis. However they are monitored, growth is usually a fundamental objective. Too often in the past, growth has been an isolated variable, disconnected from profitability; more airlines are now explicitly linking growth and profits. Some carriers serving premium segments now look at customer loyalty as a key marketplace performance criterion (the underlying drivers of which are assumed to be service quality and customer satisfaction).

Financial performance

> A billion here, a billion there.
> Pretty soon it adds up to real money.
> Everett Dirksen

Financial performance outcomes need to be assessed for an airline as a whole and for individual routes (e.g., the Revex ratio), markets, products, and segments – although route, market, product, and segment analyses are inevitably burdened by subjective decisions regarding how to allocate indirect costs and joint or common costs. Financial performance outcome metrics have been well covered in Morrell (1997). Lower level drivers can be found amongst the metrics already discussed in the areas of operational performance, cost structure, customer satisfaction and service quality, and marketplace performance. One persistent curiosity in the industry is the practice of measuring costs per unit of output produced (i.e., per ASM/ASK etc.) and revenue per unit of output sold (i.e., per RPM/RPK etc.), with the result that unit cost and yield are not directly comparable without making an adjustment to reflect achieved load factor. Yield certainly has its uses as a metric of price performance, but unit revenue (i.e., revenue per unit of output produced – per ASM/ASK etc. – rather than per unit of output sold) is a much better financial performance outcome metric to place alongside unit cost.

Rather than repeat discussions of financial performance that appear in Morrell (ibid) and other airline and aircraft finance books, what I will do here is briefly draw attention to a trend in financial performance appraisal that appears likely to have a strong influence on how airline performance is assessed in future. At the beginning of this chapter I mentioned that since the early 1990s there has been a growing interest in assessing organizational performance not just in financial terms, but on a more balanced basis which takes explicit account of what is being achieved in respect of customer satisfaction, process performance, and learning; Kaplan and Norton's (1996) balanced scorecard is the most popular example, and the strategy-performance pyramid used in this chapter comes from the same 'stable'. More recently, the primacy of financial performance has resurfaced in the guise of 'shareholder value', and there are those who believe that this is the only Level I performance outcome metric that matters – everything else going on in an organization being just a driver of shareholder value; performance management is seen as a matter of managing performance drivers in a way that maximises shareholder value. The perspective underlying the value-based management approach is founded on the following assumptions.

- **Shareholders are the most important stakeholder group** This view argues that focusing on their obligations to shareholders gives top managers a clear basis on which to act, whereas working to reconcile the often ill-defined and conflicting interests of multiple stakeholders leads inevitably to ineffective, unaccountable, and uncontrollable management. Top managers must take all stakeholders into account, but are – according to this argument – responsible only to shareholders. The primacy of financial objectives is therefore guaranteed.
- **Cash-flow is a better metric than financial accounts** Simply put, cash-flow is a fact whereas financial accounts are based in large measure on opinion. Financial accounts follow the rules of double-entry book-keeping, subject to the generally accepted practices of the jurisdiction concerned and also subject within the limits of that latitude to the practices of given industries and choices made by managers at individual firms. When airlines and other companies have to adjust their financial accounts by magnitudes of several hundred million dollars in order to re-cast results drawn-up according to one country's accounting rules and principles (with regard to aircraft depreciation or the recognition of foreign currency gains and losses, for example) into results acceptable in another country, we are clearly not talking about

facts but about interpretations. Cash-flow is not a matter of interpretation; it is either present or it is not.

- **Economic profit is a better metric than accounting profit** Not only is accounting profit susceptible to manipulation, but it takes no account of the cost of shareholders' capital. Whereas accountants define profit as the amount by which revenues exceed costs incurred dealing with external parties other than shareholders, economists consider also the opportunity cost represented by total returns forgone by shareholders as a result of not employing their capital in an alternative, equally risky, venture. Economists then go on to define as 'normal profit' the profit (after deduction of opportunity costs) required to keep capital employed in the activity in which it is currently employed. Normal profit – which therefore includes a return on capital – is treated as a cost by economists, whereas it is ignored by accountants. Value-based management looks for the investment in resources required by every activity, no matter how small in scale that activity, to generate a positive risk-adjusted cash return; if cash is spent – whether on a new service attribute, staff training, an advertising campaign, running a business unit, or buying an A380 – that cash is expected to earn more than its cost.

There has long been a concept in accounting called 'residual income', which is essentially accounting profit minus the cost of capital. What the shareholder value movement has done is 'attempt to transform accounting income (revenue minus expenses) into a number that more closely approximates economic income (cash flows in excess of the opportunity cost of capital). This calculation is similar to residual income, but is distinguished by (1) a series of adjustments to eliminate potential distortions of accrual accounting and (2) the inclusion of both debt and equity sources of capital in the calculation of cost of capital' (Simons, 2000: 176).

The shareholder value movement – founded on the primacy of cash-flow and the importance of explicitly taking into account the cost of equity capital – has progressed from academia into the world of equity analysts since the mid-1990s, and is increasingly being used by corporate managers. It is strongest in the United States and, to a lesser extent, other parts of the English-speaking world, and weakest in continental Europe and Asia. It has been mentioned here because as more airlines come to rely on global capital markets for their funding, what US analysts are paying attention to will come to matter even more than it already does.

Those airlines choosing to actively manage – rather than just pay lip-service to – shareholder value often simplify the analysis into a single metric which can then be used to align strategy (i.e., operating and investment decisions), performance measurement, and staff compensation. These metrics all share a fundamental assumption that value is being added only when cash equity returns exceed equity costs and that this, rather than any measure of accounting profit or profitability, should be the arbiter of financial performance; they differ in the way they manipulate source data and the cost of capital and in the different aspects of value that they emphasise (Black et al, 1998). Three of the most popular are the 'future (or free) cash-flow' (FCF) model, economic value added (EVA), and the cash-flow return on investment (CFROI); the latter was introduced some time ago by Qantas, for example. Explanations of all three can be found in Black et al (ibid) and Ehrbar (1998). The key point to bear in mind when using any of these approaches is that in the long run an airline in a competitive environment can only create value for its shareholders by creating value for its customers.

Several of the proprietary shareholder value metrics being marketed by financial advisers (e.g., EVA) make adjustments to compensate for a short-coming in financial accounting which sits particularly badly with many researchers in the services management field. By convention, financial accounts treat as current expenses the costs arising from activities which contribute to the further development of assets as important as human resources (e.g., training and staff development) and brand equity (e.g., advertising). In economic terms these are investments in the future. A system which treats staff training as the equivalent of paying an electricity bill is out of touch with the reality of a modern service enterprise.

Service strategy: performance-induced reassessment

> Plans will get you into things, but you gotta work your way out.
> Will Rogers

An important part of performance management is the impetus it should provide to reassess objectives in light of what has been learned from experience. There is still considerable debate amongst researchers and practitioners alike regarding whether organizations as such learn, whether people learn and organizations support learning, or whether learning is an entirely personal experience that is simply given meaning by the organizational context. Amongst those who do accept that organizational learning takes place, the idea of multiple learning loops is a popular approach to strategic reassessment.

* **Single-loop learning** (Argyris and Schön, 1978, 1996; Swieringa and Wierdsma, 1992) The issue here is whether objectives were met and, if not, what should be done to get back on course. Assessment takes place

within the boundaries of existing activities and processes. An often overlooked point is that 'one-size-fits-all' performance monitoring systems can be dangerous; because different strategies require different activities, task priorities, resource deployments, and behaviours, there is a strong argument that performance monitoring systems should be designed to have the capabilities needed to monitor whatever is particularly relevant to the intended strategy (Govindarajan and Shank, 1992).

• **Double-loop learning** (Argyris and Schön, 1978, 1996) In this case the parallel runs more closely with the idea of strategy-making as an emergent process. Environments are so complex and dynamic that it might not be possible to meet an objective, simply because the world has moved on since it was established. As environments change and tactical responses mature into strategies, it is as well to keep up a sustained questioning not only of whether to change our approach to achieving objectives but also whether the objectives themselves need changing. In other words, we should supplement the question 'Is our strategy working?' (single-loop learning) with the question 'Is our strategy still viable?' (double-loop learning).

• **Triple-loop learning** Very occasionally the strategic logic, business model, and/or underlying values of an organization are reassessed as part of the process of questioning why certain things are done and why they are done in a certain way (Swieringa and Wierdsma, 1992). 'Strategic logic' is a senior management team's 'theory of competition' or 'theory of the business', guiding how resources should be deployed to exploit perceived market opportunities and generate favourable market responses. Strategic logic is continually being 'market-tested', and responses from the marketplace should be used to help reassess the validity of its underlying assumptions – in other words, to reassess management's belief system linking certain actions, notably the deployment of resources, to desired outcomes. One advantage of jointly formulating a performance management system within the senior management team and linking it explicitly to strategy is that any latent differences of opinion regarding the airline's strategic logic/theory of the business will be exposed.

Customer satisfaction and service quality

> If the information doesn't exist, create it.
> Colin Marshall

We saw earlier in the book that there is plenty of terminological confusion amongst practitioners regarding what is meant by 'customer satisfaction' and 'service quality'. The literature itself is far from consistent in its definition of the concepts.

Definitions

The definitions adopted here follow those in chapter 4. (Note that they are not universally agreed; Grönroos (2000, chapter 4), for example, offers an alternative approach.)

*   **Customer satisfaction** This is the outcome arising from a comparison by customers of their predictive expectations of service (i.e., what probably *will* happen on a particular journey) against their perceptions of the service actually received (Zifko-Baliga, 1998).
*   **Service quality** This is the outcome arising from a comparison by customers of their ideal expectation of service (i.e., what ideally *should* happen on journeys of the type concerned) against their perceptions of the service received (ibid).

A customer might correctly predict the service likely to be received from a particular airline and therefore be 'satisfied' with that service, yet at the same time perceive it to fall short of the ideal and therefore be deficient in 'quality'. There is some degree of consensus that 'customer satisfaction is a transaction-specific short-term measure, whereas service quality is an attitude formed by a long-term, overall evaluation of performance' (Hoffman and Bateson, 1997: 298).

Although research into customer satisfaction has been under way for several decades, only over the last 20 years has attention been paid to customer-perceived service quality (as different from specification-driven 'technical' quality, which has been a subject of study – at least in the context of manufacturing industry – for a considerable time). Indeed, some writers still treat customer satisfaction and customer-perceived service quality as synonymous (Hill, 1996). There are textbooks which argue that service quality is not a result of customers comparing perceptions against prior expectations, but is a generalised outcome driven by the satisfaction derived from each past service experience (Kurtz and Clow, 1998); others consider service quality a background assessment which influences satisfaction with current service experiences (Cronin and Taylor, 1992). In fact, there is no general agreement on how to define either construct, how many dimensions each has (i.e., what the components of each construct are as far as customers are concerned), or how they are related.

Returning to the definition I have chosen to use, we can see that there are implications for the design of surveys intended to assess an airline's performance from customers' perspectives. The first step must be to decide what it is we need to measure – satisfaction, quality, or both; the answer depends entirely upon whether our customers are believed to use 'predictive' or 'ideal' expectations as the benchmark against which perceptions of service are measured – and this takes us back to the importance of customer understanding that was stressed in chapter 3. Using surveys designed to monitor customer satisfaction can help establish whether we are perceived to be delivering services in line with customers' predictions; if not, we might need to look into how closely the design of our services matches customers' expectations, whether we are effectively managing expectations (e.g., through marketing communications) to help customers better predict the services they will receive, and whether we are failing to deliver service in conformity with specifications. Surveys designed to monitor service quality can be used to identify what we need to be doing in order to move our value proposition closer to what targeted customers consider to be ideal.

A closer look at service quality

Very broadly, we can think of quality in the following terms.

1. **Innate quality** Unhelpfully difficult to measure, this is essentially a 'you know it when you see it' approach (e.g., without stating exactly why, we might simply define a flight in first class as 'higher quality' than a flight at the back end of a widebody).
2. **Product quality** Here the concern is with the quantitative specifics of service package design (e.g., *more* seat pitch denotes higher quality, as does *less* queuing to check-in).
3. **Process quality** The issue in this case is the extent to which the service delivery system actually manages to deliver the designed service package as specified. For example, if specifications require reservations telephone pick-up times of 10 seconds or less and the system delivers in conformity with this specification, 'high' quality has been achieved – irrespective of what those customers who actually have to wait close

to 10 seconds for their calls to be answered might think of the performance.

Both product and process quality measurements were addressed above
under 'operational performance', emphasising the point that several Level I
metrics in the strategy-performance pyramid can share the same lower level
performance drivers. One of the advantages of this approach to performance measurement is that drill-down metrics help underline the performance interrelatedness within each airline system. Important as they are,
however, these operational performance metrics are insufficient when it
comes to measuring service quality, because this is something judged not
by any metric of functional performance but through the perceptions of
literally millions of individual customers. Quality is not simply a matter of
getting passengers and shipments to their destinations on time and 'undam-
aged'; quality is also about customers' perceptions of each service encounter, from the initial call to make a reservation or arrange cargo pick-up to
delivery of baggage at the final destination or presentation of the shipping
invoice. The essence of quality is what customers get out of their activity
cycles rather than what airlines put into them. Conformity to customers'
expectations is ultimately more important than conformity to service design
specifications. This takes us to the fourth, and for our purposes most relevant, definition of service quality.

4. **Quality in use** This definition, the one that should matter to all profit-
    seeking airlines, focuses entirely on what customers get out of a
    service. In other words, quality is customer-defined (Grönroos, 1984).
    For example, the merits of flying in first class, of having more seat
    pitch or shorter check-in queues, and of having reservations calls
    picked up in 10 seconds or less are all evaluated by the customer rather
    than the airline. This flags the point that it is vital to understand what
    customers actually feel about specific service attributes, because some
    will inevitably matter more than others. Process improvement designed
    to shave two minutes off a check-in queue, for example, might matter
    more to perceptions of service quality than two minutes off baggage re-
    claim. The imperative is to establish what matters to the customer, and
    then devise and monitor appropriate metrics.

It is with 'quality-in-use' that we are concerned here. Two approaches have
transitioned from the literature into practice.

1. **Incident-based approaches** Examples include the critical incident
    technique and observational methods, both of which look at individual

service encounters – the former from the customer's perspective, the latter from that of the airline. Despite being oriented to specific encounters, the critical incident technique in particular is not uncommonly generalised to provide 'proxy insights' into service success and failure across the organization as a whole. The argument is that if a single incident can be assumed to be representative of other incidents (even though not all incidents), it can point to the reasons for success or failure on a general, organization-wide level.

2. **Attribute-based approaches** Two are in widespread use.

   - *Attribute performance measures* This technique involves conducting market research to find out which service attributes matter most to targeted customers, then using surveys to rate the airline's performance in respect of each on a five-point scale. (See Holloway (1998b) for a summary of airline service attributes; see also Lewis and Sinhapalin (1991), and Bowen and Headley (1999)). The logic is that absolute assessments of service performance, rather than assessments relative to prior expectations, drive overall perceptions of service quality. (Cronin and Taylor (1992, 1994) have developed an instrument called SERVPERF to measure perceptions of attribute performance.)

   - *The expectancy disconfirmation model* This is the approach used in the definition of quality I argued in favour of earlier in the section (and is, incidentally, widely used in the customer satisfaction literature): quality is seen as an assessment of the perceived service experience relative to ideal/normative expectations in respect of the experience. Perceived quality is taken to sit on a continuum stretching from unacceptable to ideal: where ideal expectations have been met (i.e., 'confirmed'), quality is high, but where there is a divergence (i.e., ideal expectations have been 'disconfirmed') quality could in some respect bear improvement.

The 'gaps model' In the course of a ground-breaking ten-year research programme investigating service quality, Parasuraman et al (1988) identified five dimensions within which customer expectations are formed: reliability, responsiveness, assurance, empathy, and tangibles. SERVQUAL is a questionnaire developed from the disconfirmation model to measure service quality, which they defined as the difference between customers' prepurchase expectations and post-purchase perceptions of outcomes along these five dimensions.

The SERVQUAL instrument uses 22 questions about customers' normative (i.e., ideal, as opposed to predictive) expectations of service in a particular industry, scoring each on a seven-point scale, and then uses the same questions to evaluate perceptions of service delivered by a given firm in that industry – also scored on a 7-point scale. Service quality is quantified by subtracting the aggregate expectations score for each dimension from the aggregate perceptions score.

- A positive figure implies performance exceeded expectations.
- Zero implies performance equated to expectations.
- A negative figure implies performance failed to match expectations.

Quality shortfalls are therefore represented by a gap between expectations of what *should* happen (with 'should' having here its 'normative/ideal/ought to' meaning rather than its 'predictive/will' meaning) and perceptions of what actually did happen. According to this customer-driven definition, the quality of a major airline's first class service can be poor and the quality of a no-frills carrier's service can be high – notwithstanding that in terms of innate quality the former might appear to be better. (For a description of the design and application of SERVQUAL, together with a summary and rebuttal of criticisms levelled against it, see Parasuraman, 1995.)

We saw above that the SERVQUAL instrument has been designed to measure any gap between customers' ideal expectations of service and the level of service perceived to have been delivered, and this gap can be used to define 'service quality'. If a gap does exist between expectations and perceptions, two questions arise: Where exactly does the problem lie? What can be done about it?

To help answer these questions, Parasuraman and his colleagues developed the 'gaps model' illustrated in figure 9.4 (Zeithaml et al, 1990). This can be used to analyse how gaps between expected and perceived service – identified as Gap 5 – might come about.

- **Gap 1** The difference between customers' ideal expectations, and what airline managers and service providers perceive them to expect. (It will be recalled from chapter 2 that the competence-based approach to competitive strategy sees the dynamics of competition as being very much a battle between managerial cognitions of what markets want now and will want in the future; airlines serving the same or similar markets might take quite different competitive actions because of differences in managers' perceptions about what customers want and how competencies should be built and leveraged.)
- **Gap 2** The difference between managers' perceptions of customers' expectations and the specifications actually established (i.e., service attributes, delivery processes, servicescapes, and physical evidence).

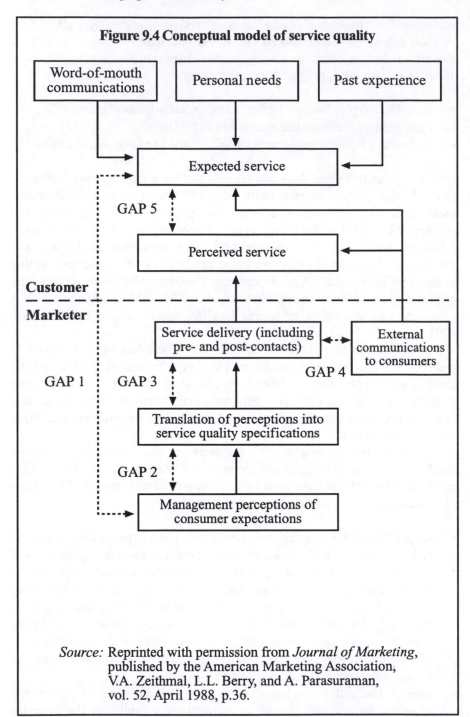

Figure 9.4 Conceptual model of service quality

Source: Reprinted with permission from *Journal of Marketing*,
published by the American Marketing Association,
V.A. Zeithmal, L.L. Berry, and A. Parasuraman,
vol. 52, April 1988, p.36.

- **Gap 3** The difference between service quality specifications and the service actually delivered (by the airline or by its various 'service partners').
- **Gap 4** The difference between the service quality promised (e.g., by marketing communications) and the service actually delivered. This is a critical area insofar as it bears on customers' expectations, which are one side of the expectations-perceptions disconfirmation model. Customers' expectations need to be managed. Specifically, their service ideals need to be formed within the context of the particular service concept being offered; an extreme example to make the point would be the irrelevance to a low-fare carrier of ideals formed around premium class international service. Another reason why this gap can be critically important is the prevalence of 'fuzzy expectations' among infrequent travellers in particular (Ojasalo, 1999).

Each gap describes a performance shortfall (technically, a source of 'post-purchase dissonance') that can be traced to one or more root causes, and an understanding of these should trigger appropriate remedial action (subject, perhaps, to an investment appraisal which relates potential lost revenue to the costs of remedying the problem, within the context of the service concept(s) concerned). These gaps can be identified fairly easily with properly designed and administered surveys aimed at unearthing customers' expectations and perceptions with regard to different service attributes. (See Lewis and Sinhapalin (1991) for an example of a Gap 1 analysis at Thai International.) Airlines with sufficient resources can aggregate responses by departure, aircraft type, cabin, airport, market segment, and across the system to identify service gaps.

Conversely, when ratings are high it is important to know why. Whilst it is necessary to uncover and address our failings, it is also critical to probe and understand the root causes of success in order to continue replicating it – always bearing in mind, of course, that the bases of today's success will not necessarily be the bases of tomorrow's.

Conclusion Compelling though all this might be, it is at best a useful framework within which to order our thoughts about service quality and customer satisfaction. Researchers are still uncertain whether customers as a whole do in fact assess service quality in terms of expectations and perceptions, whether the disconfirmation paradigm itself is fatally flawed by some of the psychometric issues arising from its application, whether service quality really is assessed along just five dimensions (and, if so, what if any their relationships are), what the nature is of any relationship between service quality, customer satisfaction, behavioural intentions, actual repurchase behaviour, and customer retention, and what role context can have in shaping expectations and perceptions. Some leading writers argue that attribute performance measures are methodologically more sound than the expectancy disconfirmation model (Grönroos, 2000). Despite its shortcomings, however, the gaps model undoubtedly advances the debate and helps us focus more clearly on the potential significance of customers' expectations and perceptions of airline service.

In the final analysis, being served is a psychological experience, affected by time, location, external cues, and the moods and attitudes of those involved. Because they are intangible, heterogeneous, and experiential incidents involving a shifting cast of participants, no service encounter is ever going to be precisely the same as any other. Each passenger enplanement and each freight shipment involves a different provider-consumer interface, and this makes inevitable the frequent 'remixture' of service – that is, the delivery of a service in a manner not envisaged when it and its delivery processes were designed. Furthermore, the fact that services are produced and consumed simultaneously means that the delivery process itself is very much subject to consumer evaluation.

This is why corporate culture is such an important performance driver. Services can never be entirely standardised; there is an understandable search for consistent standards of service delivery in some airlines, particularly those trying to leverage their corporate names into brand identities, but the ultimate goal is impossible to reach. Corporate culture, however, can serve to narrow the parameters within which variations in consistency occur.

iv. Conclusion

> I couldn't wait for success, so I went ahead without it.
> Jonathon Winter

A performance management system should tell us at least the following.

1. How much revenue we are earning from selling our services, both in aggregate and by market and segment.
2. Who we are selling to and why they are buying.
3. How/where they are buying.
4. How effectively we are communicating our chosen image and positioning to target markets and segments.
5. How much it is costing us to deliver our services, both in aggregate and wherever possible by market and product.

6. How effectively service delivery and other processes are working, and whether efficiency levels are improving.
7. The extent to which we are meeting our customers' expectations.
8. Whether we are effectively exploiting the identified competitive advantage(s) underlying our choice of service concept(s).
9. Whether we are building the competencies that reasonably plausible alternative scenarios suggest might be required in future.
10. Whether our employees are satisfied and the corporate culture is supportive of what we are trying to achieve for our customers.
11. What and how we are learning, and how we are exploiting our growing knowledge resource.
12. What shareholders are getting out of all this endeavour.

In effect, what we are doing in asking these and more detailed performance questions is using performance outcome and driver metrics to assess the marketing, operations, HRM, and financial strategies that have been put in place to implement the competitive strategy chosen to turn service concept into marketplace reality. Not all the performance metrics needed for this assessment will be available in current management or executive information systems. In particular, relatively few airlines have embraced the activity-based management system necessary to truly understand process costs; others have been slow to address employee satisfaction and even customer satisfaction issues. The situation varies widely. There is nonetheless a strong argument that if something is considered important to the success of a strategy or action plan, a way should be found to measure it. Accuracy to the third decimal place is not essential; where a high level of precision is either impossible, unduly expensive, or meaningless, the very fact that attention is being paid to a metric even if it is only subjectively measured is often sufficient to improve performance.

Whenever possible, performance metrics should be designed in a way that conveys comprehensible and actionable information to those responsible for the performance in question. For example, flight attendants might see no *direct* relationship between what they do and the financial figures reported by their employer, but most will be able to understand the need to identify and rectify service failures attributable to inflight delivery processes that could have a negative impact on customer satisfaction and, ultimately, revenue growth.

Performance information can be put to several uses.

1. It should be benchmarked against:
    *   objectives;
    *   best performance elsewhere in the airline or group (i.e., internal benchmarking), the industry (i.e., competitor and industry benchmarking), and any other industry relevant to the type of performance being benchmarked (i.e., best-in-class benchmarking);
    *   the expectations of internal and external stakeholders;
    *   customers' perceptions of competitors' performances in the same dimension.
2. It should be used to help improve or possibly even redesign the service package and/or service delivery system.
3. It should be used to communicate improvements to staff and other stakeholders.
4. It should be used as a basis for performance-related tranches of employee compensation.

In other words, benchmarked performance information should be seen as a source of learning – rather than, as in the past, control – and a stimulus for continuous improvement, innovation and other forms of change. This is the difference between performance *measurement* and performance *management*. Change and innovation are subjects of the final chapter.

10 Change, Creativity, and Innovation

> Even if you're on the right track, you'll get run over if you just sit there.
>
> Will Rogers

There is an argument that in the absence of environmental change, organizational change would be slow and haphazard (Senior, 1997). The 'rational choice' or planning model of strategy-making that we met in chapter 1 gives prominence to the diagnosis of environmental change as input into SWOT analyses, using catchy mnemonics such as PEST (Johnson and Scholes, 1997) to identify separate but interlinked political, economic, socio-cultural, and technological environments. Clearly, the airline business is being affected by at least one major change emanating from each of these: regulatory liberalisation, the impact of globalisation on business travel and of rising disposable incomes on leisure travel, ever-increasing customer expectations, and the new frontiers opened up by ultra-long-haul aircraft and by e- (and m-) commerce.

In this final chapter, I will briefly introduce the change literature, link it to the concepts of creativity and innovation, and conclude with a comment on the relevance of all three to strategic services management and to the model adopted for the present book.

i. Change

> Skate to where the puck is going, not to where it is.
>
> Wayne Gretzky

The airline industry has always been dynamic – at least on the technological side. What is different now is the pace of both technological and non-technological change emanating from increasingly complex, unstable, and turbulent environments. 'Complexity' is a measure of the number of influences and stakeholders at work and the ease with which they can be understood, whilst 'instability' reflects the dynamism of these influences, their degree of interrelatedness, and the volatility of stakeholders' expectations; the more complex and unstable an environment, the more 'turbulent' it is (Holloway, 1998b).

The change literature is vast, multi-disciplinary, and unruly (Joyce and Woods, 1996). Whilst I cannot synthesise it in this short chapter, what I do want to do is link the ideas of change, creativity, and innovation because all three are important to strategic services management – specifically, to our ability to stay in tune with (or, perhaps, lead) customers' expectations and keep ahead of the competition. Whilst brands have to remain consistent over time and retain key facets of their identities, they must nonetheless change in the sense of adapting to evolving lifestyles, cultural symbolism, values, and customer needs (Kapferer, 1997). The management challenge lies in knowing what to leave alone, what to change, how to change it, and when; it also lies in dealing with time-compression – the need to assess and reassess these variables almost continuously.

Change is constant and inevitable. The purpose of strategy is to try to influence the direction and pace of change. Strategic change in particular needs to be vision-driven – 'a missile pursuing an evasive target rather than a blue-bottle buzzing in a jar' (Martin, 1995: 20).

The characteristics of change

> Continuous improvement is better than delayed perfection.
> Mark Twain

Change has been characterised in a variety of different ways in the literature. I will highlight just three.

Change characterised by the rate at which it occurs

Grundy (1993) distinguishes between three different rates of change.

1. **Discontinuous change** This is change marked by rapid shifts in strategy, structure, and/or culture – triggered perhaps by a major internal problem or by a significant external shock. On an operational level it might be exemplified by a major process re-engineering effort. Dis-

continuous change of any sort usually requires significant prior change in people's mental models of the business.

2. **Smooth incremental change** On a strategic level, this idea is close to Quinn's (1980) concept of logical incrementalism, which we met in chapter 1. At an operational level, it is close to concepts such as kaizen or continuous improvement and was strongly espoused in the 'excellence' and TQM literatures popular in the 1980s and 1990s.

3. **Bumpy incremental change** Periods of either little or just incremental change are, according to this model, punctuated by interludes of more rapid change.

Leonard (1998: xii) puts these alternatives into context, whilst also emphasising the importance of the cognitive resources we looked at in some depth in chapter 7.

> Companies survive on their ability to adapt when necessary, and it is increasingly necessary for them to do so. Successful adaptation is not, however, a chameleon-like response to the most immediate stimuli – a quick switch to a new enterprise or an impulse acquisition. Rather, successful adaptation seems to involve the thoughtful, incremental redirection of skills and knowledge bases so that today's expertise is reshaped into tomorrow's capabilities. Of course, companies do sometimes require a dramatic shift in priorities and/or leadership; progress need not be plodding. The point is that successful adaptation builds thoughtfully from where we are. Because we cannot see the future, we can prepare for it only by planning for continuous rejuvenation of a firm's strategically important knowledge assets – its core capabilities.

Change characterised by how it comes about

In chapter 1 we met two models which explain, from opposite ends of what is in fact a continuum of managerial practices, the processes through which strategic change is brought about. Both could be extended to consider non-strategic (e.g., operational) change.

1. **Planned change** The model in this case has insightful decision-makers perceiving a need for change, planning how it should happen, and orchestrating the implementation of plans. Fogg (1999) in fact equates strategic change to the implementation of a strategic plan.

2. **Emergent change** This model sees change as the natural product of learning (a concept we met in chapters 7 and 9, as well as chapter 1). The idea that learning is continuous rather than episodic and that the change to which it gives rise is unpredictable and non-linear sits comfortably with two key principles of chaos theory – a body of work that

has during the last two decades crossed over from mathematics and the natural sciences into organization studies: first, small deviations in the assumed starting position of a change process from the actual starting position (in terms of understanding the market situation, customers' expectations, competitors' mental models, or internal relationships, for example) can have a disproportionate impact on eventual outcomes; second, outcomes are entirely path dependent – and every path is strewn with unknowns that can have unforeseeable consequences. Whether or not we buy into chaos theory or the process view of strategy-making, since the early 1990s there has been an increasingly pervasive view that collective learning underpins core competencies and capabilities and is, accordingly, a key foundation of competitive advantage (Leavy, 1996).

The need for operational change can often be diagnosed using quality improvement tools such as Ishikawa/fishbone analysis not dissimilar to those mentioned in chapter 9 in the context of diagnosing the root causes of service failure. Identifying the need for strategic change, on the other hand, tends to be a more intuitive process based on tacit knowledge and industry foresight – a black box rather than a tool box. Many of the initiatives launched by British Airways in the mid-1990s were based on an insightful appreciation of the need for strategic change: at a time of excellent financial performance when everything appeared to be going well, the senior management team looked into the future and determined that upward pressure on unit costs and downward pressure on yields would eventually squeeze profits and that this prospect justified a major company-wide cost management initiative, heavy investment in service innovation to consolidate the loyalty of premium segments, and a new (more global) corporate identity.

Midwest Express is another carrier that recently launched an improvement programme when everything appeared on the surface to be going well. Its CHIP initiative (based around **C**ustomer focus, **H**ighly involved employees, **I**nformation-based decision-making, and **P**rocess improvement – a play on the carrier's renowned, baked-onboard chocolate-chip cookies) was set in motion in the mid-1990s as a result of concern among senior executives that there was a danger of complacency arising from success.

Change characterised by its scale

Dunphy and Stace (1993) have distinguished between changes on four different scales.

1. **Fine-tuning** An ongoing process of 'fitting' strategy, structure, people, and processes.

2. **Incremental adjustment** Distinct, but not radical, adjustments to strategies, structure, and processes triggered by environmental change.
3. **Modular transformation** Major realignment of part(s) of an organization.
4. **Corporate transformation** Radical shifts in strategy, structure, and processes affecting an entire organization.

Links between change and strategy

> Reasonable men adapt themselves to the environment;
> unreasonable men try to adapt the environment to themselves.
> Thus, all progress is the result of the efforts of unreasonable men.
> George Bernard Shaw

The liberalisation of air transport markets has introduced into the industry intense pressures for change; other pressures include rapidly evolving customer expectations, and the implications that advances in information technology hold for distribution, service design, revenue management, process design, customer relationship management, supply chain management, and better-informed decision-making. What matters, however, is not just these pressures themselves but how each airline's key decision-makers perceive their effects on the industry. We saw in chapter 2 that the competence-based theory of competitive strategy casts change in large measure as an outcome of both organizational learning and managerial cognition (Sanchez et al, 1996). The resources an airline accumulates and the manner in which they are deployed – that is, the manner in which new competencies are built and existing competencies are leveraged – is according to this theory dependent upon changes in managers' cognitions regarding what resources are going to be needed to meet future objectives and how they should be deployed. We have seen that managerial cognition finds a practical outlet in strategic logic and in the one or more service concepts that flow from it. The competence-based approach also recognises the vital importance of *strategic flexibility* – the ability to change resources and/or their deployment in response to changing circumstances (Sanchez, 1993). Where available, these 'strategic options' – in effect, options to change strategy – are rarely cost-free.

Perhaps the most important link between strategy and change should be an airline's evolving service concept(s). As Grönroos (2000: 384) has noted, 'well-defined and easily understood service concepts' are necessary to guide change. Brand identity also provides a link in the chain. Because the airline industry is a high-contact service business, any significant change in culture will lead inevitably to a change in brand identity. Conversely, any programme to reshape brand identity in a major way is going to have to take into account the likely need for new attitudes and behaviours – that is, the likely need for a change in culture. We will look at culture change shortly. (See Wolff Olins (1995) for a concise overview of how to structure an identity change.)

Approaches to the management of change

> There is nothing more difficult than to achieve a new order of things,
> with no support from those who will not benefit
> and only lukewarm support from those who will.
> Machiavelli

Beyond Lewin's well-worn 'unfreeze-change-refreeze' framework, there is no widely accepted, definitive model of change management; different authors tend to focus on different aspects of the process (Leavy, 1996). The problem with a great deal of change management literature is that it is highly practitioner-oriented, and partly because of this fails to make explicit the theoretical foundations on which it is inevitably based – particularly its standpoint on the nature of wider social and economic change and on the nature of organizations (e.g., organizations as unitary, rationally manageable entities to be re-engineered, or as cultures to be interpreted and developed?). It also frequently has little or nothing to say with regard to assumptions about the nature of employees (e.g., extrinsically motivated and prone to shirking, or intrinsically motivated sources of intellectual capital waiting to be unleashed?). Neither does it have much to say about the highly contextual nature of organizational effectiveness. Gurus, hero-managers, and student-oriented texts tend to write (sometimes almost evangellically) about change as a logical, plannable, and well-ordered solution to objective problems – frequently ignoring its other persona as a social, negotiated, and quasi-experimental means of coping with 'messy' issues (Collins, 1998). Much of the popular literature acknowledges the truism that change is a process rather than an event, but then goes on to oversimplify that process into a sequence of formulaic, acontextual steps. Too often it is treated as episodic rather than as ongoing.

Two overarching approaches to the analysis of change can be identified in the literature (Senior, 1997; Collins, 1998).

1. **Rationally planned, hard systems change** This approach includes large numbers of prescriptive, mechanistic, sequential, multi-step procedures which treat change as a discrete episode (perhaps even a

'project') embedded in the otherwise stable flow of events, and which often deal somewhat naively with the social and political contexts within which it takes place. These are rational-logical models with roots in systems engineering, suited to hard, objective problems where consensus about what needs to be done is widespread and people-related issues are relatively minor. Many follow a similar format: diagnose the situation; identify desirable improvements and the constraints that impede them; specify performance metrics; generate objectives; detail selected options; evaluate those options against performance metrics; select the preferred option; develop implementation plans; implement; monitor; and adjust. Although most suited to 'hard' operational changes, this type of approach is also sometimes used to manage strategic change. As a mode of strategic change it is best exemplified by extreme examples of the 'rational planning' approach to strategy-making; Joyce and Woods (1996) refer to it in this context as the 'strategy implementation model' of strategic change, noting that it is an essentially modernist approach which sees change as a matter of deciding what needs to be done, planning how to do it (giving particular attention to structures and systems), then implementing the plan and monitoring performance.

2. **Highly socialised, soft systems models of change** At the other end of the continuum of approaches lie models drawn from the strategic HRM, organization development (OD), and soft systems literatures which stress the importance of politics, conflict, informal as well as formal relationships, commitment, and particularly culture as key variables in the management of change. Whereas hard systems models are heavily oriented to the content and control of change, soft systems models are equally concerned with process and context – particularly where there is little or no consensus on the need for change and/or how it should be accomplished. Soft systems models tend to be highly people-oriented, long-term in their perspective, and flexible rather than prescriptive; in particular, they stress the need to gain commitment to whatever vision underlies a change. However, because of their people-orientation, there must be doubts about how generalisable the research findings on which they are based would be if extended across national and cultural boundaries (Jaeger, 1986; Adler, 1997).

Given the central role ascribed by these models to culture change, it is worth repeating the point made in chapter 8 that whereas it is commonly assumed (not least in the change management literature) that culture is a manageable 'thing' that organizations *have*, there is an equally valid view that it is in fact only a metaphor used to help understand what organizations *are* (Feldman, 1986, 1989; Morgan, 1997). The following quotation summarises the importance of this latter position (Barclay, 1997: 293).

> Managers can influence the evolution of culture by being aware of the symbolic consequences of their actions and by attempting to foster desired values, but they can never control culture in the sense that many management writers advocate.
>
> Culture can and does change: that is, it can be *influenced* to change, but it cannot *be* changed. It does not exist independently of its members; rather, it is the manifestation of the values and ideals of the group. Culture will therefore change only where there is a willingness and commitment to change.

There is no incontrovertibly correct perspective, but clearly what we choose to assume will inform how we go about 'managing' change; what is also clear is that culture change, however it comes about, is a long process and can only be sustained if underlying values change (Fogg, 1999). Difficult though this is, British Airways in the 1980s and Continental in the 1990s are just two examples of it having been successfully achieved. (Brown (1998) provides excellent coverage of the more popular models of culture change; none is yet widely accepted as definitive. He also suggests some practical approaches to the management of culture change. For an account of a vision-driven culture-change initiative at Atlantic Southeast, intended to move towards a customer service culture and away from a heavy margin- and bottom-line orientation, see *Air Transport World*, January 2001.)

These 'soft' models can be used in respect of operational change as exemplified by soft systems methodology (Checkland and Scholes, 1999), but they are most generally used to effect organization-wide change in the context of a broader strategic initiative – as evidenced in the extensive OD literature. On a strategic level, the key point is that organization culture is seen not as just another implementation variable, but as something that has to be addressed *before* any other change can be effected (Joyce and Woods, 1996); some models in fact focus entirely on culture and how commitment should be built, whereas others argue that culture only changes once an organization's political forces have played out to a consensus (ibid).

In summary, 'how to' guides to change frequently treat social, cultural, and political issues superficially if at all, whilst much of the culture change literature tends to downplay the importance of organizational context and path dependency – reducing change to a question of getting people to see the need for new attitudes and behaviours (a need that is in most cases assumed to have been identified and articulated by insightful senior managers). There is no single widely accepted theory of change, and it would perhaps be unreasonable to expect one given the lack of agreement on the very nature of organizations (e.g., whether they are unitary, integrated, and readily manageable 'things' or pluralist, conflict-prone, and negotiated social constructions).

Senior (1997) has nonetheless identified four overall themes in the literature as a whole.

- There is no 'one best way' to bring about change.
- Change takes place within the context of organizational culture.
- People are central to change, and this in turn demands focus on issues of empowerment versus control.
- Creativity and innovation are necessary attributes of change.

We turn to creativity and innovation next.

ii. Creativity

> Don't worry about people stealing your ideas. If they're any good, you'll have to ram them down people's throats.
>
> Howard Aitken

West (1997: 1) defines creativity as, 'the bringing together of knowledge from different areas of experience to produce new and improved ideas'. (For a thorough review of the role of creativity in management problem-solving, see Proctor, 1995.) Creativity can be characterised as a link between change and innovation (Henry, 1991).

1. **Change and creativity** Organizational change does not take place in a vacuum and is rarely accomplished without creative thinking by somebody. Creativity can be looked upon as either a subset or a facilitator of change, but in either case its precise role in any change process will depend upon the people involved (e.g., their cognitive frames of reference, imagination, and risk-taking propensities) and the organizational context (e.g., whether or not there is a climate supportive of experimentation within the airline as a whole, and within individual departments, teams, and workgroups). ('Climate' can be defined as the feelings, attitudes, and behavioural tendencies which characterise organizational life: Nystrom, 1990.)

2. **Creativity and innovation** This linkage has been well-documented by Henry (1991: 3).

> Creativity is about the quality of originality that leads to new ways of seeing and to novel ideas. It is a thinking process associated with imagination, insight, innovation, ingenuity, intuition, inspiration and illumination. However, creativity is not just about novelty: for an idea to be truly creative it must also be appropriate and useful. The related term 'innovation' is usually used to describe the process whereby creative ideas are developed into something tangible, like a new product or practice.

Whereas creativity is the generation of new ideas, innovation is the process of actually putting new and improved services or ways of doing things into practice – something which requires the co-operation of others (West, 1997).

iii. Innovation

> You have to kiss a lot of frogs to find a prince.
> 3M slogan

For the purposes of this chapter, I will treat innovation as a change (whether incremental or radical) in either product or process intended to improve in some way on what is currently offered or done. By 'product' I mean a new or existing service package; by 'process' I am primarily referring to service delivery processes – although innovation can of course occur in other processes as well. Because service delivery processes are in many cases part of one or more service packages, we have to accept some degree of overlap.

Organizations exist in the most part to standardise and control some aspect(s) of their members' behaviour. This stacks the cards against innovation to begin with, and Quinn (1985) suggests a number of specific reasons why the institutionalisation of innovation can be such a challenge in large corporate hierarchies – including top management conservatism, cultural intolerance of innovators, excessive routinisation and bureaucracy, and short-term pay-back horizons. Innovation is nonetheless important for the following reasons.

- To generate incremental revenue from higher fares that can be earned by offering unique benefits (although any source of differentiation that is not founded on tacit or otherwise hard-to-copy resources or competencies will probably be short-lived as competitors catch up – and perhaps begin offering the same functional benefits without charging a price premium).

- To establish points of difference, even though a price premium might not be sustainable.
- To build or enhance a brand image based on being an innovator. It can be argued that this in itself is a source of competitive advantage (Kay, 1993), and the rapid growth of Emirates provides a good example of advantage consciously built on an assiduously cultivated reputation as an innovator.
- To motivate staff, encouraging them to believe in the product they are responsible for delivering.
- To close any service quality gaps (as identified at a macro-level by the 'gaps model' introduced in chapter 9, or at a micro-level by quality improvement tools such as Ishikawa/fishbone analysis and fault-tree analysis).
- To revitalise a 'stale' brand. (See Holloway (1998b) for a discussion of airline product and brand life cycles.)
- To lower process costs, or prevent them rising faster than they other-wise would.

The bottom line, however, is that in many of the market segments that full-service airlines are targeting, customers' expectations are changing more frequently than in the past. Grönroos (2000: 196) argues that, 'It is not enough to understand which values or benefits customers are seeking; one must also understand that the benefits customers are looking for will change over time, and that the customer-perceived quality and value which is provided has to change accordingly'.

It is not unreasonable to characterise innovation as a core process which, because it is associated with refreshing what each airline offers and how it creates and delivers its offer(s), is a 'generic activity associated with surv-ival and growth' (Tidd et al, 1997: 25).

Innovation as a source of competitive advantage

> Chance favours only the prepared mind.
> Louis Pasteur

An innovation can be a source of competitive advantage (particularly if it changes an industry's 'rules of engagement'), but in most service business-es such advantage is often ephemeral; an ongoing competence in the man-agement of innovation, on the other hand, can lead to more sustainable advantage (Kay, 1993). This underlines the fact that innovation should not be seen simply as a spark of creativity, but as a process – ideally a repeatable process – of harnessing good ideas and transforming them into commercially successful outcomes. Tidd et al (1997) argue that achieving a sustained competence in this respect is a function of deciding how to structure the innovation process appropriately, and how to develop the effective behavioural patterns which define how it works on a day-to-day basis.

This second point takes us back to the concept of 'routines' that we met in chapter 2: in this case the routine – which is always learned and can never be precisely copied from other firms – both drives and reflects 'how we do innovation around here' (ibid: 34). Some routines are better than others at coping with a particular airline's internal context and external (e.g., competitive) environments. An embedded innovation routine can be a source of competitive advantage or, if based on formulas more appropriate to yesterday's contexts and environments, it can be a barrier to new thinking; innovation is one of those variables that we saw in chapter 2 can be either a core competence or a core rigidity (Leonard-Barton, 1992a).

The problem here is that contrary to the normative and frequently prescriptive advice of many popular textbooks, there is considerable evidence in the occupational psychology literature that the distinct nature of different innovations and their particular individual contexts make the notion of a 'one best way' approach to the management of innovation processes highly questionable (King and Anderson, 1995). This is why there is no 'checklist' in the present chapter. Tidd et al (1997: 36) have nonetheless suggested that the following abilities (in bold type) are central to the management of innovation, and they have described the routines which contribute towards them (in plain type).

1. **Recognising** Environmental scanning and searching routines which look for external clues that trigger internal change.
2. **Aligning** The fitting of proposed change(s) to the airline's strategy – in other words, not innovating because it is fashionable or as a knee-jerk reaction to competitors but as a considered, vision-driven initiative.
3. **Acquiring** Going outside the airline for knowledge that is unavailable inhouse, and bringing it onboard to where it is needed.
4. **Generating** Having at least one source of commercially relevant creativity inhouse.
5. **Choosing** Being able to select change options which respond efficiently and effectively to the environmental trigger, are consistent with strategy, and leverage both firm-specific and firm-addressable resources.
6. **Executing** Managing product and process development projects from inception to launch.

7. **Implementing** Managing the introduction of change from both the technical and human standpoints.
8. **Learning** Being willing and able to evaluate what has been done and reflect on the lessons it provides.
9. **Developing the organization** Embedding the behaviours underlying all these routines into the fabric of the organization. Whether an airline can in fact embed an ongoing capacity for innovation will depend on the presence of the following factors (ibid: 306-307).

    - Vision, leadership, and the will to innovate.
    - An organizational structure which channels rather than stifles creativity.
    - The presence of influential people willing to champion change.
    - Effective cross-functional teams able to harness diverse perceptions and skills (and able to accommodate the conflict which open debate is likely to engender).
    - A broadly held commitment to individuals' personal and professional development.
    - Acceptance of, and participation in, organization-wide continuous improvement.
    - Consistent focus on the customer – whether internal or external.
    - A culture that supports and rewards creative endeavour.
    - Widespread recognition of the need to learn, and an active commitment to capturing and deploying new knowledge.

We have met all of the above concepts in one guise or another during the course of the present book. The question that immediately comes to mind is 'How many airlines does this list describe?' Intuitively, the answer seems likely to be 'not many'. Most airlines will in fact fall into one of the following categories.

1. **Innovator** Consistent innovation requires an organizational climate conducive to creativity and (commercial) risk-taking, good linkages to external sources of knowledge, and a thorough understanding of the customer. It can be a fundamental plank of an airline's overall brand image (e.g., Virgin Atlantic, Emirates, and British Airways). We also saw in chapter 2 that innovation can have important strategic implications insofar as it is underpinned by a sustained competence that competitors find difficult or costly to imitate (something the literature refers to as an 'outpacing' strategy).
2. **Fast follower** This strategy requires close attention to competitors and an ability to move quickly when change is warranted (e.g., Cathay Pacific).

3. **Laggard** The examples are numerous, and all presumably have confidence that a do-nothing approach will not have negative impacts on market share, revenue, and/or costs.

Whatever approach is adopted, innovation is a critical factor in any truly competitive market. Indeed, we saw in chapter 2 that more than 70 years ago there were economists who dismissed equilibrium as the normal state of affairs in competitive markets and identified innovation as the primary source of the 'creative destruction' that really characterises such markets.

Where to innovate

> We need to distinguish between true, copper-bottomed mistakes like wearing a black bra under a white blouse or, to take a more masculine example, starting a land war in Asia, and mistakes that at the time they were committed did have a chance.
> John Cleese

In a more academic vein than John Cleese, Leonard (1998: 118) has distinguished between what she calls 'intelligent failure' and 'unnecessary failure', and argued the important role of failure in building knowledge. Innovation is very much a case of 'nothing ventured, nothing gained'. It can emerge in several fields – service design, communication, processes, and organizational structures and systems, for example. We will look briefly at just service and process innovation.

Service innovation

> The telephone has too many shortcomings to be seriously considered as a means of communication. The device is inherently of no use to us.
> Western Union, 1876

In chapter 4 we distinguished between 'service design' (i.e., the mapping out of what is to be delivered to customers) and 'service development' (i.e., the wider process of moving from first recognition that a new service or a change to an existing service is necessary through to implementation – a process of which design is just one part). Much of the early literature focused on trying to understand what constitutes an innovation (Gopalkrishnan and Damanpour, 1997) and why innovation matters (Lengnick-Hall, 1992), turning later to consideration of how innovation processes work; attention was primarily oriented to manufactured goods until work on service innovation began in earnest during the 1990s (Johnson, et al,

2000). Research suggests that much innovation in service firms arises from ad hoc development projects rather than embedded, replicable routines (ibid); anecdotally, these findings would appear to apply to much of the airline industry – although growing numbers of more forward-looking carriers do now appear to recognise the need to embed a capacity to innovate.

Service innovation occurs when a customer or potential customer perceives something new about a service. We can distinguish three types (Rice, 1997).

1. **Continuous innovation** This takes the form of incremental modification(s) to existing services. These modifications may affect customers' perceptions of value, but they are unlikely to have a significant effect on overall patterns of purchase behaviour; they could, however, help prevent customer defections. An example might be the upgrading of inflight meal options. Modifications can be developed as part of an autonomous effort to improve the product, or in response to problems uncovered by root cause analysis (which we met in chapter 9).
2. **Dynamically continuous innovation** The introduction of a significant new service attribute or a major improvement to an existing attribute might be sufficient to influence purchase behaviour. For example, the opening of extensive and appealing new lounge facilities at a major hub could affect consumer choice.
3. **Discontinuous innovation** This involves the introduction of a totally new type of service with a significant impact on consumer purchase behaviour. An example might be the launching of a new low-fare or regional service concept by a carrier not presently serving these segments. (See Rao and Steckel (1998), chapter 3, for a comprehensive review of techniques available for uncovering unmet customer needs.)

The impetus behind an innovation might be competitors' initiatives, rising and explicit customer expectations, or the creativity of an airline's people (Trott, 1998). Innovation can be brought to bear on any service attribute, but the most visible examples are found in airport lounges and – in particular – aircraft cabins. Major changes in cabin interiors are complex projects with design and functionality the central issues (e.g., aesthetics, ergonomics, and overall visual brand identity), but inevitably set within the parameters laid down by space constraints and by regulatory requirements. These projects are truly cross-functional insofar as they require the co-operation of marketing, engineering, scheduling, revenue management, catering, and service delivery personnel. Technology is clearly having an influence on service innovation both in the air (e.g., inflight entertainment and communications options, and improved galley equipment such as dry-steam ovens) and on the ground (e.g., distribution technologies and pass-enger facilitation).

Regarding any innovation affecting a service attribute, several questions need to be asked.

- What additional benefit(s) will it provide to customers?
- What use will it make of existing resources and competencies? Will new resources and competencies be required in order to deliver it?
- What will it do for the brand?
- What are the financial costs, risks, and paybacks? (Major product innovations are investments and should be analysed as such; see Heskett et al (1997), and Zeithaml and Bitner (2000) for models that can be used to examine the financial case for service improvements.)
- What is the lead-time for introduction?

Given that it can take up to two years for an airline to introduce a major cabin redesign across a substantial fleet and bearing in mind that some leading full-service carriers are now refreshing their various cabins (partic-ularly long-haul cabins) on a three-to-five year cycle, the development and implementation of major service innovations can be more or less ongoing processes. In addition to major redesign initiatives, many smaller changes are constantly taking place to individual service attributes and delivery processes. One approach is to go for, say, a six-year design life subject to a mid-life upgrade. However, because the product life cycle is likely to cont-inue to accelerate, there will quite possibly be a move to modular design concepts in long-haul premium cabins; these will allow more or less cont-inuous upgrades, focusing on different elements of the onboard service-scape in sequence rather than going for 'big-bang' re-launches at increas-ingly shorter intervals (Pilling, 2001).

Service innovation involves economic and design challenges. The econ-omic challenge is to balance consumers' needs for onboard living space against the fact that cabin floor-space is one of any airline's core revenue-generating resources; the service concept should provide a context for this trade-off. The design challenge is to maximise consumers' physical and psychological comfort and also maximise attribute (e.g., IFE) availability and accessibility subject to the confines of the space available and to the economic imperatives of the service concept. The stakes are getting very high in some markets. In early 2000, British Airways launched a £600 million revamp of its long-haul first and business class cabins, which most notably introduced the industry's first flat-bed business class seats; these innovations were specifically targeted at premium travellers who were no longer seeing value for money in the airline's prices given competitors' service improvements, and they were consistent with its strategy of focusing attention on top-end segments in long-haul markets.

Because of the nature of airline services, any service innovation is likely to have broad, multi-functional implications. Changing seat-pitch will involve people from marketing, engineering, scheduling, revenue management, catering, and cabin services among others; changing something as simple as stemware used for meal service will involve 'training, purchasing, catering, cabin attendants, marketing, sales, stores, station operations, and flight operations' (Needham, 1998: 227).

Process innovation

> If you only have a hammer, you tend to see every problem as a nail.
> Abraham Maslow

Process innovation can have one of three objectives.

1. Do what we already do, but more efficiently and/or effectively – perhaps focusing on particular tasks and activities (the way they are performed and the value they add), on individual cost drivers (input costs and/or resource productivity), or on linkages between processes.
2. Do something we do not yet do.
3. Stop doing something – either altogether, or by outsourcing it.

When process innovations are undertaken on an incremental scale, we are in the field of kaizen or continuous improvement (something which is not simply the tool of TQM that it is often painted as, but is in part an artefact of organizational culture underpinned by service-oriented values); when undertaken on a 'breakthrough' scale, we are in the territory of business process re-engineering (something that has been around since the Taylorism and 'scientific management' of the early 1900s but was repackaged and brought up to date in the 1990s). In either case, process innovation might be systemwide or local – with the latter perhaps destined to remain an isolated initiative or instead intended to pilot wider adoption. An example of the benefits of piloting innovations can be found in some of the initiatives pioneered at the United Shuttle and subsequently introduced into the mainline operation; for an interesting account of how ground-handling processes were re-engineered to help the Shuttle achieve faster gate turnarounds, higher aircraft utilisation, and unit costs around three cents per ASM lower than the mainline carrier, see Kimes and Young (1997).

Process innovation might affect service delivery processes (back- and front-office) or any other business process. Blueprinting (touched on in chapter 5) can be used to change a service by re-designing some aspect of its delivery; this might involve minor changes, or it could involve significant variations in the levels of complexity and divergence (also explained in chapter 5) which characterise the service. Innovative work processes away from the front line can be encouraged by creative building design. This is exemplified by British Airways' campus-style 'office of the future' at Harmondsworth near London Heathrow – designed both for easy reconfiguration as business unit structures change, and also to facilitate staff interaction at cafes along a central street linking the six buildings or 'houses' and at designated 'innovation points'. The symbolism, as well as the functionality, of this type of innovation can have a potent influence on attitudes and behaviours; it can be used as an artefact of a new culture.

Benchmarking might be an important thread in process innovation. The story of Southwest benchmarking its aircraft turnaround process against Indianapolis 500 pit crews is widely cited in the services management literature (Fitzsimmons and Fitzsimmons, 1998).

Box 10.1 lists a comprehensive set of recommendations for improving service quality suggested by Berry et al (1993).

Box 10.1: Recommendations for improving service quality

1. Listening: *Understand what customers really want through continuous learning about the expectations and perceptions of customers and non-customers (e.g., by means of a service quality information system).*
2. Reliability: *Reliability is the single most important dimension of service quality and must be a service priority.*
3. Basic service: *Service companies must do the basic things well and, above all else, keep the promises that customers buying into a service feel have been made to them.*
4. Service design: *Develop a holistic view of the service while managing its many details.*
5. Recovery: *To satisfy customers who encounter a service problem, service companies should encourage customers to complain (and make it easy for them to do so), respond quickly and personally, and develop a problem resolution system.*
6. Surprising customers: *Although reliability is the most important dimension in meeting customers' service expectations, process dimensions (e.g., assurance, responsiveness, and empathy) are most important in exceeding customer expectations, such as by surprising customers with uncommon swiftness, grace, courtesy, competence, commitment, and understanding.*

7. Fair play: *Service companies must make special efforts to be fair and to demonstrate fairness to customers and employees.*
8. Teamwork: *Teamwork is what enables large organizations to deliver service with care and attentiveness by improving employee motivation and capabilities.*
9. Employee research: *Conduct research with employees to reveal why service problems occur and what companies must do to solve problems.*
10. Servant leadership: *Quality service comes from inspired leadership throughout the organization; from excellent service-system design; from the effective use of information and technology; and from a slow-to-change, invisible, all-powerful, internal forced called corporate culture.*

Source: Berry et al (1993), quoted in Keller (1998: 615).

It is essential to keep firmly in mind that high levels of customer satisfaction today are no guarantee of future success (Hamel and Prahalad, 1994). This is why learning, strategic thinking, industry foresight, and an understanding of customers and how their expectations are likely to change are even more significant in the long term than customer satisfaction figures – critical though these undoubtedly are. And neither – except perhaps in an oligopoly situation – are competitors likely to stand still; we therefore need to keep updating our positioning maps in order to monitor 'competitor drift' as well as 'customer drift' (Mercer, 1997).

iv. Conclusion

> If at first an idea is not absurd, then there is no hope for it.
> Albert Einstein

Senior (1997: 308) has this to say on the topics covered in the present chapter.

> In summary, the close connection between creativity, innovation and change is evidenced by the number of books and articles which consider them, in many ways, to be inseparable. The conclusion here is that responding to, or planning, change involves forms of creative thinking which are varied in focus and means. All people are creative, but creative in different ways. The challenge for all members of organisations is to understand further these differences and to value the strengths of those who are different from themselves. Looking for complementary ways of thinking rather than only those which match one's own is a way of ensuring appropriate innovation as a component

of any change. However, encouraging creativity of outlook is not sufficient in today's changeable, turbulent environments. Constructing an organisational climate which is conducive to creative thinking and idea-handling is important if the full benefits of a creatively oriented staff are to be felt.

But change, creativity, and innovation need a frame of reference, and that is provided by vision. In particular, vision informs innovation (West, 1997), and innovation moves us towards our vision. It is rarely possible to motivate people with a SWOT analysis. What leads people to change, to create, and to innovate – often against their own instincts – is belief in a vision which paints a plausible picture of a better future. That innovation often has uncertain outcomes and that vision presents us with a moving target is what makes travelling the iterative loop mapped out by this book so much fun.

Let me leave you with one final thought. From a services management perspective, there are really only two types of airline: those with a customer service department, and those with a customer service soul.

References

Aaker, D.A. (1995), *Strategic Market Management*, (4th edition), Wiley, New York.

Aaker, D.A. (1996), *Building Strong Brands*, The Free Press, New York.

Aaker, D.A. (1997), 'Dimensions of Brand Personality', *Journal of Marketing Research*, 34, August.

Aaker, D.A. and Biel, L. (1993), *Brand Equity and Advertising*, Lawrence Erbaum Associates, Hillsdale NJ.

Adler, N.J. (1997), *International Dimensions of Organizational Behaviour* (3rd edition), South Western College Publishing, Cincinnati OH.

Albrecht, K. (1988), *At America's Service*, Dow Jones-Irwin, Homewood, IL.

Amit, R.H. and Schoemaker, P.J.H. (1993), 'Strategic Assets and Organizational Rents', *Strategic Management Journal*, 14, 1.

Anderson, K. (1999), 'Standards for Service: From Countability to Accountability' in Zemke, R. and Woods, J.A., (eds) *Best Practices in Customer Service,* AMACOM, New York.

Argyris, C. (1990), *Overcoming Organizational Defenses: Facilitating Organizational Learning*, Prentice-Hall, Englewood Cliffs NJ.

Argyris, C. and Schön, D.A., (1978), *Organizational Learning: A Theory-action Perspective,* Addison-Wesley, Reading MA.

Argyris, C. and Schön, D.A., (1996), *Organizational Learning II: Theory, Method, and Practice*, Addison-Wesley, Reading MA.

Arino, A. and de la Torre, J. (1998), 'Learning From Failure: Towards an Evolutionary Model of Collaborative Ventures', *Organization Science*, 9, 3.

Assael, H. (1995), *Consumer Behaviour and Marketing Action* (5th edition), South-Western Publishing, Cincinnati OH.

Baden-Fuller, C. and Volberda, H.K. (1997), 'Strategic Renewal in Large Complex Organizations: A Competence-based View', in Heene, A. and Sanchez, R. (eds), *Competence-based Strategic Management*, Wiley, Chichester.

Band, W.A. (1991), *Creating Value for Customers*, Wiley, New York.

Barclay, C. (1997), 'Culture: The Prime Differentiator', in Murley, P. (ed), *Handbook of Customer Service*, Gower, Aldershot.

Barley, S., Meyer, G., and Gash, D. (1988), 'Cultures of Culture: Academics, Practitioners and the Pragmatics of Normative Control', *Administrative Science Quarterly*, 33, 1.

Barney, J.B. (1986a), 'Organizational Culture: Can it be a Source of Sustained Competitive Advantage?', *Academy of Management Review*, 11, 3.

Barney, J.B. (1986b), 'Strategic Factor Markets: Expectations, Luck, and Business Strategy', *Management Science*, 32, 3.

Barney, J.B. (1991), 'Firm Resources and Sustained Competitive Advantage', *Journal of Management*, 17, 1.

Barney, J.B. (1997), *Gaining and Sustaining Competitive Advantage*, Addison-Wesley, Reading MA.

Barney, J.B. and Hesterley, W. (1996), 'Organizational Economics: Understanding the Relationship Between Organizations and Economic Analysis', in Clegg, S.R., Hardy, C., and Nord, W.R. (eds), *Handbook of Organisation Studies*, Sage, London.

Bateson, J.E.G. (1985), 'Perceived Control and the Service Encounter', in Czepiel, J.A., Solomon, M.R., and Surprenant, C.F. (eds), *The Service Encounter*, Lexington Books, Lexington MA.

Bateson, J.E.G. (1995), *Managing Services Marketing* (3rd edition), The Dryden Press, Fort Worth TX.

Bauer, K. (1998), 'Delivering Consistent Comfort in a Mixed Fleet', in Butler, G.F. and Keller, M.R. (eds), *Handbook of Airline Marketing*, Aviation Week Group, New York.

Berger, P.L. and Kluckmann, T. (1966), *The Social Construction of Reality*, Doubleday, New York.

Berry, L.L. (1999), *Discovering the Soul of Service*, The Free Press, New York.

Berry, L.L., Lefkowith, E.F., and Clark, T. (1988), 'In Services, What's in a Name?', *Harvard Business Review*, September-October.

Bhat, S. and Reddy, S.K. (1998), 'Symbolic and Functional Positioning of Brands', *Journal of Consumer Marketing*, 15, 1.

Bissessur, A. and Alamdari, F. (1998), 'Factors Affecting the Operational Success of Strategic Airline Alliances', *Transportation Journal* 25, 331-355.

Bitner, M.J. (1992), 'Servicescapes: The Impact of Physical Surroundings on Customers and Employees', *Journal of Marketing*, 56, 4.

Bitner, M.J., Booms, B.M,, and Tereault, M. (1990), 'The Service Encounter: Diagnosing Favourable and Unfavourable Incidents', *Journal of Marketing*, 54, 1.

Black, A., Wright, P., and Bachman, J.E. (1998), *In Search of Shareholder Value: Managing the Drivers of Performance*, Pitman, London.

Bleeke, J. and Ernst, D. (1993), 'The Way to Win in Cross-border Alliances', in Bleeke, J. and Ernst, D. (eds), *Collaborating to Compete*, Wiley, Chichester.

Bogner, W.C. and Thomas, H. (1994), 'Core Competence and Competitive Advantage: A Model and Illustrative Evidence from the Pharmaceutical Industry', in Hamel, G. and Heene, A. (eds), *Competence-based Competition*, Wiley, Chichester.

Bogner, W.C. and Thomas, H. (1996), 'From Skills to Competences: The "Play-out" of Resource Bundles Across Firms', in Heene, A. and Sanchez, R. (eds.), *Competence-based Strategic Management*, Wiley, Chichester.

Booms, B.H. and Bitner, M.J. (1981), 'Marketing Strategies and Organization of Service Firms', in Donnelly, J. and George, W.R. (eds), *Marketing of Services*, American Marketing Association, Chicago IL.

Boulding, K.E. (1956), *The Image*, University of Michigan Press, Ann Arbor MI.

Bounds, G., Yorks, L., Adams, M., and Ranney, G. (1994), *Beyond Total Quality Management*, McGraw-Hill, New York.

Bowen, B.D. and Headley, D. (1999), *The Airline Quality Rating 1999*, University of Nebraska at Omaha, Aviation Institute and Wichita State University, W. Frank Barton School of Business.

Bowman, C. and Ambrosini, V. (1998), 'Value Creation Versus Value Capture: Towards A Coherent Definition of Value in Strategy – An Exploratory Study', *Cranfield School of Management*, Working Paper SWP 14/98.

Bowman, C. and Faulkner, D. (1997), *Competitive and Corporate Strategy*, Irwin, London.

Bradley, F. (1995), *Marketing Management: Providing, Communicating, and Delivering Value*, Prentice Hall, Hemel Hempstead.

Brews, P.J. and Hunt, M.R. (1999), 'Learning to Plan and Planning to Learn: Resolving the Planning School/Learning School Debate', *Strategic Management Journal*, 20, 10.

Brown, A. (1998), *Organizational Culture* (2nd edition), Pitman, London.

Bruce, M. and Morris, B. (1998), 'In-house, Outsourced or a Mixed Approach to Design', in Bruce, M. and Jevnaker, B.H. (eds), *Management of Design Alliances*, Wiley, Chichester.

Burgoyne, J. (1988), 'Management Development for the Individual and the Organization', *Personnel Management*, 20, 6.

Butler, G.F. and Keller, M.R. (1998) (eds), *Handbook of Airline Marketing*, Aviation Week Group, New York.

Butler, R. (1991), *Designing Organisations*, Routledge, London.

Campbell, A, Goold, M., and Alexander, M. (1995), 'Corporate Strategy: The Quest for Parenting Advantage', *Harvard Business Review*, 73, March-April.

Campbell-Hunt, C. (2000), 'What Have We Learned About Generic Competitive Strategy? A Meta-analysis', *Strategic Management Journal*, 21, 2.

Chamberlin, E.H. (1933), *The Theory of Monopolistic Competition*, Harvard University Press, Cambridge MA.

Chandler, A.D. Jr. (1962), *Strategy and Structure: Chapters in the History of Industrial Enterprise*, MIT Press, Cambridge MA.

Chapman, P. (1997), 'Roles Not Jobs', in Murley, P. (ed), *Handbook of Customer Service*, Gower, Aldershot.

Chase, R.B. (1978), 'Where Does the Customer Fit in a Service Operation?', *Harvard Business Review*, November-December.

Chase, R.B. and Hayes, R.H. (1991), 'Beefing Up Operations in Service Firms', *Sloan Management Review*, Fall.

Checkland, P. and Scholes, J. (1999), *Soft Systems Methodology in Action*, Wiley, Chichester.

Chiesa, V. and Manzini, R. (1997), 'Competence Levels Within Firms: A Static and Dynamic Analysis', in Heene, A. and Sanchez, R. (eds), *Competence-based Strategic Management*, Wiley, Chichester.

Child, J. and Faulkner, D. (1998), *Strategies of Cooperation: Managing Alliances, Networks, and Joint Ventures*, Oxford University Press, Oxford.

Collier, R.A. (1995), *Profitable Product Management*, Butterworth-Heinemann, Oxford.

Collins, D. (1998), *Organizational Change: Sociological Perspectives*, Routledge, London.

Cray, D. and Mallory, G.R. (1998), *Making Sense of Managing Culture*, International Thomson Business Press, London.

Cronin, J.J. Jr. and Taylor, S.A. (1992), 'Measuring Service Quality: A Reexamination and Extension', *Journal of Marketing*, 56, July.

Cronin, J.J. Jr. and Taylor, S.A. (1994), 'SERVPERF Versus SERVQUAL: Reconciling Performance-Based and Perceptions-Minus-Expectations Measurement of Service Quality', *Journal of Marketing*, 58, 125-131.

Cronshaw, M. and Thompson, D.J. (1991), *Sources of Rent and Airline Deregulation in Europe*, Centre for Business Strategy Working Paper, London Business School.

Cross, R.G. (1998), 'Trends in Airline Revenue Management', in Butler, G.F. and Keller, M.R. (eds), *Handbook of Airline Marketing*, Aviation Week Group, New York.

Czepiel, J.A., Solomon, M.R., and Surprenant, C.F. (eds) (1985), *The Service Encounter*, Lexington Books, New York.

Dasburg, J.H. (1998a) 'Northwest Airlines AirCares: A Community Support Program Combining Community Relations, Marketing, Promotion, and Public Relations', in Butler, G.F. and Keller, M.R. (eds), *Handbook of Airline Marketing*, Aviation Week Group, New York.

Dasburg, J.H. (1998b) 'Northwest is for MEmphis Campaign Supports Successful Hub Market Turnaround', in Butler, G.F. and Keller, M.R. (eds), *Handbook of Airline Marketing*, Aviation Week Group, New York.

D'Aveni, R.A. (1994), *Hypercompetition: Managing the Dynamics of Strategic Maneuvering*, The Free Press, New York.

Davenport, T. (1993), *Process Innovation: Reengineering Work Through Information Technology*, Harvard Business School Press, Boston MA.

Day, G.S. and Nedungadi, P. (1994), 'Managerial Representations of Competitive Advantage', *Journal of Marketing*, 58, April.

Deal, T.E. and Kennedy, A.A. (1982), *Corporate Cultures: The Rites and Rituals of Corporate Life*, Addison-Wesley, Reading MA.

de Chernatony, L. (1999a), 'Brand Management Through Narrowing the Gap Between Brand Identity and Brand Reputation', *Journal of Marketing Management*, 15, 157-179.

de Chernatony, L. (1999b), 'The Challenge of Services Branding: Knowledge Management to the Rescue?', *The Journal of Brand Management*, 6, 4.

de Chernatony and Dall'Olmo Riley, F. (1997), 'Brand Consultants' Perspectives on the Concept of the Brand', *Marketing and Research Today*, 25-42.

de Chernatony, L., Daniels, K., and Johnson, G. (1995), 'Managers' Perceptions of Competitors' Positioning: A Replication Study', Paper presented at TIMS Marketing Science Conference, Sydney, July 1995.

de Chernatony, L. and McDonald, M. (1998), *Creating Powerful Brands* (2nd edition), Butterworth-Heinemann, Oxford.

deGeus, A. (1988), 'Planning as Learning', *Harvard Business Review*, March-April.

DeSouza, G. (1992), 'Designing a Customer-Retention Plan', *The Journal of Business Strategy*, March/April.

Dierickx, I. and Cool, K. (1988), 'Competitive Advantage', INSEAD Working Paper 88/07.

DiMaggio, P.J. and Powell, W.W. (1983), 'The Iron Cage Revisited: Institutional Isomorphism and Collective Rationality in Organizational Fields,' *American Sociological Review*, 48, 147-160.

Dosi, G. and Teece, D. (1998), 'Organizational Competencies and the Boundaries of the Firm', in Arena, R. and Longhi, C. (eds), *Markets and Organizations*, Springer-Verlag, New York.

Douma, S. and Schroeder, H. (1998), *Economic Approaches to Organizations* (2nd edition), Prentice Hall, Harlow.

Doyle, P. (1994), *Marketing Management and Strategy*, Prentice Hall, Englewood Cliffs NJ.

Doyle, P. (1997), 'Radical Strategies for Profitable Growth', *Warwick Business School Working Paper*.

Dryburgh, I. (2000), 'First Revolution', *Aircraft Interiors International*, September.

Dunphy, D. and Stace, D. (1993), 'The Strategic Management of Corporate Change', *Human Relations*, 45, 8.

Durand, T. (1997), 'Strategizing for Innovation: Competence Analysis in Assessing Strategic Change', in Heene, A. and Sanchez, R. (eds), *Competence-based Strategic Management*, Wiley, Chichester.

Dussauge, R. and Garrette, B. (1995), 'Determinants of Success in International Strategic Alliances: Evidence from the Global Aerospace Industry', *Journal of International Business Studies,* 26, 505-530.

Dussauge, R. and Garrette, B. (1999), *Cooperative Strategy: Competing Successfully Through Strategic Alliances*, Wiley, Chichester.

Easton, G. and Araujo, L. (1996), 'Characterizing Organizational Competences: An Industrial Networking Approach', in Sanchez, R., Heene, A., and Thomas, H. (eds), *Dynamics of Competence-Based Competition: Theory and Practice in the New Strategic Management*, Pergamon, Oxford.

Eden, C. and Ackermann, F. (1998), *Making Strategy*, Sage, London.

Edvardsson, B. (1992), 'Service Breakdowns: A Study of Critical Incidents in an Airline', *International Journal of Service Industry Management*, 3, 4.

Ehrbar, A. (1998), *EVA: The Real Key to Creating Wealth*, Wiley, New York.

Ehrenburg, A.S.C. (1972), *Repeat Buying: Theory and Applications*, North Holland, London.

Elfring, T. and Baven, G. (1996), 'Spinning-off Capabilities: Competence Development in Knowledge-intensive Services', in Sanchez, R., Heene, A., and Thomas, H. (eds), *Dynamics of Competence-Based Competition: Theory and Practice in the New Strategic Management*, Pergamon, Oxford.

Elfring, T. and Volberda, H.W. (2001), 'Schools of Thought in Strategic Management: Fragmentation, Integration, and Synthesis', in Volberda, H.W. and Elfring, T. (eds), *Rethinking Strategy*, Sage, London.

Erramilli, M.K. (1996), 'Nationality and Subsidiary Ownership Patterns in Multinational Corporations', *Journal of International Business Studies*, 27, 225-248.

Fahey, L. (1999), *Competitors*, Wiley, New York.

Farquhar, P. (1989), 'Managing Brand Equity', *Marketing Research*, 1, September.

Favart-Andrieux, C. (1998), 'Developments in Aircraft Interior Design', in Baldwin, R. (ed), *Developing the Future Aviation System*, Ashgate, Aldershot.

Feldman, S.P. (1986), 'Management in Context: An Essay on the Relevance of Culture to the Understanding of Organizational Change', *Journal of Management Studies*, 23, 6.

Feldman, S.P. (1989), 'The Business Wheel: The Inseparability of Autonomy and Control within Organizations', *Journal of Management Studies*, 26, 2.

Feldwick, P. (1991), 'Defining a Brand', in Cowley, D. (ed), *Understanding Brands*, Kogan Page, London.

Fill, C. (1995), *Marketing Communications*, Prentice Hall, Hemel Hempstead.

Fitzsimmons, J.A. and Fitzsimmons, M.J. (1998), *Service Management: Operations, Strategy, and Information Technology* (2nd edition), McGraw-Hill, New York.

Fogg, C.D. (1999), *Implementing Your Strategic Plan*, AMACOM, New York.

Ford, D., Gadde, L-E., Håkansson, H., Lundgren, A., Snehota, I., Turnbull, P., and Wilson, D. (1998), *Managing Business Relationships*, Wiley, Chichester.

Fors, N.J. (1996), 'Knowledge-based Approaches to the Theory of the Firm: Some Critical Comments', *Organization Science*, 7, 5.

Foss, N.J. (1997), 'Resources and Strategy: A Brief Overview of Themes and Contributions', in Foss, N.J. (ed), *Resources, Firms, and Strategies*, Oxford University Press, Oxford.

Garvett, D.S. and Avery, A.A. (1998), 'Frequent Traveler Programs: Moving Targets', in Butler, G.F. and Keller, M.R. (eds), *Handbook of Airline Marketing*, Aviation Week Group, New York.

Gattorna, J.L. and Walters, D.W. (1996), *Managing The Supply Chain: A Strategic Perspective*, Macmillan, Basingstoke.

Gittell, J.H. (1997), 'Horizontal Relationships and the Quality of Communication: Coordinating the Airline Departure Process', *Harvard Business School Working Paper*.

Gittell, J.H. (1999), 'Coordinating Services Across Functional Boundaries', in Zemke, R, and Woods, J.A. (eds), *Best Practices in Customer Service*, HRD Press, Amherst MA.

Goodman, J. (1999), 'Quantifying the Impact of Great Customer Service', in Zemke, R. and Woods, J.A. (eds), *Best Practices in Customer Service*, AMACOM, New York.

Gopalkrishnan, S. and Damanpour, F. (1997), 'A Review of Innovation Research in Economics, Sociology, and Technology Management', *Omega*, 25, 1.

Gorman, P., Thomas, H., and Sanchez, R. (1996), 'Industry Dynamics in Competence-Based Competition', in Sanchez, R., Heene, A., and Thomas, H. (eds), *Dynamics of Competence-Based Competition: Theory and Practice in the New Strategic Management*, Pergamon, Oxford.

Govindarajan, V. and Shank, J.K. (1992), 'Strategic Cost Management: Tailoring Controls to Strategies', *Journal of Cost Management for the Manufacturing Industry*, 6, 3.

Gowler, D. and Legge, K. (1986), 'Images of Employees in Company Reports: Do Company Chairmen View Their Most Valuable Asset as Valuable?', *Personnel Review*, 15, 5.

Grant, R.M. (1991), 'The Resource-Based Theory of Competitive Advantage', *California Management Review*, 33, 3.

Grant, R.M. (1996), 'A Knowledge-based Theory of Inter-firm Collaboration', *Organization Science*, 7, 375-387.

Grant, R.M. (1998), *Contemporary Strategy Analysis,* Blackwell, Malden MA.

Grönroos, C. (1984), *Strategic Management and Marketing in the Service Sector*, Chartwell-Brat, Bromley.

Grönroos, C. (2000), *Service Management and Marketing: A Customer Relationship Management Approach* (2nd edition), Wiley, Chichester.

Grönroos, C. and Lindberg-Repo, K. (1998), 'Integrated Marketing Communications: The Communications Aspect of Relationship Marketing', *Integrated Marketing Communications Research Journal*, 4, 1.

Grove, S.J. and Fisk, R.P. (1983), 'The Dramaturgy of Services Exchange: An Analytical Framework for Services Marketing', in Berry, L.L., Shostack, G.L., and Upah, G.D. (eds), *Emerging Perspectives on Services Marketing*, American Marketing Association, Chicago IL.

Grove, S.J., Fisk, R.P, and John, J. (2000), 'Services as Theater: Guidelines and Implications', in Swartz, T.A. and Iacobucci, D. (eds), *Handbook of Services Marketing and Management*, Sage, Thousand Oaks CA.

Grundy, T. (1993), *Managing Strategic Change*, Kogan Page, London.

Gudmundsson, S.V. (1998), *Flying Too Close to the Sun: The Success and Failure of New-entrant Airlines*, Ashgate, Aldershot.

Håkansson, H. Sharma, D.D. (1996), 'Strategic Alliances in a Network Perspective', in Iacobucci, D. (ed), *Networks in Marketing*, Sage, Thousand Oaks CA.

Hallowell, R. and Schlesinger, L.A. (2000), 'The Service Profit Chain: Intellectual Roots, Current Realities, and Future Prospects', in Swartz, T.A. and Iacobucci, D. (eds), *Handbook of Services Marketing and Management*, Sage, Thousand Oaks CA.

Hamel, G. (1991), 'Competition for Competence and Inter-partner Learning Within International Strategic Alliances', *Strategic Management Journal*, 12, special issue, 83-103.

Hamel, G. and Prahalad, C.K. (1989), 'Strategic Intent', *Harvard Business Review*, May-June.

Hamel, G. and Prahalad, C.K. (1992), letter to *Harvard Business Review*, May-June.

Hamel, G. and Prahalad, C.K. (1993), 'Strategy as Stretch and Leverage', *Harvard Business Review*, March-April.

Hamel, G. and Prahalad, C.K. (1994), *Competing for the Future*, Harvard Business School Press, Boston MA.

Hammer, M. (1996), *Beyond Reengineering*, HarperCollins, London.

Handy, C.B. (1985), *Understanding Organizations* (3rd edition), Penguin, London.

Hardy, L. (1987), *Successful Business Strategy: How to Win in the Market-place*, Kogan Page, London.

Hargie, O. and Tourish, D. (2000) (eds), *Handbook of Communication Audits for Organizations*, Routledge, London.

Harrigan, K.R. (1988), 'Strategic Alliances and Partner Assymetries', in Contractor, F.J. and Lorange, P. (eds), *Cooperative Strategies in International Business*, Lexington Books, Lexington MA.

Heath, R.L. (1997), *Strategic Issues Management: Organizations and Public Policy Challenges*, Sage, Thousand Oaks CA.

Henderson, B. (1974), *The Experience Curve Reviewed III – How Does it Work?*, Boston Consulting Group.

Hendry, C. and Pettigrew, A. (1990), 'Human Resource Management: An Agenda for the 1990s', *International Journal of Human Resource Management*, 1, i.

Henry, J. (1991), 'Making Sense of Creativity', in Henry, J. (ed), *Creative Management*, Sage, London.

Hergert, M. and Morris, D. (1989), 'Accounting Data for Value Chain Analysis', *Strategic Management Journal*, 10, 175-188.

Herzberg, F., Mausner, B., and Snyderman, B. (1959), *The Motivation to Work* (2nd edition), Wiley, New York.

Heskett, J.L. (1995), 'Strategic Services Management: Examining and Understanding It', in Glyn, W.J. and Barnes, J.G. (eds), *Understanding Services Management*, Wiley, Chichester.

Heskett, J.L, Jones, T.O., Loveman, G.W., Sasser, W.E. Jr., and Schlesinger, L.A. (1994), 'Putting The Service-Profit Chain to Work', *Harvard Business Review*, March-April.

Heskett, J.L., Sasser, W.E. Jr., and Schlesinger, L.A. (1997), *The Service-Profit Chain*, The Free Press, New York.

Hill, N. (1996), *Handbook of Customer Satisfaction Measurement*, Gower, Aldershot.

Hitt, M., Dacin, T., Tyler, B., and Park, D. (1997), 'Understanding the Differences in Korean and US Executives' Strategic Orientations', *Strategic Management Journal*, 18, 2.

Hodgkinson, G.P., Bown, N.J., Maule, A.J., Glaister, K.W., and Pearman, A.D. (1999), 'Breaking the Frame: An Analysis of Strategic Cognition and Decision-making Under Uncertainty', *Strategic Management Journal*, 20, 10.

Hoffman, K.D. and Bateson, J.E.G. (1997), *Essentials of Services Marketing*, The Dryden Press, Fort Worth TX.

Hofstede, G. (1980), *Culture's Consequences: International Differences in Work-Related Values*, Sage, Beverly Hills CA.

Hofstede, G. and Bond, M.H. (1988), 'The Confucius Connection: From Cultural Roots to Economic Growth', *Organizational Dynamics*, 16, 4.

Holloway, S. (1997), *Straight and Level: Practical Airline Economics*, Ashgate, Aldershot.

Holloway, S. (1998a), *Changing Planes: A Strategic Management Perspective on an Industry in Transition (Vol. 1: Situation Analysis)*, Ashgate, Aldershot.

Holloway, S. (1998b), *Changing Planes: A Strategic Management Perspective on an Industry in Transition (Vol. 2: Strategic Choice, Implementation, and Outcome)*, Ashgate, Aldershot.

Hope, C. and Müehlemann, A. (1997), *Service Operations Management: Strategy, Design, and Delivery*, Prentice Hall, Hemel Hempstead.

Howard, J.A. and Sheth, J.N. (1969), *The Theory of Buyer Behaviour*, Wiley, New York.

Ind, N. (1997), *The Corporate Brand*, Macmillan, Basingstoke.

Irons, K. (1997a), *The World of Superservice*, Addison-Wesley, Harlow.

Irons, K. (1997b), *The Marketing of Services*, McGraw-Hill, Maidenhead.

Jaeger, A.M. (1986), 'Organization Development and National Culture: Where's the Fit?', *Academy of Management Review*, 11, 1.

Jenkins, K.J. (1992), 'Service Quality in the Skies', *Business Quarterly*, Autumn.

Jenkins, M. (1997), *The Customer Centred Strategy*, Pitman, London.

Johnson, G. (1987), *Strategic Change and the Management Process*, Blackwell, Oxford.

Johnson, G. and Scholes, K. (1997), *Exploring Corporate Strategy* (4ᵗʰ edition), Prentice Hall, Hemel Hempstead.

Johnson, S.P., Menor, L.J., Roth, A.V., and Chase, R.B. (2000), 'A Critical Evaluation of the New Service Development Process: Integrating Service Innovation and Service Design', in Fitzsimmons, J.A. and Fitzsimmons, M.J. (eds), *New Service Development: Creating Memorable Experiences*, Sage, Thousand Oaks CA.

Jones, T.O. and Sasser, W.E. Jr. (1995), 'Why Satisfied Customers Defect', *Harvard Business Review*, November-December.

Joyce, P. and Woods, A. (1996), *Essential Strategic Management: From Modernism to Pragmatism*, Butterworth-Heinemann, Oxford.

Kamoche, K. (1996), 'Human Resources as Strategic Assets: An Evolutionary Resource-based Theory', *Journal of Management Studies*, 33, 8.

Kanter, R.M. (1994), 'Collaborative Advantage: The Art of Alliances', *Harvard Business Review*, July-August.

Kapferer, J.N. (1997), *Strategic Brand Management*, Kogan Page, London.

Kaplan, R.S. and Norton, D.P. (1996), *The Balanced Scorecard*, Harvard Business School Press, Boston MA.

Kay, J. (1993), *Foundations of Corporate Success*, Oxford University Press, Oxford.

Keaveney, S. (1995), 'Customer Switching Behaviour in Service Industries: An Exploratory Study', *Journal of Marketing*, 59, August.

Keller, K. (1993), 'Conceptualizing, Measuring, and Managing Customer-based Brand Equity', *Journal of Marketing*, 57, 1.

Keller, K.L. (1998), *Strategic Brand Management: Building, Measuring, and Managing Brand Equity*, Prentice Hall, Upper Saddle River NJ.

Kimes, S.E. and Young, F.S. (1997), 'The Shuttle by United', *Interfaces*, 27, 3.

King, N. and Anderson, N. (1995), *Innovation and Change in Organization*, Routledge, London.

Kogut, B. (1993), *Country Competitiveness: Technology and the Organizing of Work*, Oxford University Press, New York.

Kogut, B. and Zander, U. (1997), 'Knowledge of the Firm, Combinative Capabilities, and the Replication of Technology', in Foss, N.J. (ed), *Resources, Firms, and Strategies*, Oxford University Press, Oxford.

Kotler, P. (1984), 'Kotler: Rethink the Marketing Concept', *Marketing News*, 14, September.

Kotter, J.P. and Heskett, J.L. (1992), *Corporate Culture and Performance*, The Free Press, New York.

Kurtz, D.L. and Clow, K.E. (1998), *Services Marketing*, Wiley, New York.

Lamming, R. (1993), *Beyond Partnership: Strategies for Innovation and Lean Supply*, Prentice Hall, Hemel Hempstead.

Langeard, E., Bateson, J., Lovelock, C., and Eiglier, P. (1981), *Marketing of Services: New Insights from Consumers and Managers*, Report no. 81-104, Marketing Sciences Institute, Cambridge MA.

Lawrence, J. (1993), 'Integrated Mix Makes Expansion Fly', *Advertising Age*, 64, November 8.

Leavy, B. (1996), *Key Processes in Strategy: Themes and Theories*, International Thomson Business Press, London.

Lengnick-Hall, C.A. (1992), 'Innovation and Competitive Advantage: What We Know and What We Need to Learn', *Journal of Management*, 18, 2.

Leonard, D. (1998), *Wellsprings of Knowledge*, Harvard Business School Press, Boston MA.

Leonard-Barton, D. (1992a), 'Core Capabilities and Core Rigidities: A Paradox in Managing New Product Development', *Strategic Management Journal*, 13, Summer Special Issue.

Leonard-Barton, D. (1992b), 'The Factory as a Learning Laboratory', Working Paper No. 92-023, *Harvard Business School*.

Levitt, B. and March, J. (1988), 'Organizational Learning', *Annual Review of Sociology*, 14, 319-340.

Levitt, T. (1980), 'Marketing Success Through Differentiation of Anything', *Harvard Business Review*, 58, January-February.

Levitt, T. (1983), *The Marketing Imagination*, The Free Press, New York.

Lewis, B.R. and Sinhapalin, D. (1991), 'Service Quality: An Empirical Study of Thai Airways', *Proceedings of The European Institute for Advanced Studies in Management*, Brussels, May.

Lewis, M.A. and Gregory, M.J. (1996), 'Developing and Applying a Process Approach to Competence Analysis', in Sanchez, R., Heene, A., and Thomas, H. (eds), *Dynamics of Competence-Based Competition: Theory and Practice in the New Strategic Management*, Pergamon, Oxford.

Lindblom, L. (1959), 'The Science of Muddling Through', *Public Administration Review*, 19, Spring.

Lovelock, C. (1996), *Services Marketing* (3rd edition), Prentice Hall, Upper Saddle River NJ.

Lynch, R. (1997), *Corporate Strategy*, Pitman, London.

Mabey, C., Salaman, G., and Storey, J. (1998), *Human Resource Management: A Strategic Introduction* (2nd edition), Blackwell, Oxford.

Mahoney, J.T. and Sanchez, R. (1997), 'Competence Theory Building: Reconnecting Management Research and Management Practice', in Heene, A. and Sanchez, R. (eds), *Competence-Based Strategic Management*, Wiley, Chichester.

Makadok, R. (1999), 'Interfirm Differences in Scale Economies and the Evolution of Market Shares', *Strategic Management Journal*, 20, 10.

Marion, R. (1999), *The Edge of Organization: Chaos and Complexity Theories of Formal Social Systems*, Sage, Thousand Oaks CA.

Martin, C.L. and Clark, T. (1996), 'Networks of Customer-to-Customer Relationships in Marketing', in Iacobucci, D. (ed), *Networks in Marketing*, Sage, Thousand Oaks CA.

Martin, J. (1992), *Cultures in Organizations: Three Perspectives*, Oxford University Press, New York.

Martin, J. (1995), *The Great Transition*, AMACOM, New York.

Maslow, A. (1964), *Motivation and Personality*, Harper & Row, London.

Mason, K.J. and Gray, R. (1995), 'Short-haul Business Travel in the European Union: A Segmentation Approach', *Journal of Air Transport Management*, 2, 3-4.

Matlin, M.W. (1998), *Cognition* (4th edition), Harcourt Brace & Company, Fort Worth TX.

McCarthy, D.C. (1997), *The Loyalty Link*, Wiley, New York.

McDonald, M. and Dunbar, I. (1998), *Market Segmentation* (2nd edition), Macmillan, Basingstoke.

McDonald, M. and Payne, A. (1996), *Marketing Planning for Services*, Butterworth-Heinemann, Oxford.

Mercer, D. (1997), *New Marketing Practice: Rules for Success in a Changing World*, Penguin Books, London.

Miller, D. (1996), 'Configurations Revisited', *Strategic Management Journal*, 17, 505-512.

Mintzberg, H. (1994), *The Rise and Fall of Strategic Planning*, Prentice Hall, Hemel Hempstead.

Mintzberg, H. and Waters, J.A. (1978), 'Patterns in Strategy Formation', *Management Science*, 24, 934-948.

Moingeon, B. and Edmondson, A. (1996), *Organizational Learning and Competitive Advantage*, Sage, London.

Morecroft, J.D.W. (1992), 'Executive Knowledge, Models, and Learning', *European Journal of Operational Research*, 59, 9-27.

Morgan, G. (1997), *Images of Organization*, Sage, Thousand Oaks CA.

Morrell, P.S. (1997), *Airline Finance*, Ashgate, Aldershot.

Morrow, M. (1992), *Activity-based Management*, Woodhead-Faulkner, Hemel Hempstead.

Mueller, F. (1996), 'Human Resources as Strategic Assets: An Evolutionary Resource-based Theory', *Journal of Management Studies*, 33, 6.

Murley, P. (ed) (1997), *Handbook of Customer Service*, Gower, Aldershot.

Murray, A.I. (1988), 'A Contingency View of Porter's "Generic Strategies"', *Academy of Management Review*, 13, 2.

Murtha, T. and Lenway, S.A. (1994), 'Country Capabilities and the Strategic State: How National Political Institutions Affect Multinational Corporations' Strategies', *Strategic Management Journal*, 15, Summer Special Issue.

Musson, G. and Cohen, L. (1999), 'Understanding Language Processes: A Neglected Skill in the Management Curriculum', *Management Learning*, 30, 1.

Needham, J.P. (1998), 'Continuous Quality Improvement: A Vehicle for Creating Competitive Advantage', in Butler, G.F. and Keller, M.R. (eds), *Handbook of Airline Marketing*, Aviation Week Group, New York.

Neely, A. (1998), *Measuring Business Performance*, The Economist Books, London.

Nelson, R.R., and Winter, S.G. (1982), *An Evolutionary Theory of Economic Change*, Belknap Press, Cambridge MA.

Normann, R. (1984), *Service Management: Strategy and Leadership in Service Businesses*, Wiley, Chichester.

Normann, R. and Ramírez, R. (1993), 'From Value Chain to Value Constellation: Designing Interactive Strategy', *Harvard Business Review*, July-August.

O'Brien, F.A. and Meadows, M. (1998), 'Future Visioning: A Case Study of a Scenario-based Approach', in Dyson, R.G. and O'Brien, F.A., *Strategic Development: Methods and Models*, Wiley, Chichester.

Ojasalo, J. (1999), *Quality Dynamics in Professional Services*, Helsinki/Helsingfors, Swedish School of Economics, Finland/CERS, cited in Grönroos, 2000: 89.

Oliver, C. (1990), 'Determinants of Interorganizational Relationships: Integration and Future Directions', *Academy of Management Review*, 15, 2.

Olve, N-G., Roy, J., and Wetter, M. (1999), *Performance Drivers: A Practical Guide to Using the Balanced Scorecard*, Wiley, Chichester.

O'Sullivan, L. and Geringer, J.M. (1993), 'Harnessing the Power of Your Value Chain', *Long Range Planning*, 26, 3.

Pai, S-W. and Trefzger, D. (1998), 'Service Recovery in the Air Cargo Business: Action Instead of Reaction', in Butler, G.F. and Keller, M.R. (eds), *Handbook of Airline Marketing*, Aviation Week Group, New York.

Palick, L.E., Cardinal, L.B., and Miller, C.C. (2000), 'Curvilinearity in the Diversification-Performance Linkage: An Examination of Over Three Decades of Research', *Strategic Management Journal*, 21, 2.

Parasuraman, A. (1995), 'Measuring and Monitoring Service Quality', in Glynn, W.J. and Barnes, J.G., *Understanding Services Management*, Wiley, Chichester.

Parasuraman, A. (1997), 'Reflections on Gaining Competitive Advantage Through Customer Value', *Journal of the Academy of Marketing Science*, 25, 2.

Parasuraman, A., Zeithaml, V.A., and Berry, L.L. (1988), 'SERVQUAL: A Multiple-Item Scale for Measuring Consumer Perceptions of Service Quality', *Journal of Retailing*, 64, 12-40.

Payne, A. (1995), *Advances in Relationship Marketing*, Butterworth-Heinemann, Oxford.

Payne, A. and Clark, M. (1995), 'Marketing Services to External Markets', in Glynn, W.J. and Barnes, J.G. (eds), *Understanding Services Management*, Wiley, Chichester.

Pearn, M., Roderick, C., and Mulrooney, C. (1995), *Learning Organizations in Practice*, McGraw-Hill, Maidenhead.

Penrose, E.T. (1959), *Theory of the Growth of the Firm*, Basil Blackwell, London.

Peppard, J. and Rowland, P. (1995), *The Essence of Business Process Reengineering*, Prentice Hall, Hemel Hempstead.

Peters, T.J. and Waterman, R.H. (1982), *In Search of Excellence: Lessons from America's Best-Run Corporations*, Harper & Row, New York.

Pettigrew, A. (1979), 'On Studying Organizational Cultures', *Administrative Science Quarterly*, December.

Pettigrew, A. and Whipp, R. (1991), *Managing Change for Competitive Success*, Blackwell, Oxford.

Pfeffer, J. and Salancik, G.R. (1978), *The External Control of Organizations: A Resource Dependence Perspective*, Harper & Row, New York.

Piercy, N. (1997), *Market-Led Strategic Change* (2nd edition), Butterworth-Heinemann, Oxford.

Pilling, M. (2001), 'Flights of Fancy', *Airline Business*, January.

Polanyi, M. (1962), *Personal Knowledge*, Harper, New York.

Polanyi, M. (1966), *The Tacit Dimension*, Anchor Day Books, New York.

Porter, M.E. (1980), *Competitive Strategy*, The Free Press, New York.

Porter, M.E. (1985), *Competitive Advantage*, The Free Press, New York.

Porter, M.E. (1990), *The Competitive Advantage of Nations*, The Free Press, New York.

Porter, M.E. (1991), 'Towards a Dynamic Theory of Strategy', *Strategic Management Journal*, 12, Winter, Special Edition.

Porter, M.E. (1996), 'What is Strategy?', *Harvard Business Review*, November-December.

Prahalad, C.K. and Hamel, G. (1990), 'The Core Competence of the Corporation', *Harvard Business Review*, May-June.

Pranter, C.A. and Martin, C.L. (1991), 'Compatibility Management: Roles in Service Performance', *Journal of Services Marketing*, Spring.

Proctor, T. (1995), *The Essence of Management Creativity*, Prentice-Hall, Hemel Hempstead.

Quinn, J.B. (1980), *Strategies for Change: Logical Incrementalism*, Irwin, Homewood IL.

Quinn, J.B. (1985), 'Managing Innovation: Controlled Chaos', *Harvard Business Review*, May-June.

Rao, V.R. and Steckel, J.H. (1998), *Analysis for Marketing Strategy*, Addison Wesley Longman, Reading MA.

Ravald, A. and Grönroos, C., (1996), 'The Value Concept and Relationship Marketing', *European Journal of Marketing*, 30, 2.

Reed, R. and DeFillippi, R.J. (1990), 'Causal Ambiguity, Barriers to Imitation, and Sustainable Competitive Advantage', *Academy of Management Review*, 15, 1.

Regnér, P. (2001), 'Complexity and Multiple Rationalities in Strategy Processes', in Volberda, H.W. and Elfring, T. (eds), *Rethinking Strategy*, Sage, London.

Reichheld, F.F. (1996), *The Loyalty Effect*, Harvard Business School Press, Boston MA.

Reichheld, F.F. and Sasser, W.E. (1990), 'Zero Defections: Quality Comes to Service', *Harvard Business Review*, September-October.

Rice, C. (1997), *Understanding Customers* (2nd edition), Butterworth-Heinemann, Oxford.

Rindova, V.P. and Fombrun, C.J. (1999), 'Constructing Competitive Advantage: The Role of Firm-Constituent Interactions', *Strategic Management Journal*, 20, 8.

Ringland, G. (1998), *Scenario Planning: Managing for the Future*, Wiley, Chichester.

Rispoli, M. (1996), 'Competitive Analysis and Competence-based Strategies in the Hotel Industry', in Sanchez, R., Heene, A., and Thomas, H. (eds), *Dynamics of Competence-Based Competition: Theory and Practice in the New Strategic Management*, Pergamon, Oxford.

Roberts, J. (1992), 'Human Resource Strategies and the Management of Change', *B884 Human Resource Strategies, Supplementary Readings 1*, Open University, Milton Keynes.

Robinson, J. (1934), 'What is Perfect Competition?', *Quarterly Journal of Economics*, 49, 104-120.

Rumelt, R.P. (1984), 'Towards a Strategic Theory of the Firm', in Lamb R. (ed), *Competitive Strategic Management*, Prentice-Hall, Englewood Cliffs NJ.

Rumelt, R.P. (1987), 'Theory, Strategy, and Entrepreneurship', in Teece, D. (ed), *Competitive Strategic Management*, Prentice-Hall, Englewood Cliffs NJ.

Salaman, G. (1996), 'Indian Snacks: Changing and Continuity', in Storey, J. (ed), *New Perspectives on Human Resource Management*, Blackwell, Oxford.

Sanchez, R. (1993), 'Strategic Flexibility, Firm Organization, and Managerial Work in Dynamic Markets: A Strategic Options Perspective', *Advances in Strategic Management*, 9, 251-291.

Sanchez, R. (1995), 'Strategic Flexibility in Product Competition', *Sloan Management Review*, Summer.

Sanchez, R. (2001), 'Building Blocks for Strategy Theory: Resources, Dynamic Capabilities and Competencies', in Volberda, H.W. and Elfring, T. (eds), *Rethinking Strategy*, Sage, London.

Sanchez, R. and Heene, A. (1996) 'A Systems View of the Firm in Competence-Based Competition', in Sanchez, R., Heene, A., and Thomas, H. (eds), *Dynamics of Competence-Based Competition: Theory and Practice in the New Strategic Management*, Pergamon, Oxford.

Sanchez, R. and Heene, A. (1997), 'Competence-Based Strategic Management: Concepts and Issues for Theory, Research, and Practice', in Heene, A. and Sanchez, R. (eds), *Competence-Based Strategic Management*, Wiley, Chichester.

Sanchez, R., Heene, A., and Thomas, H. (1996), 'Introduction: Towards The Theory and Practice of Competence-Based Competition', in Sanchez, R., Heene, A., and Thomas, H. (eds), *Dynamics of Competence-Based Competition: Theory and Practice in the New Strategic Management*, Pergamon, Oxford.

Sasser, W.E. and Klein, N. (1994), 'British Airways: Using Information Systems to Better Service the Customer', Case No. 9-935-065, Harvard Business School Publishing, Boston MA.

Sasser, W.E. Jr., Hart, C.W.L., and Heskett, J.L. (1991), *The Service Management Course*, The Free Press, New York.

Schein, E.H. (1985), *Organizational Culture and Leadership*, Jossey-Bass, San Francisco CA.

Scheuing, E.E. (1998), 'Delighting Your Customers: Creating World-Class Service', in Zemke, R. and Woods, J.A. (eds), *Best Practices in Customer Service*, AMACOM, New York.

Schneider, S.C. (1989), 'Strategy Formulation: The Impact of National Culture', *Organization Studies*, 10, 149-168.

Schneider, S.C. and Angelmar, R. (1993), Cognition in Organizational Analysis: Who's Minding the Store?', *Organizational Studies*, 14.

Schneider, B. and Bowen, D.E. (1993), 'The Service Organization: Human Resources Management is Crucial', *Organizational Dynamics*, Spring.

Schultz, D.E. and Barnes, B.E. (1999), *Strategic Brand Communication Campaigns*, NTC Business Books, Lincolnwood IL.

Selznick, P. (1957), *Leadership in Administration: A Sociological Interpretation*, Harper & Row, New York.

Senge, P. (1990), *The Fifth Discipline*, Doubleday, New York.

Senior, B. (1997), *Organizational Change*, Pitman, London.

Shenkar, O. and Zeira, Y. (1992), 'Role Conflict and Role Ambiguity of Chief Executive Officers in International Joint Ventures', *Journal of International Business Studies*, 23, 55-75.

Shostack, G.L. (1977), 'Breaking Free from Product Marketing', *Journal of Marketing*, 41, 2.

Shostack, G.L. (1984), 'Designing Services That Deliver', *Harvard Business Review*, January-February.

Siehl, C. and Martin, J. (1984), 'The Role of Symbolic Management: How Can Managers Effectively Transmit Organizational Culture?', in Hunt, J.D., Hosking, D., Schriesheim, C., and Stewart, R. (eds), *Leaders and Managers: International Perspectives on Managerial Leadership and Behaviour*, Pergamon, New York.

Simons, R. (2000), *Performance Measurement and Control Systems for Implementing Strategy*, Prentice-Hall, Upper Saddle River NJ.

Sinclair, M.T. and Stabler, M. (1997), *The Economics of Tourism*, Routledge, London.

Slack, N., Chambers, S., Harland, C., Harrison, A., and Johnston, R. (1998), *Operations Management* (2nd edition), Pitman, London.

Smith, K.G., Grimm, C.M., Gannon, M.J., and Chen, M. (1991), 'Organizational Information Processing, Competitive Responses and Performance in the US Domestic Airline Industry', *Academy of Management Journal*, 34, 60-85.

Spender, J-C. (2001), 'Business Policy and Strategy as a Professional Field', in Volberda, H.W. and Elfring, T. (eds), *Rethinking Strategy*, Sage, London.

Spreng, R.D., Harrell, G.D., and Mackay, R.D. (1995), 'Service Recovery: Impact on Satisfaction and Intentions', *Journal of Services Marketing*, 9, 1.

Stacey, R.D. (1996), *Strategic Management and Organisational Dynamics* (2nd edition), Pitman, London.

Stalk, G., Evans, P., and Shulman, L.E. (1992), 'Competing on Capabilities: The New Rules of Corporate Strategy', *Harvard Business Review*, March-April.

Stein, J. (1997), 'On Building and Leveraging Competences Across Organizational Borders: A Socio-Cognitive Perspective', in Heene, A. and Sanchez, R. (eds), *Competence-based Competition*, Wiley, Chichester.

Stewart, T.A. (1997), *Intellectual Capital: The New Wealth of Organizations*, Nicholas Brealey, London.

Storey, J. (1992), *Developments in the Management of Human Resources: An Analytical Review*, Blackwell, Oxford.

Sutton, C. (1998), *Strategic Concepts*, Macmillan, Basingstoke.

Sveiby, K.E. (1997), *The New Organizational Wealth*, Berrett Koehler, San Francisco CA.

Swieringa, G. and Wierdsma, A. (1992), *Becoming a Learning Organization*, Addison-Wesley, Reading MA.

Tallman, S. and Atchison, D.L. (1996), 'Competence-Based Competition and the Evolution of Strategic Configurations', in Sanchez, R., Heene, A., and Thomas, H. (eds), *Dynamics of Competence-Based Competition: Theory and Practice in the New Strategic Management*, Pergamon, Oxford.

Tansik, D.A. and Smith, W.L. (2000), 'Scripting the Service Encounter', in Fitzsimmons, J.A. and Fitzsimmons, M.J. (eds), *New Service Development: Creating Memorable Experiences*, Sage, Thousand Oaks CA.

Tapp, A. (1997), *Principles of Direct & Database Marketing*, Pitman, London.

Tax, S.S. and Brown, S.W. (1998), 'Recovering and Learning from Service Failure', *Sloan Management Review*, Fall.

Teece, D.J. (1984), 'Economic Analysis and Strategic Management', *California Management Review*, Spring.

Teece, D.J., Pisano, G., and Shuen, A. (1997), 'Dynamic Capabilities and Strategic Management', *Strategic Management Journal*, 18, 7.

Tenner, A.R. and DeToro, I.J. (1997), *Process Redesign: The Implementation Guide for Managers*, Addison-Wesley, Reading MA.

Thomas, L.G. III and Waring, G. (1999), 'Competing Capitalisms: Capital Investment in American, German, and Japanese Firms', *Strategic Management Journal*, 20, 8.

Thornett, B. (1997), 'Customer Information Systems', presentation to the IATA *Information Management 97* conference, Atlanta, 4th-8th May.

Tidd, J., Bessant, J., and Pavitt, K. (1997), *Managing Innovation: Integrating Technological, Market, and Organizational Change*, Wiley, Chichester.

Treacy, M. and Wiersma, F. (1995), *The Discipline of Market Leaders*, HarperCollins, London.

Trott, P. (1998), *Innovation Management & New Product Development*, Pitman, London.

Usunier, J-C. (1996), *Marketing Across Cultures* (2nd edition), Prentice Hall, Hemel Hempstead.

van der Heijden, K. (1996), *Scenarios: The Art of Strategic Conversation*, Wiley, Chichester.

Vandermerwe, S. (1993), *From Tin Soldiers to Russian Dolls: Creating Added Value Through Services*, Butterworth-Heinemann, Oxford.

van Maanen, J. and Barley, S.R. (1984), 'Occupational Communities: Culture and Control in Organizations', in Staw, B.M. and Cummings, L.L. (eds), *Research in Organizational Behaviour*, JAI Press, Greenwich CT.

Volberda, H.W. (1996), 'Flexible Configuration Strategies Within Philips Semiconductors: A Strategic Process of Entrepreneurial Revitalization', in Sanchez, R., Heene, A., and Thomas, H. (eds), *Dynamics of Competence-Based Competition: Theory and Practice in the New Strategic Management*, Pergamon, Oxford.

von Krogh, G., Roos, J., and Slocum, K. (1994), 'An Essay on Cooperative Epistemology', *Strategic Management Journal*, 15,1.

Ward, J.C. and Reingen, P. (1996), 'A Network Perspective on Crossing the Micro-Macro Divide in Consumer Behaviour Research', in Iacobucci, D. (ed), *Networks in Marketing*, Sage, Thousand Oaks CA.

Wayland, R.E. and Cole, P.M. (1997), *Customer Connections: New Strategies for Growth*, Harvard Business School Press, Cambridge MA.

Webster, F.E. (1994), *Market-driven Management*, Wiley, New York.

Weick, K.E. (1995), *Sensemaking in Organizations*, Sage, Thousand Oaks CA.

Wernerfelt, B. (1984), 'A Resource-Based View of the Firm', *Strategic Management Journal*, 5, 2.

West, M.A. (1997), *Developing Creativity in Organizations*, BPS Books, Leicester.

Wilkström, S. and Normann, R. (1994), *Knowledge and Value*, Routledge, London.

Winterscheid, B.C. and McNabb, S. (1996), 'From National to Global Product Development Competence in the Telecommunications Industry: Structure and Process in Leveraging Core Capabilities', in Sanchez, R., Heene, A., and

Thomas, H. (eds), *Dynamics of Competence-Based Competition: Theory and Practice in the New Strategic Management*, Pergamon, Oxford.

Wolff Olins (1995), *The New Guide to Identity*, Gower, Aldershot.

Womack, J.P., Jones, D.I., and Roos, D. (1990), *The Machine That Changed the World*, Rawson, New York.

Wong-Rieger, D. and Rieger, F. (1989), 'The Influence of Societal Culture on Corporate Culture, Business Strategy, and Performance in the International Airline Industry', in Osigweh, C.A.B. (ed), *Organizational Science Abroad: Constraints and Perspectives*, Plenum, New York.

Woodruff, R.B. (1997), 'Customer Value: The Next Source of Competitive Advantage', *Journal of the Academy of Marketing Science*, 25, 2.

Worcester, R.M. (1997), 'Tomorrow's Company is the Company You Keep', *Journal of Communication Management*, February.

Zakreski, E. (1998), 'Beyond Frequent Flyers: Knowing Customers as a Foundation for Airline Growth', in Butler, G.F. and Keller, M.R. (eds), *Handbook of Airline Marketing*, Aviation Week Group, New York.

Zeithaml, V.A. (2000), 'Service Quality, Profitability and the Economic Worth of Customers', *Journal of the Academy of Marketing Science*, January.

Zeithaml, V.A. and Bitner, M.J. (2000), *Services Marketing: Integrating Customer Focus Across the Firm* (2nd edition), McGraw-Hill, New York.

Zeithaml, V.A., Berry, L.L., and Parasuraman, A. (1993), 'The Nature and Determinants of Customer Expectations of Services', *Journal of the Academy of Marketing Science*, 21, Winter.

Zeithaml, V.A., Parasuraman, A., and Berry, L.L. (1990), *Delivering Service Quality: Balancing Customer Perceptions and Expectations*, The Free Press, New York.

Zifko-Baliga, G.M. (1998), 'What customers Really Want: How That Affets What Service to Deliver', in Zemke, A. and Woods, J.A. (eds), *Best Practices In Customer Service*, AMACOM, New York.

Zou, S. and Cavusgil, S.T. (1996), 'Global Strategy: A Review and an Integrated Conceptual Framework', *European Journal of Marketing*, 30, 1.

Index

activities (and activity systems) (*see also: value chains*) 27-28, 32, 268, 338
   activity-based costing and management 262, 267, 315, 362, 381
   and branding 189
   and internal communications 223
   and processes 235, 248-249
   as a source of competitive advantage 254, 261-262
advertising (*see also: customers, expectations, management of*) 96, 145, 177, 217, 220, 229, 230, 231, 325, 339
   as a brand element 192, 202, 203, 207, 302, 366
Aeroflot 200
agency theory 330, 331
Air Canada 177, 362
Air France 177, 197
AirLiance Materials 362
AirOne 93
Alitalia 93
alliances (*see also: collaboration; collusion*) 271, 323-324, 362
   and branding 197-198, 204, 333-334
   and culture *see: culture*
   and distribution 221
   and pricing 141
   and product/geographical scope 79
   and service consistency 114, 158, 351
   as industry recipe 48
   competence-related 45
     and resources 249
   internal communication 227-228
   management 256, 296, 324, 327-335
   motives 327-329
   nature and scope 325-327

   complementary 327
   horizontal 326
   vertical (*see also: scope, vertical*) 325-326, 332
American Airlines 33, 70, 141, 181, 183, 201, 289, 310, 314, 329
American Eagle 210
American Productivity and Quality Center 236
assets, firm-specific 31
Atlantic Southeast Airlines 390

BAA 201
Balair/CTA 17, 78
balanced scorecard *see: performance, balanced scorecard*
barriers to entry 13, 27, 37, 49, 52, 53, 65, 99, 135, 140, 252, 295, 323, 324, 329
benchmarking *see: performance, benchmarking*
benefits (provided by a service) (*see also: service, augmented; service, core; service, expected; value chains*) 90, 123-124, 129, 132-139, 152, 342, 393
   and alliances 198
   and branding 192, 198, 367
   and communications 218, 367
   and market positioning 101, 303
   and the activity system 262-263
   emotional/symbolic 103, 125, 131, 139, 144, 145, 152-153, 156, 166, 244, 250, 300
     and branding 187-189, 196, 199
   functional (utilitarian) 125-126, 130, 139, 145, 147, 156, 300
     and branding 187-189
blueprinting *see: processes, service delivery, blueprinting*

Boston Box 14
boundary conflicts 170-173
brand 151
    alignment 196-197
    and emotional benefits 144
    architecture 209-210
    as a service attribute 196
    as a social construction 52, 188-189
    as a source of competitive advantage 195
    association 90, 191, 199, 200-201, 203-204, 208, 209
    awareness 202, 208, 209, 212, 217, 231, 366
        alliances 228
        awareness set 212, 216
        prompted 188
        spontaneous/unprompted 188
    brand contacts 302
    charter 192-193
    definition 105, 187-189
    elements 155, 192, 195, 198-205, 213, 215, 228-232, 286, 300, 301, 366
    evoked (consideration) set 212, 216
    equity 199-200, 201, 218, 304-305
    identity 85, 104, 105-106, 145, 151, 185-198, 211, 386
        and alliances 227
        and culture 289, 387-388
        and image contrasted 180-194
        as a social construction 283
        management of 194-197, 232
            communications 205-210, 229, 257, 365
            visual 178-179, 180-181, 183, 201-202, 306, 397
                alliances 228
    image (*see also: perception*) 42, 51, 93, 103, 105-106, 130, 131, 136, 139, 145-147, 152, 155, 156, 157, 185-198, 250, 254, 280, 299, 300, 301, 305, 318, 335, 247, 393
        and alliances 158, 333-334
        and communications 223, 365, 366
        and competitive advantage 54, 96
        and identity contrasted 189-194
        and organizational culture 192, 294, 380
        and reputation contrasted 147,

188-189
    and pricing 140, 142
    fragmentation 188-189
    impact of servicescape 178-179, 183
    management of 194-197, 236
    reducing purchase risk 111, 367
    knowledge 206, 213, 365, 366
    logo 189, 192, 286
    loyalty (*see also: marketing, relationship; customer, loyalty*) 73, 132, 147, 190, 201, 218, 247, 288, 294, 301, 305, 306, 365
    management 100, 106, 111, 189, 190, 215, 256, 301, 366
        and internal communication 223
    master-brand 87, 97, 208, 209-210
    name 189, 192, 198-201, 365
    oral clues 203
    personality 106, 190, 194, 206, 258, 303, 304
        brand values 106, 111, 125, 144, 190, 204, 209, 223, 228, 229, 289, 366
    physical/tangible evidence/clues *see: physical evidence*
    points of difference (*see also: positioning, market; value chains*) 99, 102-103, 124-125, 134, 147, 151, 155, 156, 157, 189, 230, 257, 359, 365, 393
        and alliances 198, 228
        and differentiation compared 102, 125, 129-132, 142, 392
        and the activity system 262-263
        role of employees 168, 244-245, 257-260
    points of similarity 99, 124, 134, 147
    recall 202, 206, 209, 301, 367
    recognition 206, 209, 301, 367
    strap-lines 202
    sub-brand 85, 167, 192, 203, 205, 209-210, 211, 218, 222
        Club Europe 200, 302
        Club World 200, 210, 227, 302, 305
        Mid Class 217
        Upper Class 217
        World Business Class 197
        World Traveller 210
British Airways 11, 16, 67, 82, 142,

153, 156, 177, 182, 183, 187-189, 196,
197, 200, 201, 202, 208, 211, 236, 273,
289, 302, 305, 327, 329, 344, 346, 352,
386, 390, 395, 398, 400
  British Airways World Cargo 210
  British Airways World Offers 210
British Midland (bmi international) 199-
200
BT 201
buying centre 211, 312
Buzz 87, 208, 209

Canon 236
Cathay Pacific Airways 17, 197, 203,
218, 395
capabilities 36, 46, 239, 252, 253, 385
  dynamic 46-47
capacity management 112, 116, 131,
135, 140, 152, 216, 241, 245-246, 323,
364
  and the need for customer queuing
  and waiting 160-163, 246, 248
causal ambiguity 33-34, 36, 42, 53-54,
55, 102, 132, 139, 239, 252, 257, 295
centralisation and decentralisation 268,
269, 270, 288
CFROI 371
change (*see also: creativity; innovation*)
4, 382, 383-391, 401
  competence rigidity 45
  culture *see: culture, organizational,*
  change
  discontinuous 384-385
  effect of structure 272
  incremental 385
  management 388-391
  operational 384, 385, 386, 390
  strategic 2, 7, 8, 11-12, 384, 386
chaos theory 385-386
charter airlines 78, 80, 84, 180, 304
Civil Aviation Authority (UK) 181
code-sharing 79, 114, 152, 158, 166,
197, 209, 229, 326, 331, 332
collaboration 13, 331-335
  collaborative advantage 269-270,
  322-330
collusion 322, 324
commitment, employee 136, 170, 224,
226, 260, 261, 282, 292, 296, 298, 321,
335, 349, 351, 356, 358, 389
communication 145, 184, 280, 325
  and branding (*see also: brand,*

elements) 190, 194, 195, 196, 204,
205-210, 300
  audits and performance 229, 364-
367
  economies of scale 207, 209-210
  external, customers 210-220
  external, other stakeholders 221-
222
  in support of product launch 138
  integrated 195, 204, 216, 228-232
  internal (*see also: organization,*
  architecture, structure) 223-228,
  243, 282, 286, 287, 296, 358, 364
    within alliances 227-228
  marketing (*see also: customers,*
  expectations, management of) 73, 84,
  85, 88, 93, 164, 211, 220, 221, 228-
232, 306, 307, 326, 359
    and branding 188, 192, 301
    and market positioning 99
    and pricing 140
    and product 151, 155
    as internal communication 224
    importance of consistency 105,
    228-232
    mix 71, 72, 206, 228-232
  objectives 205-210, 228
  strategic messaging 205-206
  tactical messaging 206-207, 220
communities of practice 255
compensation, employee 223
competencies (*see also: value chain*) 16,
19, 54, 66, 74, 82, 94, 104, 106, 136,
249, 257, 398
  and alliances 328, 333, 335
  and the activity system 263
  -building 44, 45, 358, 387
  contrasted with processes 236-239
  contrasted with routines 37
  core 15, 42-43, 45, 133, 252, 386,
  394
  distinctive 38, 41, 253, 276
  firm-specific 41, 109, 125, 236, 253
  identification of 43
  in brand management 106
  industry-specific 38, 124, 253
  in product development (*see also:*
  innovation) 132
  integrative 279, 322, 329
  -leveraging 44, 45, 387
  rigidity of 45, 394
  strategy-specific 38-39, 109, 253

competence-based theory (*see also: strategy, competitive*) 36-47, 259, 358, 377, 387
competition law 322, 326
competitive advantage (*see also: collaboration, collaborative advantage*) 2, 16, 19, 54-55, 74, 75, 87, 88, 96, 104, 127, 133, 138, 381
    and cost structure 140, 216
    and market position 98, 100, 130
    and employees 172, 243, 250-251
    definition 23-24
    protecting 52-54, 55, 239
    sources 24-52, 55, 68, 69-70, 71, 109, 195, 252, 254, 256, 257, 259-260, 276, 288, 290, 294, 295, 321, 322, 325, 358, 386, 393, 393-396
        activity systems 262-263
        value chains 263-267
            competitors 97, 100, 138, 140, 141, 147, 195, 205, 219, 319, 320, 365, 384, 392, 397, 401
    multi-market contact 323
complaints (*see also: service failure*) 154, 175, 176, 320, 321, 341, 344-347, 400
    as input into service design 120, 133
    management system 345
complexity theory 339
concept testing 135
configuration, strategic 38, 276-277
conjoint analysis 129
consistency (*see also: variability*) 56, 96, 99, 101, 104-106, 113-114, 118, 123, 126, 136-137, 144, 145, 165, 187, 194, 198, 210-211, 215, 218, 224, 228-232, 249, 271, 287, 291, 380, 384
    strategic 27, 105
consumer behaviour (*see also: physical evidence; risk; service evaluation*) 72, 118, 147, 157, 179, 380
    influence of brand image 106, 152, 187, 195, 199, 301
    influence of communications 205, 206-207, 211-220, 365
    influence of service design 132, 133, 135, 154, 258, 311, 397-398
    involvement 212
    repeat purchasing (*see also: service delivery; service encounters; servicescape*) 161, 166, 179, 215, 219, 220, 303, 306, 308, 313, 314,
318, 343, 350
consumers, contrasted with customers 89-90, 117
contestability theory 13, 324
Continental Airlines 390
Continental Lite 208
contingency theory 259, 328
continuous improvement 30, 175, 248, 251, 382, 385, 395, 399
core business 13, 16
cost (*see also: activities; value chains*)
    and customer retention 314-315
    base/structure (*see also: productivity*) 76, 79, 93, 94, 95, 103, 132, 138, 140, 143, 144, 216, 362-364, 368, 386, 393
    leadership *see: positioning, strategic*
    management 93-94, 95, 104, 241, 244-247, 273, 306, 330, 386
        and alliances 325, 326
        and the activity system 262-263
    marginal 142
creativity (*see also: change; innovation*) 258, 261, 391-392, 394, 395, 397, 401
credence product 214
critical incident technique 134, 347, 375
critical (key) success factors 74, 97, 101, 147, 338-339
Crossair 17, 87
    EuroCross 210
culture 282-296, 359
    defined 282
    national 49, 114, 126, 152, 156, 157, 176, 179, 182, 183, 200, 203, 256, 281, 282-284, 295, 359, 389
        and alliances 158, 273, 334-335
    organizational 11, 42, 49, 284, 285-296, 399-400
        and alliances 198, 289, 295-296, 313, 324, 328, 331, 333, 335, 349, 359
        and brand image 192, 194, 204-205, 294
        and competencies 47, 259
        and competitive advantage 53, 54, 255, 261, 288, 290
        and consistency 105, 113, 114, 123, 137, 144, 294, 380
        and human resource policies (*see also: HRM*) 172
        and internal communication 226
        and performance 381

and points of difference 125,
131, 139, 152
and routines 253, 257
as an integrative 'mechanism'
268
as a social construction 283
as metaphor 51, 388, 389
change 48, 292, 387-388, 389
compatibility with strategy 95
creation of 290-291
defined 285
effect on service 102, 103, 170
in relation to cognition,
knowledge, and learning 48-49,
357
service culture (ethic) 123, 139,
173, 225, 285, 399
sources 104
subculture 194, 272, 284, 289, 292
customer (*see also: service delivery, role
of customers*) 347
activity cycles 166, 169, 240, 375
advocacy ('word-of-mouth') 76,
126, 161, 213, 215, 219, 220, 298,
302, 303, 317
negative 344
communication with (*see also:
communication*) 210-220, 229
contrasted with consumer 89-90,
117
defection (*see also: customer,
retention; service failure; service
recovery*) 318-321, 321, 349, 351
expectations (*see also: service,
failure; service quality*) 44, 76, 85,
88, 89, 92, 101, 144, 147, 159, 165,
286, 306, 314, 316, 321, 341, 342,
343, 381, 384, 386, 387, 397
and alliances 158
and branding 199, 304
importance of exceeding 260,
309
input into service design 96,
113, 119, 120-122, 123, 129,
133, 157, 247, 256, 393
management of 196-197, 230
impact of servicescape 178-
179
impact of communications (*see
also: communications,
marketing*) 217-218, 219, 220,
374, 379

minimum expected level of
service 124, 127, 301
predictive and ideal/normative
120, 373, 376
feedback from (*see also: complaints*)
113, 120, 133, 136, 138, 171, 297,
306, 346
impact of other customers 165, 166,
173-175, 218-219
investment in 316
lifetime-value 70, 73, 301, 303, 306,
308, 309, 315, 317, 318, 350
full profit potential 309
loyalty (*see also: brand, loyalty;
customer, retention; FFPs;
marketing, relationship*) 58, 73, 76,
79, 119, 139, 151, 156, 165, 199,
215, 260, 300, 303, 305-312, 313,
318, 321, 349, 351, 368, 386
perceptions *see: perceptions,
customers'*
perspective on organizations 58
portfolio 316
preference 216, 247, 301, 306, 311
relationships 194, 299-321, 387
retention (*see also: customer,
defection; service failure*) 165, 206,
298, 300, 308, 312-318, 321, 351,
380
satisfaction (*see also: customer,
expectations; perception, customers',
of service; service evaluation;
service quality*) 58, 119, 164, 240,
241, 258, 260, 271, 280, 297, 314,
320, 338, 345, 355, 363, 364, 401
and branding 199
and customer loyalty 297, 305,
306, 309, 368
and demand peaking 166, 349
and service design 134, 138,
145, 156, 157, 167
and service scripting 177
as a leading indicator 338
definition 373
effect of culture (*see also:
culture*) 102, 294
impact of service encounters *see:
service encounters*
links to employee satisfaction
see: service-profit chain
surveys 306
outcome 137

understanding 54, 67-71, 104, 106,
119-123, 143, 211, 218, 252, 304,
307, 317, 374, 395, 400-401
    misunderstanding 171
value *see: value, customer*
cycle of failure 298
Cyprus Airways 202

Dan-Air 180
data mining 311, 317
data warehousing 311, 317
de-layering 270, 273
Delta Air Lines 32, 173, 177, 197, 208,
281
Delta Express 78, 208
demand *see: market, demand*
departure control 241-243, 399, 400
deregulation 13, 383, 387
design 157, 178, 204-205, 211
differentiation *see: brand, points of
difference*
Directional Policy Matrix 14
direct marketing 217, 220, 227, 231,
252, 302, 303, 316
discounting (*see also: revenue
management*) 142
Disney 169
distinctiveness *see: brand, points of
difference*
distribution 72, 88, 95, 221, 280-281,
309, 314, 322, 325, 326, 362, 387
    and pricing 140, 142
diversification 14-15, 19, 82, 208, 222,
270
dramaturgy 169-170

easyJet 82, 200, 208, 221
e-commerce 16, 18, 19, 153, 154, 162,
165, 323, 325, 326
economies of scale (*see also:
communication, economies of scale*) 25,
87, 208, 324, 326, 363
economies of scope 14-15, 87, 208, 324,
326, 363
Emirates 201, 393, 395
employee
    conflict 168-173
    satisfaction *see: service-profit chain*
empowerment (*see also: HRM*) 113,
139, 169, 172, 177, 224, 240, 258-259,
261, 270, 288, 349, 351, 391
enactment theory 51

environmental influencing 222
ERP 241
e-ticketing 16, 18, 95, 153, 326
EVA 371
evolutionary economics 29
experience curve 25
experience product (*see also: service, as
an experience*) 198, 214

fault-tree analysis 347
FCF 371
FedEx 172
FFPs (*see also: customer, loyalty*) 217,
231, 252, 305, 309-311, 316, 318, 319,
320, 344, 345, 350
    and alliances 158, 204, 326, 327,
    329, 332
    as service attributes 90, 93, 127,
    154
        databases 70, 73, 252
        elite tiers 71
feedback 340
finance theory 38
five-forces model (*see also: positioning,
strategic; structure-conduct-
performance model*) 13-14, 26, 66, 90,
321
focus groups 135, 137, 344, 347, 365
franchising 79, 209, 323, 328-329
frequencies, in relation to service
concept 84
Frontier Airlines 84

game theory 323, 327, 331
Gandalf 93
Go 200, 208
government relations 280
groupthink 37, 289, 334

Honda 236
hierarchies 255, 263, 268, 270, 271,
272, 273, 332, 392
HRM (*see also: culture; empowerment*)
172, 225-226, 230, 243, 250, 251-260,
261, 290, 295, 298, 389
    and alliances 334-335
hypercompetition 52

Impulse 84
Indian Airlines 93
industrial organization (IO) economics
13-14, 25, 38

industrial relations 296-297
industry attractiveness 13
industry recipe 48, 71, 72, 284
industry relations 280
information 311, 320, 333, 337, 340-341, 344, 349, 350
    and alliances 328, 332
    individual 256
    IS/IT 250, 255, 269, 271, 326, 357, 358, 363, 387
    organizational 252
innovation (*see also: change; creativity; process, design; service design*) 76, 251, 325, 382, 392-401
    as investment 398
    effect of culture 28
    and competitive advantage 29, 53, 54, 55, 95
    institutionalisation of 392
    process 382, 399-401
    product (service) 134-135, 177, 229, 257, 303, 307, 359, 382, 396-399
inseparability (or simultaneity) of service production and consumption 112-113, 160, 164, 214, 235, 240, 349
institutional theory 327-328
intangibility (of services) (*see also: service, as an experience*) 111-112, 160, 288
intellectual capital 251, 252
internal marketing 225-226
International Benchmarking Clearinghouse 236
investor relations 280
Ishikawa technique *see: root cause analysis*
issues, strategic 222, 226, 231, 280, 284, 285, 289-290, 296

JALways 78
Japan Airlines 201
Jet Airways 93
job design 261
joint ventures 222, 274, 323-324, 329, 330, 332

KLM 11, 197, 201, 208, 218
KLMuk 87
know-how 31, 252
knowledge (*see also: brand, knowledge; customer, understanding; learning*) 37, 47, 54, 66, 82, 381, 394

-based theory 36, 253
declarative and procedural 251
individual 255-256, 358
in relation to cognition, culture, and learning 48-49, 253, 356, 357
in relation to product development 132, 395
maps 255
organizational 251-255, 358-359, 385
stocks and flows 255
tacit (*see also: tacitness*) 33, 54, 69, 133, 239, 252, 253, 257, 290, 357, 386
types 256-257

leadership, the (and senior management) 4, 224, 282, 284, 286, 288, 290, 291, 295, 298, 337, 338, 339, 341, 355, 359, 385, 386, 391, 392, 395, 401
learning (*see also: knowledge*)
    in alliances 325, 331, 334
    individual learning 356-357
    in relation to cognition, culture, and knowledge 48-49, 252, 290-293
    model of strategy-making 7-11, 46, 357, 385-386
    organizational (*see also: complaints*) 30, 31, 43, 46, 54, 269, 344, 345, 347, 351, 357, 358, 359, 371, 381, 386, 387, 395, 400, 401
        as metaphor 51
        effect of structure 272
    the learning organization 254, 356, 357
Legend 93
leverage (operating and financial) 116, 246
lifetime value (of customers) *see: customer, lifetime-value*
line of visibility 164, 240
logical incrementalism 7, 259, 385
low-cost/ -fare airlines 42, 53, 69, 75, 78, 79, 80, 84, 92, 94-95, 124, 131, 142-143, 143-144, 144, 157, 160, 169, 180, 184, 200, 207, 221, 247, 249, 259, 304, 316, 318, 377, 379
    and the activity system 262-263
loyalty *see: customer, loyalty*
Lufthansa 16, 141, 197, 323, 362
    InfoFlyway 210
Lufthansa Technik 19, 210

managerial cognition (*see also: perception, managers'*) 29, 38, 40-41, 44, 47-52, 54, 333, 338, 377, 387
    cognitive mapping 40, 49
market
    analysis of opportunities 64-67
    demand 66-67, 77, 117
        peaking 94, 117, 165, 182, 342
    development 82
    penetration 82
    positioning *see: positioning, market*
    research 66-67, 68, 69-70, 99, 120, 133, 147, 157, 183, 200, 231, 365, 376
        for customer value analysis 100
    segmentation 71-75, 88, 101, 107, 127, 133, 138, 303, 399
        and branding 188, 196, 209-210
        and communication 217, 228-229, 302
        as social a construction 52
        positioning within a segment 97, 128, 145-147
        procedure 72-74
        segment-of-one 302, 316, 321
    structure 66
marketing (*see also: direct marketing*)
    agreements 332
    departments 271
    exchanges 299-300
    relationship (*see also: customer, loyalty; customer, retention*) 300-304, 310, 312, 317
    tactical and strategic contrasted 118
marketing concept 306
marketing mix (*see also: advertising; price; promotion; public relations; service, design*) 117-118, 141, 300
    services marketing mix 106, 118, 300
marketplace performance 368
market share 45, 298, 309, 318, 328, 368
    economic benefits of 25,
    pricing for 140
MedLink 156
mental models 7, 36, 37, 38, 99, 104, 106, 132, 253, 256, 359, 385, 386
    or mindset 37, 38, 256, 284
microeconomics 2, 13, 29, 141, 264
Midwest Express 84, 144, 199, 386
mission 3, 76

moments of truth 113, 114, 165
motivation, employee 223, 225, 227, 258-260, 261, 292, 321, 356, 388, 393
MRO business 16, 323, 325, 361, 362
multi-attribute decision analysis 135

national environment, contribution to competitive advantage 28-29, 55
needs gap analysis 134
network (route) 77, 79, 93, 256, 326, 330, 363
    and pricing 142
    as a resource 250
    in relation to service concept 84, 85, 152, 157, 162
Northwest Airlines 197, 201, 222, 231

objectives 3, 6, 104, 192, 195, 223, 226, 267, 269, 294, 306, 330, 331, 338, 339, 355, 369, 371, 372, 381
observation 375
oneworld 228
open skies 29
operations 97, 183, 240, 241-243, 244, 321, 326, 329, 331, 335, 338, 339, 347, 355, 357, 384, 385, 386, 390
    consistency 105
    operating strategy (*see also: activities; value, customer, cost management strategy; value, customer, revenue strategy; value chains*) 244-247, 289, 362, 363
    performance 360-362, 368
organizations
    architecture 42, 45, 263-276
        external relationships *see: relationships, external*
        structure (*see also: processes; value chains*) 139, 261, 267-274, 285, 338, 395
            and strategy 269
    as social constructions 50-52, 126, 271, 391
    customer perspective 58
    development (OD) 389, 390, 395
    nature of 50-52, 258
    network 269, 279-281
        as metaphor 51
    shareholder perspective 58
outsourcing (*see also: stakeholders; suppliers*) 274, 275-276, 280, 291, 325, 343, 361, 362, 363, 399

activities 263
competencies 44
impact on service quality 173
overbooking 154

Pan Am 200
partnerships *see: alliances*
path dependency 30, 32, 33, 36, 42, 45,
190, 266, 268, 274, 276, 386, 390
perception 191-192, 228
brand (*see also: brand, image*) 105,
126, 145-147, 152, 188-189, 190,
204-205, 282, 299, 302, 303, 304,
312, 333
customers', of service (*see also:
service, as an experience; service
encounters; service quality*) 91, 122,
127, 159, 166, 219, 301, 321, 342,
345, 360
effect of queuing and waiting
160-163
effect of scripting 177
impact of other customers *see:
customer, impact of other
customers*
customers', of market position 97,
99, 101, 130, 365
and communication 210-220
impact of servicescape 178-179
customers' of staff 171
managers' (*see also: managerial
cognition*) 48, 49, 51, 52, 72, 104,
283, 387, 395
perceptual mapping 134, 365
perfect competition 13
performance 6, 15, 16, 19, 87, 106-107,
352-382
and brand image 194
and culture 290, 291-295
balanced scorecard 352, 369
benchmarking 381-382, 400
drivers and outcomes compared 338,
381
importance of people 260
management 335, 337-341
and measurement contrasted 337
networks 280, 325, 327
service (*see also: service, attribute,
specification*) 160
strategy-performance pyramid 352-
373
perishability (of services) 112

personal selling 220
physical (or tangible) evidence (or clues)
(*see also: risk, reassurance; service
evaluation*) 118, 159, 165, 167, 168,
198, 203
planning 5
model of strategy-making (*see also:
strategy, emergent*) 6-7, 340, 383,
385, 389
portfolio planning (*see also: strategy,
corporate*) 3, 14-15
positioning 97-98, 128
as a social construction 52
market (*see also: brand, points of
difference; value chains*) 88, 97-101
and branding 188, 190, 195,
200, 206, 213, 364-365
and brand personality/values
106, 111
and culture 294
and service design 138, 147,
152, 160, 347
and the activity system 263, 363
and the marketing mix 118, 143
determinants 99-100
positioning maps 365, 401
price-performance combination
98-99, 131
procedure 98
repositioning 100, 103, 177
role of servicescape 178-179
rules 100
strategic (*see also: activities; five
forces model; structure-conduct-
performance model*) 25-28, 36, 38,
54, 87, 140, 142-143, 321
price 72, 131-132, 139-143, 145, 219,
323
cost-plus 94
elasticity 301
functions of 140-141
price-quality relationship 112
strategic/price platforms, 141, 141-
143, 147
tactical 140-141, 143
Pro Air 84
processes (*see also: activities; value
chains*) 235-249, 338, 381
back-office 169, 240-241, 258, 360-
361
contrasted with competencies 236-
239

design (*see also: innovation; service design*) 241, 248, 250, 363, 387
  complexity and divergence 248-249, 400
service delivery (front-office) (*see also: line of visibility; service, as an experience; service delivery; service encounters*) 76, 112, 118, 164-165, 169, 240-243, 249, 258, 288, 293, 304, 342, 360-361, 399
  as service attributes 151, 156, 158-163
  blueprinting (*see also: service failure, fail-safe*) 136, 159-160, 174, 240, 399
    walk-through audit 160
  defined 236, 239
  types 235-236
product 111, 115
  development (*see also: service, design*) 82
productivity (*see also: cost, base/structure; culture, organization*) 54, 94, 95, 159, 160, 166, 246, 252, 256, 261, 296, 297, 362-364
  and the servicescape 180, 183
project 247
promotion 141, 143, 216, 217, 230, 306, 366
prosumer 240
public relations 96, 145, 207, 217, 220, 222, 231, 325, 366

Qantas 197
Qualiflyer Group 17, 328
quality function deployment 134
Quality of Working Life Movement 260
queue modelling 161

re-engineering 2, 291, 363, 384, 399
  as metaphor 51, 388
regional airlines 80, 84
relationships 42, 45, 56, 228
  customer *see: customer*
    and brand personality/values 106
  external (*see also: alliances; collaboration; customer; organization, architecture; outsourcing; suppliers*) 42, 45, 269-270, 274-276
    knowledge of 255

  partnership 275
  internal (*see also: communication, internal; HRM; internal marketing*) 42, 45, 145, 226, 281, 386
  investment in 303
reputation 156, 188-189, 335, 365, 393
  contrasted with brand image 147
resources (*see also: brand; culture, organization; HRM; value chain*) 2, 14, 16, 19, 54-55, 66, 82, 87, 104, 106, 126, 136, 260, 300, 398
  and alliances 279, 324, 328, 334-335
  and market position 98, 130
  brand as a resource 190, 199, 206
  cognitive 250-257, 385
  contribution to tasks, activities, and processes 236, 244, 249-263
  employees as a resource 281, 294
  identification of 34-36
  non-cognitive 250
  tacit 36, 139, 392
resource-based theory (*see also: strategy, competitive*) 29, 31-36, 221, 239, 254, 259, 264, 290, 322, 324
resource-dependence theory 221-222, 327, 331
revenue management (*see also: discounting*) 75, 131, 141, 142, 143, 152, 154, 218, 252, 256, 361, 387
risk (consumers') (*see also: consumer behaviour; physical evidence; service evaluation*)
  purchase 111, 208, 212, 214-215, 367
  reassurance 111, 125, 167, 206-207, 219, 367
ROI 303
roles (*see also: service delivery, role of customers; service delivery, role of staff*)
  role ambiguity 171
  role conflict 169-170
  role theory 169-173
Rolls Royce 17
root-cause analysis (*see also: service failure, analysis of*) 175, 288, 293, 320, 321, 346, 347, 351, 379, 386, 397
  fault-tree analysis 347, 393
  Ishikawa/fishbone/cause-and-effect analysis 347, 386, 393
routines 29-31, 33, 36, 42, 44, 45, 133, 252, 253, 333, 357, 359, 394

contrasted with competencies 37
Ryanair 78, 84, 144

Sabena 17
safety 122, 143-144, 152, 157, 170, 180
SAirGroup 17
SAS 82, 165, 323, 324
satisfaction *see: customer, satisfaction*
scenario planning 6, 10, 37, 358, 381
scheduling 152, 241, 250, 252, 347
   and alliances 329
   in relation to service concept 84,
   152, 162
scope
   competitive 61-64, 76-87, 88, 102,
   119, 155, 218
   geographical 77, 78-84, 88, 102, 152
   industrial 12-18, 19
   product 77, 78, 79-84, 88, 102-104,
   152
   vertical *(see also: alliances, nature
   and scope, vertical; outsourcing)*
   12, 18-19, 222, 269-270, 274-276,
   280-299, 323
scripts 105, 113, 169, 176-177, 219, 314
search product 198, 214
seat accessibility 154
seat availability 154
segment *see: market, segmentation*
service 76, 258
   acceptable (ideal, desired, adequate)
   121, 133
   as an experience *(see also: experience product; intangibility;
   perceptions, customers' of service;
   processes, service delivery)* 112,
   116, 123, 125, 136, 145, 156, 159,
   167, 240, 244, 258, 260, 288, 343,
   376, 380
      and alliances 158, 197
   as a performance 123, 166-167, 169-
   171
   as a social construction 52
   attributes *(see also: benefits;
   processes, service delivery; service,
   design; service encounters; servicescapes)* 91, 123, 127, 139, 143, 144,
   145-147, 157, 203, 241, 341, 358-
   359, 360, 397, 398-399
      and customer value analysis
      100, 128-129, 359
      and pricing 139-140, 143

   and the service concept 127,
   138
   and zones of tolerance 122,
   133, 138
   bundled into a service package
   125, 136, 143, 144, 145, 152,
   153, 159, 244
   impact on costs 246
   improvement *see: innovation*
   in relation to brand image *see:
   brand, image*
   in relation to strategic context
   132
   links to benefits 134, 157
   menu of 152-156
   process 127-129, 240, 360
   specification 123, 136-137,
   159-160, 248, 360, 374-375
   what is done and how it is
   done *(see also: culture,
   organization)* 123-124, 139,
   145, 171, 258
   augmented 44, 80, 103, 124, 125,
   127, 130, 131, 144, 145, 147, 157,
   341
      and branding 188, 365
   characteristics 105, 111-115, 125-
   126, 136, 160, 213
   characteristics of airline service
   115-117
   concept 64, 75, 77, 87-101, 102,
   119, 126, 144, 145, 153, 155, 244,
   245, 294, 298, 313, 321, 347, 358-
   359, 360, 387
      and brand architecture 209-210
      and branding 194, 195, 196, 301
      and pricing 140, 141-143
      and the activity system 263, 363
      as problem solving 123
      contribution to service design
      127, 138, 160, 183, 398
      employees' roles 169, 260
      portfolio of concepts 85-87, 88,
      97, 127, 209-210
      single-concept focus 84-85, 88,
      97, 127
   core 44, 124, 127, 143, 144, 157,
   167, 258, 341
   design *(see also: benefits;
   complaints; conjoint analysis;
   concept testing; critical incident
   technique; customer, expectations,*

input into service design; customers, feedback from; focus groups; innovation; multi-attribute decision analysis; needs gap analysis; network; perception, perceptual mapping; processes, service delivery; quality function deployment; schedule; service, attributes; value, customer) 72, 88, 173, 216, 244-245, 308, 314, 320, 321, 325, 340, 342, 363, 364, 387
  and competitive strategy 119-127
  and market positioning 99
  influence of front-line staff 116, 134, 136, 171, 257-260
  process (*see also: innovation; process, design*) 127-139, 349, 364, 387
    expeditionary marketing 138, 359
    time-compressed 138
  expected *see: customer, expectations*
  outcomes, contrasted with outputs 127, 134, 137, 139, 164, 167, 233, 244, 252, 257
service delivery (*see also: culture, organization; processes; service, attributes, what is done and how it is done; value chains*) 116, 134, 143, 148, 247, 280, 284, 291, 297, 301, 313, 321, 325, 342, 356
  and internal communications 223-224, 226-227
  and market positioning 99
  and the activity system 263
  as a source of reassurance 206
  functionality 125, 139
  impact on brand image 197, 202, 204, 218, 219-220, 232, 233, 302
  link to service concept 233
  processes *see: processes, service delivery*
  role of customers 159, 166-168, 169, 174, 240
  role of servicescapes 180
  role of staff 113, 114, 118, 156, 159, 165, 169, 175, 240, 250-251, 257-260, 401
    role ambiguity 171
    role conflict 169-170

style and tone 53, 54, 113, 114, 123-124, 130, 139, 144, 145, 244, 254
  as reassurance 125
  effect of culture 102, 103, 114, 287, 290, 295
  personality 258
system (*see also: capacity management; processes, service delivery*) 18, 45, 71, 72, 73, 74, 87, 90, 95, 113, 114, 127, 135, 151, 159, 247, 288, 289, 320, 342, 346, 347, 351
  under-serving and-over-serving 107
  queuing and waiting for service 160-163, 167
service encounter (*see also: culture, organization; processes, service delivery; scripts; service delivery, role of customer; service delivery, role of staff; servicescapes; variability*) 96, 113, 114, 126, 148, 164-177, 240, 241, 290, 294, 303, 319, 342, 344, 349, 360, 375-376
  and branding 105-106, 196, 202, 210, 219, 302
  and communication 229
  and market positioning 99
  and zones of tolerance 122, 133, 138, 160
  as a battle for control 163
  as a service attribute 151
  defined 164-165
  design of 175-177
  functionality 125
  individuality in 177
  people involved 166-174
  specification 137
  types 165
service evaluation (*see also: customer, expectations; customer, satisfaction; perception, customers' of service; physical evidence; risk, reassurance*) 167-168, 213, 219-220, 230, 240, 349
service failure (*see also: complaints; customer, defection; root cause analysis*) 136, 159, 248, 258, 289, 303, 306, 317, 319, 320, 341-348
  analysis of (*see also: root cause analysis*) 342-343
  detection (*see also: complaints*) 344-347, 374, 381
  fail-safe (*see also: processes, service delivery, blueprinting*) 136, 159,

314, 342, 347
service-price offers 91, 92, 102-103,
131, 141, 143, 143-145, 145, 244, 247,
263, 285, 288, 313, 318, 320
service-profit chain 168, 172, 225-226,
297-299, 356
service providers *see: service delivery,
role of staff*
service quality (*see also: customer,
satisfaction*) 144, 301, 319, 325, 342,
364, 366, 368, 373-380, 400-401
    definition 373
    gaps model 376-380, 393
    SERVQUAL 376-380
service recovery 258, 303, 306, 317,
319, 320, 343, 345, 349-352, 365
    designed-in procedures 159
service remixture 380
services
    distinguished from customer service
    115
    distinguished from goods 56, 111,
    115
    management literature 56
servicescape 178-184, 230, 240, 398
    and service delivery 159, 160
    as a brand element 192, 202, 219,
    302
    as a service attribute 151, 154-155,
    156
    design criteria 183-184
    design elements 180-182
    impact on queuing and waiting 163
    impact on service encounters 165
services management 'trinity' 56, 230,
245
servuction system 112, 240
Shuttle by United 87, 208, 399
signage 181, 202
simultaneity of production and
consumption *see: inseparability of
service production and consumption*
Singapore Airlines 16, 112, 191, 323
skills, individual 256, 258
social constructions 50-52, 126, 147,
188, 283
Southwest Airlines 78, 84, 102, 131,
144, 187, 188, 190, 199, 202, 209, 217,
230, 236, 241-243, 261, 263, 289, 294,
356, 400
span of control 268
Spirit 84

stakeholders (*see also: competitors;
customers; distribution; suppliers*) 16,
29, 56, 191-192, 194, 196, 204-205, 221-
222, 227-229, 287, 289, 301, 333, 340,
366, 369, 381, 384
    stakeholder networks 279-281
Star Alliance 228, 250, 331
strategic description (of an airline) 74,
77
strategic (or industry) foresight 10, 44,
45, 46, 55, 386, 401
strategic groups 38
strategic intent 3, 202
strategic logic 36, 37-38, 45, 105, 132,
244, 249, 270, 333, 358, 372
    and the activity system 263
strategic management 4, 7, 357
strategic options 38, 45
strategic performance 371-372
strategic space 55
strategic themes 10, 55, 59, 223, 259,
269
strategic thinking 8, 9, 352, 358, 401
strategy 1-5, 19, 253, 259, 335, 338
    and internal communications 223-
    224, 226
    as a social construction 52
    competitive (*see also: competence-
    based theory; resource-based
    theory; structure-conduct-
    performance model*) 3, 12, 19, 20,
    24, 87, 88, 94, 101, 102, 104, 322,
    381
        and brand extension 207
        and design 204
        and the activity system 262-263
        generic 27, 102-103
    co-operative 321-335
    corporate (*see also: portfolio
    planning*) 12-19, 82, 88, 322, 330
    emergent (*see also: planning, model
    of strategy-making*) 8, 46, 251, 259,
    269, 292, 331, 357, 372, 385-386
    strategy-making processes 5-12
structure-conduct-performance model
(*see also: five forces model; positioning,
strategic; strategy, competitive; value
chains*) 25-28, 31, 259, 321
suppliers 222, 229, 271, 322, 343, 360,
361-362
    relationship management 256
    supply chain 280, 293, 325, 326,

361, 387
Swissair 16, 201, 328
systems and systems theory 239, 279, 280, 285, 342, 355
   soft systems 389-390

TACA Group 328
tacitness (*see also: knowledge, tacit*) 33, 36, 42
tapered integration 275
tasks 175, 261
   and processes 235
teams and teamwork 136, 241-243, 251, 261, 268, 269, 271, 273, 334, 395, 401
   and alliances 331
Thai International 191, 197, 218
ticket conditionality 87, 90, 152, 154
total quality management 2, 58, 134, 342, 385, 399
Touch and Go Airlines 200
touchpoints 220
training 117, 123, 168, 169, 171, 172, 177, 182, 221, 223, 227, 230, 251, 254, 258-260, 262, 291, 298, 320, 321, 334, 335, 343, 347, 349, 356, 358, 364
   in support of service launch 137, 138
transaction cost theory 18, 274, 327
trust 281, 303, 312, 324, 330, 331, 335
TWA 203

United Airlines 16, 70, 87, 141, 197, 202, 208, 286, 310, 362
USAirways (USAir) 200

value
   customer (*see also: value chains*) 42, 43, 68, 73, 76, 88, 89-97, 126, 139, 143, 144, 159
      analysis 100, 128-129, 359
      and augmented service 125, 144
      and branding 198, 199
      and the activity system 262-263, 363
      as a context for service design 138, 161, 235, 247, 347
      as a service outcome 127-129
      cost management strategy 93-94, 244-247, 273-274, 298
      developing a value proposition 96-97, 119, 144, 273, 306, 312, 374

revenue strategy 92-93, 273-274, 298
   shareholder 58, 140, 274, 298, 300, 305, 306, 307, 316, 325, 330, 369
value chains (*see also: activities; processes*) 18, 263-267, 323
   analysis of resources 34
   contrived and natural 266-267
   in the SCP model (*see also: strategy-conduct-performance model*) 26-28, 263-267, 322
value constellations *see: organizations, network*
values 105, 144, 156, 282, 286, 286-289, 290, 291, 292, 295, 297, 356, 372, 390, 399
   and internal communication 224, 226
   as a source of competitive advantage 251, 257, 288
   underpinning the brand 190, 194, 195, 198
ValuJet 200
Vanguard Airlines 84
variability (or heterogeneity) of services (*see also: consistency; processes, service delivery; service encounters*) 113, 136, 160, 165, 194, 214
Varig 197
vertical integration (*see: scope, vertical*)
Virgin 190, 208
Virgin Atlantic Airways 67, 156, 172, 180, 191, 196, 217, 287, 367, 395
Virgin Blue 84
virtuous circle 298
vision 3-4, 19, 54, 76, 88, 96, 101, 131, 232, 313, 384, 389, 394, 395, 402
   and branding 194, 196
   and internal communication 223
   as a tool for evaluating market opportunities 65-66, 75

waiting for service 161-163
walk-through audit 160

Xerox 308

yield 94, 95, 116, 368-369, 386

zero defects 320, 342
zone of tolerance 121, 122, 133, 138, 247